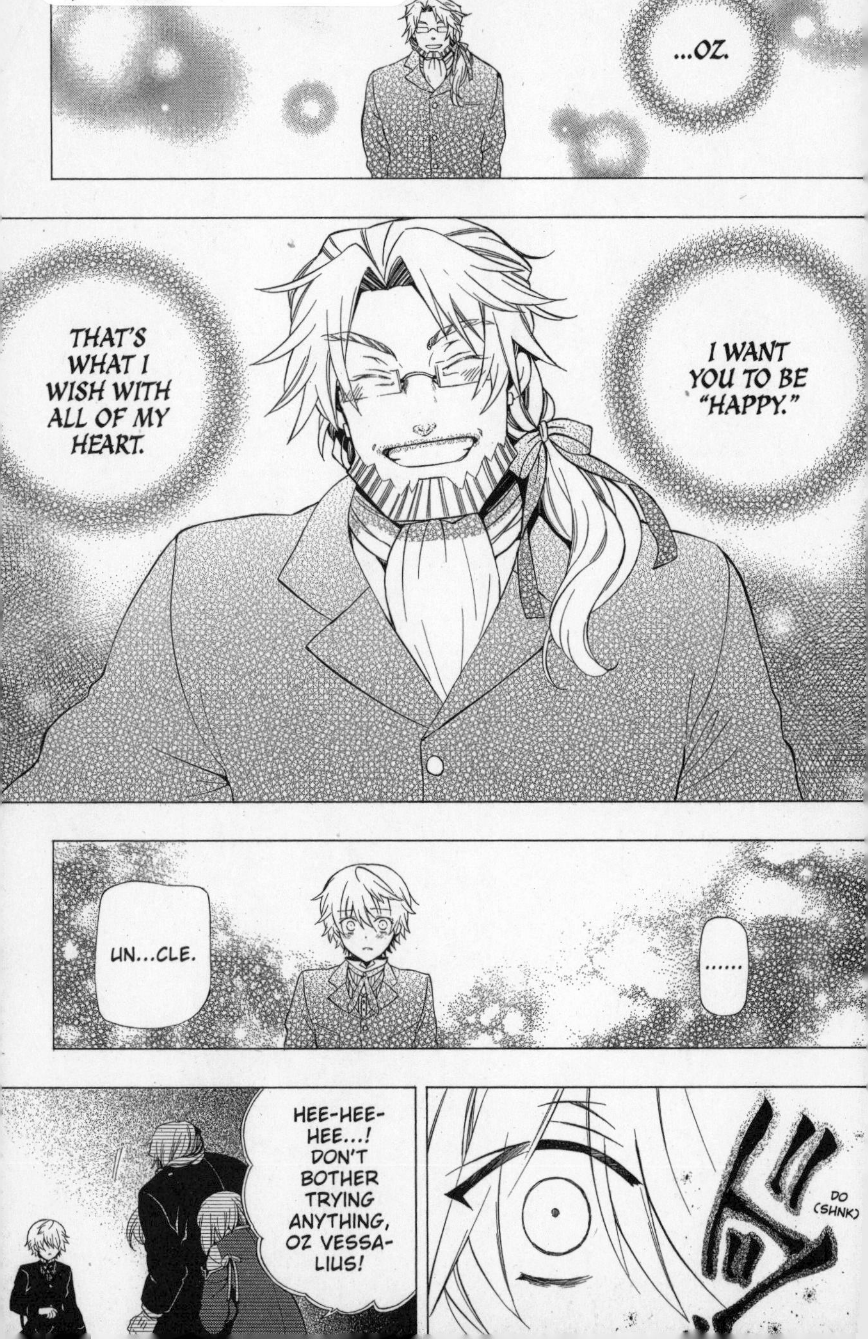
...OZ.
I WANT YOU TO BE "HAPPY."
THAT'S WHAT I WISH WITH ALL OF MY HEART.
......
UN...CLE.
DO (SHNK)
HEE-HEE-HEE...! DON'T BOTHER TRYING ANYTHING, OZ VESSA-LIUS!

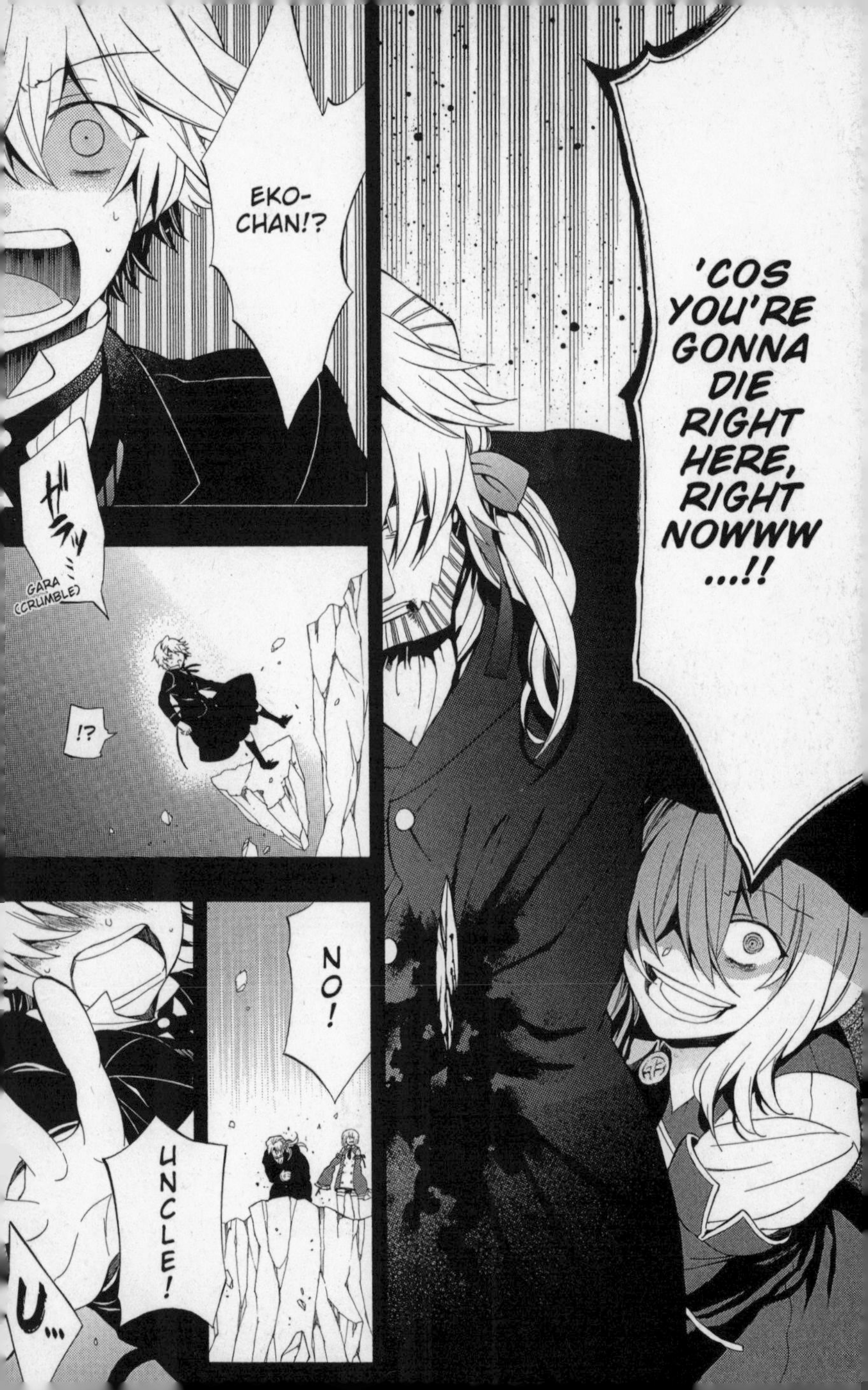
'COS YOU'RE GONNA DIE RIGHT HERE, RIGHT NOWWW ...!!
EKO-CHAN!?
GARA (CRUMBLE)
!?
NO! UNCLE!
U...

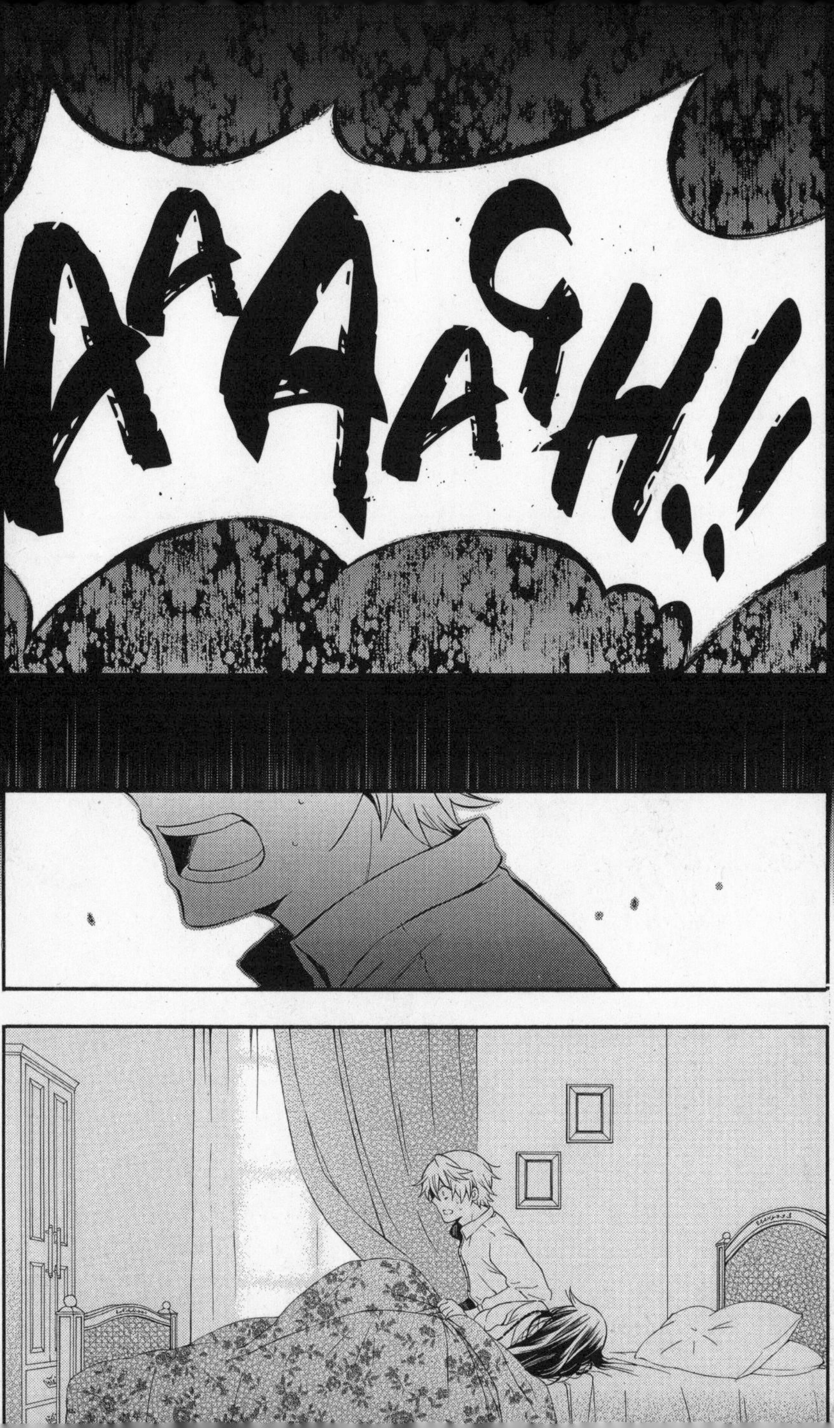
AAAAGH!!

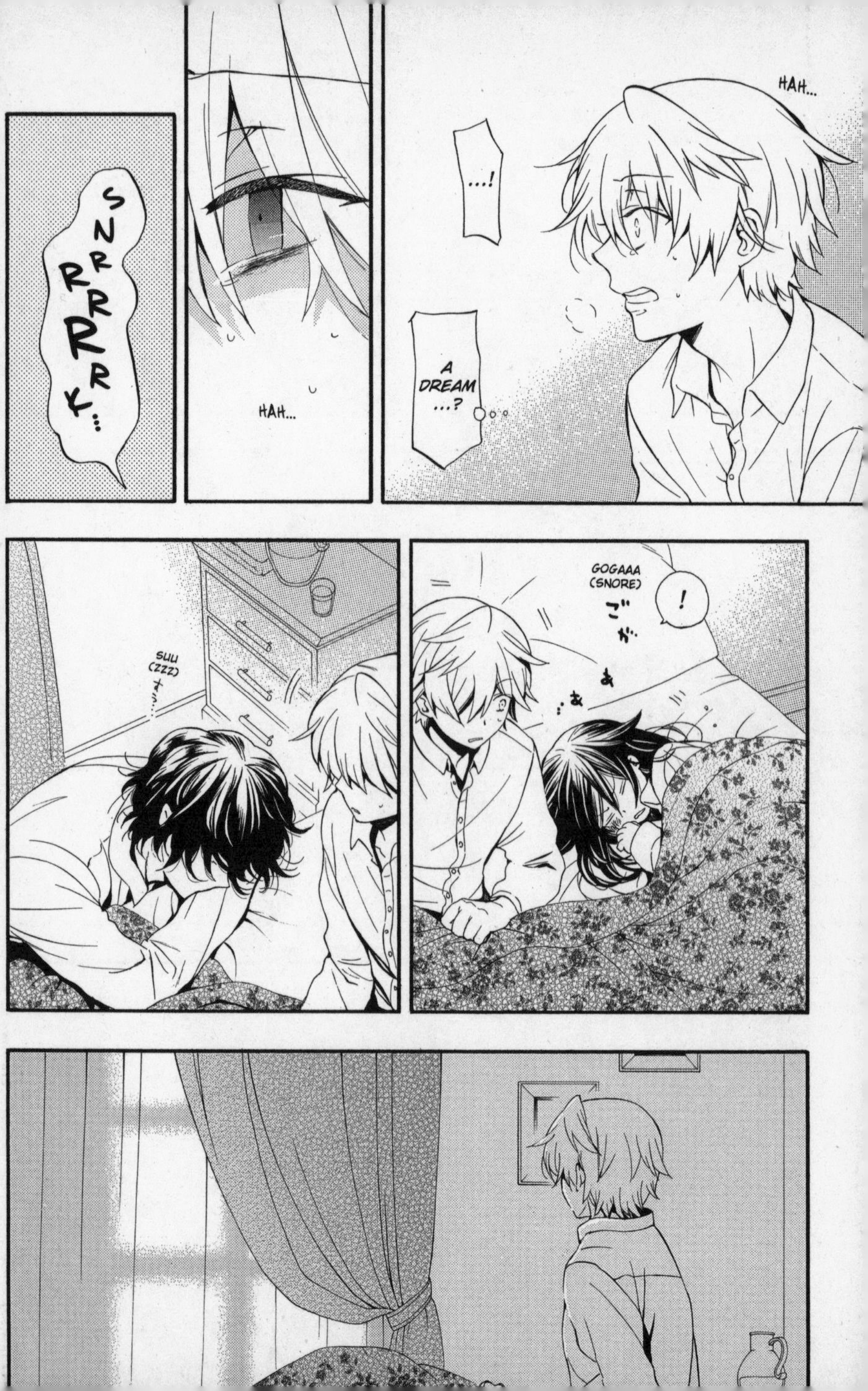
HAH...
...!
A DREAM ...?
HAH...
SNRRRRRK...
GOGAAA (SNORE)
!
SUU (ZZZ)

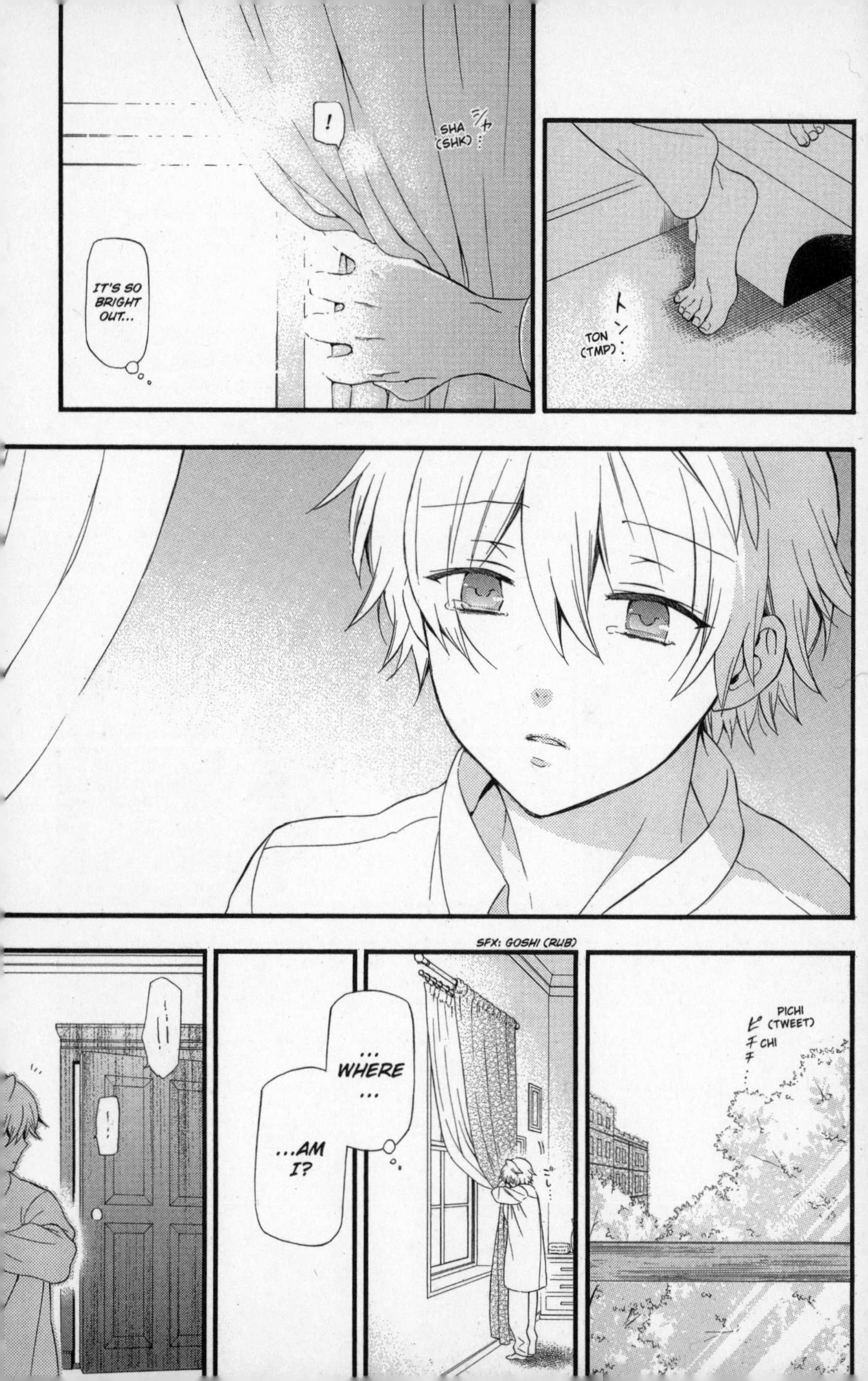
トン
TON (TMP)
シャ
SHA (SHK)
!
IT'S SO BRIGHT OUT...
ピチチ
PICHI (TWEET) CHI
SFX: GOSHI (RUB)
...WHERE...
...AM I?
!!
!?

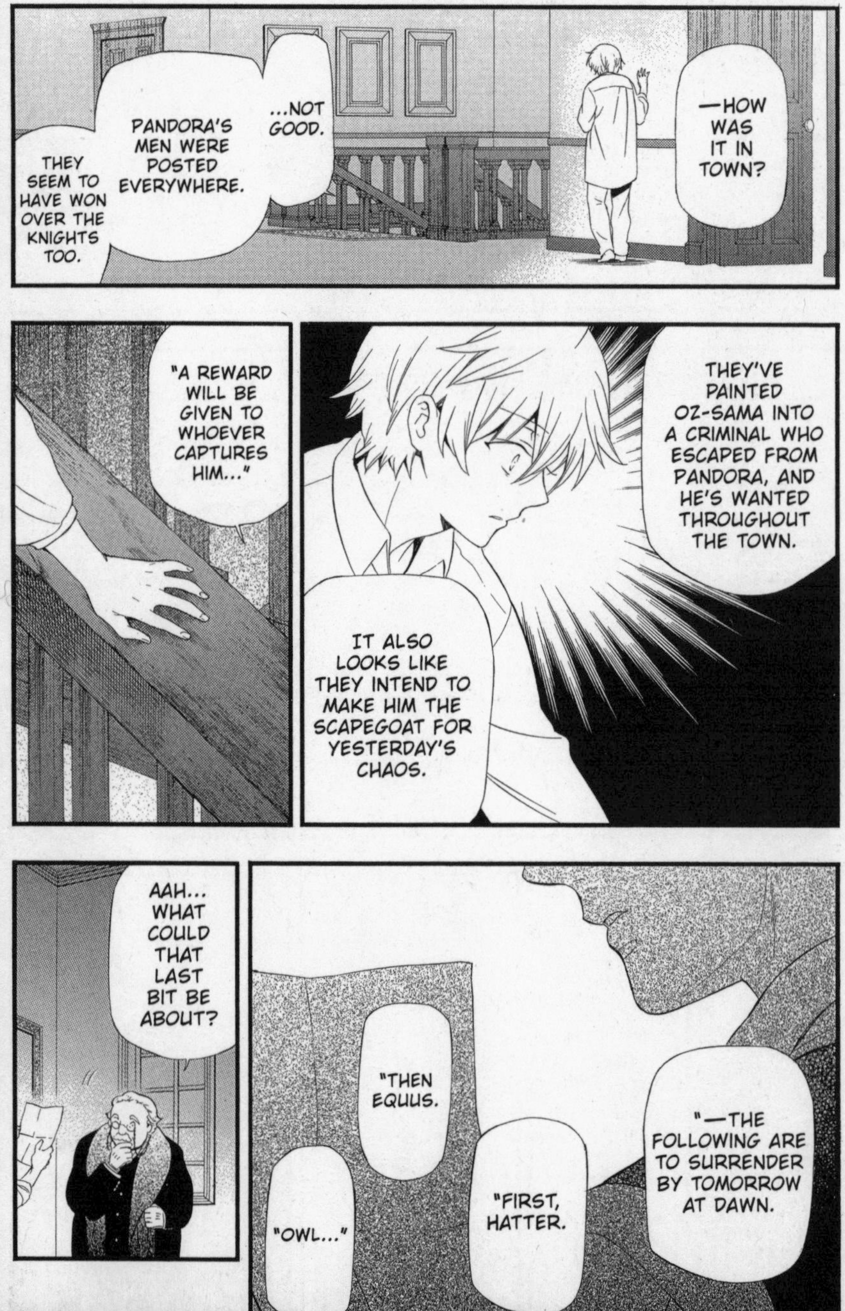
—HOW WAS IT IN TOWN?
...NOT GOOD.
PANDORA'S MEN WERE POSTED EVERYWHERE.
THEY SEEM TO HAVE WON OVER THE KNIGHTS TOO.
THEY'VE PAINTED OZ-SAMA INTO A CRIMINAL WHO ESCAPED FROM PANDORA, AND HE'S WANTED THROUGHOUT THE TOWN.
IT ALSO LOOKS LIKE THEY INTEND TO MAKE HIM THE SCAPEGOAT FOR YESTERDAY'S CHAOS.
"A REWARD WILL BE GIVEN TO WHOEVER CAPTURES HIM..."
"—THE FOLLOWING ARE TO SURRENDER BY TOMORROW AT DAWN.
"FIRST, HATTER.
"THEN EQUUS.
"OWL..."
AAH... WHAT COULD THAT LAST BIT BE ABOUT?

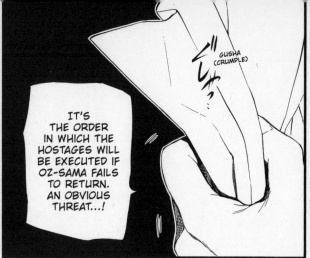

GUSHA (CRUMPLE)

IT'S THE ORDER IN WHICH THE HOSTAGES WILL BE EXECUTED IF OZ-SAMA FAILS TO RETURN. AN OBVIOUS THREAT...!

GYAH!

DON (SLAM)

!

BATA (FLAIL)

BATA (FLAIL)

GORON (ROLL)

BATAN (WHAM)

!?

OOOOZ —!!!

9

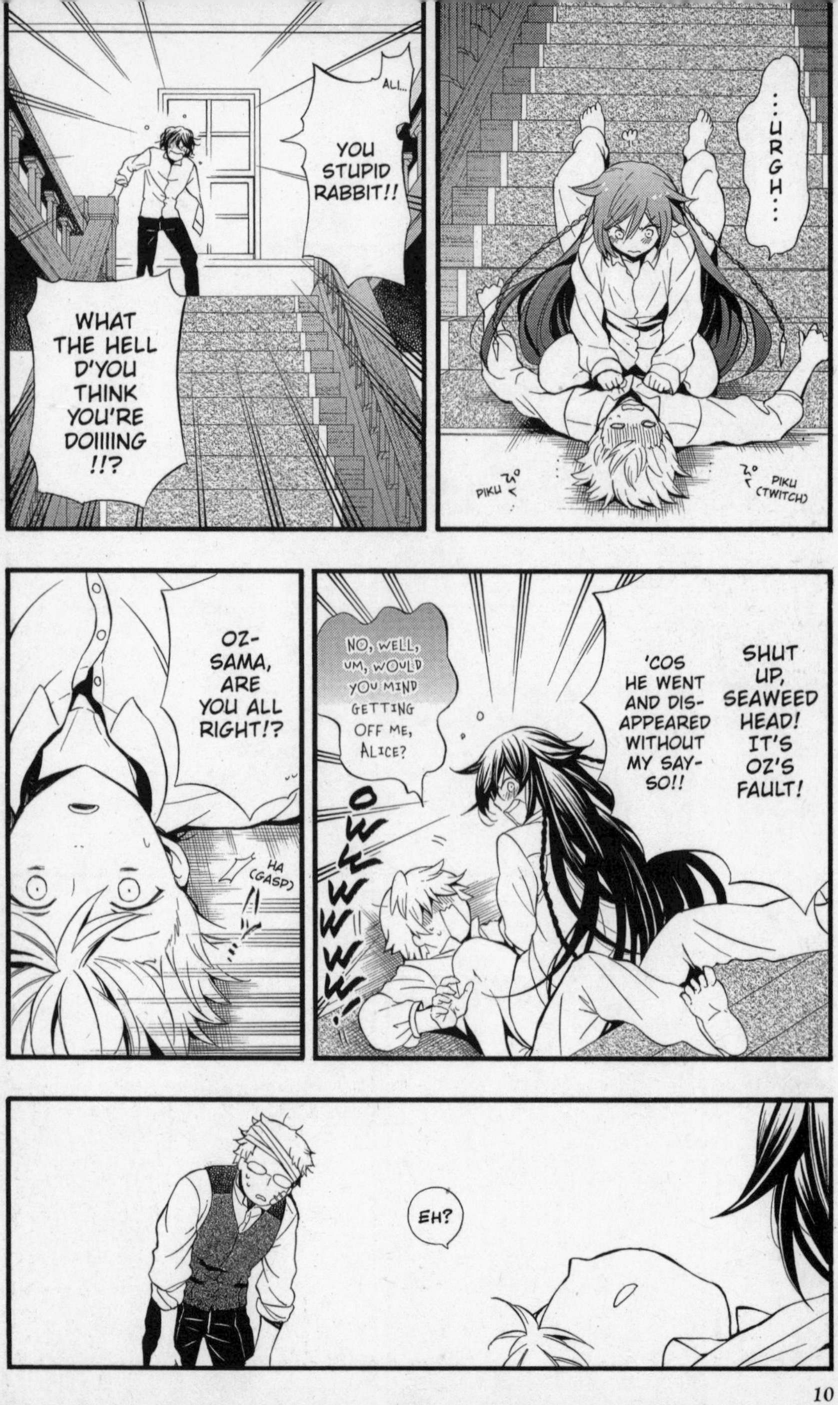
...URGH...
PIKU
PIKU (TWITCH)
ALI...
YOU STUPID RABBIT!!
WHAT THE HELL D'YOU THINK YOU'RE DOIIIING!!?
SHUT UP, SEAWEED HEAD! IT'S OZ'S FAULT!
'COS HE WENT AND DIS-APPEARED WITHOUT MY SAY-SO!!
NO, WELL, UM, WOULD YOU MIND GETTING OFF ME, ALICE?
OWWWWWWWW!
OZ-SAMA, ARE YOU ALL RIGHT!?
HA (GASP)
EH?

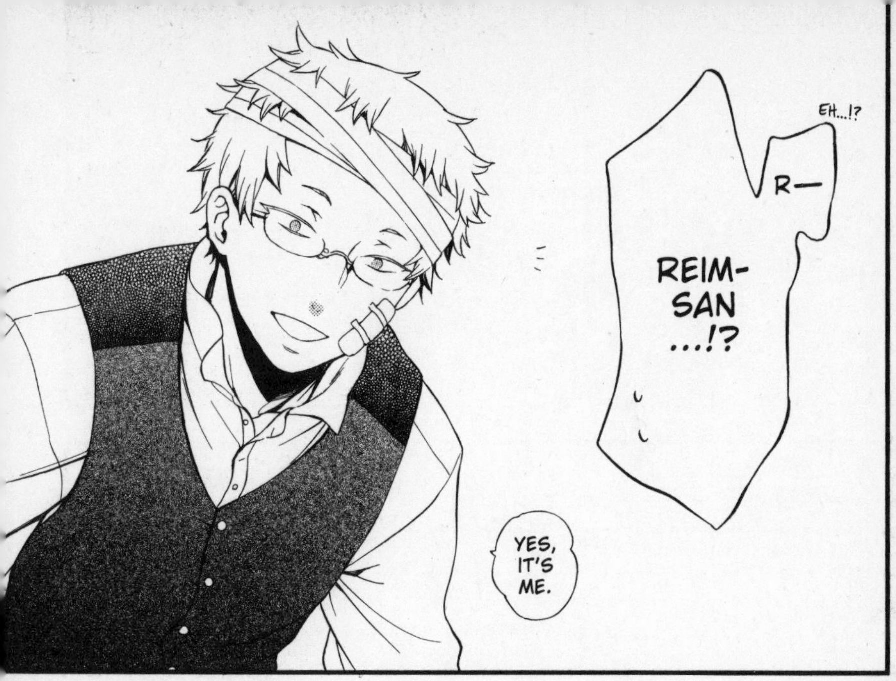
EH...!?
R—
REIM-SAN ...!?
YES, IT'S ME.

Retrace:LXXXIII

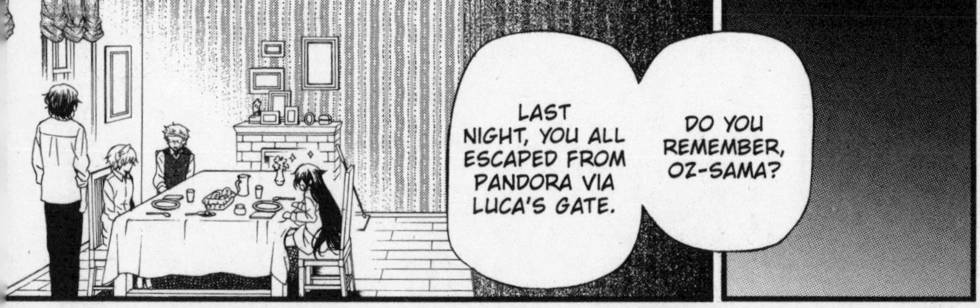
DO YOU REMEMBER, OZ-SAMA?
LAST NIGHT, YOU ALL ESCAPED FROM PANDORA VIA LUCA'S GATE.

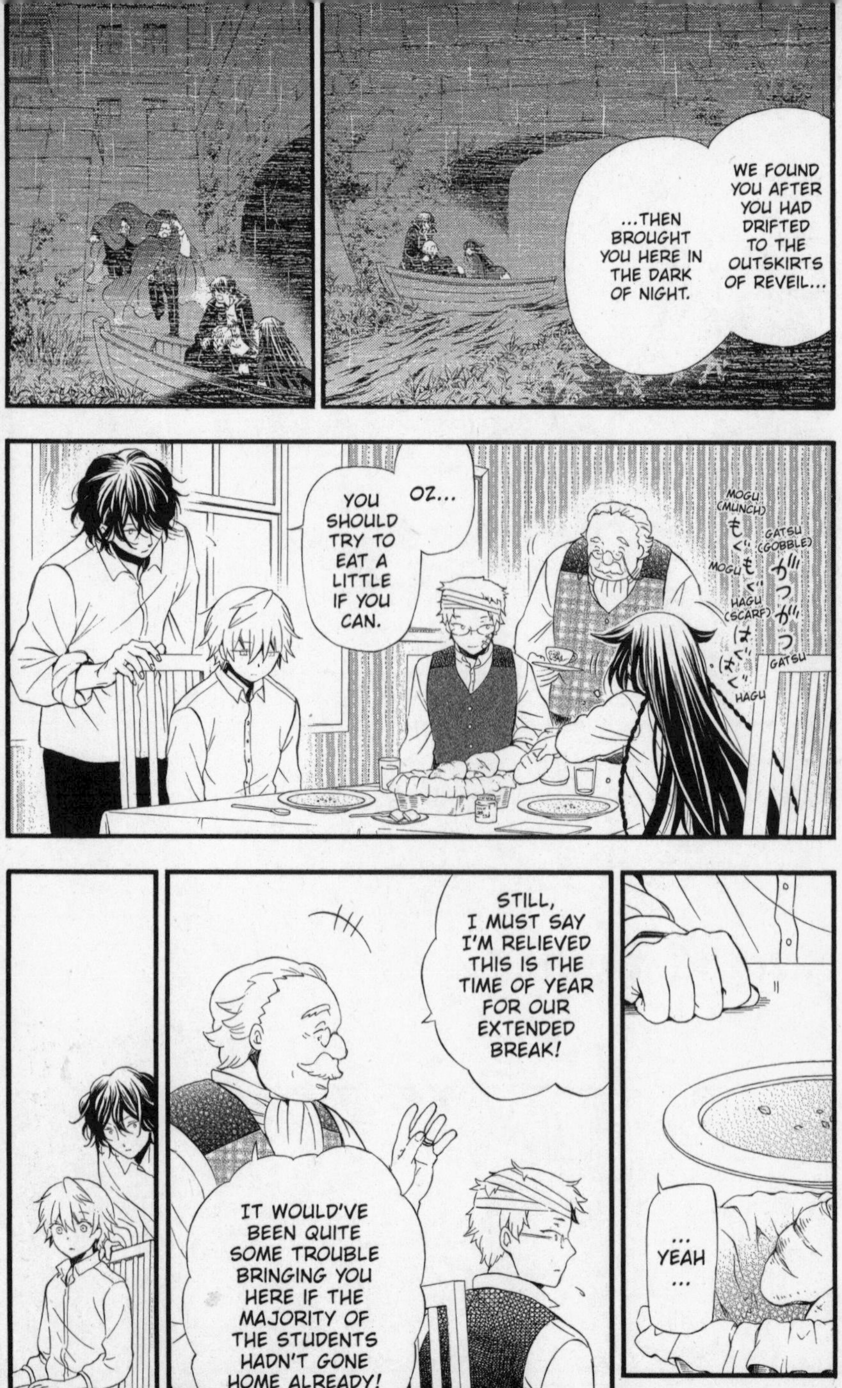
WE FOUND YOU AFTER YOU HAD DRIFTED TO THE OUTSKIRTS OF REVEIL...
...THEN BROUGHT YOU HERE IN THE DARK OF NIGHT.
MOGU (MUNCH) もぐ
MOGU もぐ
GATSU (GOBBLE) がつ
がつ GATSU
HAGU (SCARF) はぐ
はぐ HAGU
OZ...
YOU SHOULD TRY TO EAT A LITTLE IF YOU CAN.
... YEAH ...
STILL, I MUST SAY I'M RELIEVED THIS IS THE TIME OF YEAR FOR OUR EXTENDED BREAK!
IT WOULD'VE BEEN QUITE SOME TROUBLE BRINGING YOU HERE IF THE MAJORITY OF THE STUDENTS HADN'T GONE HOME ALREADY!

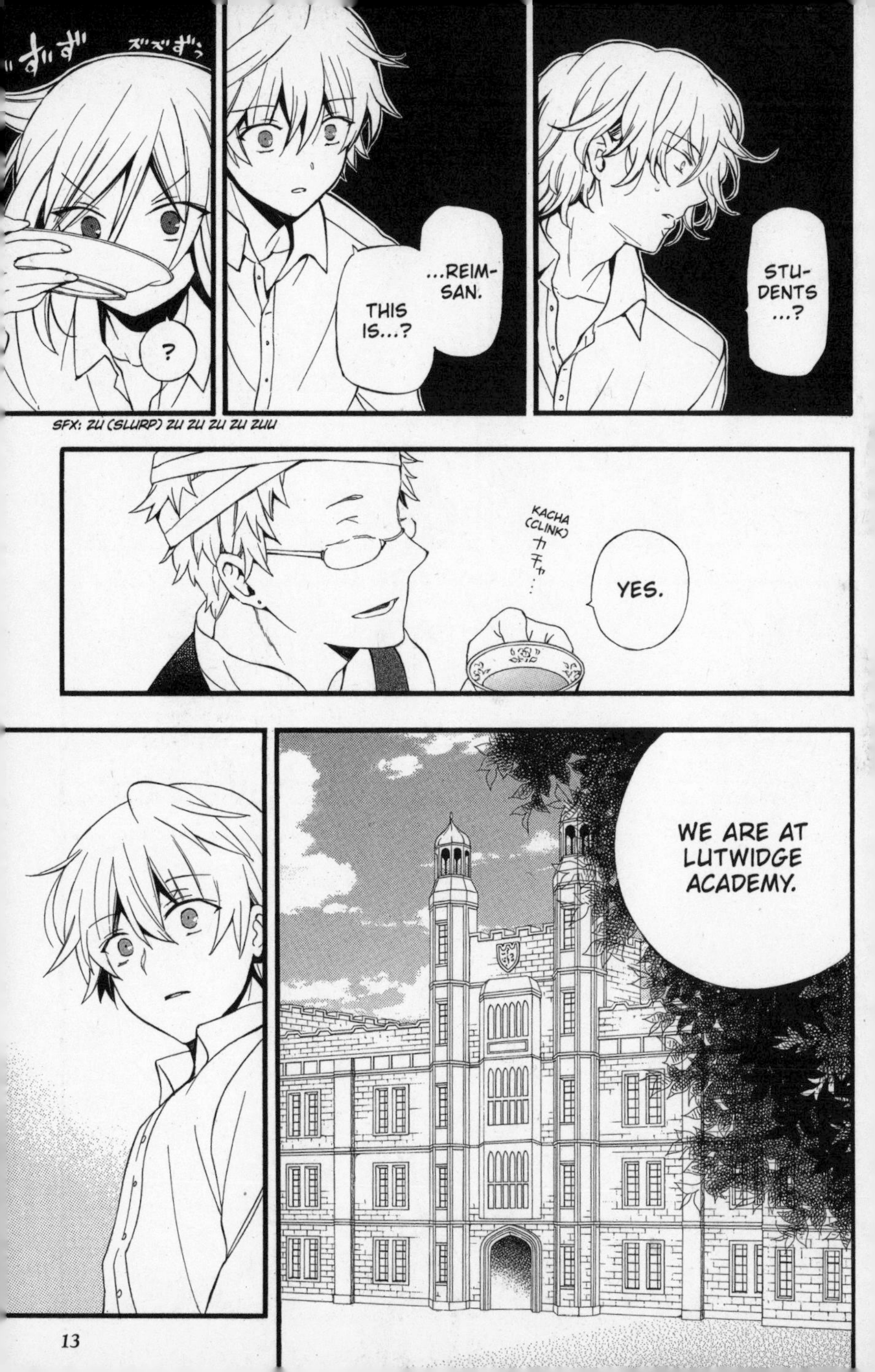
STU-DENTS ...?
...REIM-SAN.
THIS IS...?
?
SFX: ZU (SLURP) ZU ZU ZU ZU ZUU
KACHA (CLINK)
YES.
WE ARE AT LUTWIDGE ACADEMY.

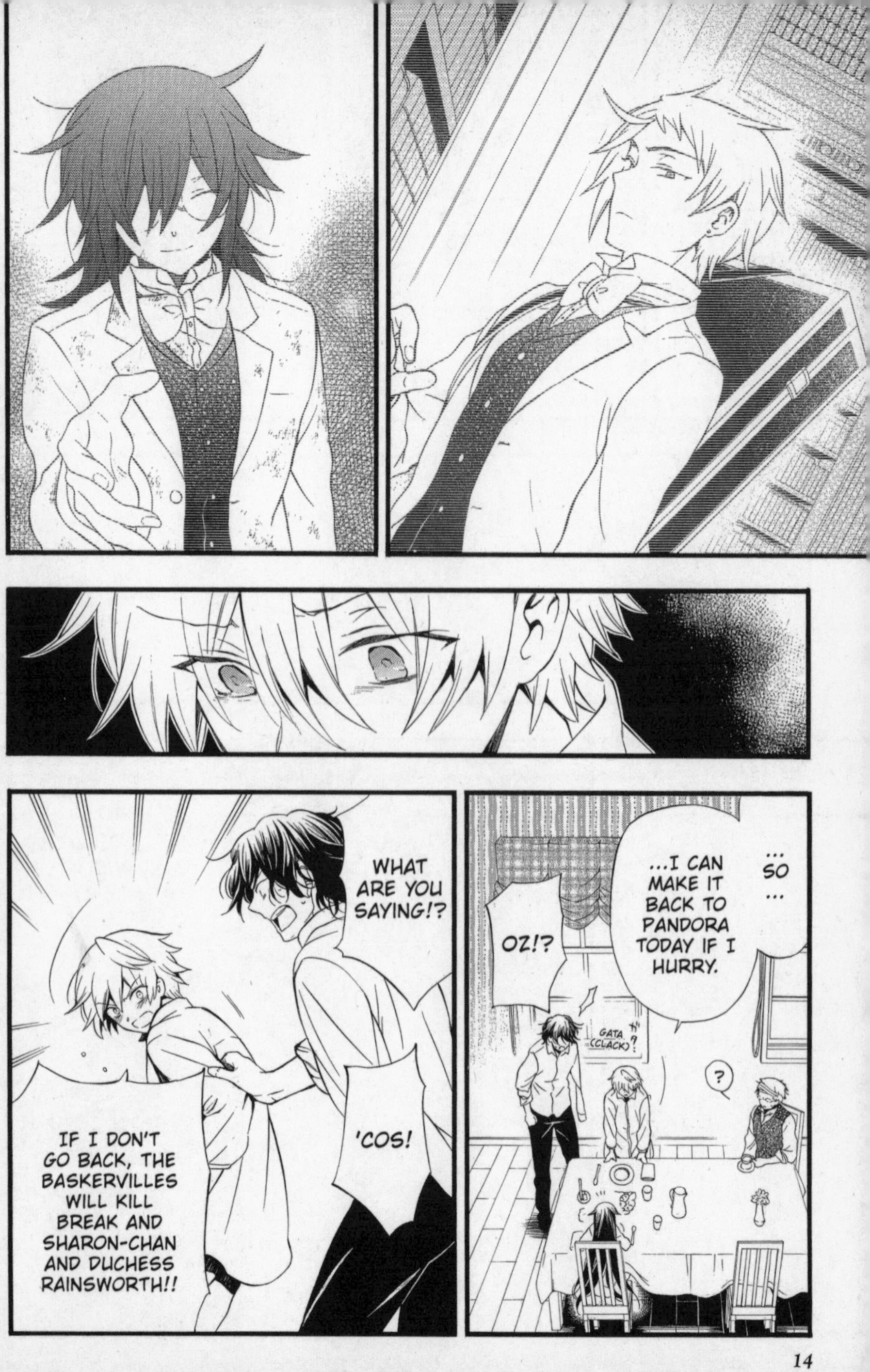
... SO ...
...I CAN MAKE IT BACK TO PANDORA TODAY IF I HURRY.
OZ!?
GATA (CLACK)
?
WHAT ARE YOU SAYING!?
'COS!
IF I DON'T GO BACK, THE BASKERVILLES WILL KILL BREAK AND SHARON-CHAN AND DUCHESS RAINSWORTH!!

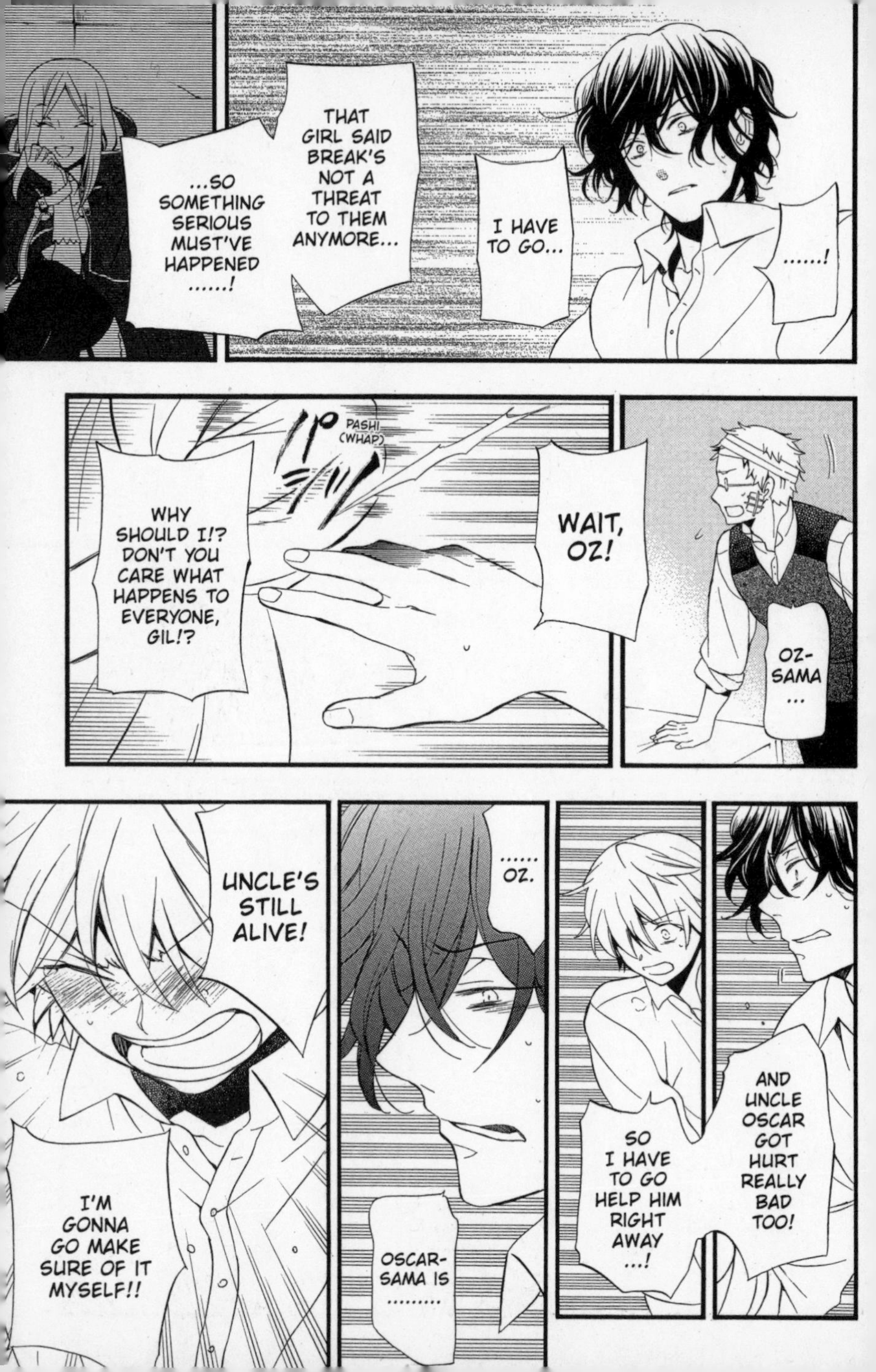
......!
I HAVE TO GO...
THAT GIRL SAID BREAK'S NOT A THREAT TO THEM ANYMORE...
...SO SOMETHING SERIOUS MUST'VE HAPPENED ......!
OZ-SAMA ...
WAIT, OZ!
PASHI (WHAP)
WHY SHOULD I!? DON'T YOU CARE WHAT HAPPENS TO EVERYONE, GIL!?
AND UNCLE OSCAR GOT HURT REALLY BAD TOO!
SO I HAVE TO GO HELP HIM RIGHT AWAY ...!
...... OZ.
OSCAR-SAMA IS ....
UNCLE'S STILL ALIVE!
I'M GONNA GO MAKE SURE OF IT MYSELF!!

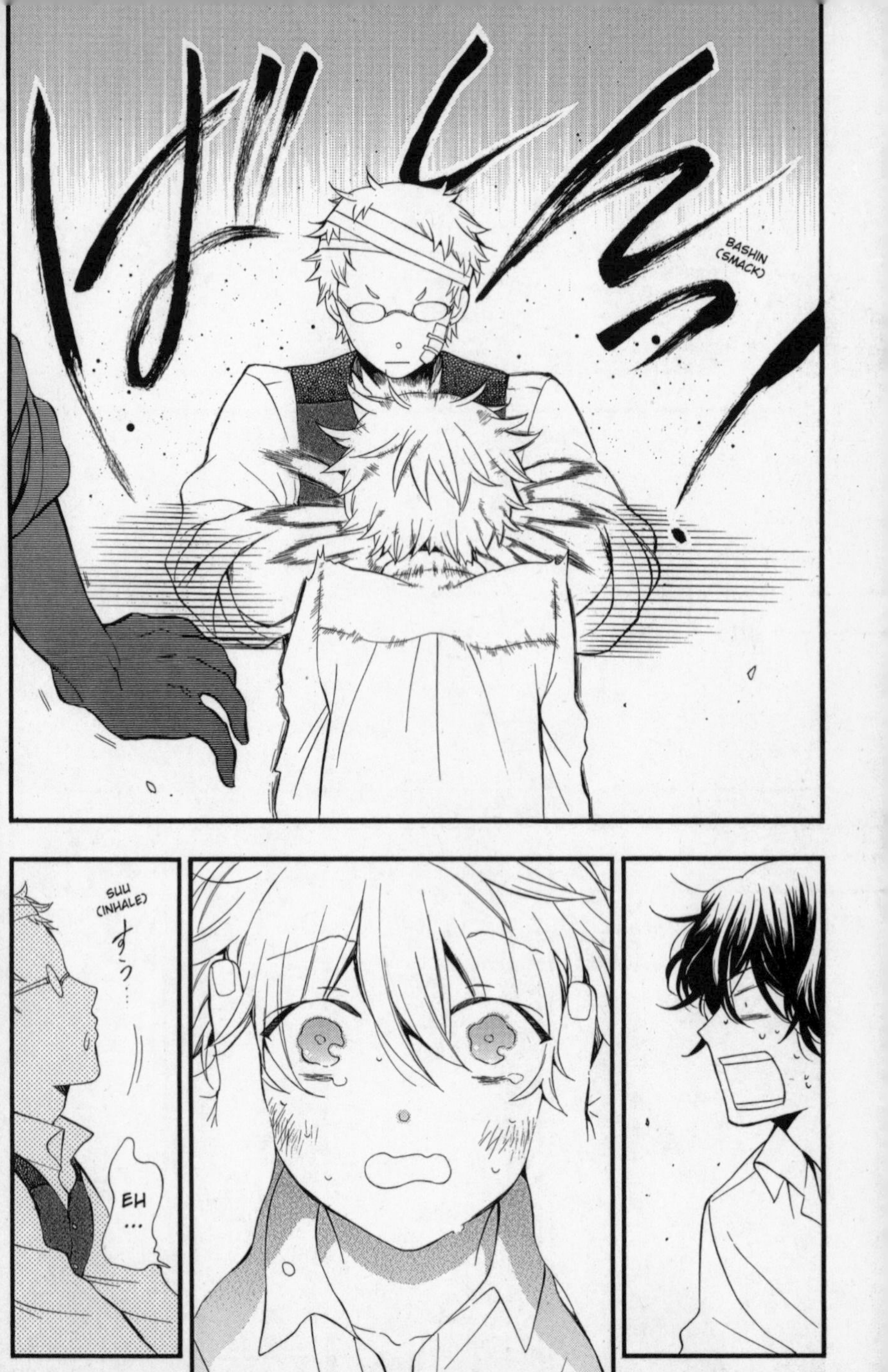
ばしんっ!
BASHIN (SMACK)
SUU (INHALE)
すっ…
EH ...

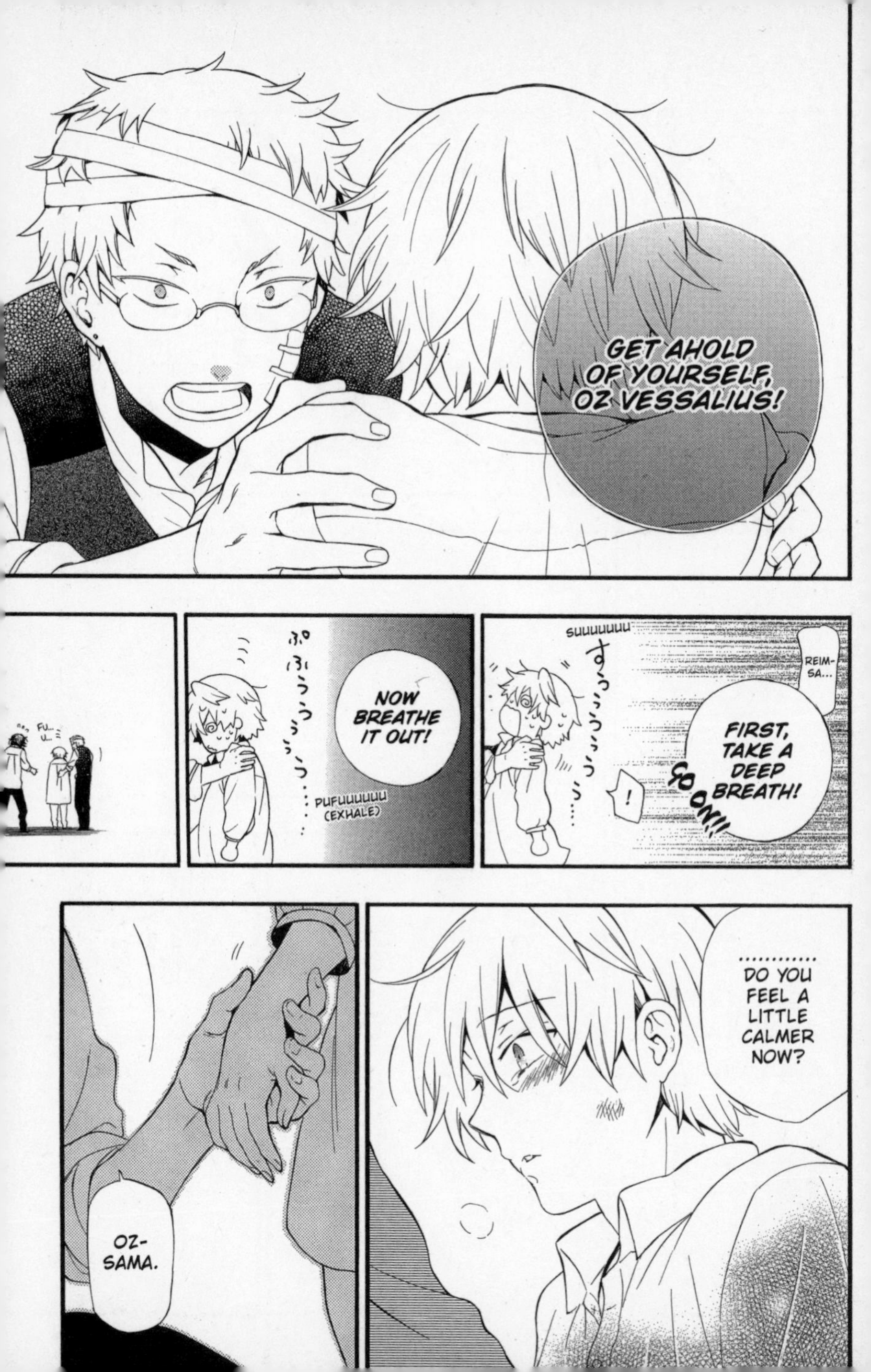
GET AHOLD OF YOURSELF, OZ VESSALIUS!
SUUUUUUU
REIM-SA...
FIRST, TAKE A DEEP BREATH!
!
GO ON!!
NOW BREATHE IT OUT!
PUFUUUUUU (EXHALE)
FU... U...
.... DO YOU FEEL A LITTLE CALMER NOW?
OZ-SAMA.

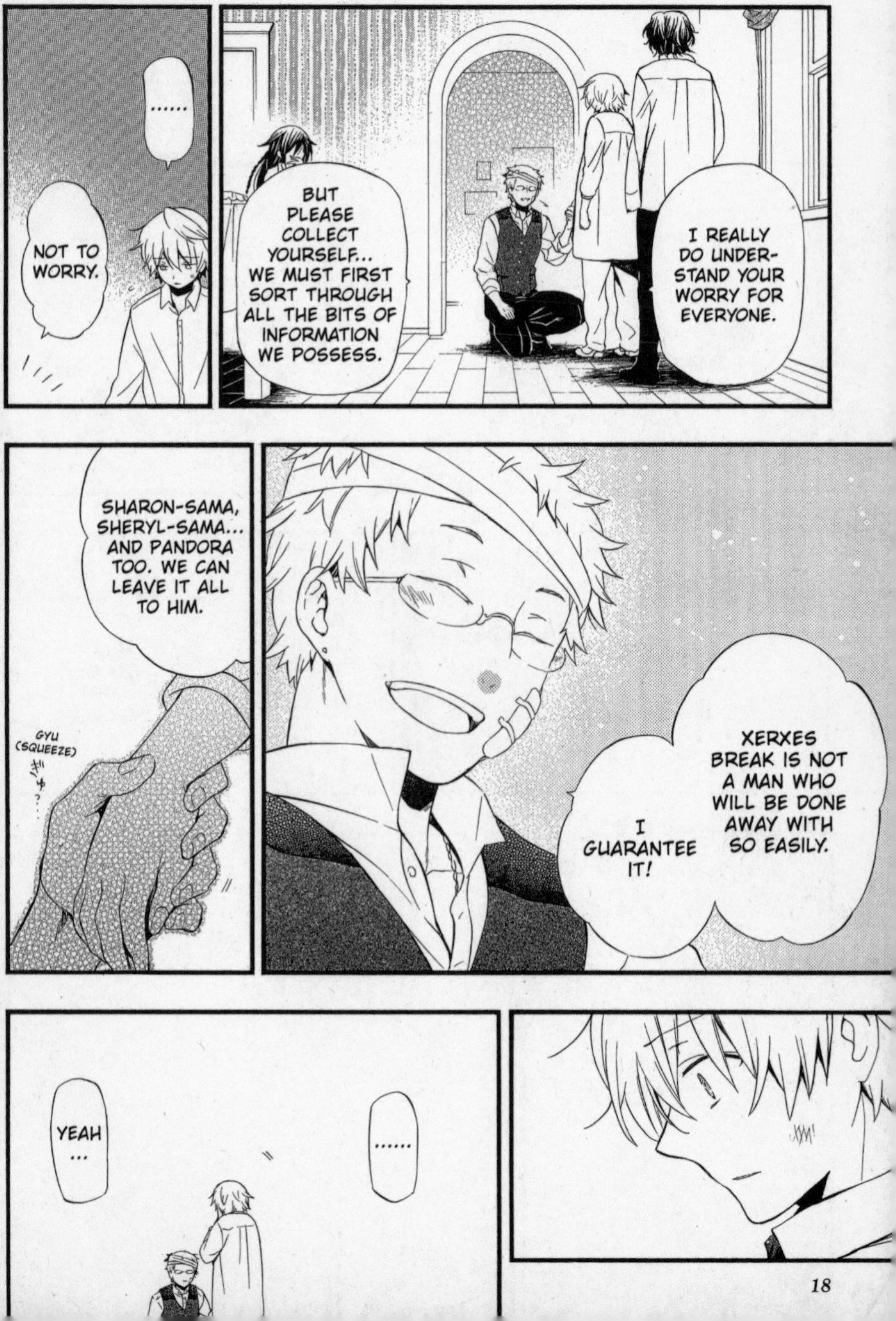
I REALLY DO UNDER-STAND YOUR WORRY FOR EVERYONE.
BUT PLEASE COLLECT YOURSELF... WE MUST FIRST SORT THROUGH ALL THE BITS OF INFORMATION WE POSSESS.
......
NOT TO WORRY.
XERXES BREAK IS NOT A MAN WHO WILL BE DONE AWAY WITH SO EASILY.
I GUARANTEE IT!
SHARON-SAMA, SHERYL-SAMA... AND PANDORA TOO. WE CAN LEAVE IT ALL TO HIM.
GYU (SQUEEZE)
......
YEAH ...

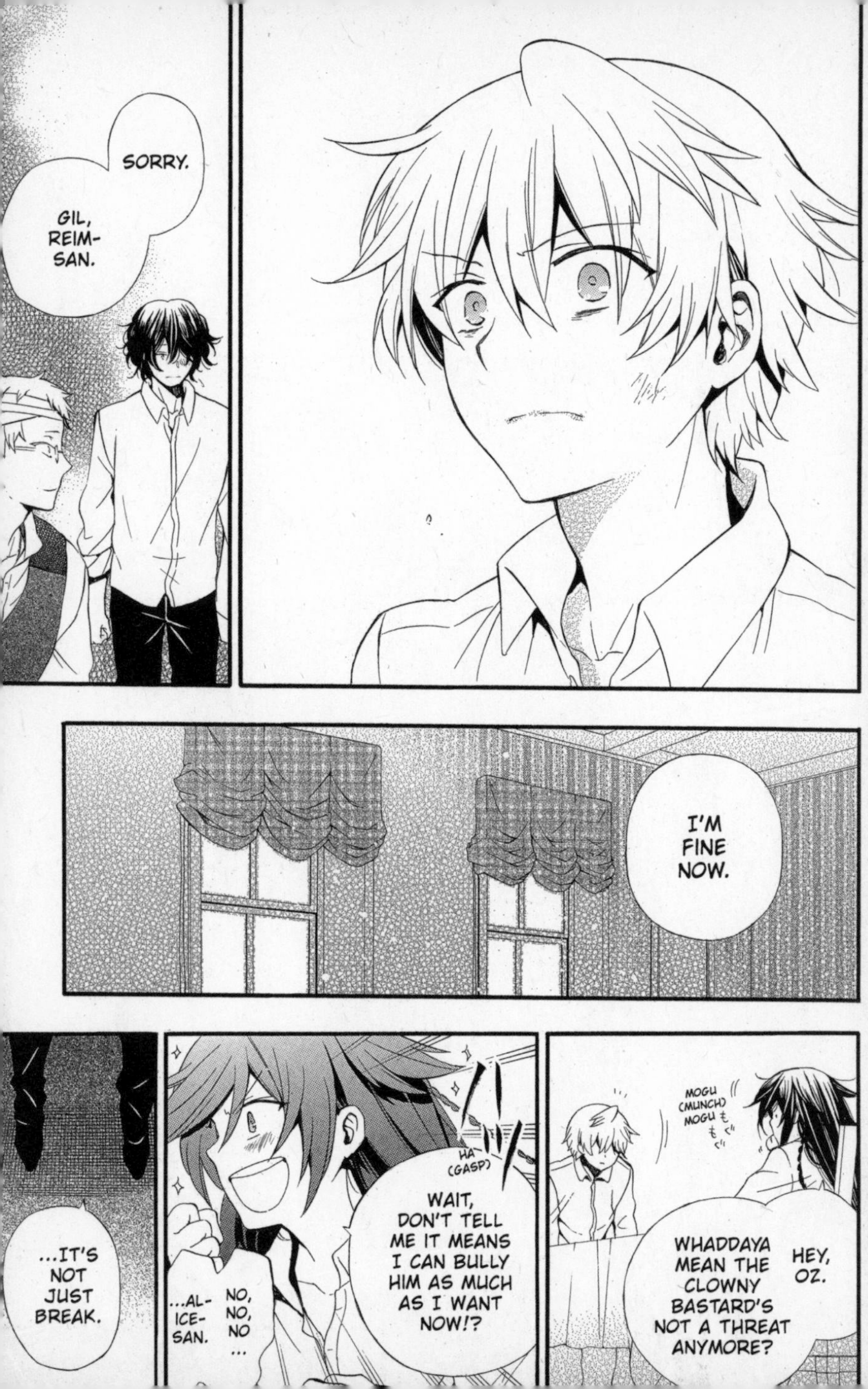
SORRY.
GIL, REIM-SAN.
I'M FINE NOW.
MOGU (MUNCH) MOGU
HEY, OZ.
WHADDAYA MEAN THE CLOWNY BASTARD'S NOT A THREAT ANYMORE?
HA (GASP)
WAIT, DON'T TELL ME IT MEANS I CAN BULLY HIM AS MUCH AS I WANT NOW!?
NO, NO, NO ...
...AL-ICE-SAN.
...IT'S NOT JUST BREAK.

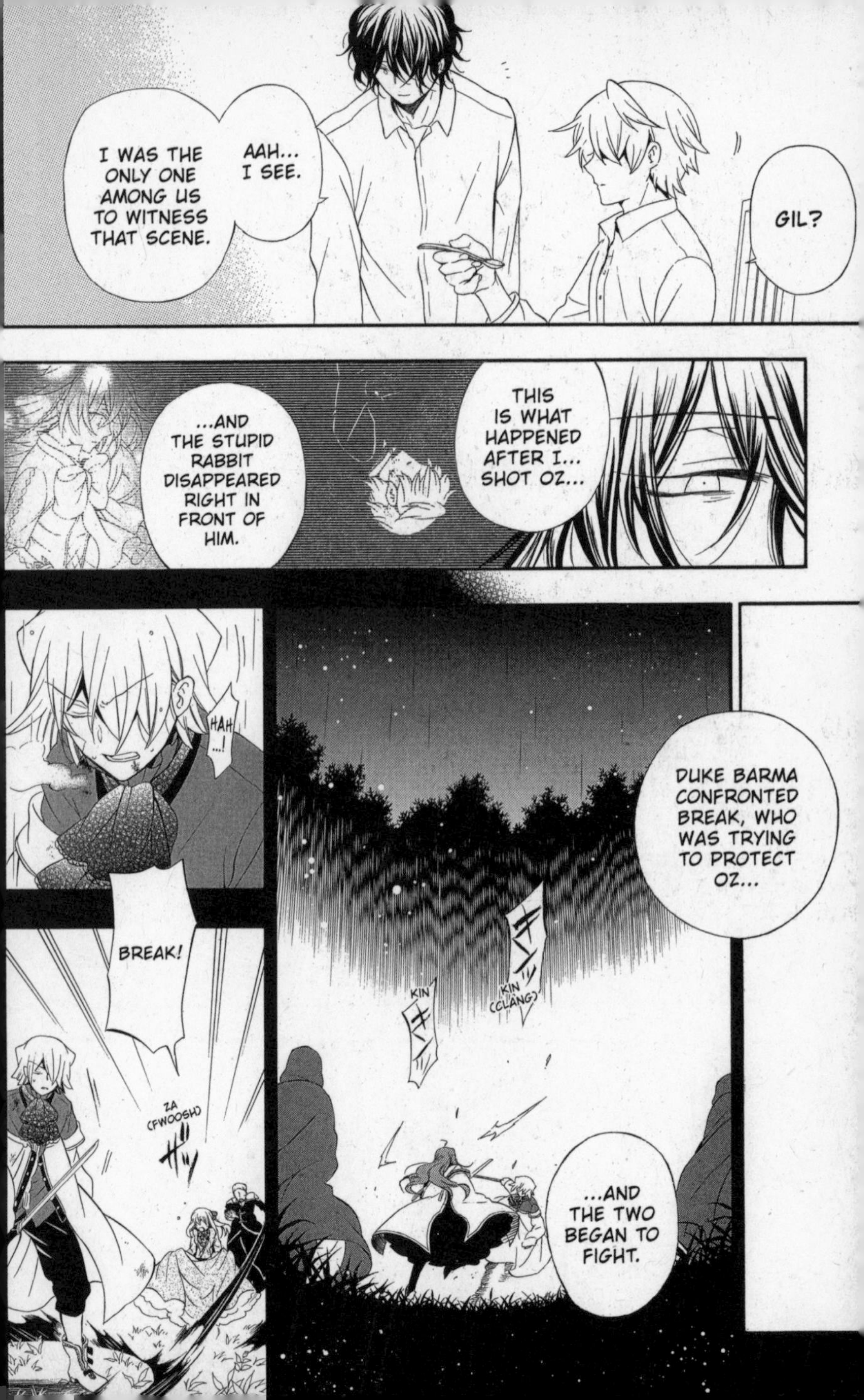
GIL?
AAH... I SEE.
I WAS THE ONLY ONE AMONG US TO WITNESS THAT SCENE.
THIS IS WHAT HAPPENED AFTER I... SHOT OZ...
...AND THE STUPID RABBIT DISAPPEARED RIGHT IN FRONT OF HIM.
DUKE BARMA CONFRONTED BREAK, WHO WAS TRYING TO PROTECT OZ...
KIN (CLANG)
KIN
...AND THE TWO BEGAN TO FIGHT.
HAH ...!
BREAK!
ZA (FWOOSH)

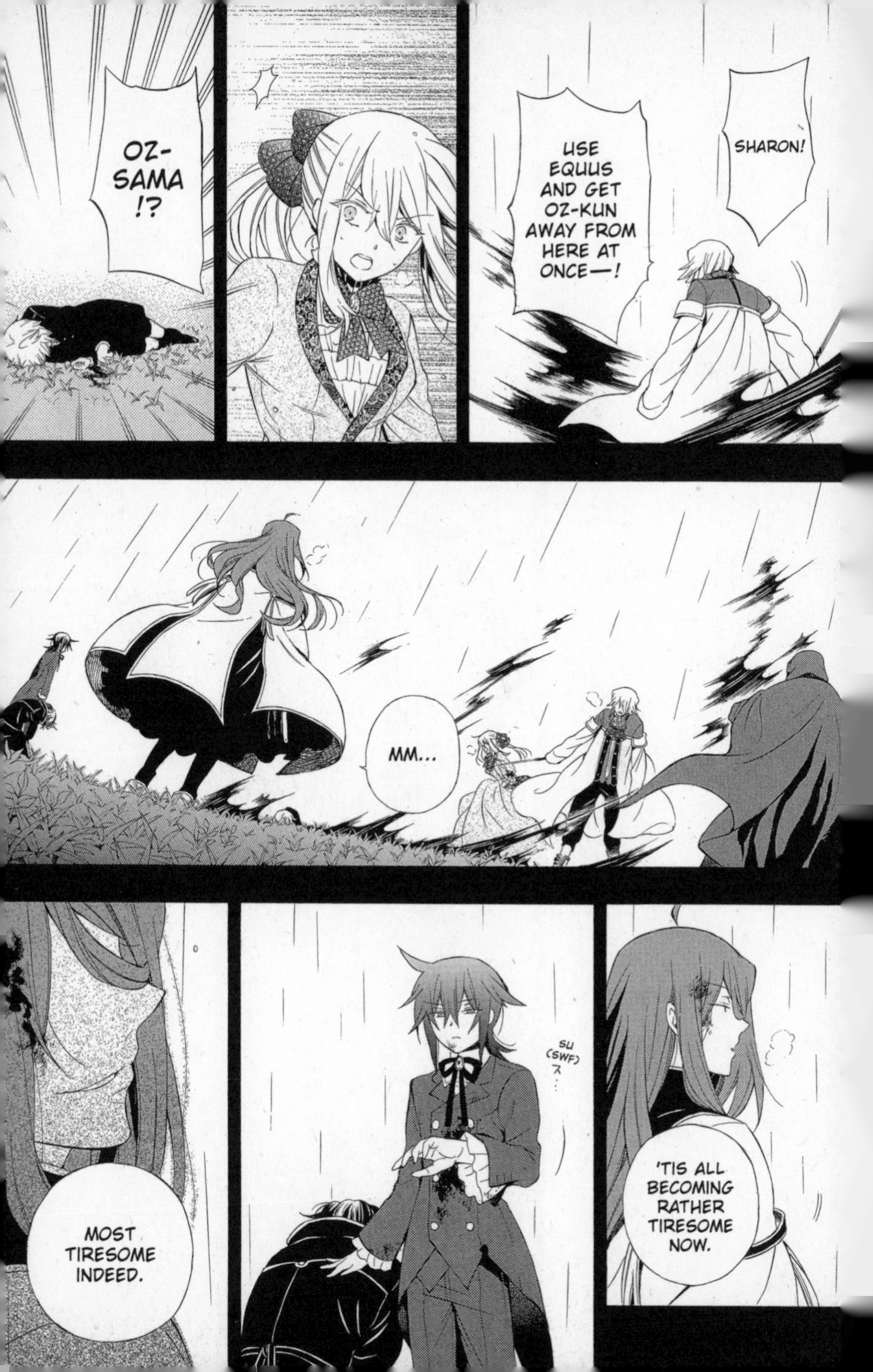
SHARON!
USE EQUUS AND GET OZ-KUN AWAY FROM HERE AT ONCE—!
OZ-SAMA!?
MM...
'TIS ALL BECOMING RATHER TIRESOME NOW.
SU (SWF)
ス…
MOST TIRESOME INDEED.

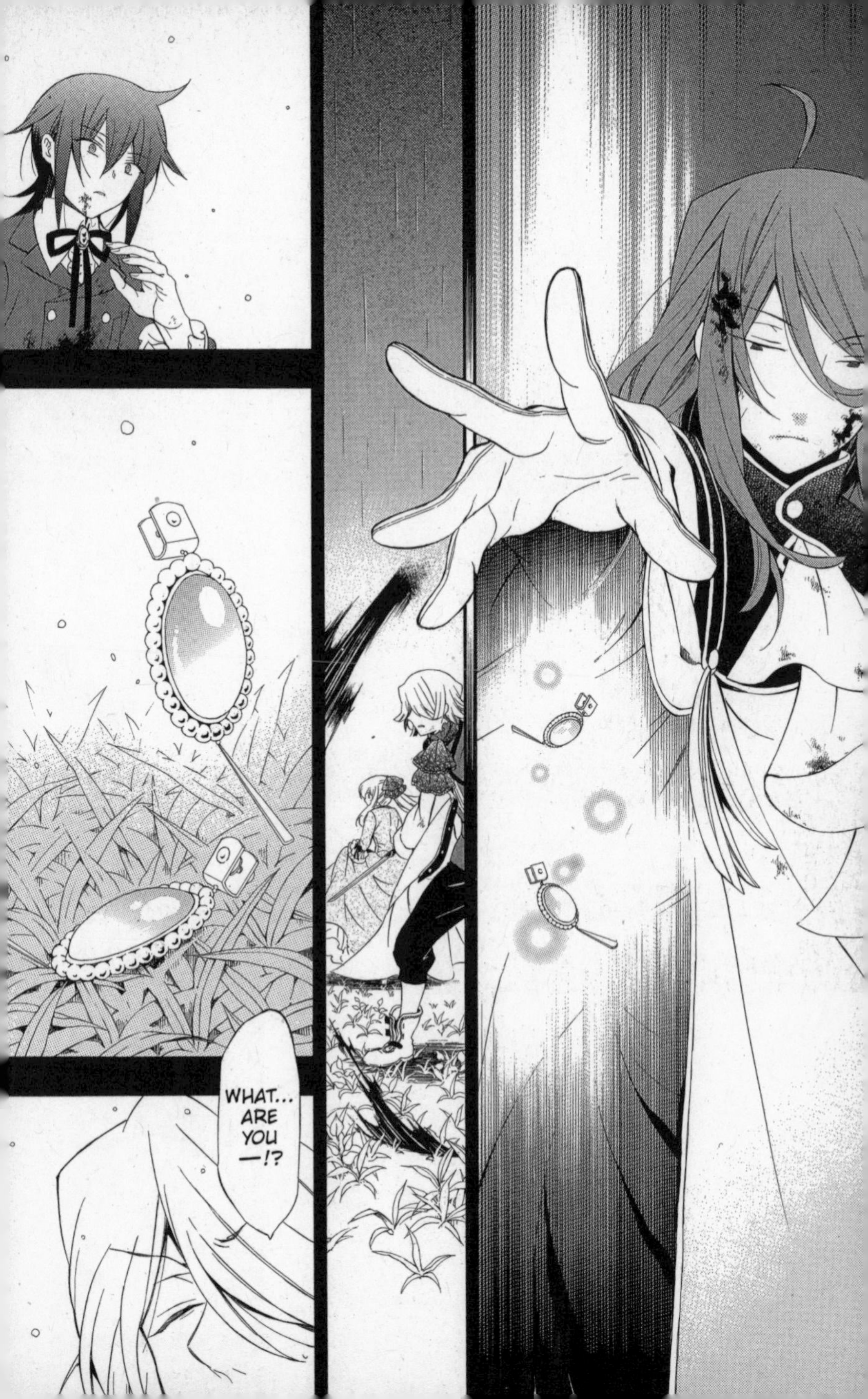
WHAT... ARE YOU —!?

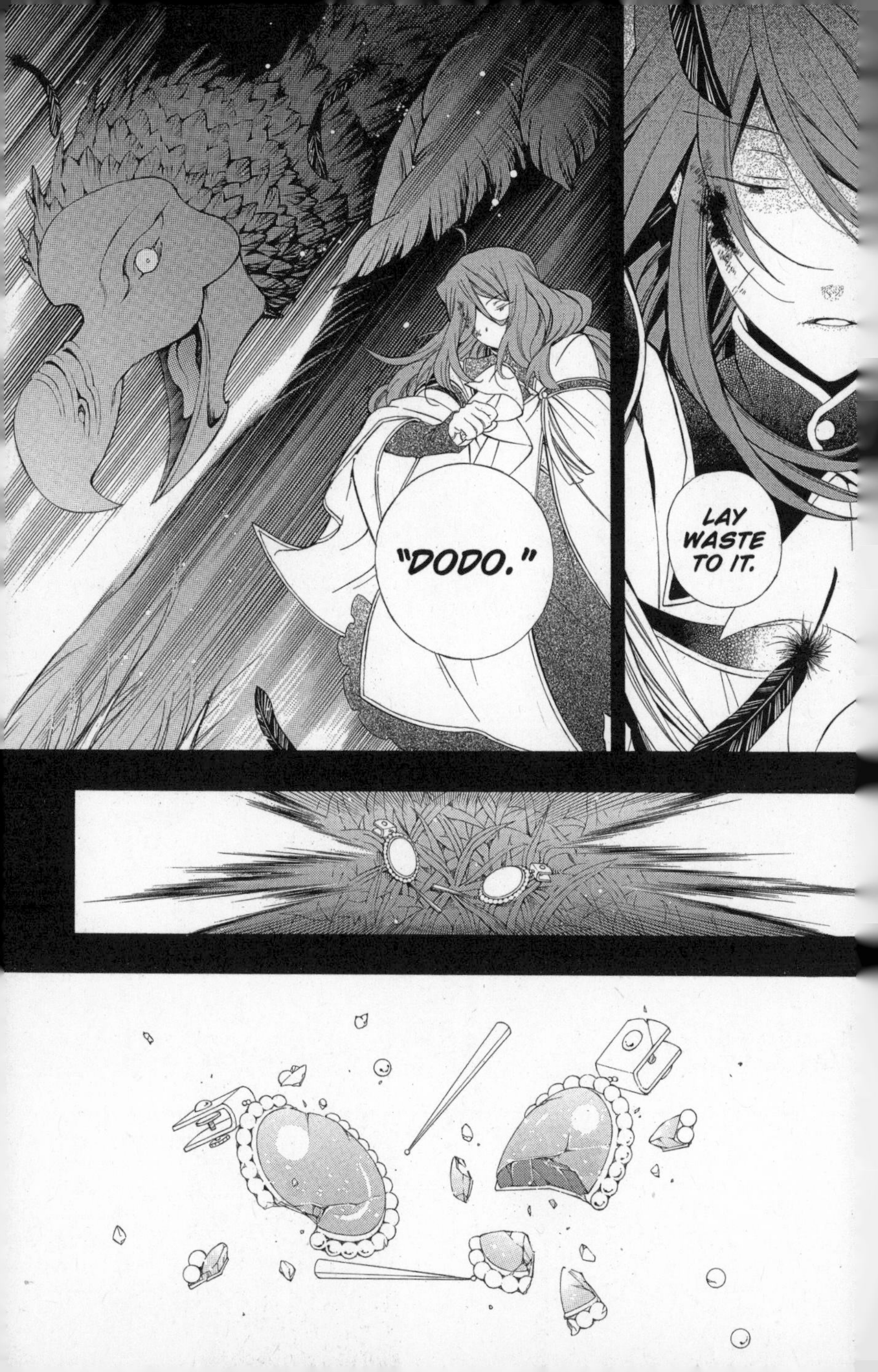
LAY WASTE TO IT.
"DODO."

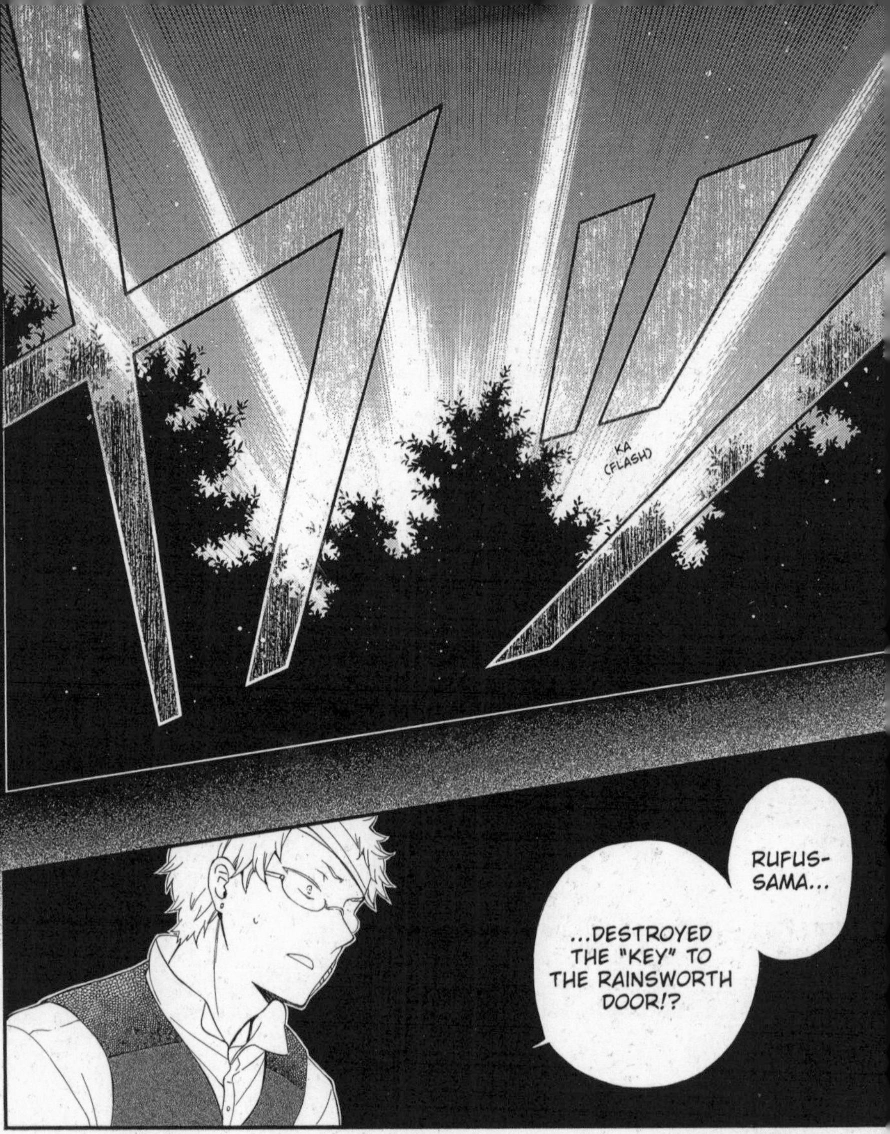
KA (FLASH)
RUFUS-SAMA...
...DESTROYED THE "KEY" TO THE RAINSWORTH DOOR!?

SFX: GYUUUU (SQUEEZE)

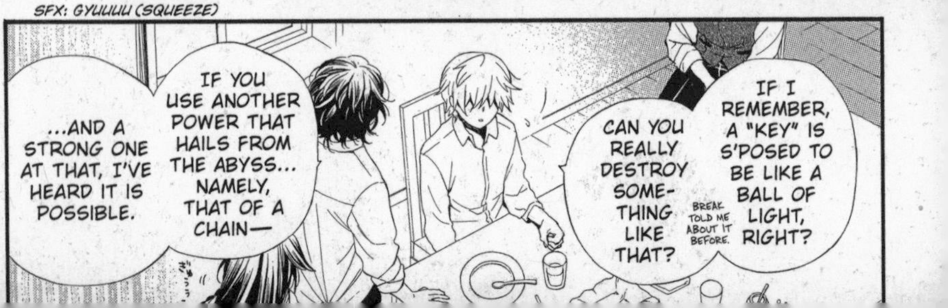
IF I REMEMBER, A "KEY" IS S'POSED TO BE LIKE A BALL OF LIGHT, RIGHT?
BREAK TOLD ME ABOUT IT BEFORE.
CAN YOU REALLY DESTROY SOME-THING LIKE THAT?
IF YOU USE ANOTHER POWER THAT HAILS FROM THE ABYSS... NAMELY, THAT OF A CHAIN—
...AND A STRONG ONE AT THAT, I'VE HEARD IT IS POSSIBLE.

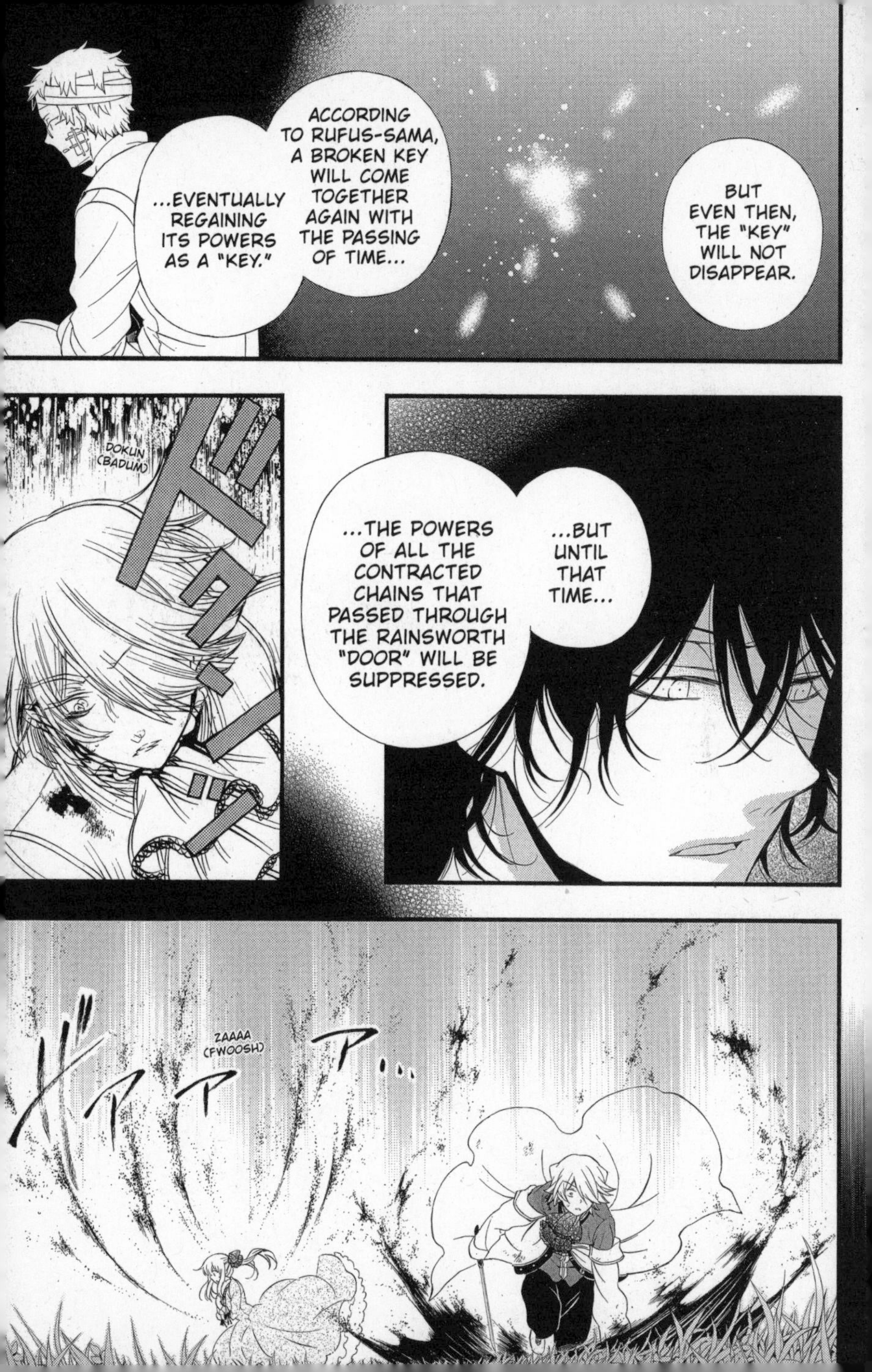
BUT EVEN THEN, THE "KEY" WILL NOT DISAPPEAR.
ACCORDING TO RUFUS-SAMA, A BROKEN KEY WILL COME TOGETHER AGAIN WITH THE PASSING OF TIME...
...EVENTUALLY REGAINING ITS POWERS AS A "KEY."
...BUT UNTIL THAT TIME...
...THE POWERS OF ALL THE CONTRACTED CHAINS THAT PASSED THROUGH THE RAINSWORTH "DOOR" WILL BE SUPPRESSED.
DOKUN (BADUM)
ZAAAA (FWOOSH)

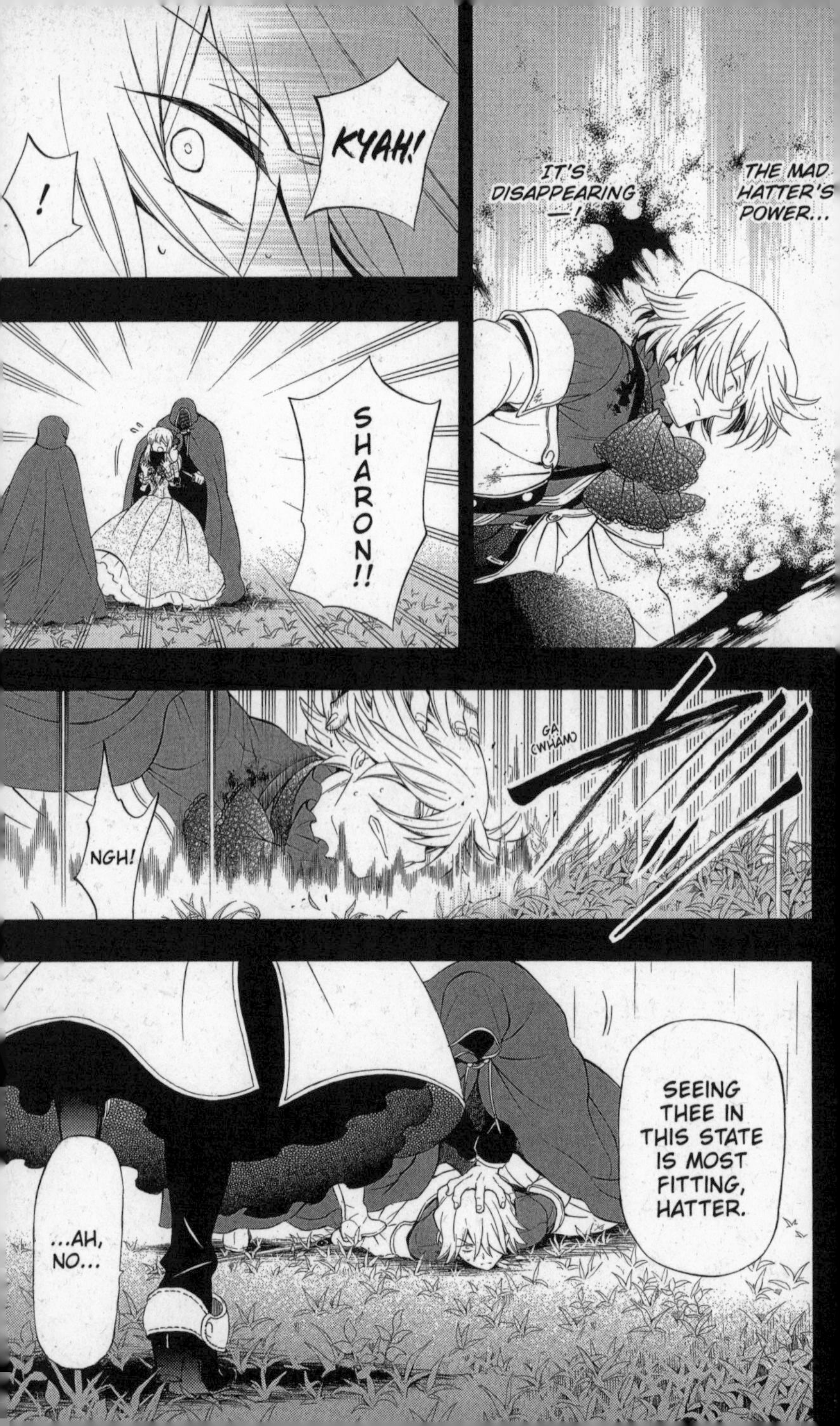
THE MAD HATTER'S POWER...
IT'S DISAPPEARING—!
KYAH!
!
SHARON!!
GA (WHAM)
NGH!
SEEING THEE IN THIS STATE IS MOST FITTING, HATTER.
...AH, NO...

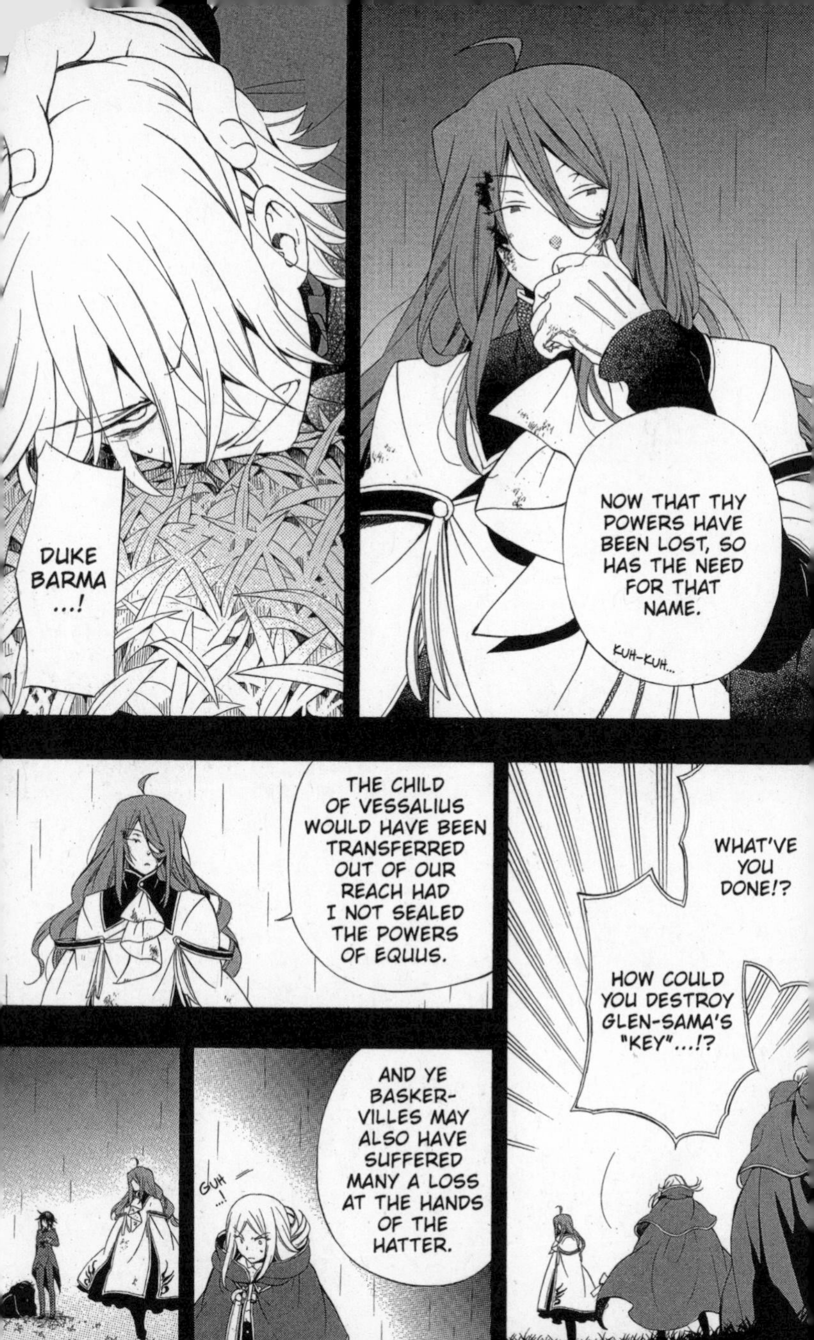
NOW THAT THY POWERS HAVE BEEN LOST, SO HAS THE NEED FOR THAT NAME.
KUH-KUH...
DUKE BARMA ...!
WHAT'VE YOU DONE!?
HOW COULD YOU DESTROY GLEN-SAMA'S "KEY"...!?
THE CHILD OF VESSALIUS WOULD HAVE BEEN TRANSFERRED OUT OF OUR REACH HAD I NOT SEALED THE POWERS OF EQUUS.
AND YE BASKER-VILLES MAY ALSO HAVE SUFFERED MANY A LOSS AT THE HANDS OF THE HATTER.
GUH ...!

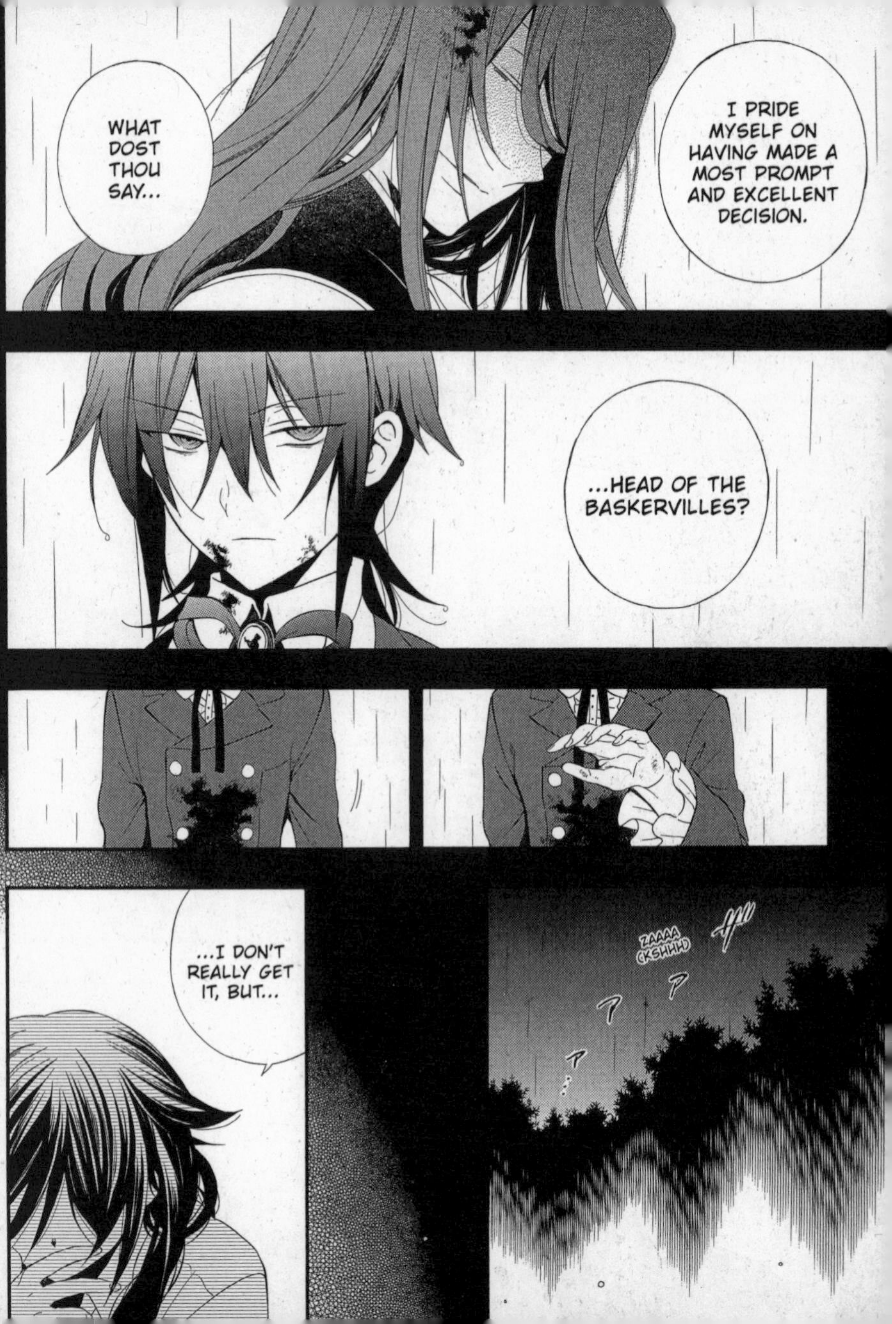
I PRIDE MYSELF ON HAVING MADE A MOST PROMPT AND EXCELLENT DECISION.
WHAT DOST THOU SAY...
...HEAD OF THE BASKERVILLES?
ZAAAA (KSHHH)
...I DON'T REALLY GET IT, BUT...

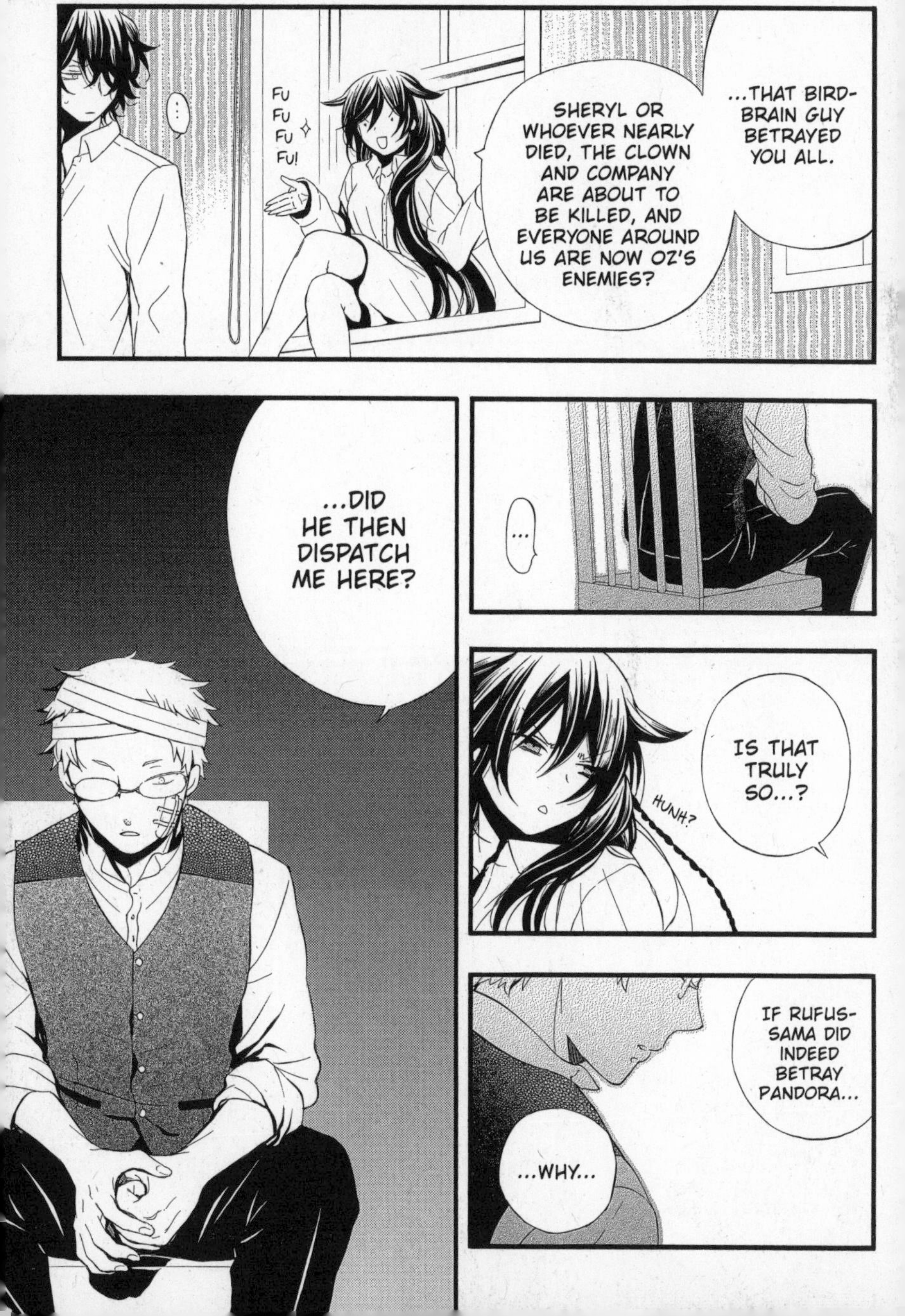
...THAT BIRD-BRAIN GUY BETRAYED YOU ALL.
SHERYL OR WHOEVER NEARLY DIED, THE CLOWN AND COMPANY ARE ABOUT TO BE KILLED, AND EVERYONE AROUND US ARE NOW OZ'S ENEMIES?
FU FU FU FU!
...
...
IS THAT TRULY SO...?
HUNH?
IF RUFUS-SAMA DID INDEED BETRAY PANDORA...
...WHY...
...DID HE THEN DISPATCH ME HERE?

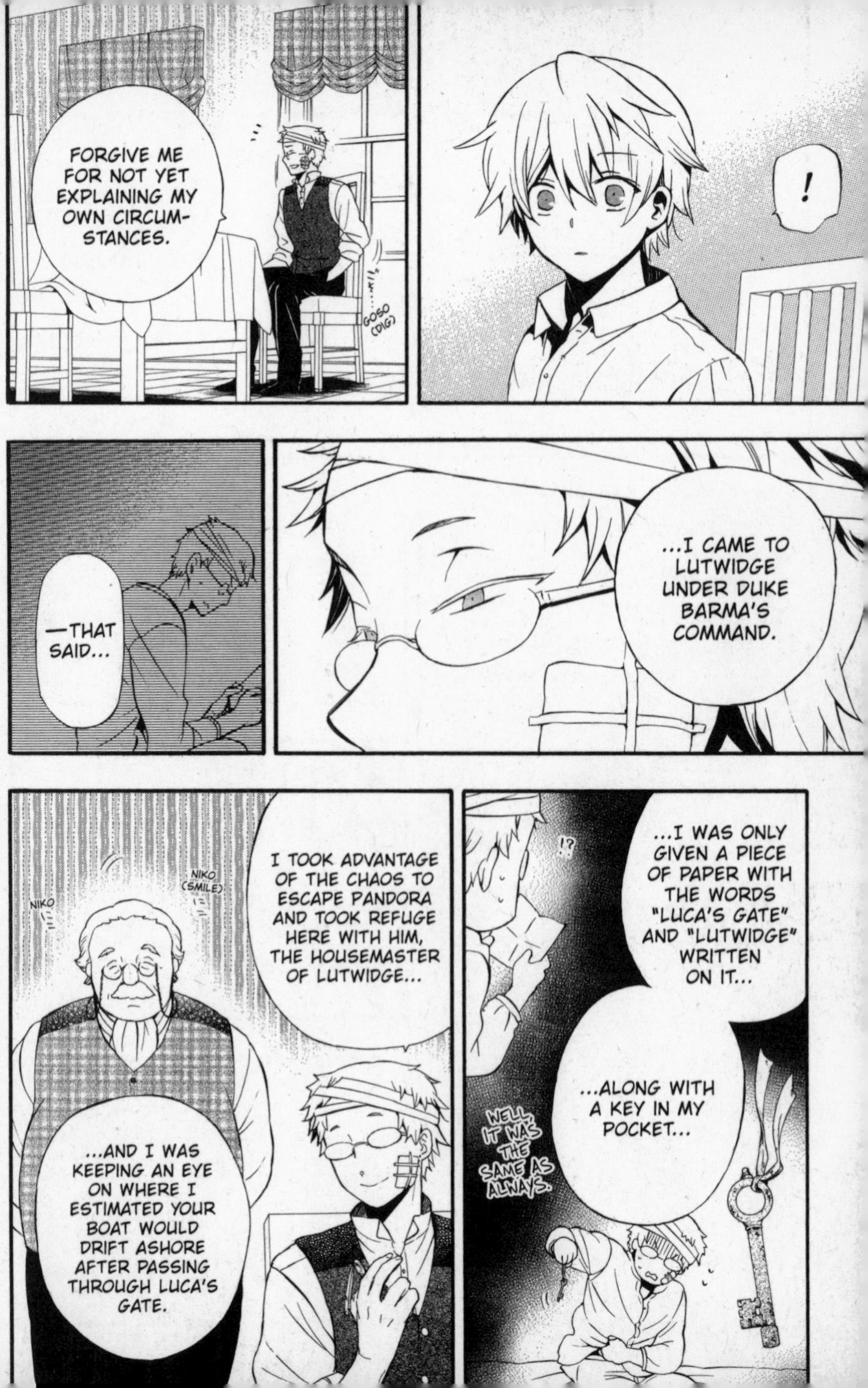
!
FORGIVE ME FOR NOT YET EXPLAINING MY OWN CIRCUM-STANCES.
GOSO (DIG)
...I CAME TO LUTWIDGE UNDER DUKE BARMA'S COMMAND.
—THAT SAID...
...I WAS ONLY GIVEN A PIECE OF PAPER WITH THE WORDS "LUCA'S GATE" AND "LUTWIDGE" WRITTEN ON IT...
!?
...ALONG WITH A KEY IN MY POCKET...
WELL, IT WAS THE SAME AS ALWAYS.
I TOOK ADVANTAGE OF THE CHAOS TO ESCAPE PANDORA AND TOOK REFUGE HERE WITH HIM, THE HOUSEMASTER OF LUTWIDGE...
NIKO (SMILE)
NIKO
...AND I WAS KEEPING AN EYE ON WHERE I ESTIMATED YOUR BOAT WOULD DRIFT ASHORE AFTER PASSING THROUGH LUCA'S GATE.

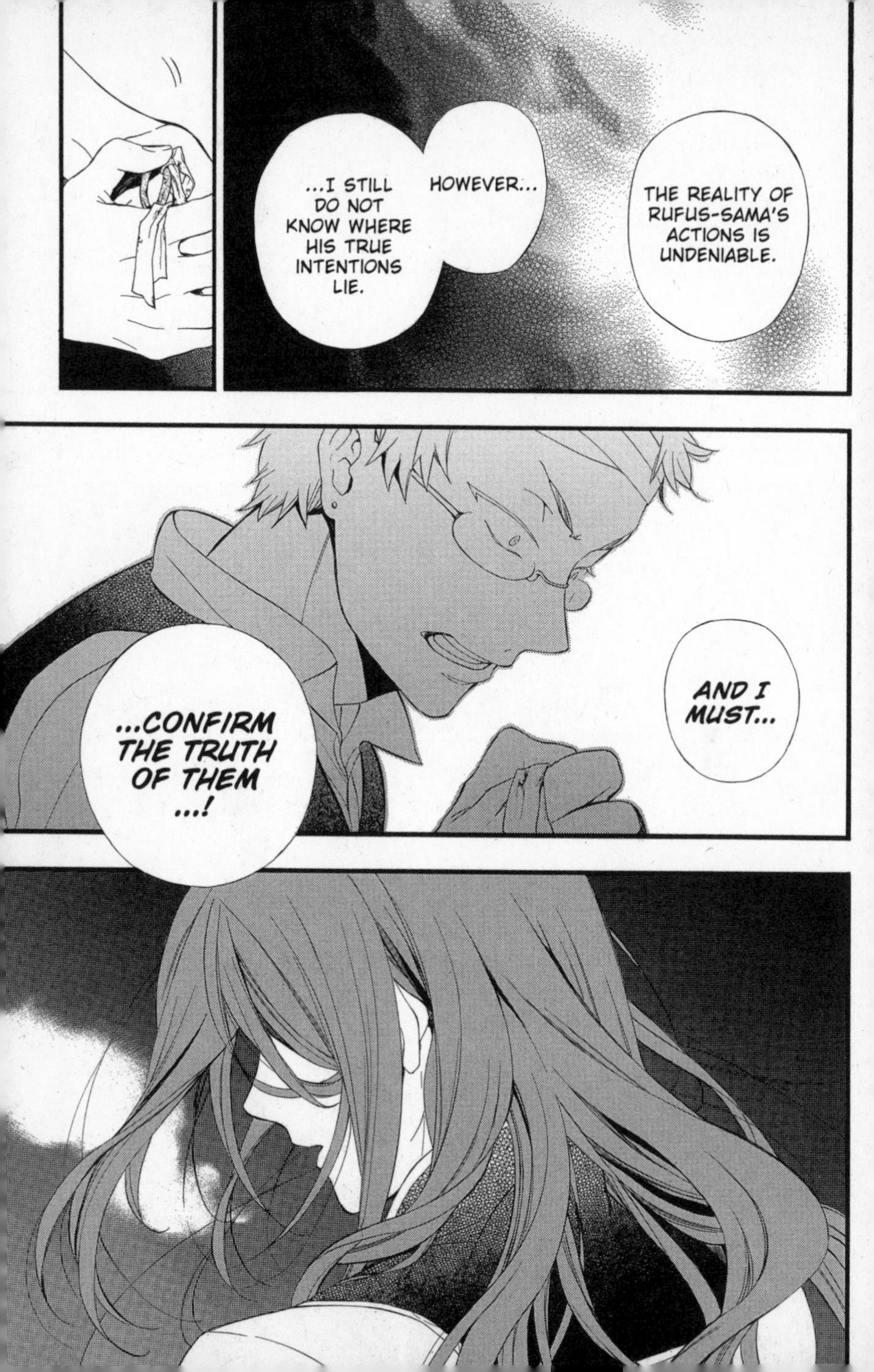
THE REALITY OF RUFUS-SAMA'S ACTIONS IS UNDENIABLE.
HOWEVER...
...I STILL DO NOT KNOW WHERE HIS TRUE INTENTIONS LIE.
AND I MUST...
...CONFIRM THE TRUTH OF THEM ...!

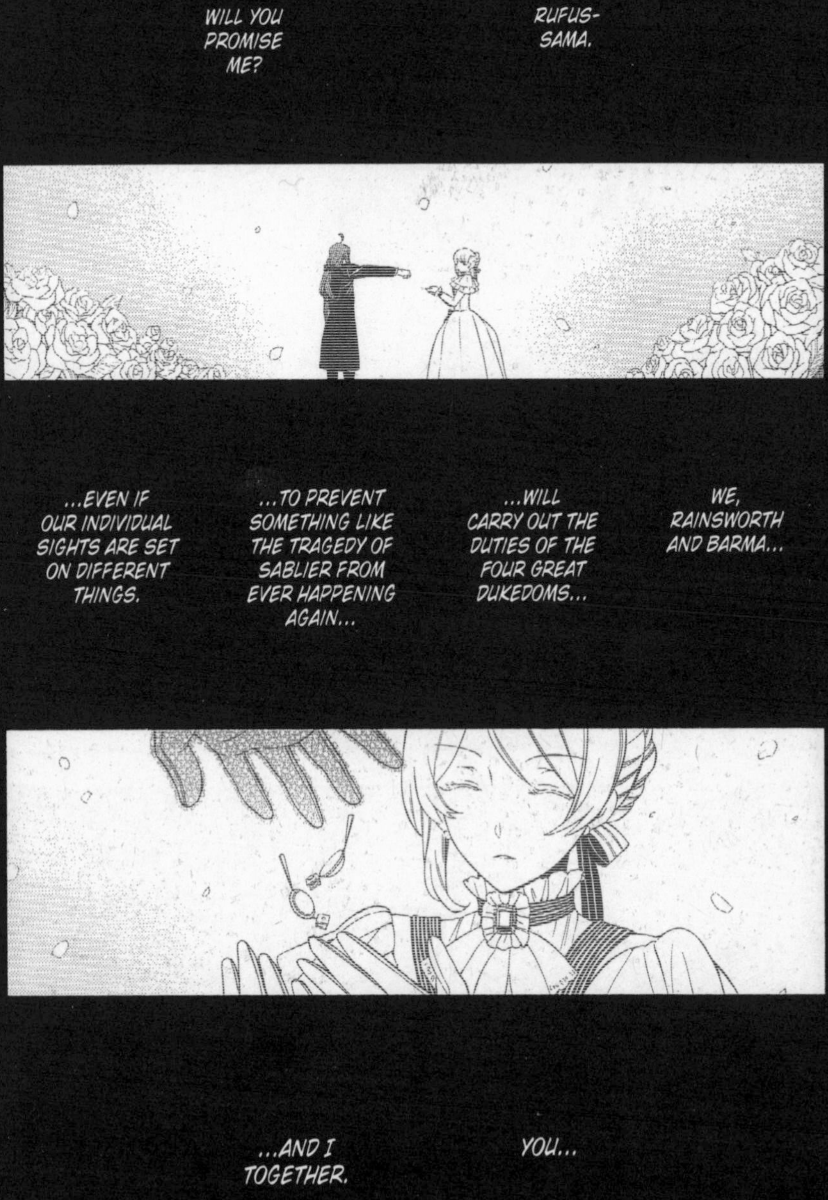
RUFUS-SAMA.
WILL YOU PROMISE ME?
WE, RAINSWORTH AND BARMA...
...WILL CARRY OUT THE DUTIES OF THE FOUR GREAT DUKEDOMS...
...TO PREVENT SOMETHING LIKE THE TRAGEDY OF SABLIER FROM EVER HAPPENING AGAIN...
...EVEN IF OUR INDIVIDUAL SIGHTS ARE SET ON DIFFERENT THINGS.
YOU...
...AND I TOGETHER.

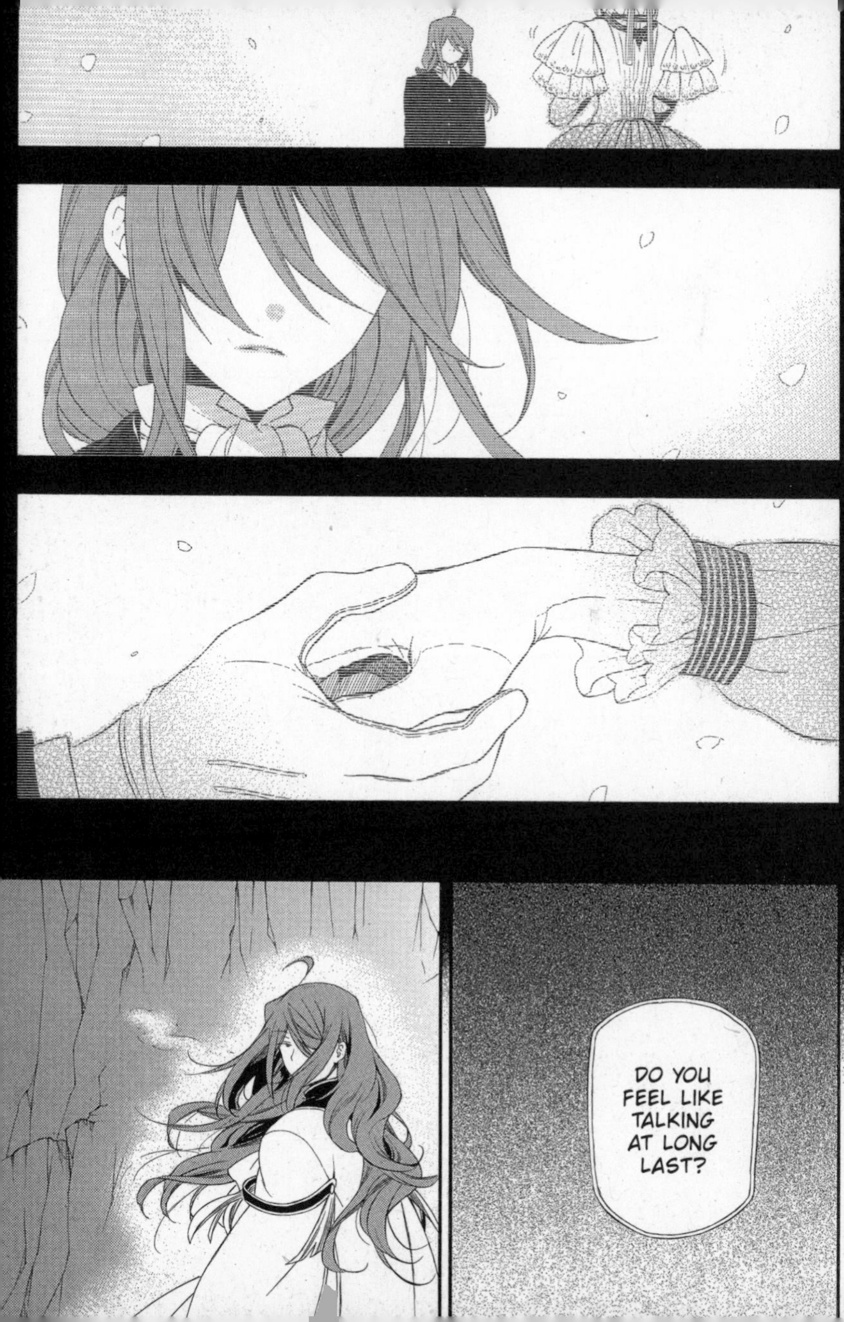
DO YOU FEEL LIKE TALKING AT LONG LAST?

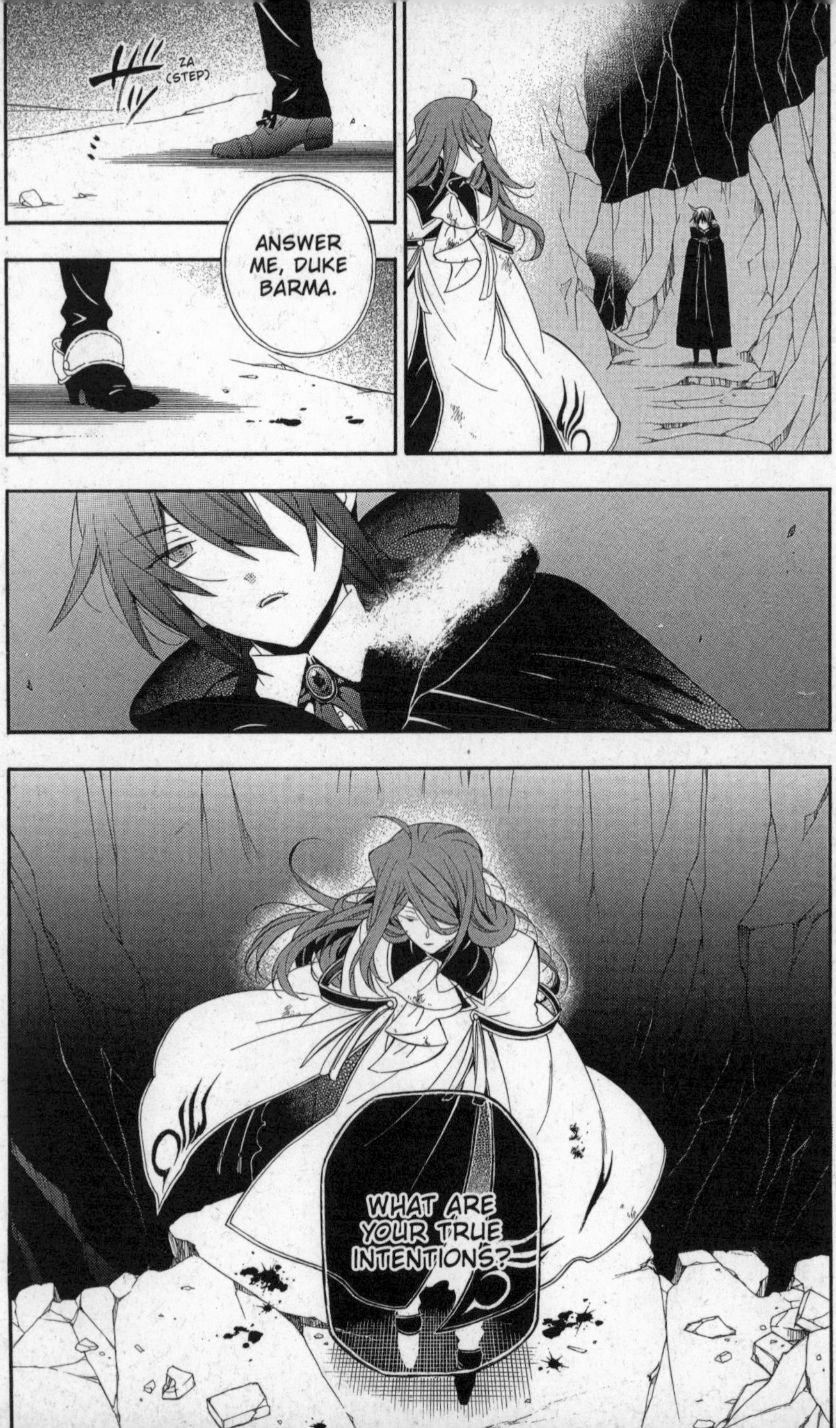
ZA (STEP)
ANSWER ME, DUKE BARMA.
WHAT ARE YOUR TRUE INTENTIONS?

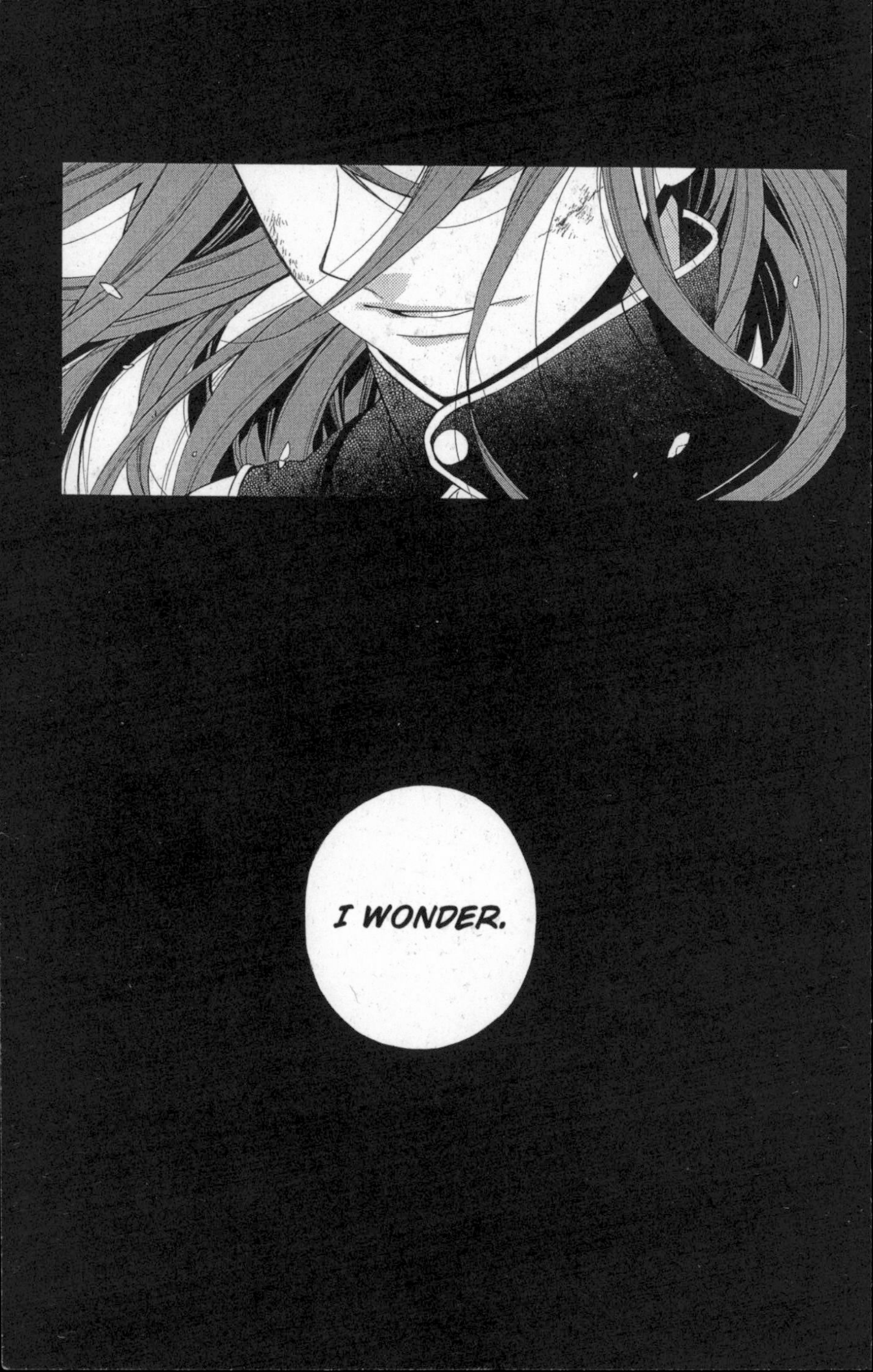
I WONDER.

Retrace : LXXXIII After the rain

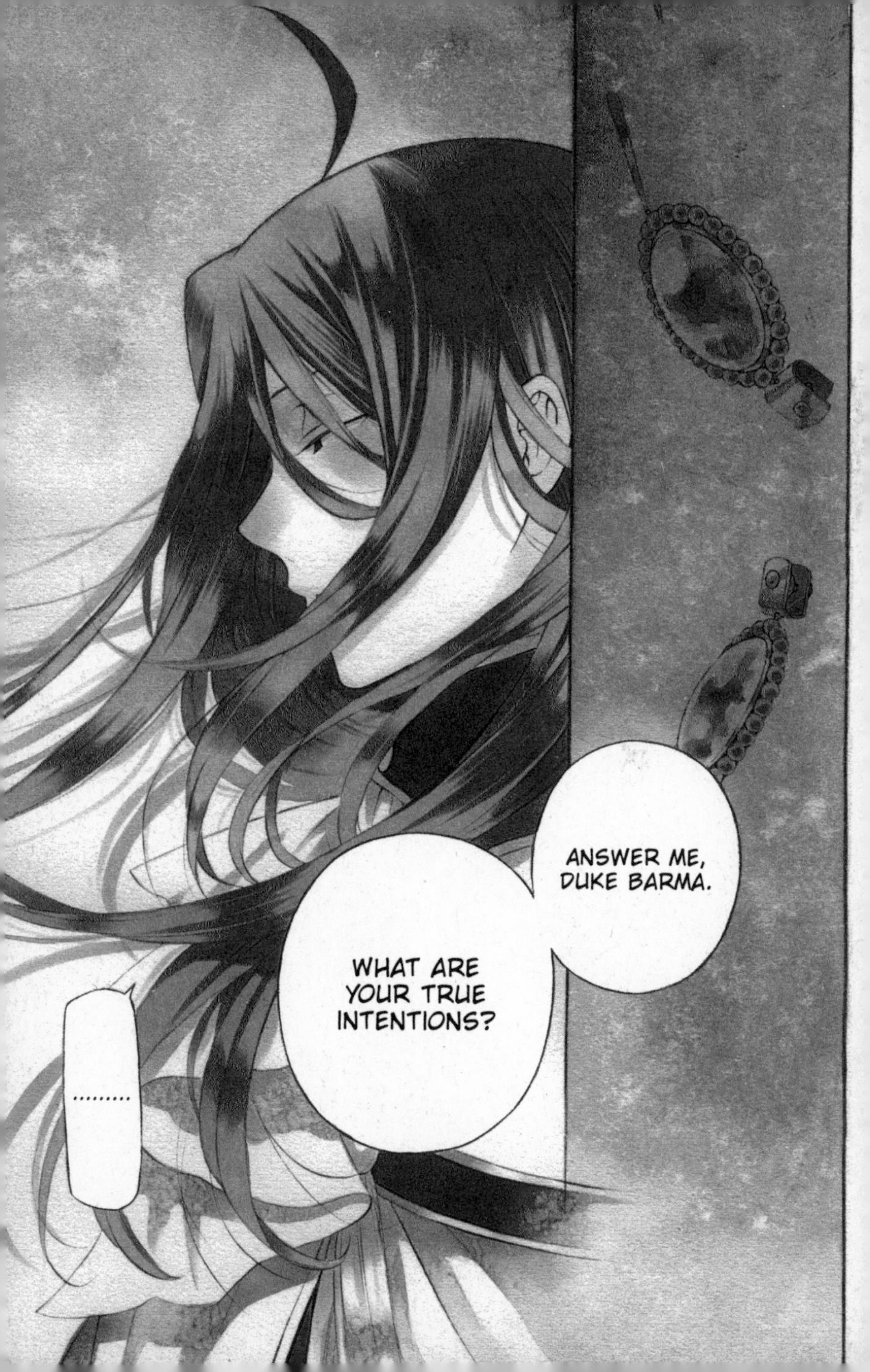
ANSWER ME, DUKE BARMA.
WHAT ARE YOUR TRUE INTENTIONS?
....

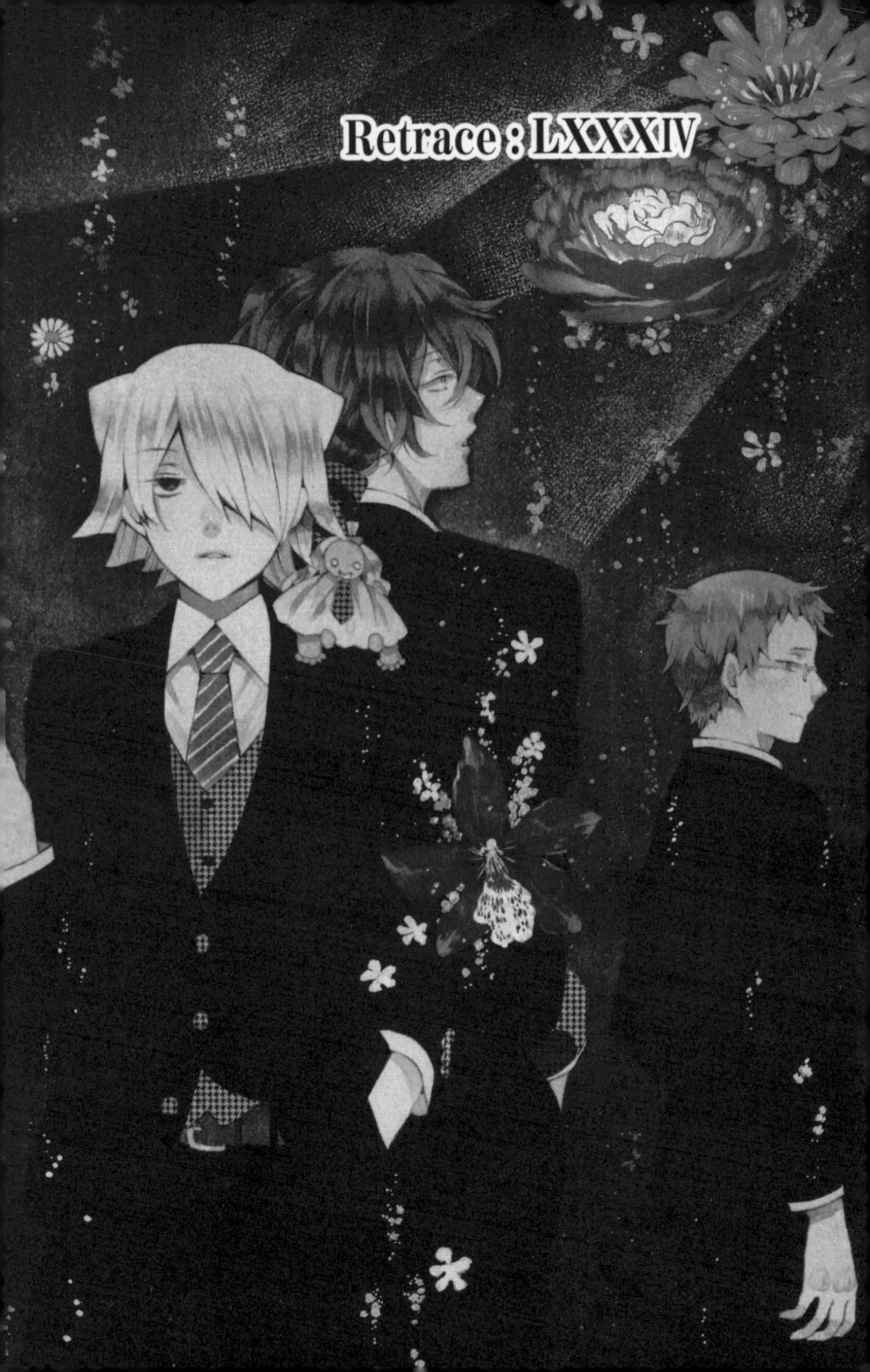
Retrace : LXXXIV

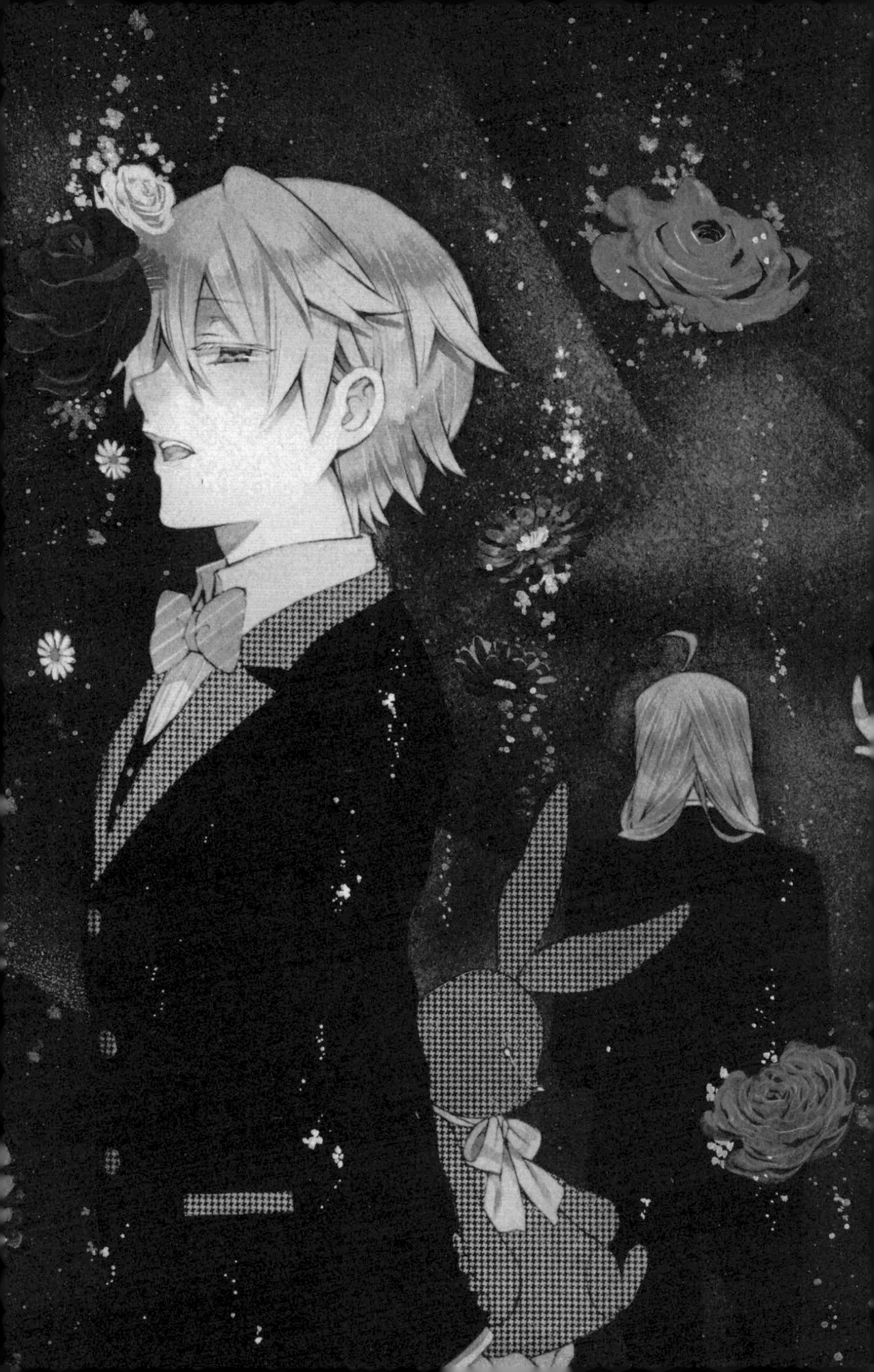

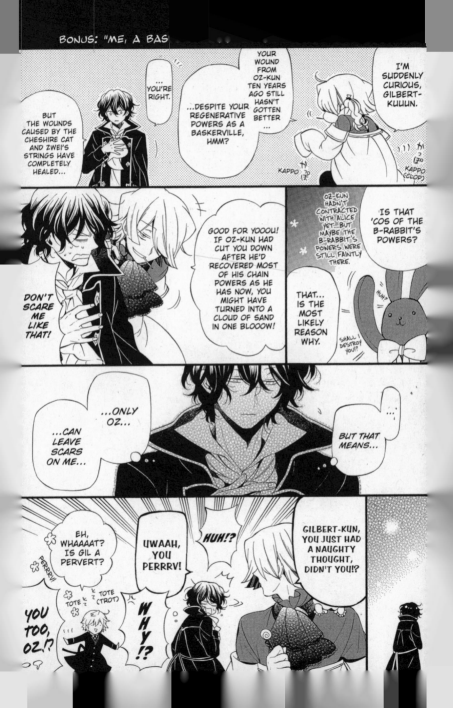

BONUS: "ME, A BAS[redacted]

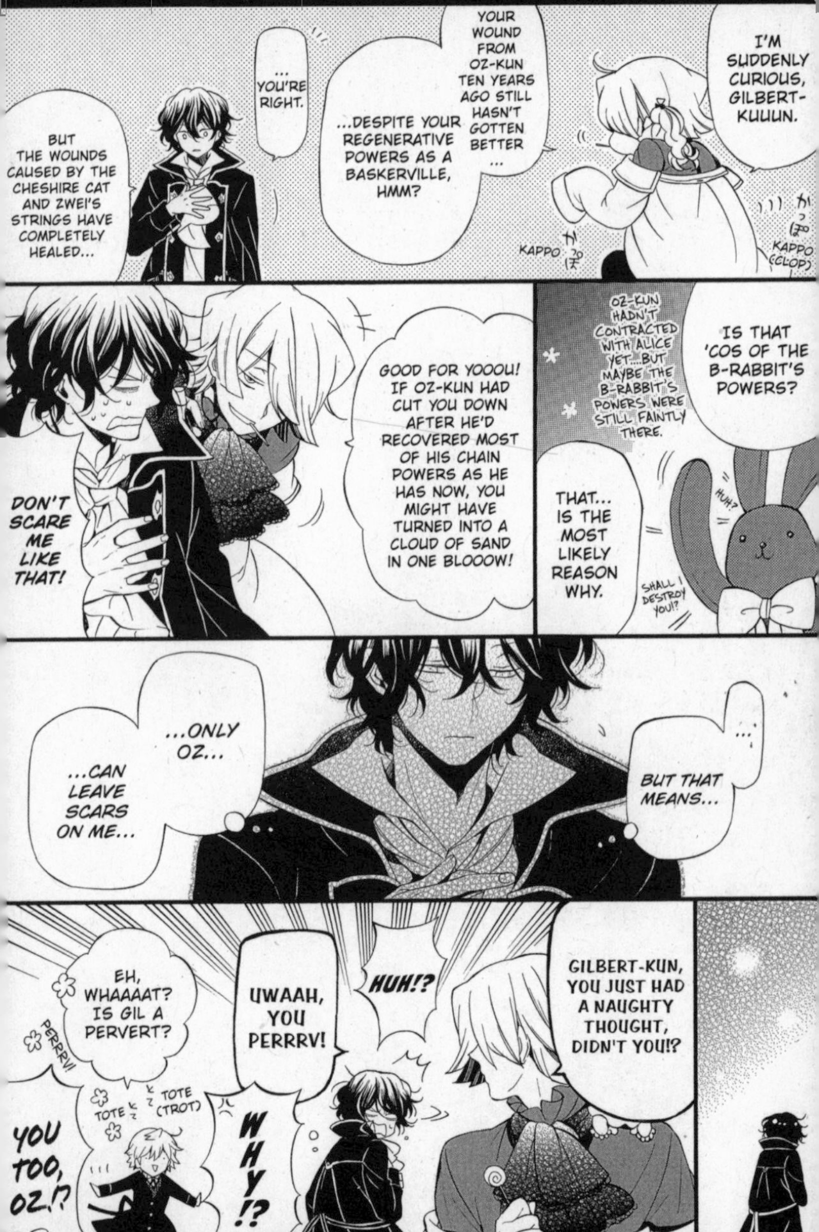
I'M SUDDENLY CURIOUS, GILBERT-KUUUN.
KAPPO (CLOP)
KAPPO
YOUR WOUND FROM OZ-KUN TEN YEARS AGO STILL HASN'T GOTTEN BETTER...
...DESPITE YOUR REGENERATIVE POWERS AS A BASKERVILLE, HMM?
...YOU'RE RIGHT.
BUT THE WOUNDS CAUSED BY THE CHESHIRE CAT AND ZWEI'S STRINGS HAVE COMPLETELY HEALED...
IS THAT 'COS OF THE B-RABBIT'S POWERS?
OZ-KUN HADN'T CONTRACTED WITH ALICE YET...BUT MAYBE THE B-RABBIT'S POWERS WERE STILL FAINTLY THERE.
THAT... IS THE MOST LIKELY REASON WHY.
HUH?
SHALL I DESTROY YOU!?
GOOD FOR YOOOU! IF OZ-KUN HAD CUT YOU DOWN AFTER HE'D RECOVERED MOST OF HIS CHAIN POWERS AS HE HAS NOW, YOU MIGHT HAVE TURNED INTO A CLOUD OF SAND IN ONE BLOOOW!
DON'T SCARE ME LIKE THAT!
...
BUT THAT MEANS...
...ONLY OZ...
...CAN LEAVE SCARS ON ME...
GILBERT-KUN, YOU JUST HAD A NAUGHTY THOUGHT, DIDN'T YOU!?
HUH!?
UWAAH, YOU PERRRV!
EH, WHAAAAT? IS GIL A PERVERT?
PERRRV!
TOTE TOTE (TROT)
WHY!?
YOU TOO, OZ!?

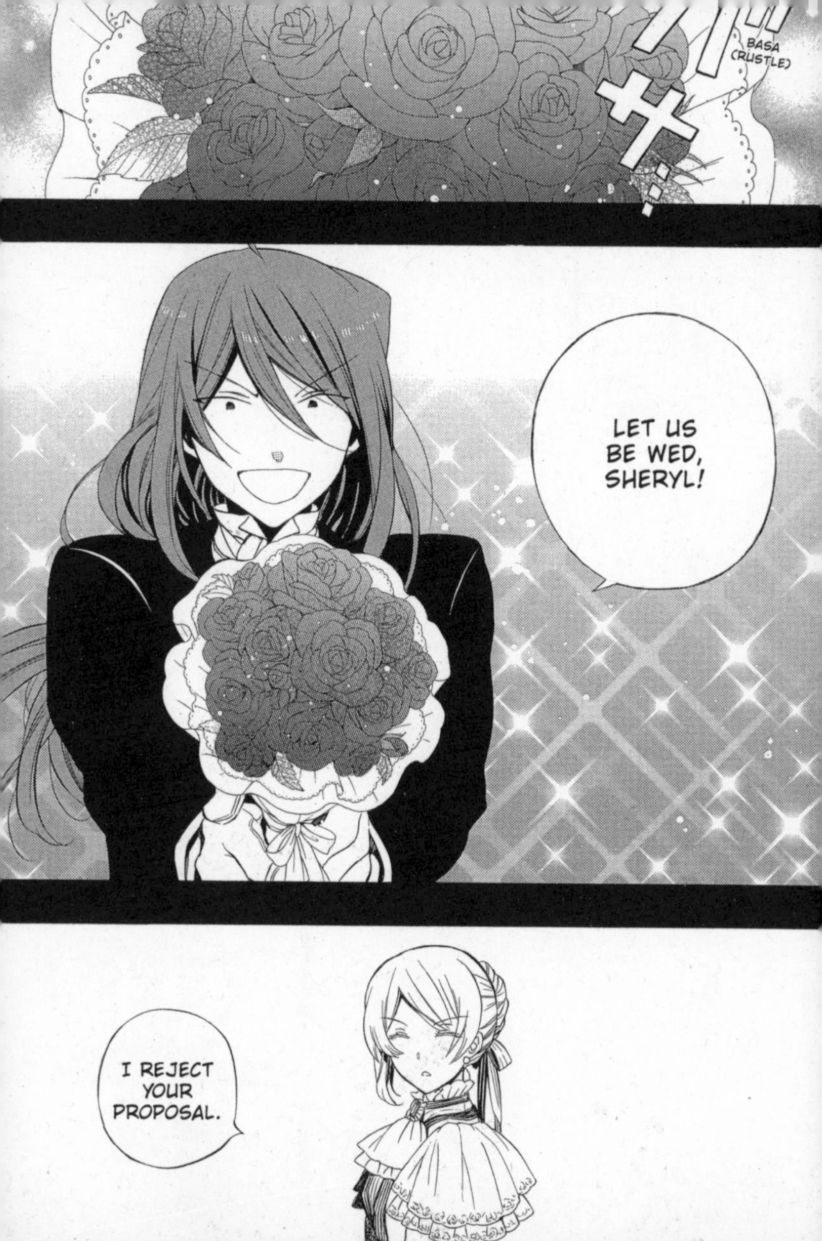
BASA (RUSTLE)
LET US BE WED, SHERYL!
I REJECT YOUR PROPOSAL.

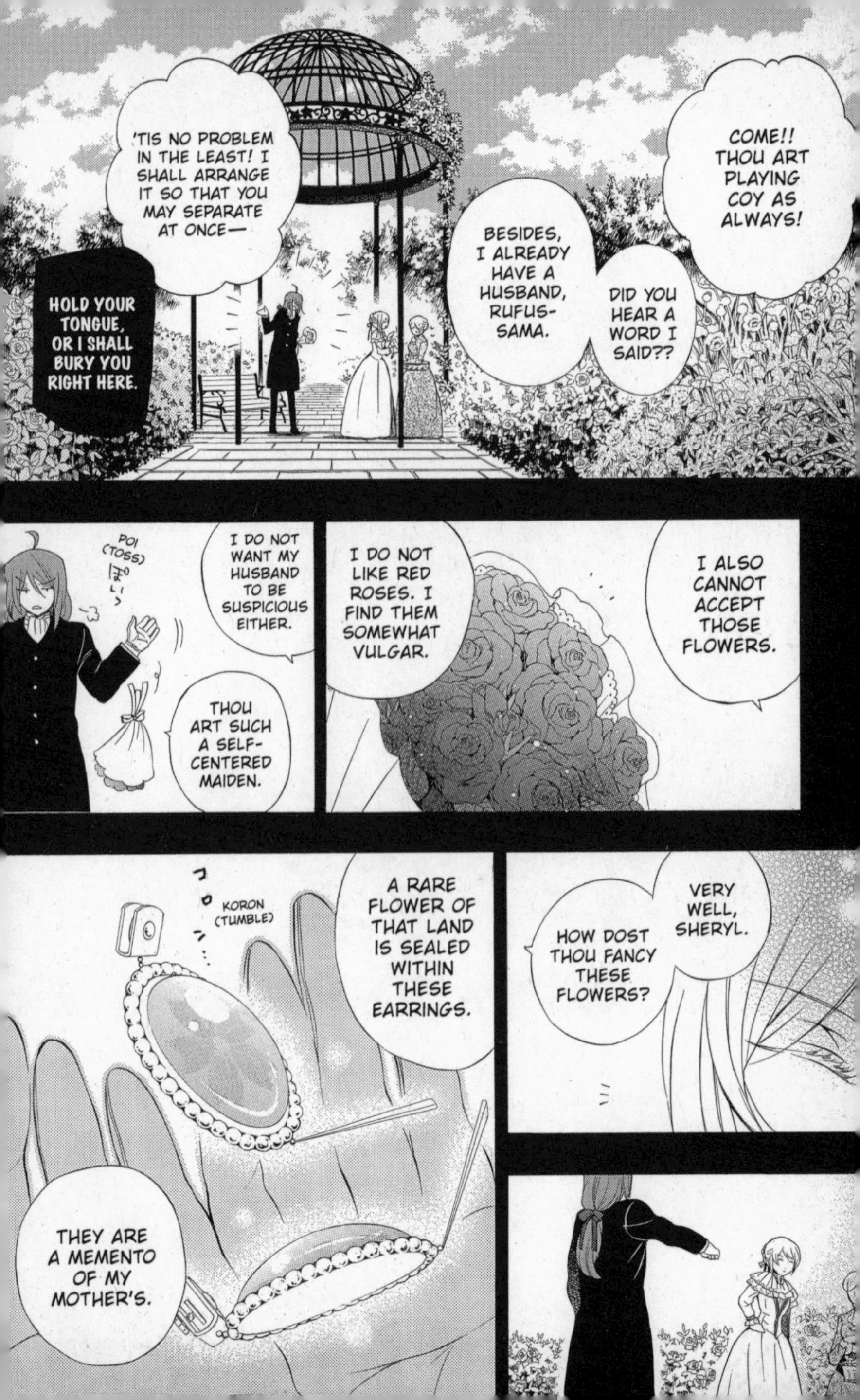
COME!! THOU ART PLAYING COY AS ALWAYS!
DID YOU HEAR A WORD I SAID??
BESIDES, I ALREADY HAVE A HUSBAND, RUFUS-SAMA.
'TIS NO PROBLEM IN THE LEAST! I SHALL ARRANGE IT SO THAT YOU MAY SEPARATE AT ONCE—
HOLD YOUR TONGUE, OR I SHALL BURY YOU RIGHT HERE.
I ALSO CANNOT ACCEPT THOSE FLOWERS.
I DO NOT LIKE RED ROSES. I FIND THEM SOMEWHAT VULGAR.
I DO NOT WANT MY HUSBAND TO BE SUSPICIOUS EITHER.
POI (TOSS)
THOU ART SUCH A SELF-CENTERED MAIDEN.
VERY WELL, SHERYL.
HOW DOST THOU FANCY THESE FLOWERS?
A RARE FLOWER OF THAT LAND IS SEALED WITHIN THESE EARRINGS.
KORON (TUMBLE)
THEY ARE A MEMENTO OF MY MOTHER'S.

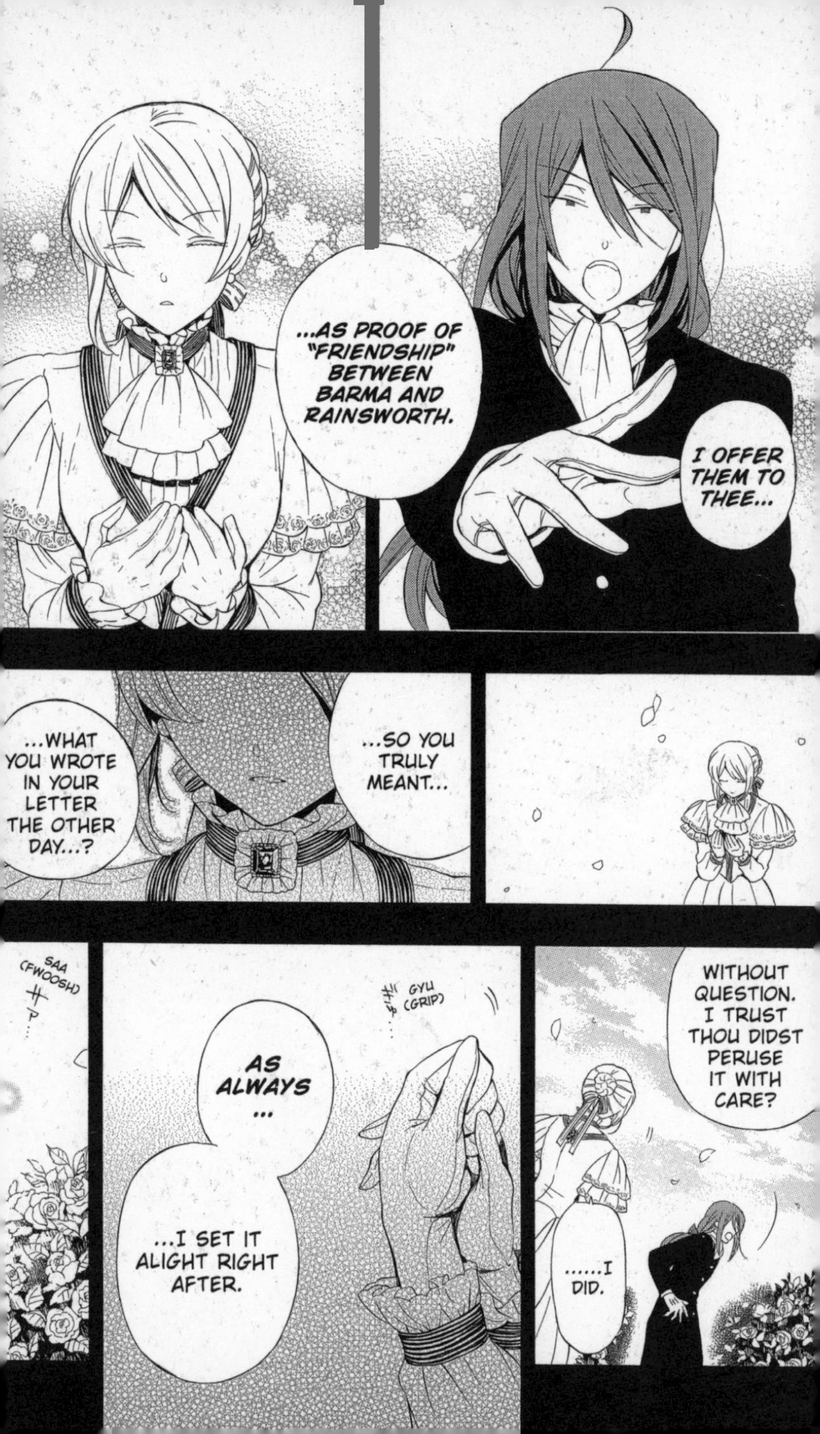
I OFFER THEM TO THEE...
...AS PROOF OF "FRIENDSHIP" BETWEEN BARMA AND RAINSWORTH.
...SO YOU TRULY MEANT...
...WHAT YOU WROTE IN YOUR LETTER THE OTHER DAY...?
WITHOUT QUESTION. I TRUST THOU DIDST PERUSE IT WITH CARE?
......I DID.
GYU (GRIP)
AS ALWAYS...
...I SET IT ALIGHT RIGHT AFTER.
SAA (FWOOSH)

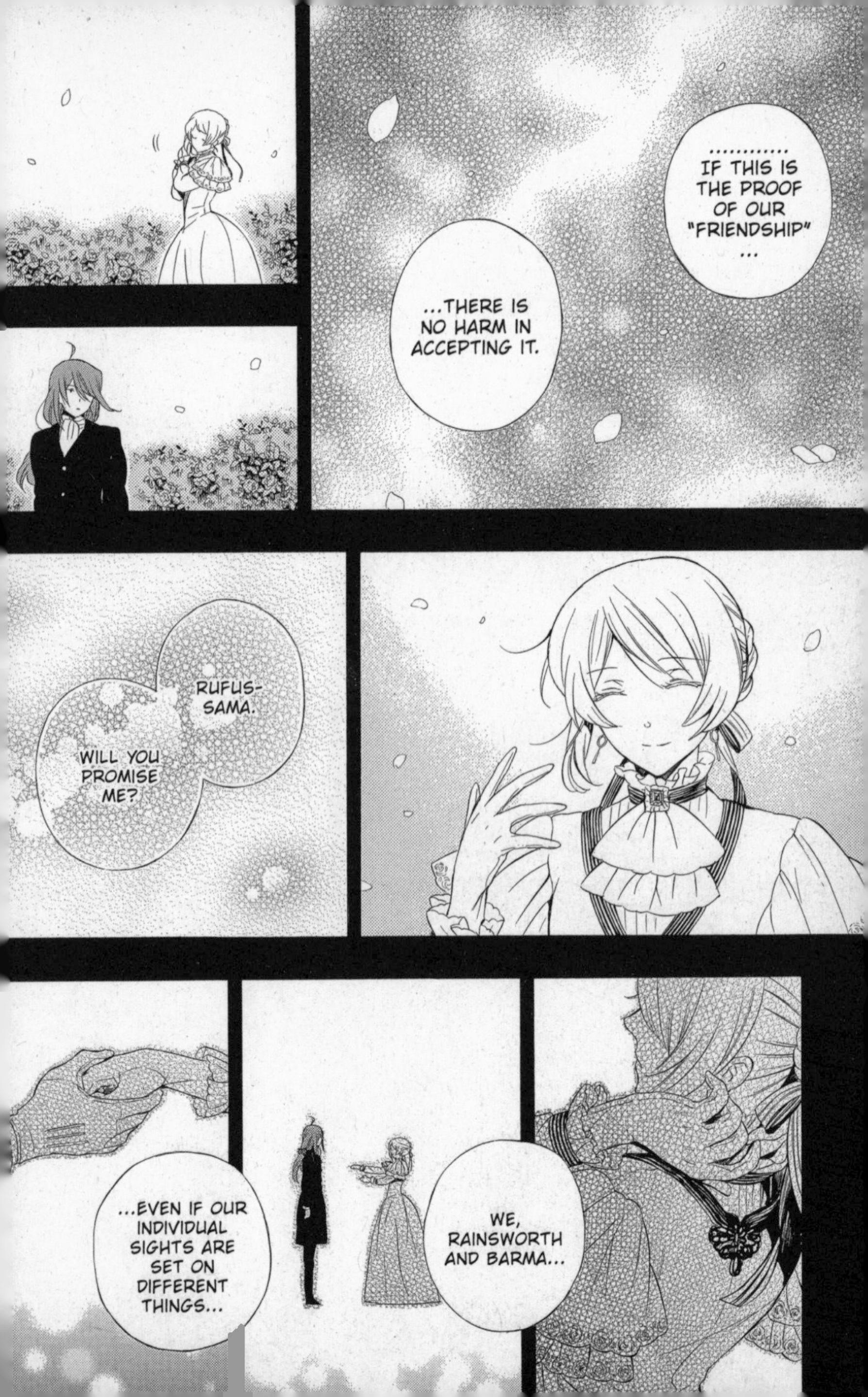
.... IF THIS IS THE PROOF OF OUR "FRIENDSHIP" ...
...THERE IS NO HARM IN ACCEPTING IT.
RUFUS-SAMA.
WILL YOU PROMISE ME?
WE, RAINSWORTH AND BARMA...
...EVEN IF OUR INDIVIDUAL SIGHTS ARE SET ON DIFFERENT THINGS...

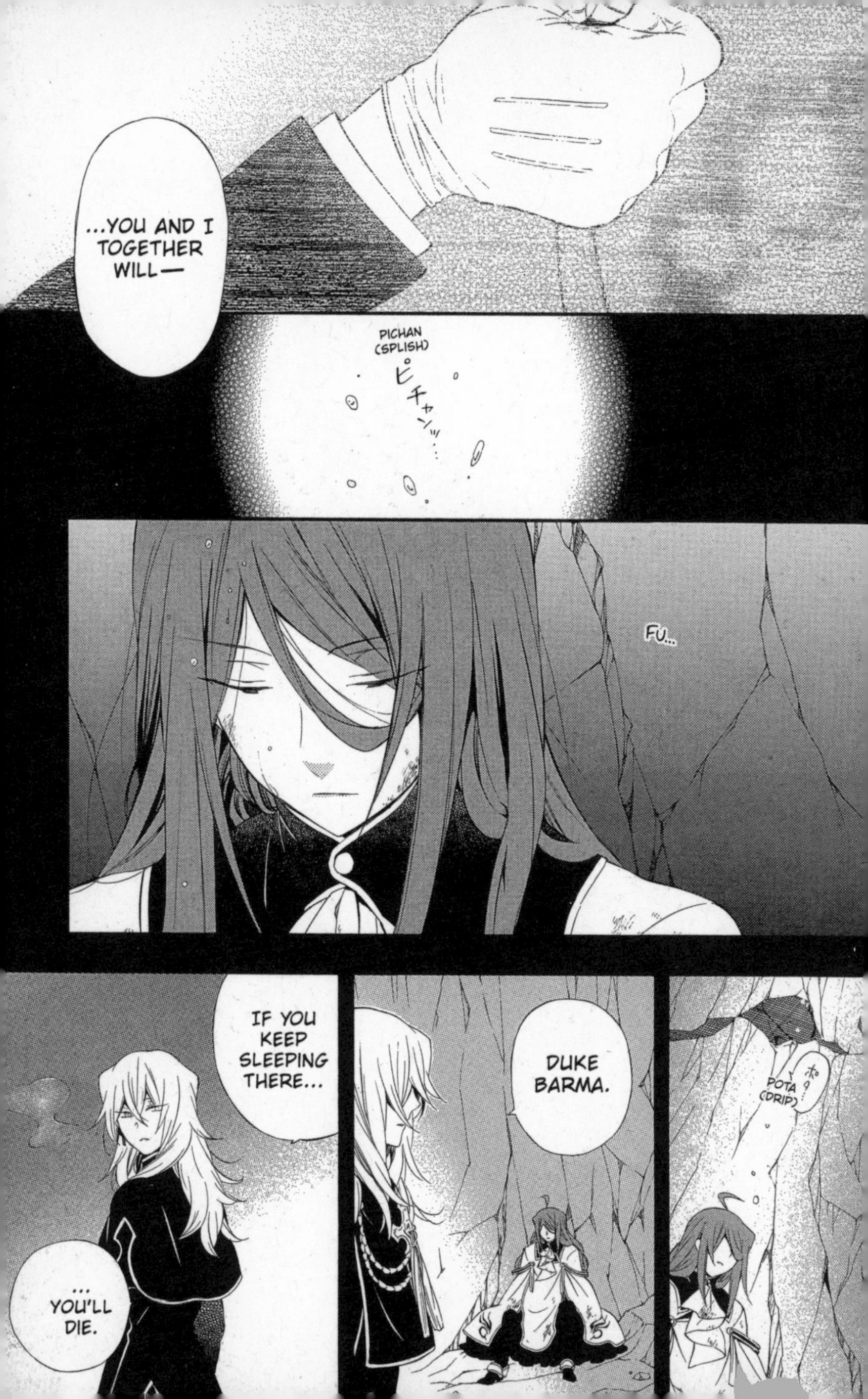
...YOU AND I TOGETHER WILL—
PICHAN (SPLISH)
ピチャンッ…
FU...
POTA (DRIP)
ポタ…
DUKE BARMA.
IF YOU KEEP SLEEPING THERE...
...YOU'LL DIE.

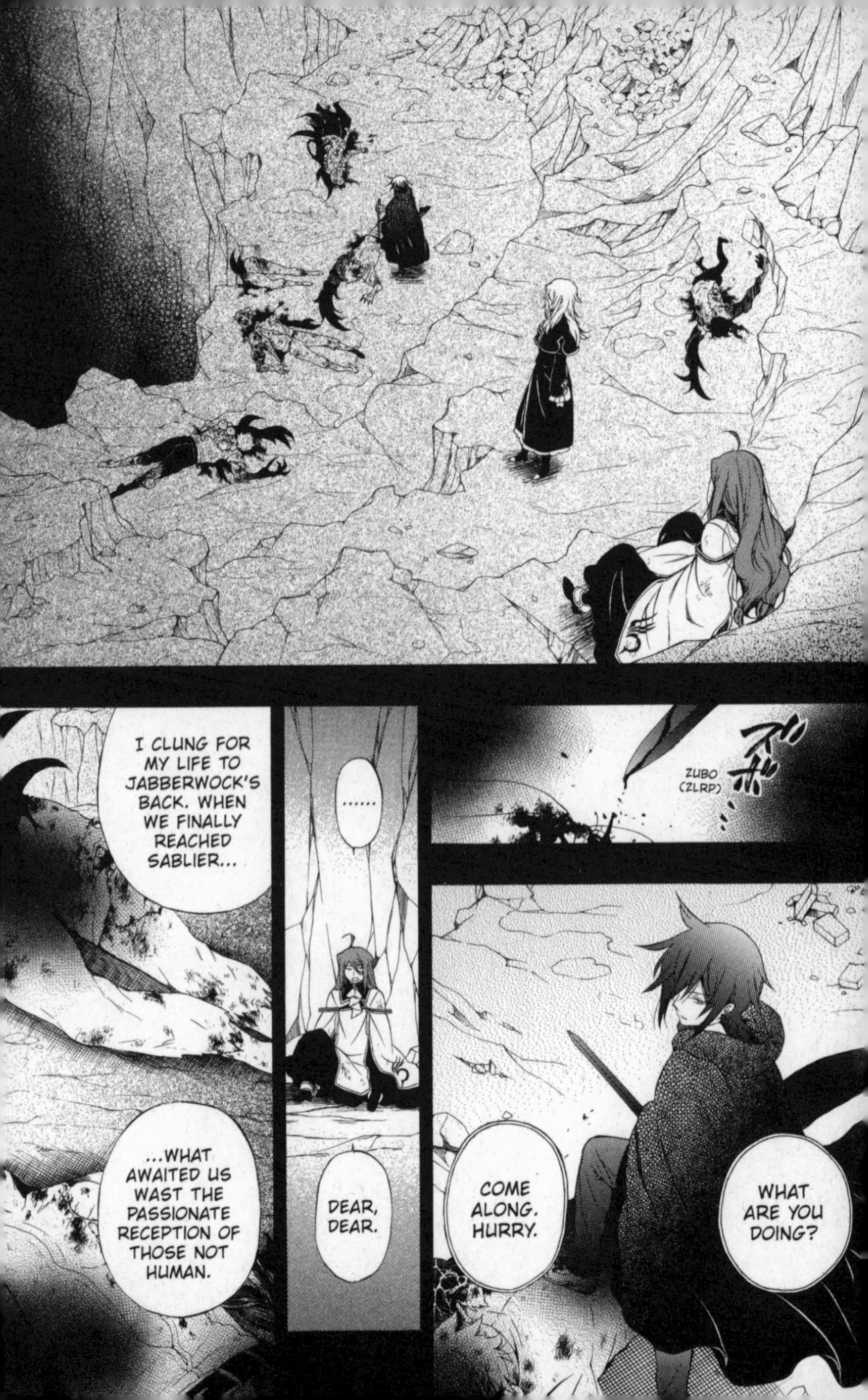
ZUBO (ZLRP)
WHAT ARE YOU DOING?
COME ALONG. HURRY.
......
DEAR, DEAR.
I CLUNG FOR MY LIFE TO JABBERWOCK'S BACK. WHEN WE FINALLY REACHED SABLIER...
...WHAT AWAITED US WAST THE PASSIONATE RECEPTION OF THOSE NOT HUMAN.

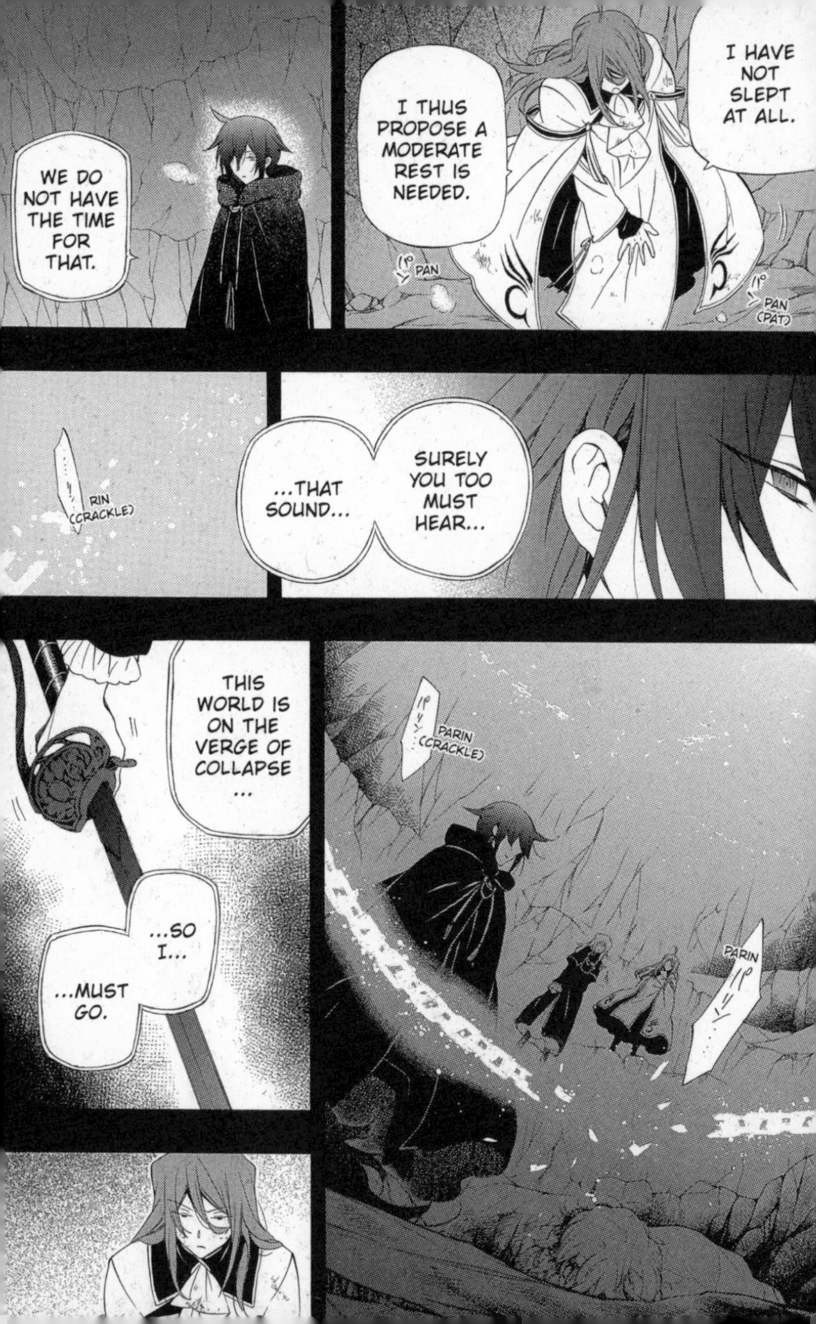
I HAVE NOT SLEPT AT ALL.
I THUS PROPOSE A MODERATE REST IS NEEDED.
PAN
PAN (PAT)
WE DO NOT HAVE THE TIME FOR THAT.
SURELY YOU TOO MUST HEAR...
...THAT SOUND...
RIN (CRACKLE)
PARIN (CRACKLE)
PARIN
THIS WORLD IS ON THE VERGE OF COLLAPSE ...
...SO I...
...MUST GO.

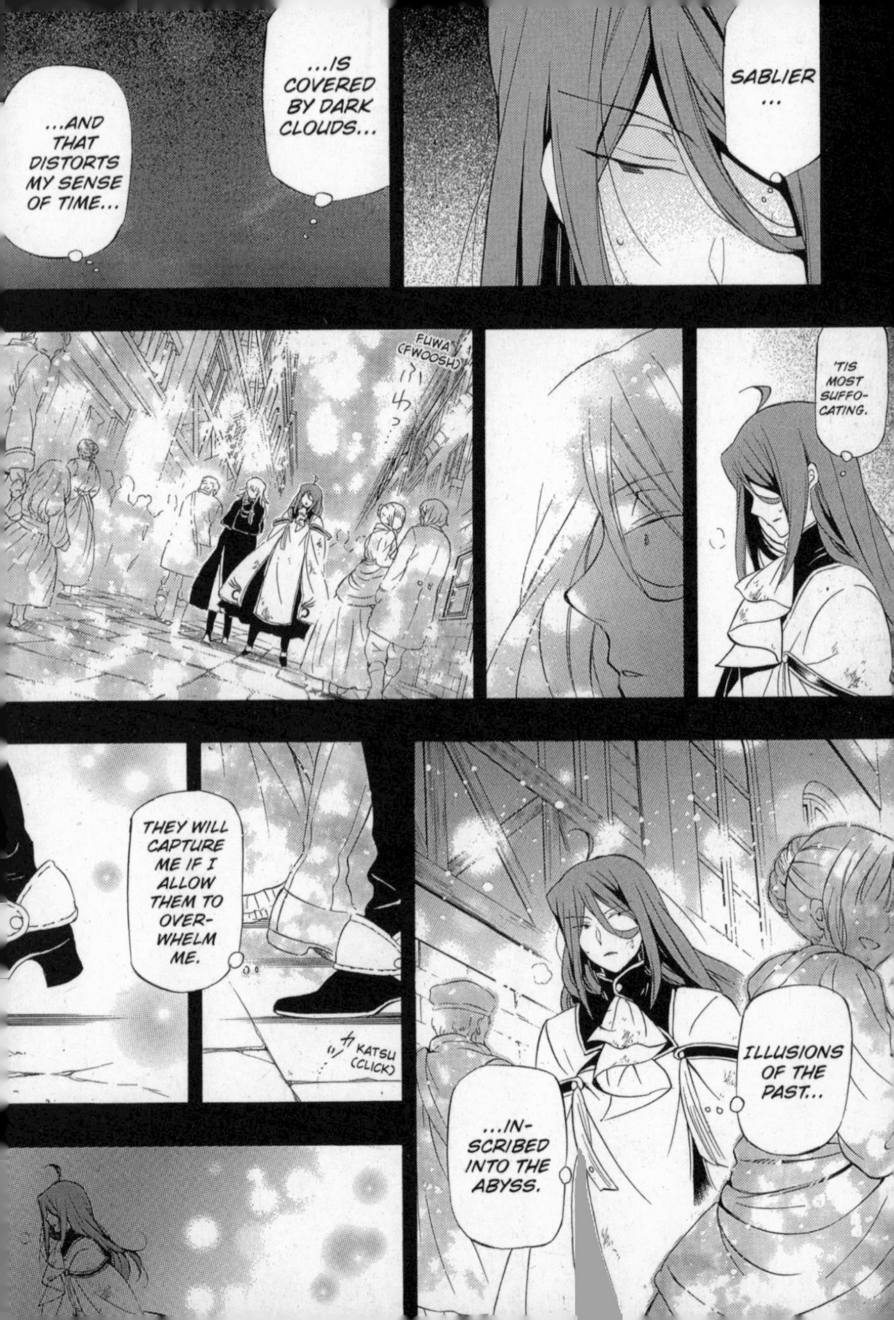
SABLIER ...
...IS COVERED BY DARK CLOUDS...
...AND THAT DISTORTS MY SENSE OF TIME...
'TIS MOST SUFFOCATING.
FUWA (FWOOSH)
ふわっ
ILLUSIONS OF THE PAST...
...IN-SCRIBED INTO THE ABYSS.
THEY WILL CAPTURE ME IF I ALLOW THEM TO OVER-WHELM ME.
カツッ
KATSU (CLICK)

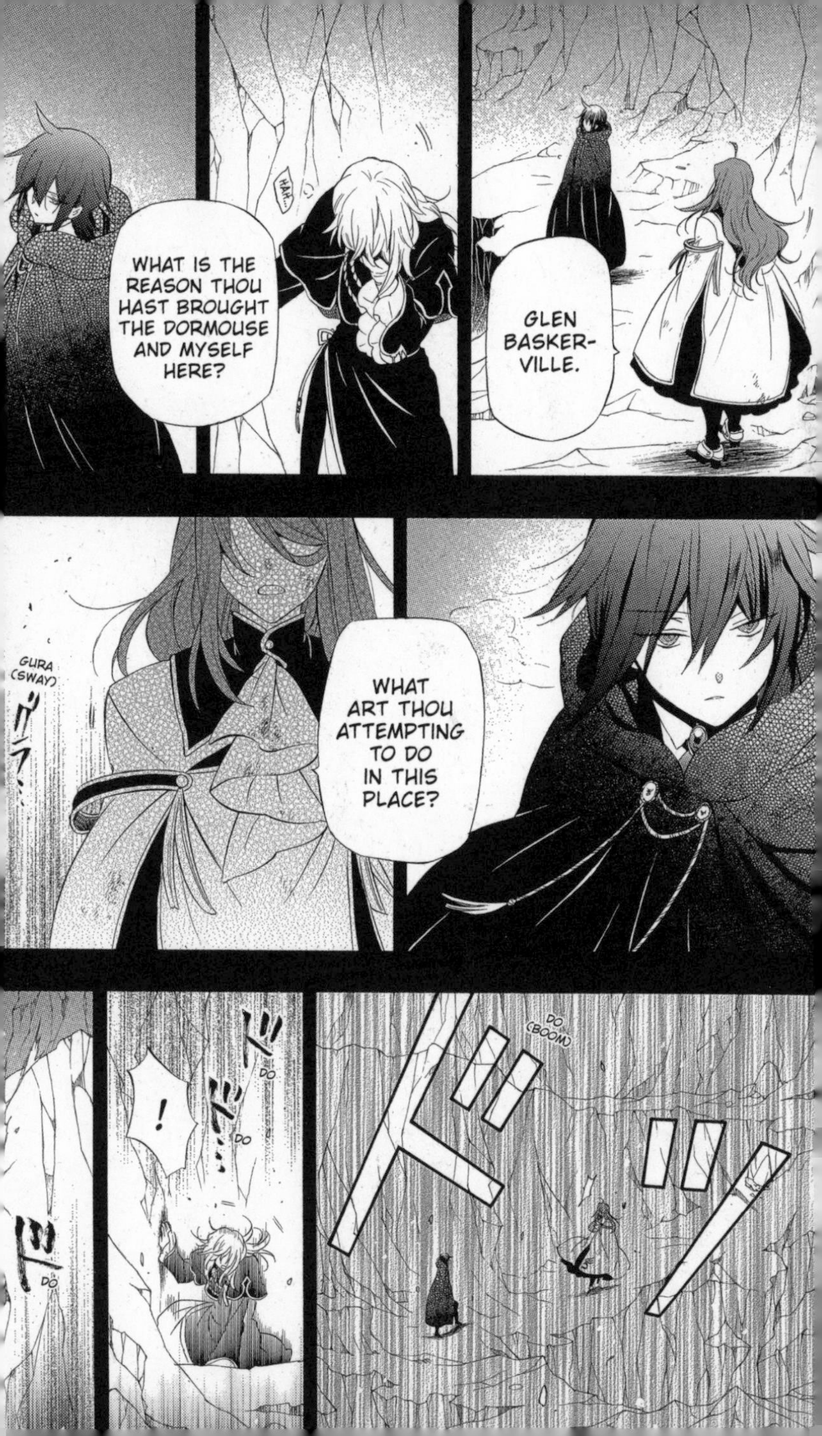
GLEN BASKER-VILLE.
HAH...
WHAT IS THE REASON THOU HAST BROUGHT THE DORMOUSE AND MYSELF HERE?
WHAT ART THOU ATTEMPTING TO DO IN THIS PLACE?
GURA (SWAY)
DO (BOOM)
DO
DO
!
DO

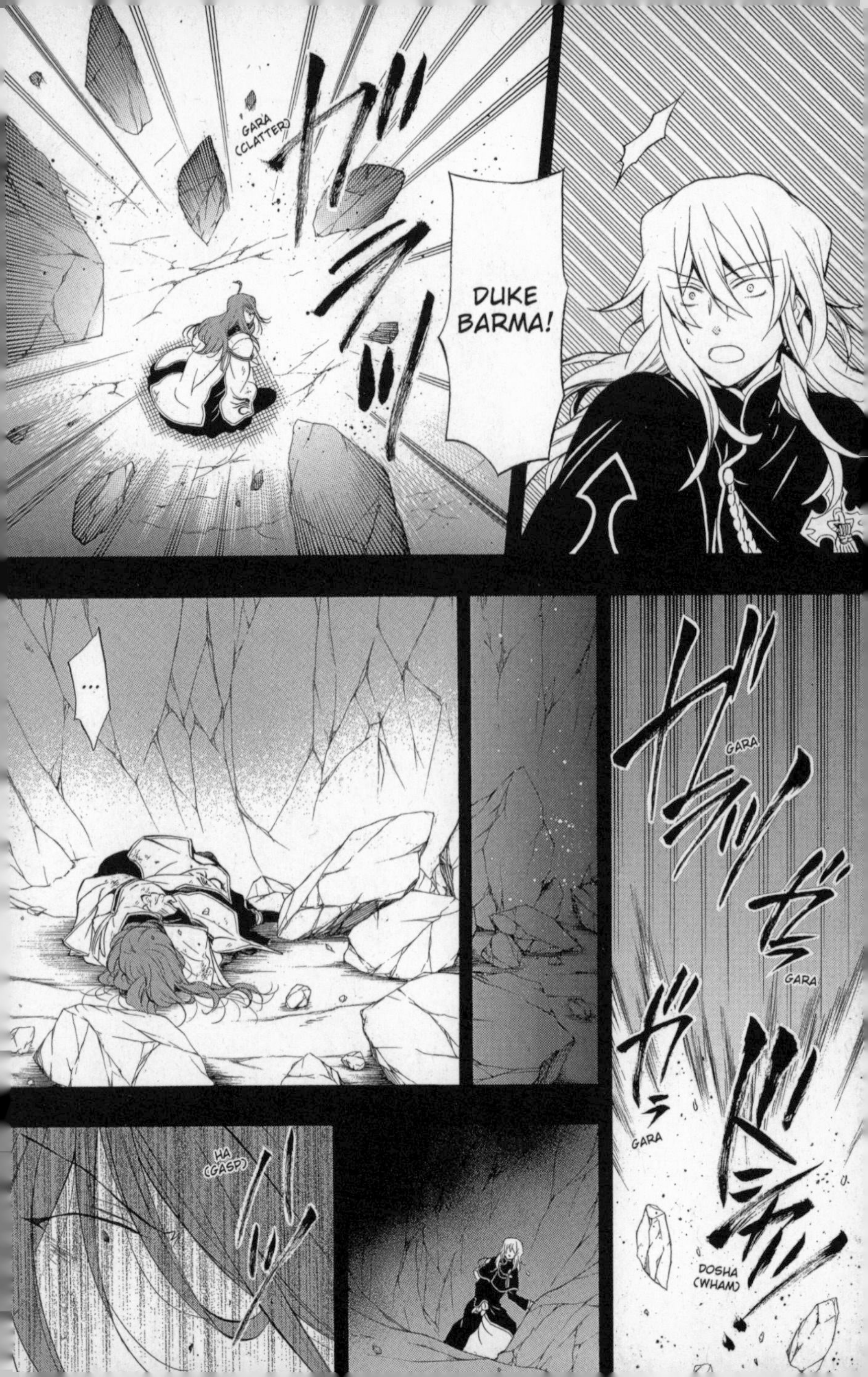
DUKE BARMA!
GARA (CLATTER)
GARA
GARA
GARA
DOSHA (WHAM)
...
HA (GASP)

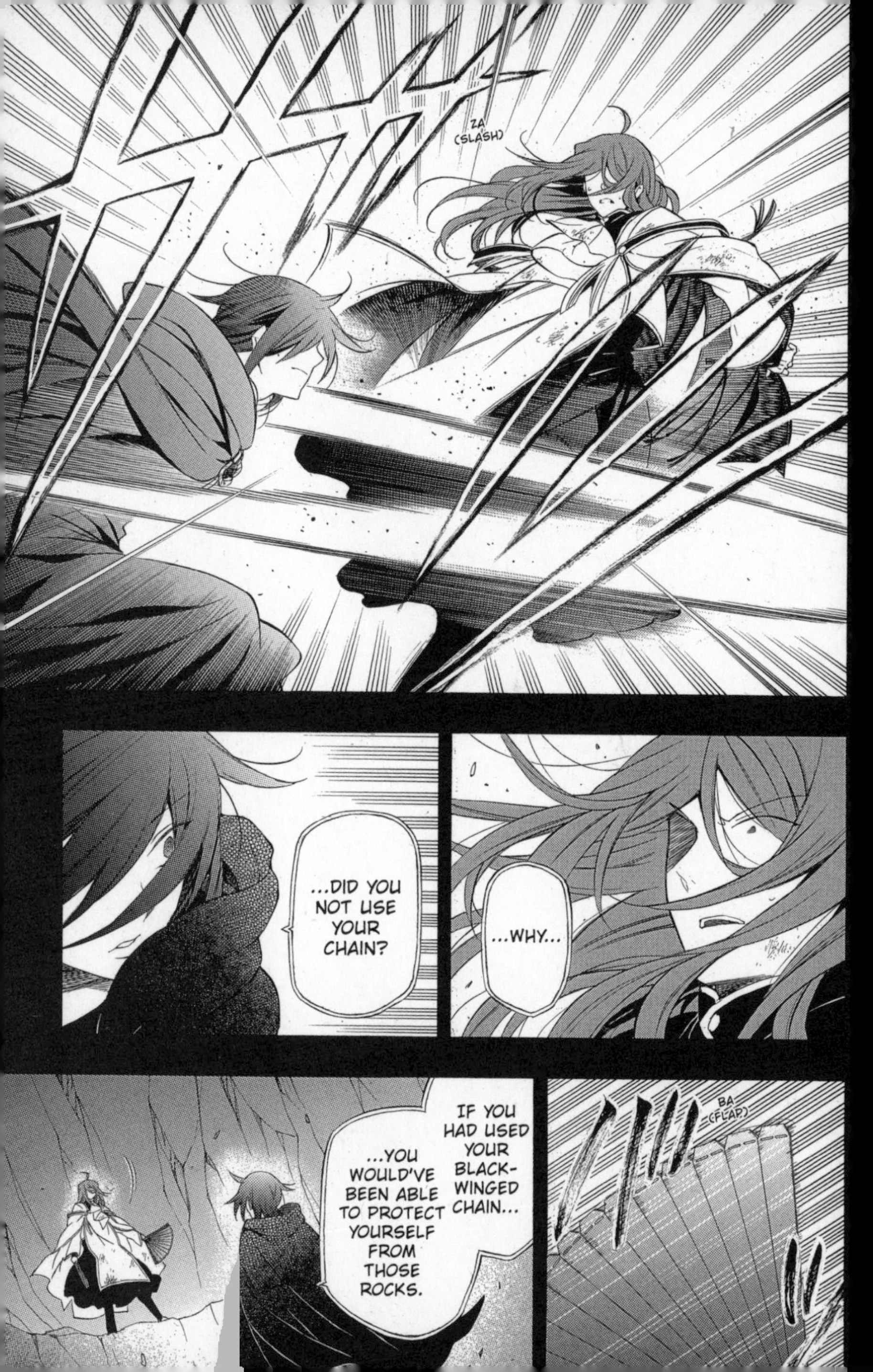

ZA (SLASH)
...WHY...
...DID YOU NOT USE YOUR CHAIN?
BA (FLAP)
IF YOU HAD USED YOUR BLACK-WINGED CHAIN...
...YOU WOULD'VE BEEN ABLE TO PROTECT YOURSELF FROM THOSE ROCKS.

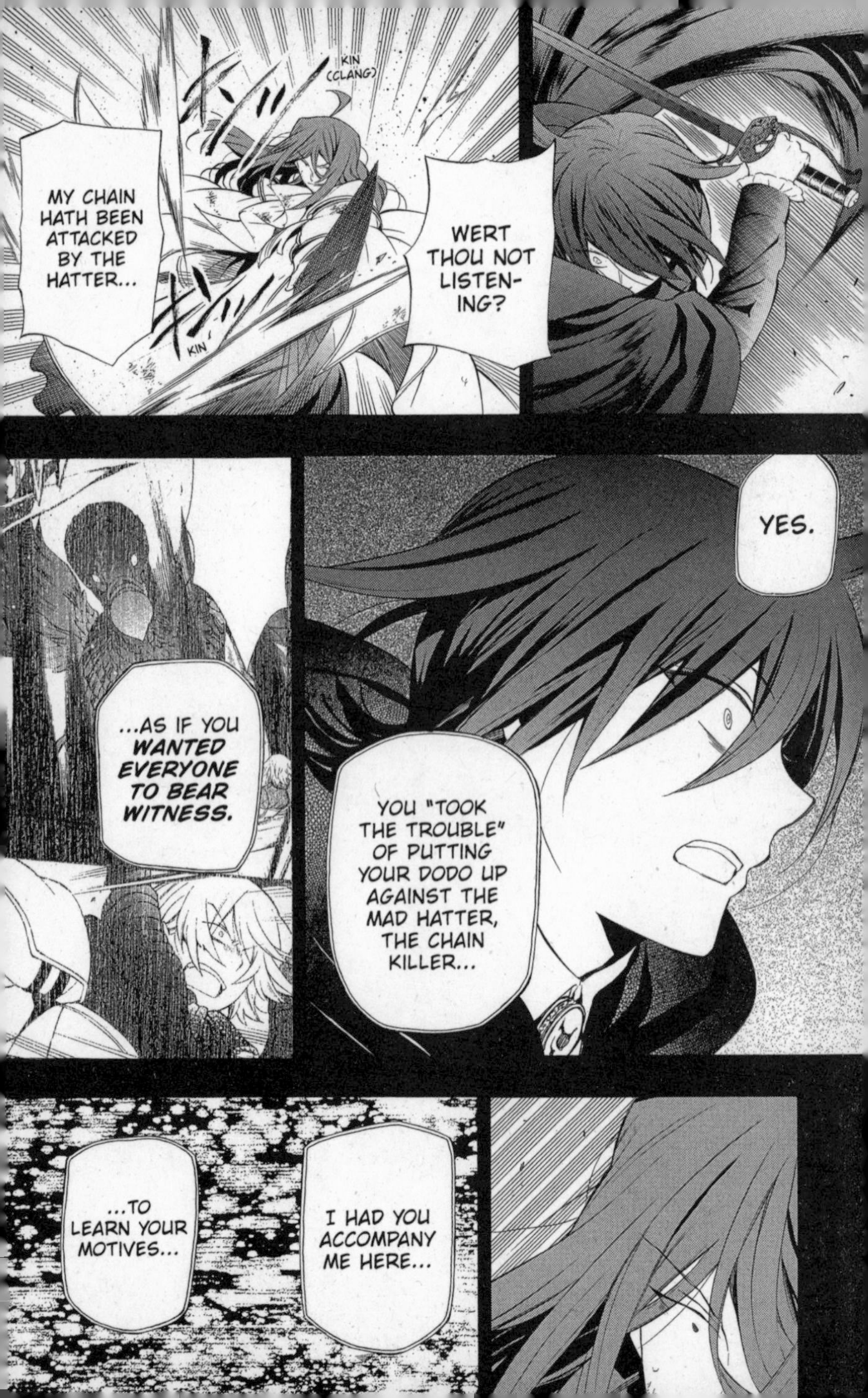
WERT THOU NOT LISTENING?
KIN (CLANG)
MY CHAIN HATH BEEN ATTACKED BY THE HATTER...
KIN
YES.
YOU "TOOK THE TROUBLE" OF PUTTING YOUR DODO UP AGAINST THE MAD HATTER, THE CHAIN KILLER...
...AS IF YOU *WANTED EVERYONE* TO BEAR WITNESS.
I HAD YOU ACCOMPANY ME HERE...
...TO LEARN YOUR MOTIVES...

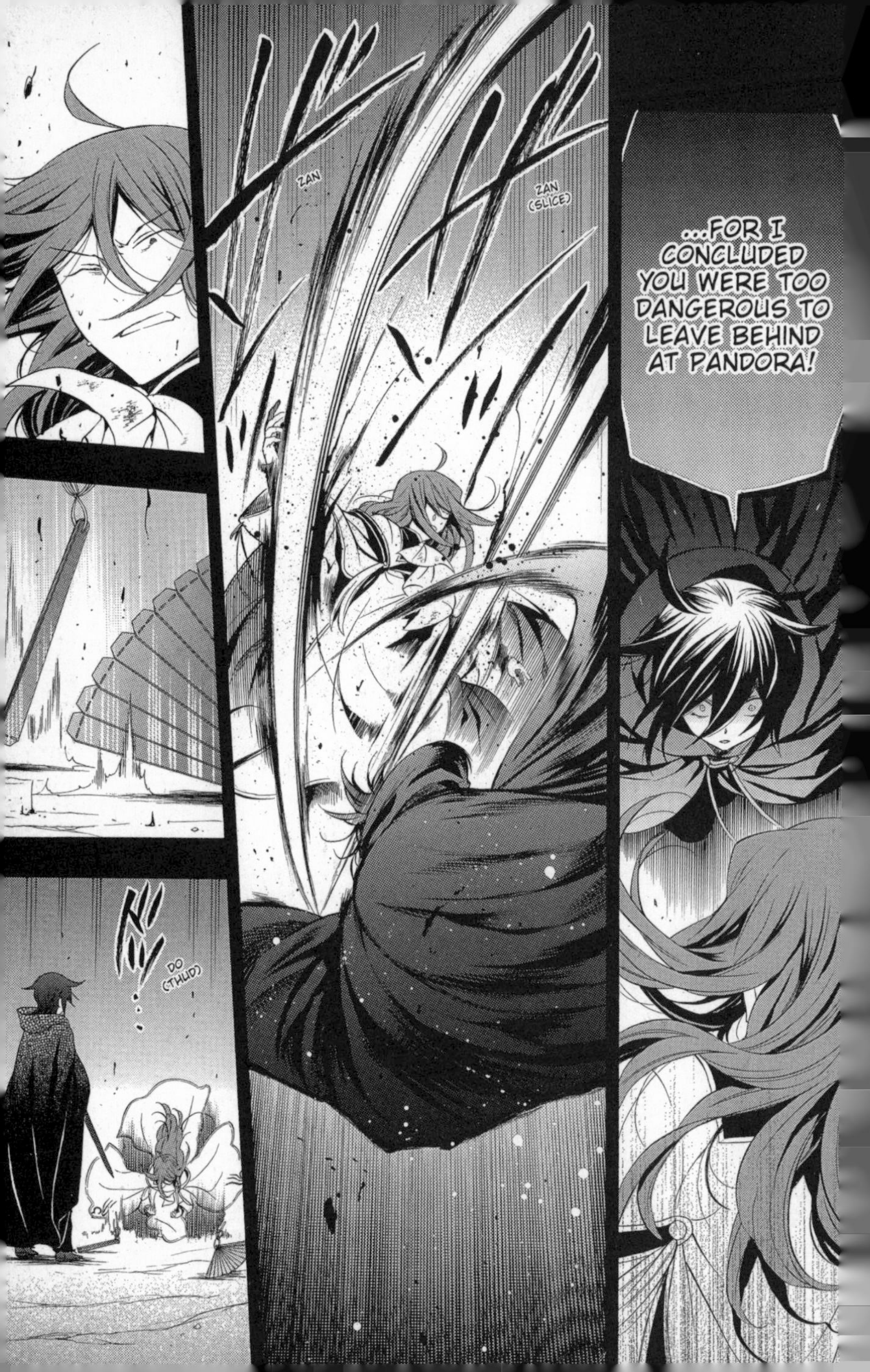
...FOR I CONCLUDED YOU WERE TOO DANGEROUS TO LEAVE BEHIND AT PANDORA!
ZAN (SLICE)
ZAN
DO (THUD)

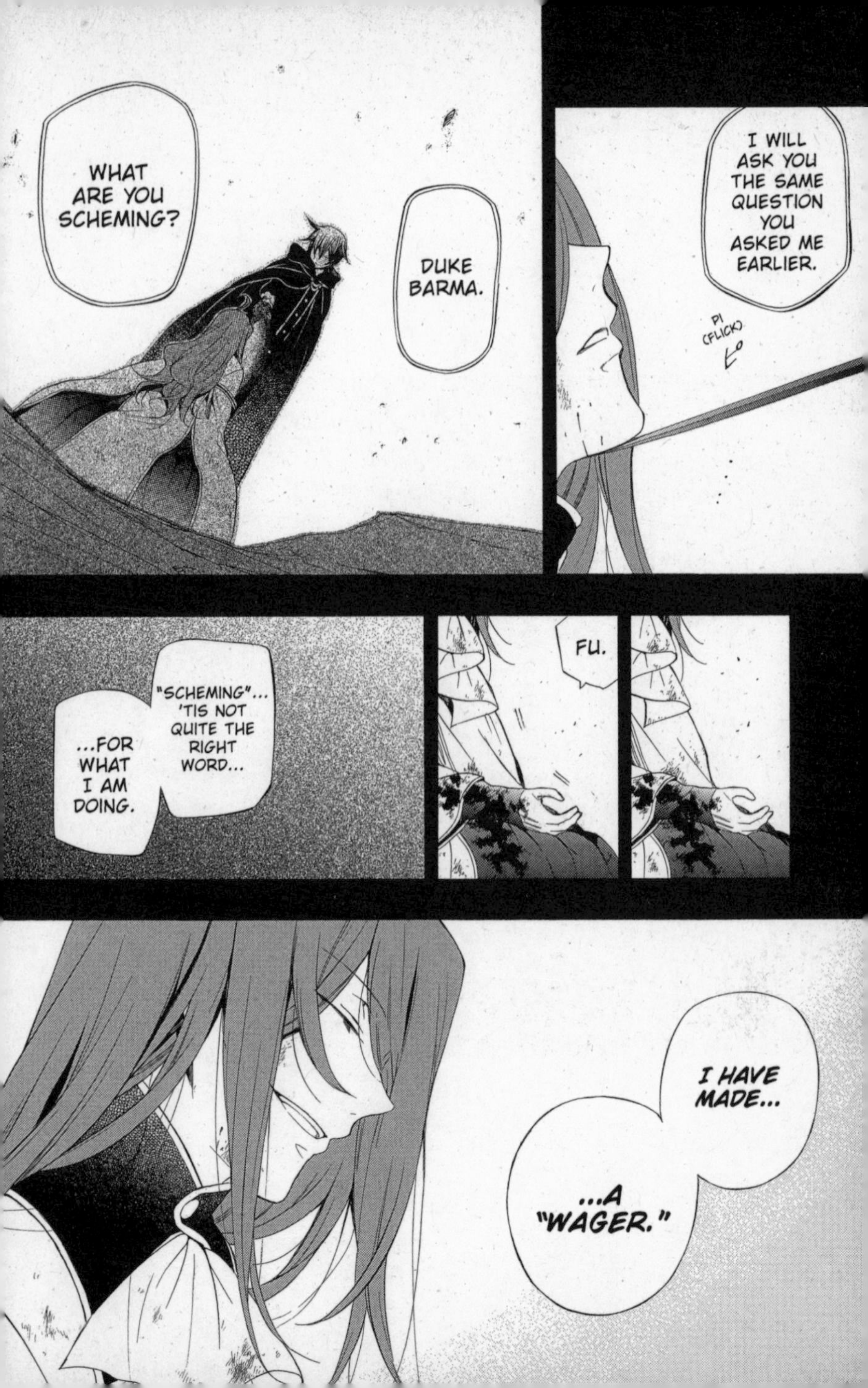
I WILL ASK YOU THE SAME QUESTION YOU ASKED ME EARLIER.
PI (FLICK)
DUKE BARMA.
WHAT ARE YOU SCHEMING?
FU.
"SCHEMING"... 'TIS NOT QUITE THE RIGHT WORD...
...FOR WHAT I AM DOING.
I HAVE MADE...
...A "WAGER."

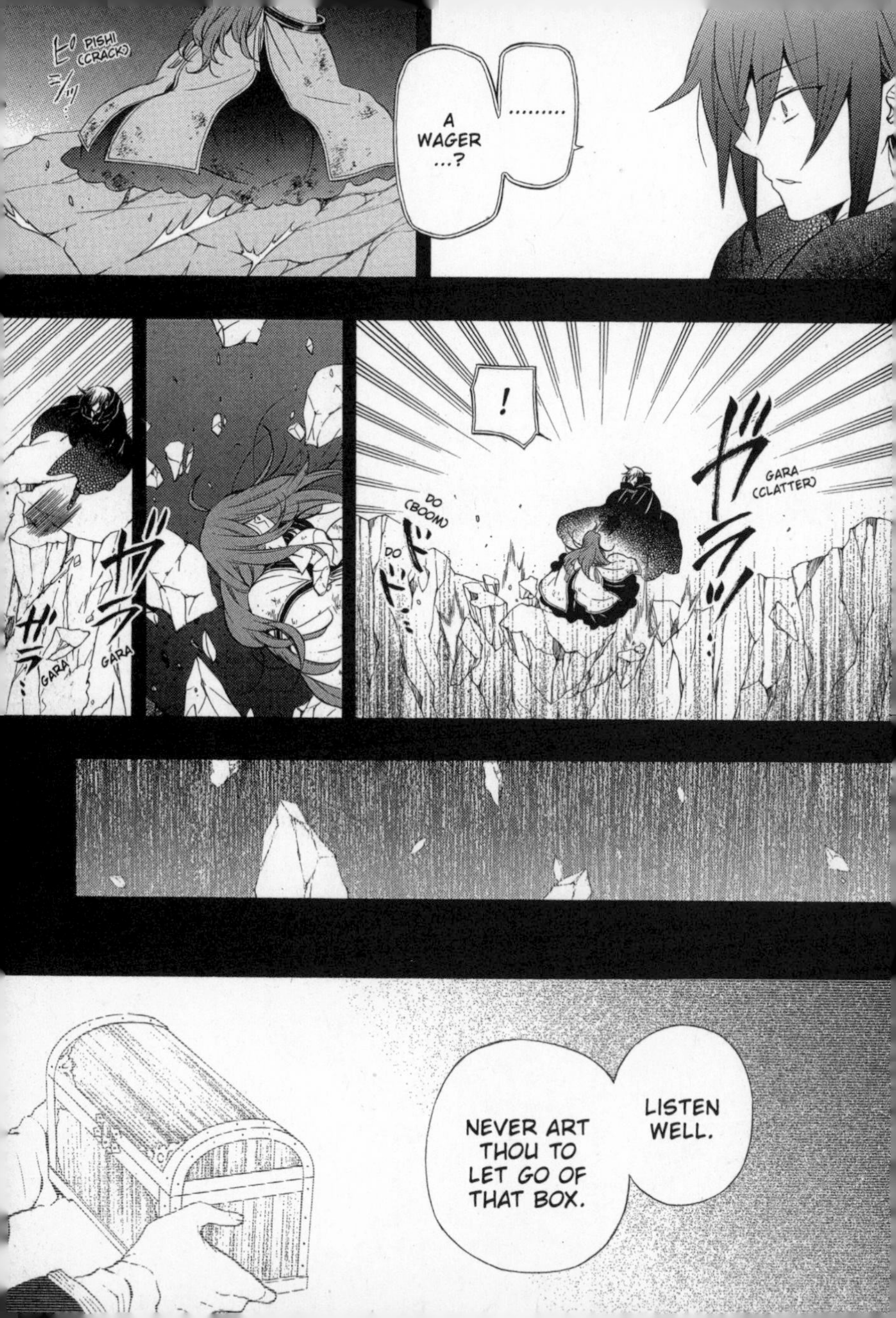
....
A WAGER ...?
ピシッ
PISHI (CRACK)
!
ガラッ
GARA (CLATTER)
ドドド
DO (BOOM) DO
ガラ
GARA
ガラ
GARA
LISTEN WELL.
NEVER ART THOU TO LET GO OF THAT BOX.

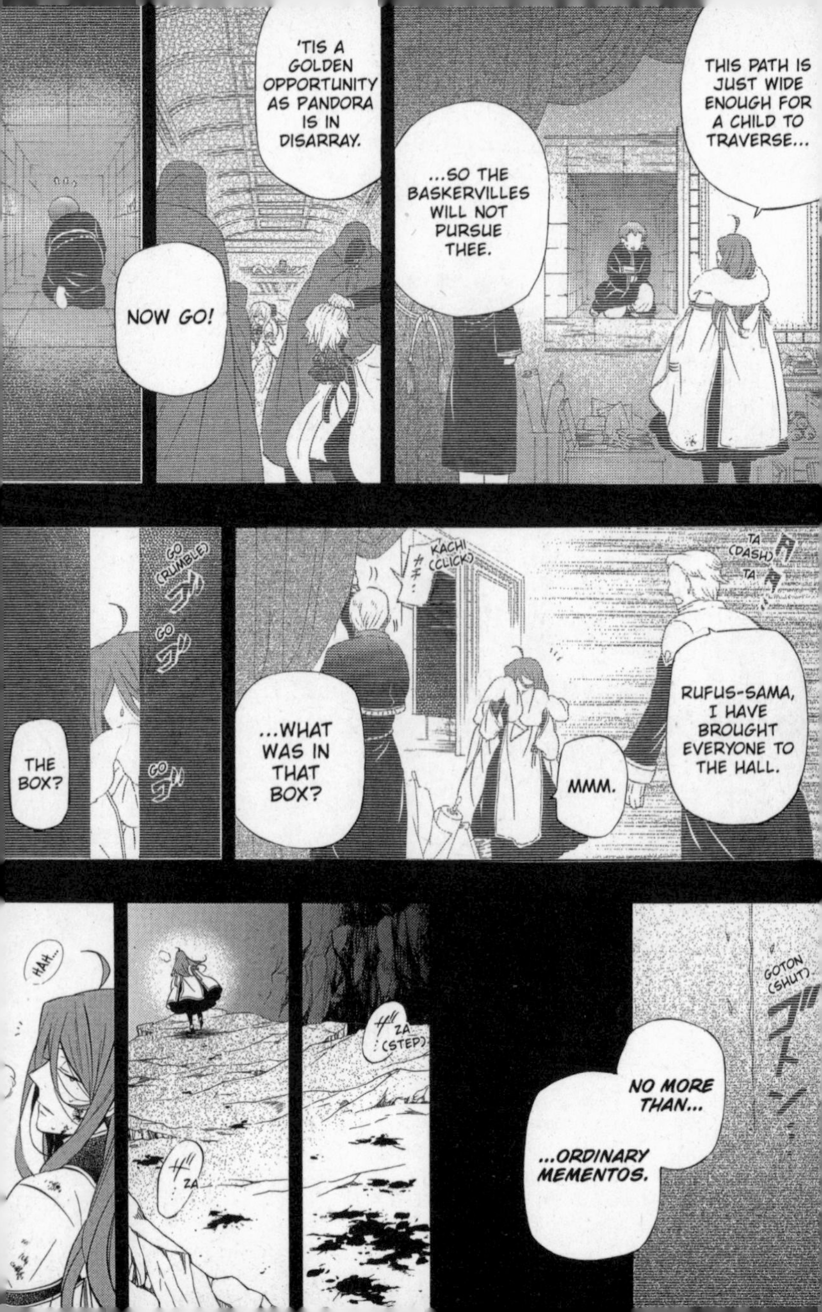
THIS PATH IS JUST WIDE ENOUGH FOR A CHILD TO TRAVERSE...
...SO THE BASKERVILLES WILL NOT PURSUE THEE.
'TIS A GOLDEN OPPORTUNITY AS PANDORA IS IN DISARRAY.
NOW GO!
TA (DASH) TA
RUFUS-SAMA, I HAVE BROUGHT EVERYONE TO THE HALL.
MMM.
KACHI (CLICK)
...WHAT WAS IN THAT BOX?
GO (RUMBLE) GO GO
THE BOX?
GOTON (SHUT)
NO MORE THAN...
...ORDINARY MEMENTOS.
ZA (STEP)
ZA
HAH...

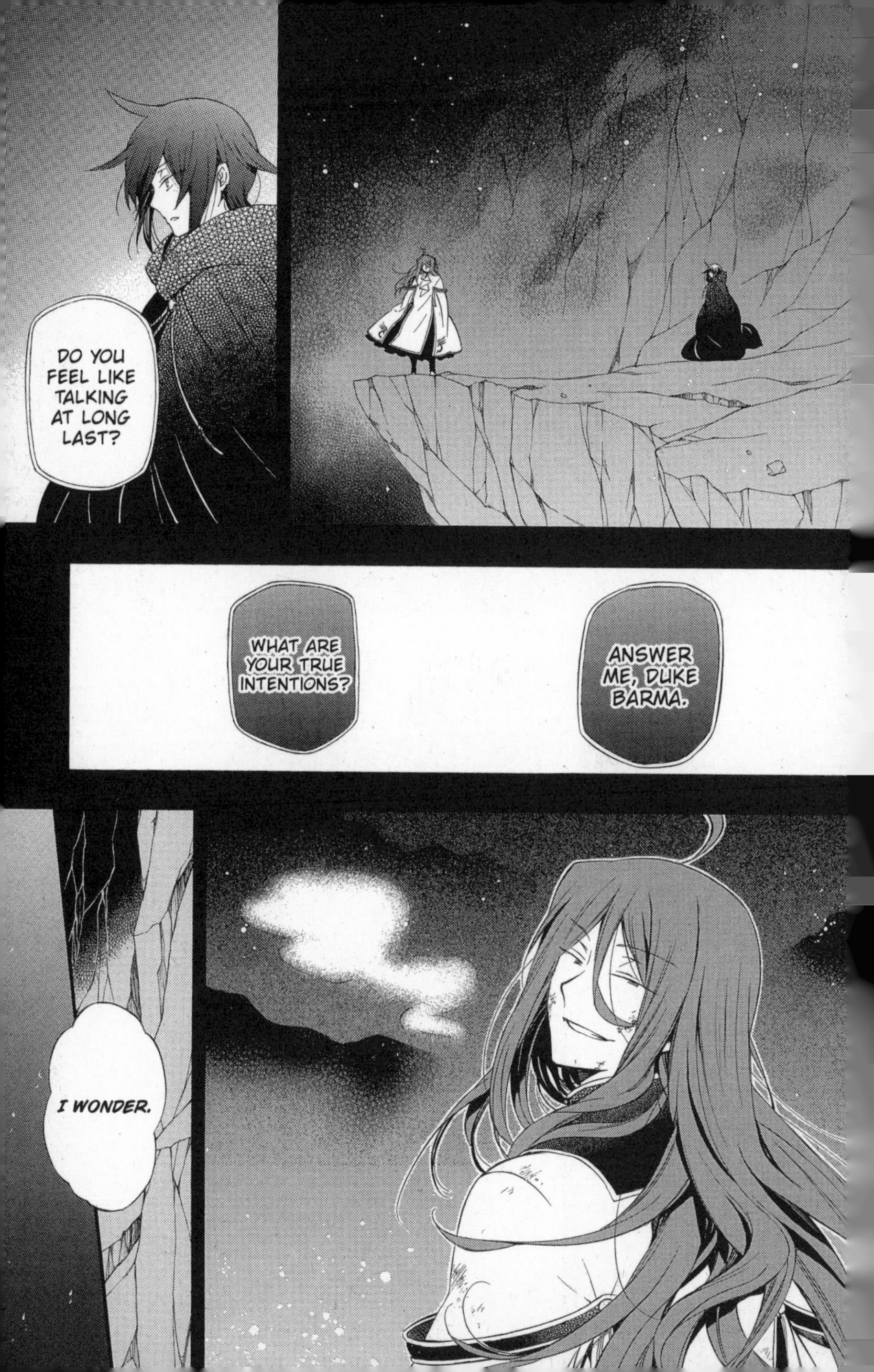
DO YOU FEEL LIKE TALKING AT LONG LAST?
ANSWER ME, DUKE BARMA.
WHAT ARE YOUR TRUE INTENTIONS?
I WONDER.

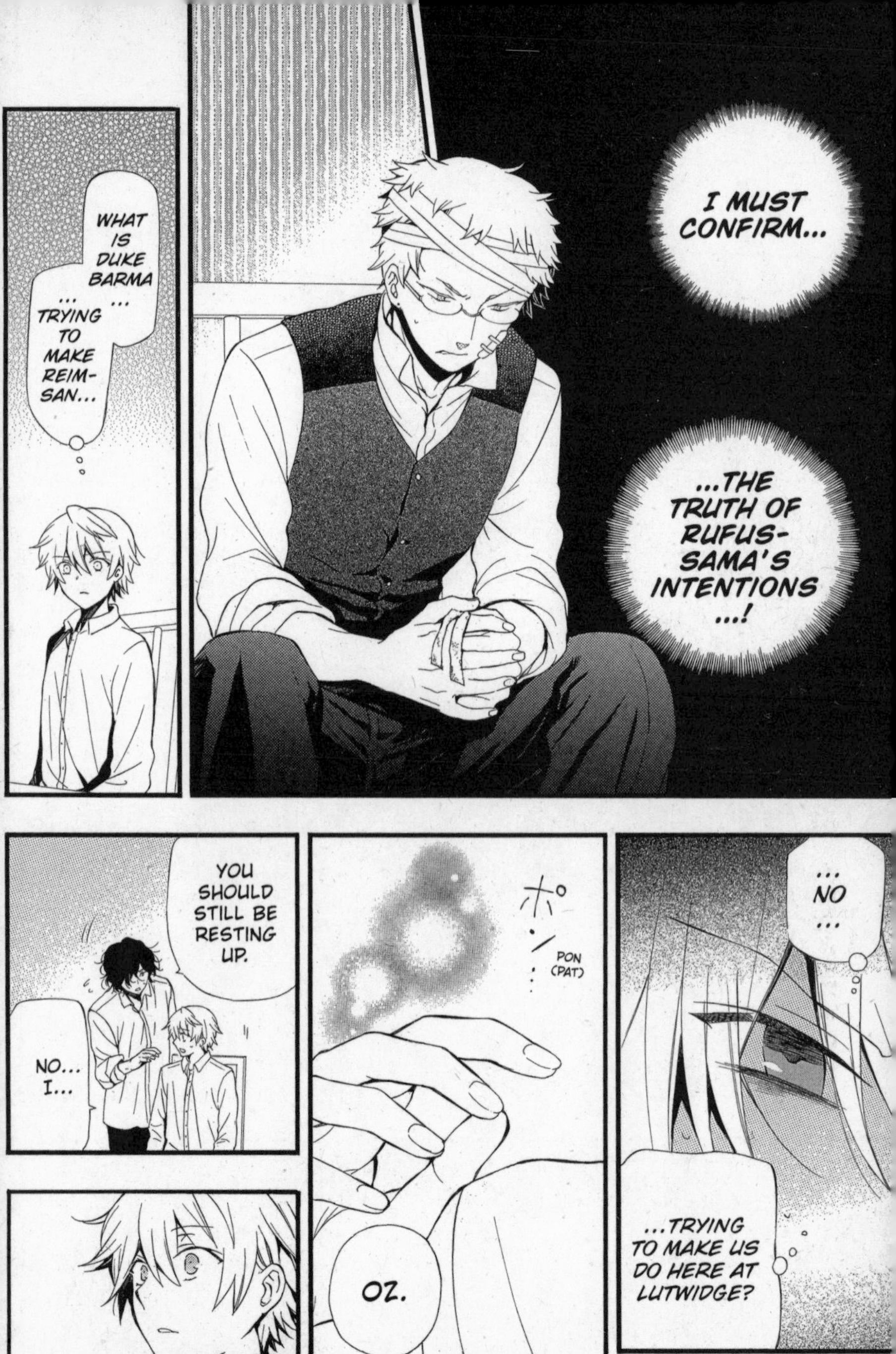
I MUST CONFIRM...
...THE TRUTH OF RUFUS-SAMA'S INTENTIONS...!
WHAT IS DUKE BARMA... ...TRYING TO MAKE REIM-SAN...
...NO...
...TRYING TO MAKE US DO HERE AT LUTWIDGE?
ポ・ン
PON (PAT)
OZ.
YOU SHOULD STILL BE RESTING UP.
NO... I...

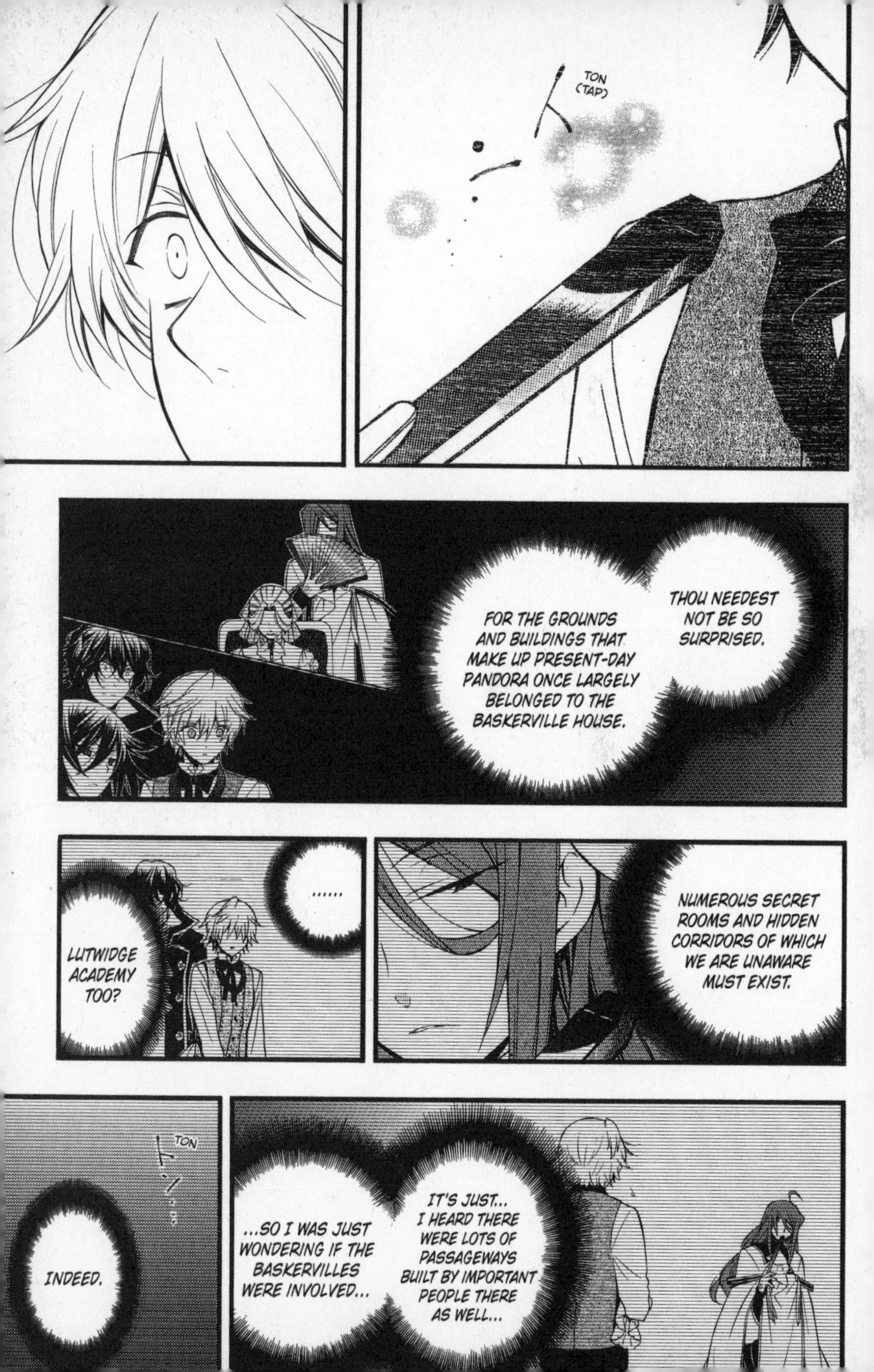
TON (TAP)
THOU NEEDEST NOT BE SO SURPRISED.
FOR THE GROUNDS AND BUILDINGS THAT MAKE UP PRESENT-DAY PANDORA ONCE LARGELY BELONGED TO THE BASKERVILLE HOUSE.
NUMEROUS SECRET ROOMS AND HIDDEN CORRIDORS OF WHICH WE ARE UNAWARE MUST EXIST.
......
LUTWIDGE ACADEMY TOO?
IT'S JUST... I HEARD THERE WERE LOTS OF PASSAGEWAYS BUILT BY IMPORTANT PEOPLE THERE AS WELL...
...SO I WAS JUST WONDERING IF THE BASKERVILLES WERE INVOLVED...
TON
INDEED.

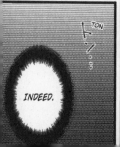

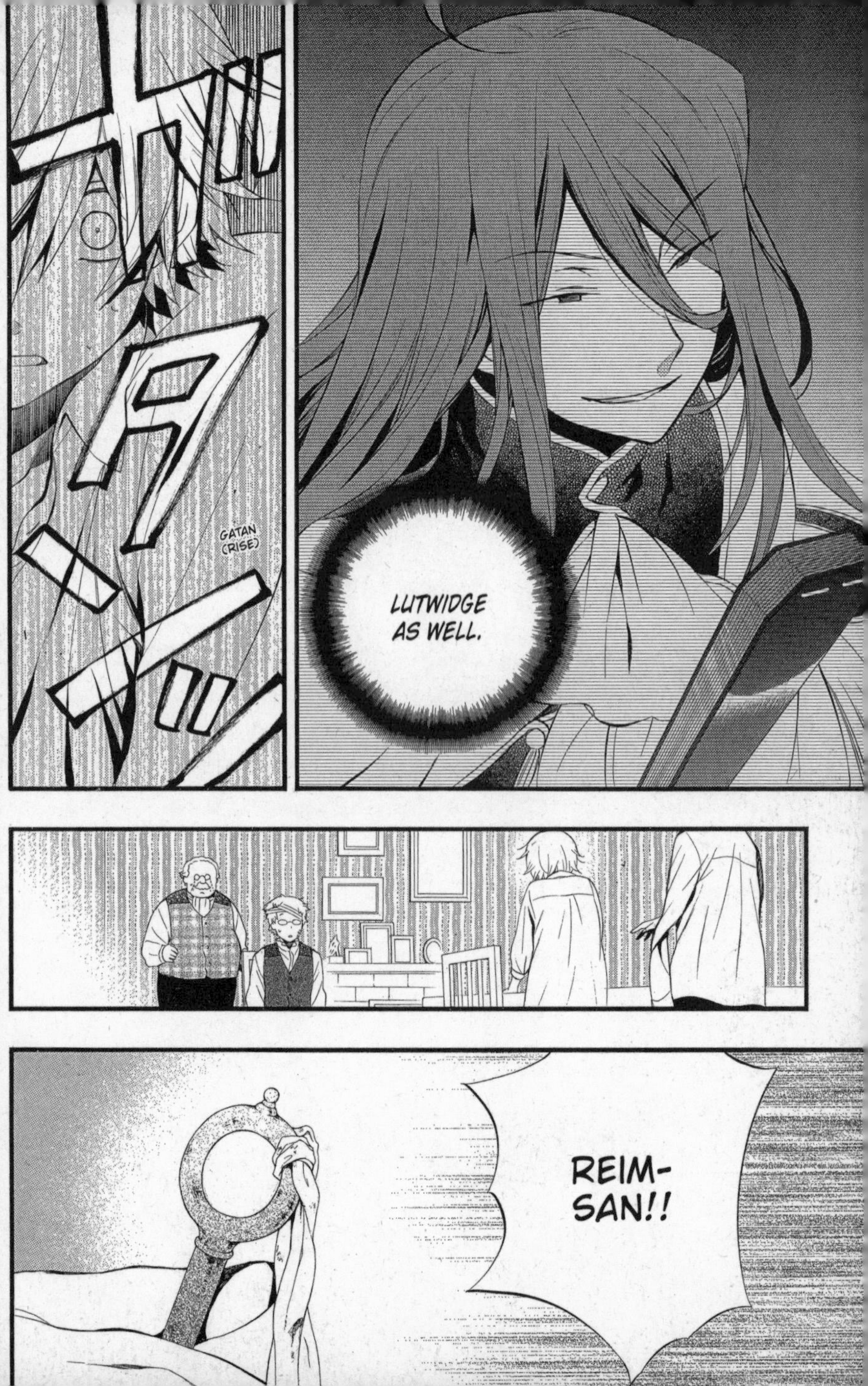
LUTWIDGE AS WELL.
GATAN (RISE)
REIM-SAN!!

Retrace : LXXXIV   Trickster

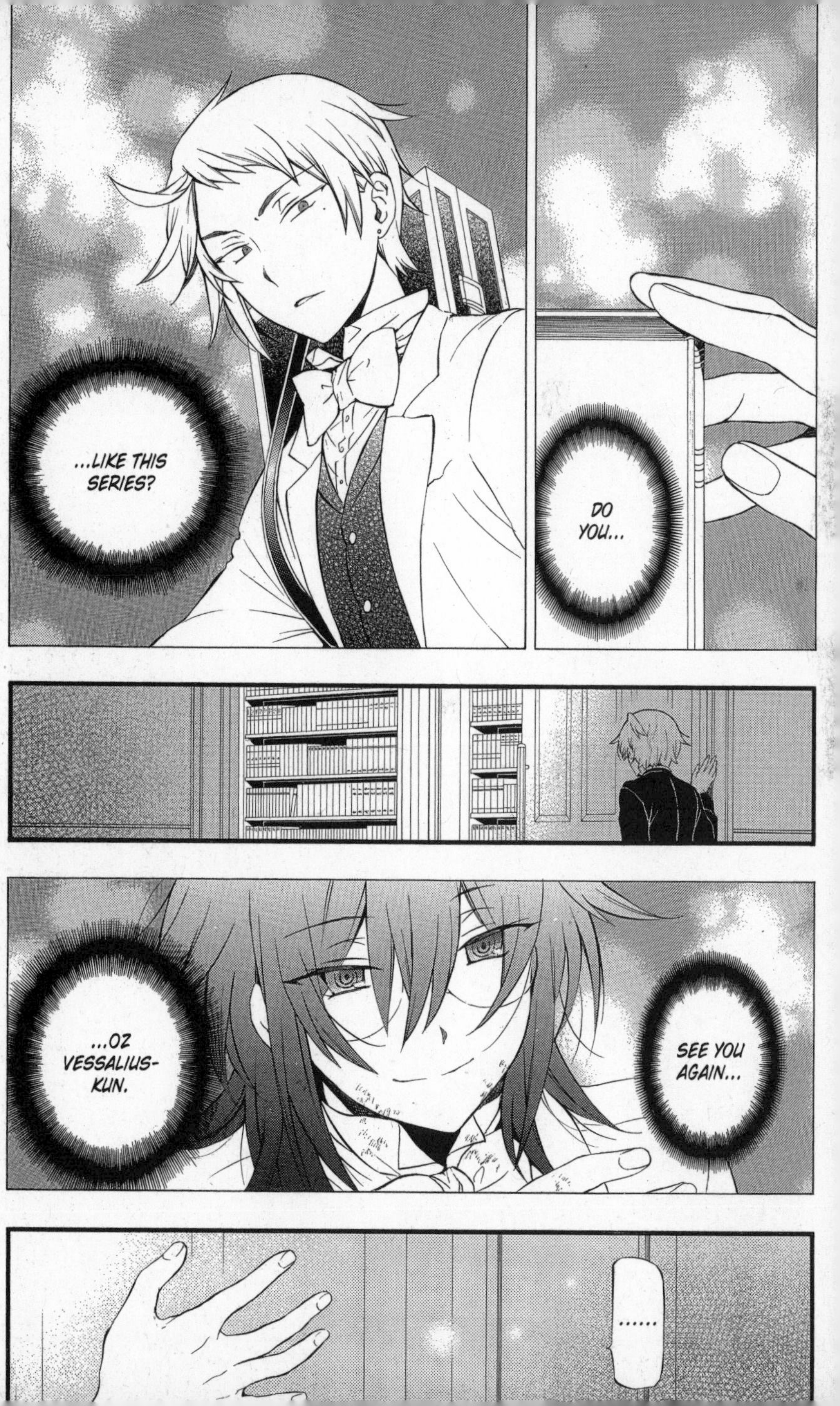
DO YOU...
...LIKE THIS SERIES?
SEE YOU AGAIN...
...OZ VESSALIUS-KUN.
......

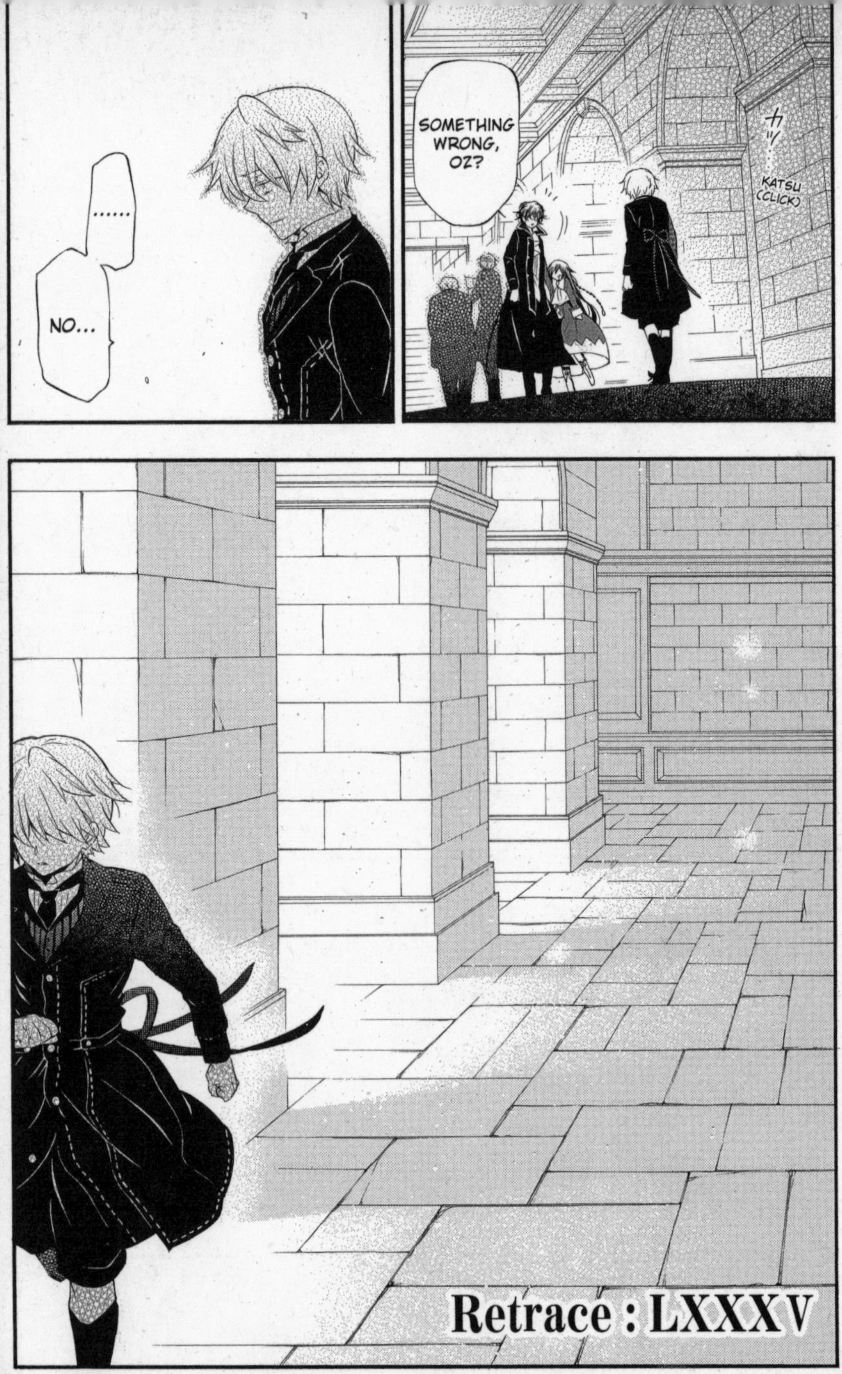
SOMETHING WRONG, OZ?
KATSU (CLICK)
......
NO...
Retrace : LXXXV

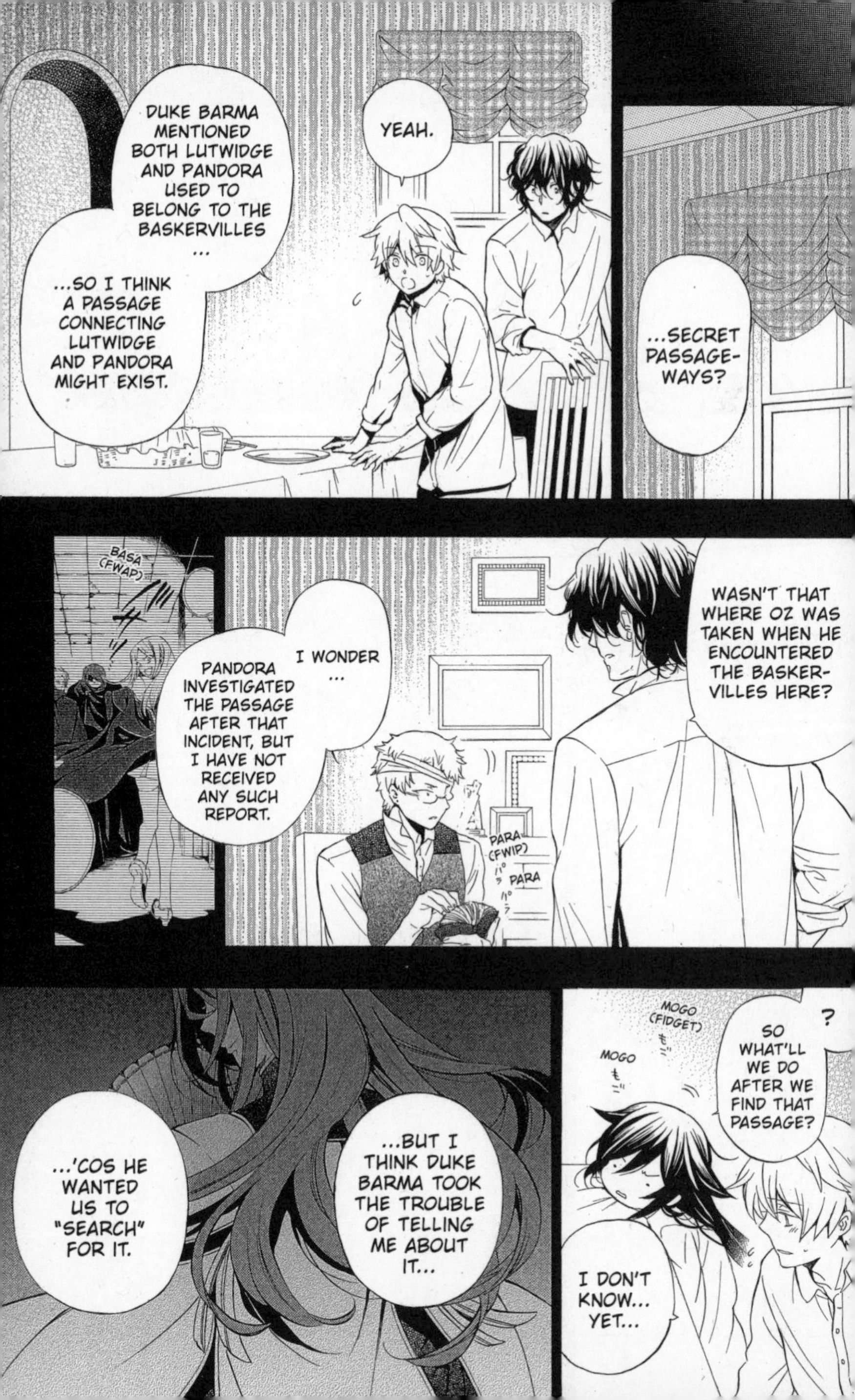
...SECRET PASSAGE-WAYS?
YEAH.
DUKE BARMA MENTIONED BOTH LUTWIDGE AND PANDORA USED TO BELONG TO THE BASKERVILLES ...
...SO I THINK A PASSAGE CONNECTING LUTWIDGE AND PANDORA MIGHT EXIST.
WASN'T THAT WHERE OZ WAS TAKEN WHEN HE ENCOUNTERED THE BASKER-VILLES HERE?
PARA (FWIP) PARA
I WONDER ...
PANDORA INVESTIGATED THE PASSAGE AFTER THAT INCIDENT, BUT I HAVE NOT RECEIVED ANY SUCH REPORT.
BASA (FWAP)
?
SO WHAT'LL WE DO AFTER WE FIND THAT PASSAGE?
MOGO (FIDGET)
MOGO
I DON'T KNOW... YET...
...BUT I THINK DUKE BARMA TOOK THE TROUBLE OF TELLING ME ABOUT IT...
...'COS HE WANTED US TO "SEARCH" FOR IT.

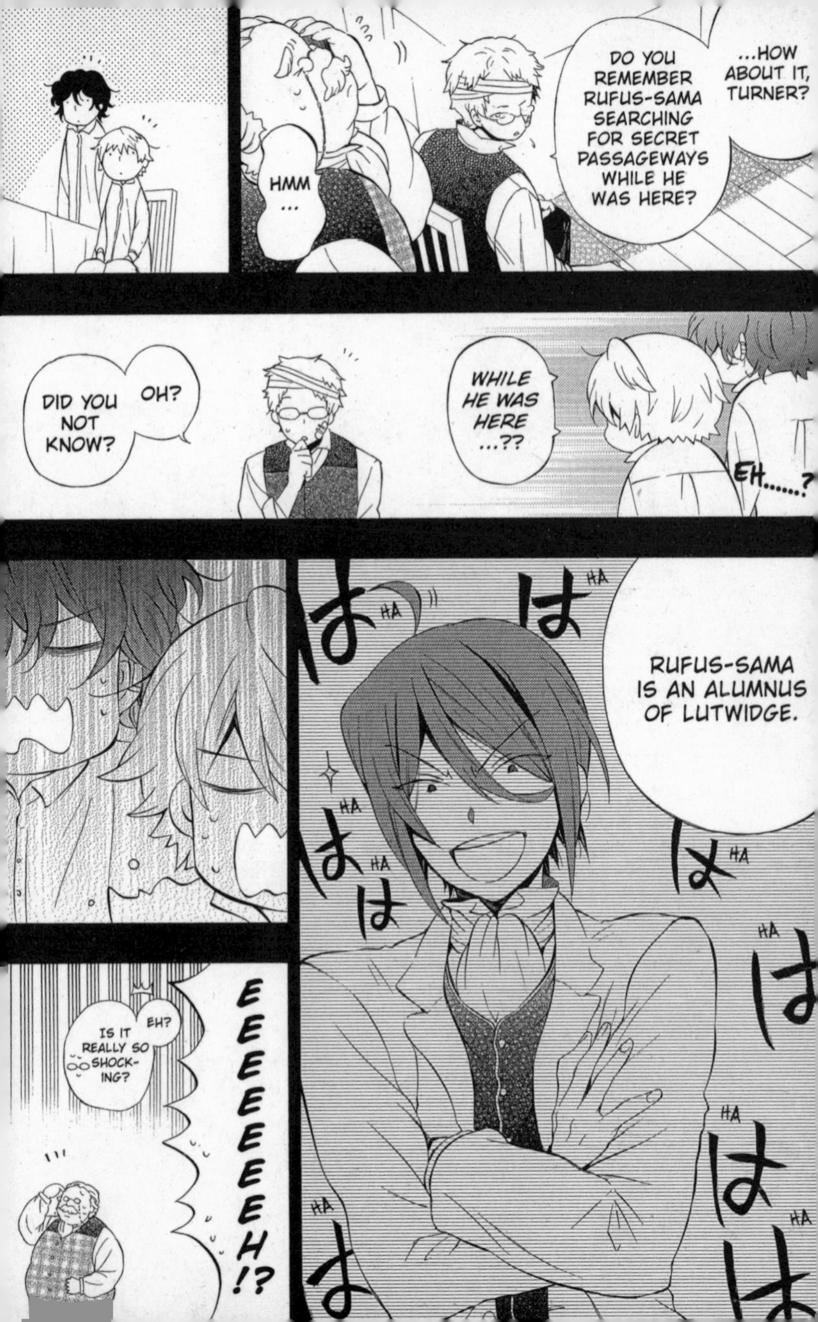
...HOW ABOUT IT, TURNER?
DO YOU REMEMBER RUFUS-SAMA SEARCHING FOR SECRET PASSAGEWAYS WHILE HE WAS HERE?
HMM ...
EH......?
WHILE HE WAS HERE ...??
OH?
DID YOU NOT KNOW?
RUFUS-SAMA IS AN ALUMNUS OF LUTWIDGE.
は HA
は HA
は HA
は HA
は HA
は HA
は HA
は HA
EEEEEEEEEEH!?
EH?
IS IT REALLY SO SHOCKING?

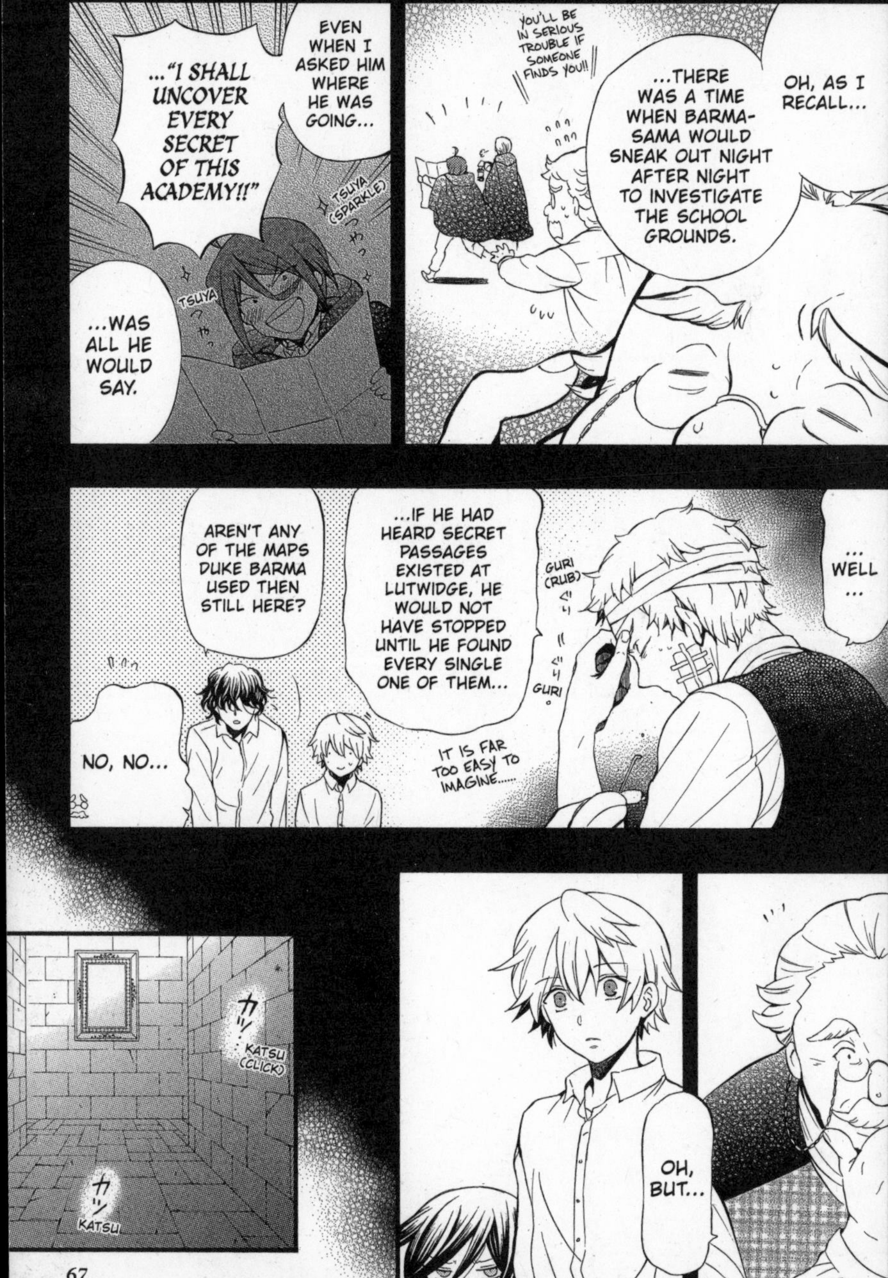
OH, AS I RECALL...
...THERE WAS A TIME WHEN BARMA-SAMA WOULD SNEAK OUT NIGHT AFTER NIGHT TO INVESTIGATE THE SCHOOL GROUNDS.
YOU'LL BE IN SERIOUS TROUBLE IF SOMEONE FINDS YOU!!
EVEN WHEN I ASKED HIM WHERE HE WAS GOING...
..."I SHALL UNCOVER EVERY SECRET OF THIS ACADEMY!!"
TSUYA (SPARKLE)
TSUYA
...WAS ALL HE WOULD SAY.
...WELL...
GURI (RUB)
GURI
...IF HE HAD HEARD SECRET PASSAGES EXISTED AT LUTWIDGE, HE WOULD NOT HAVE STOPPED UNTIL HE FOUND EVERY SINGLE ONE OF THEM...
IT IS FAR TOO EASY TO IMAGINE.....
AREN'T ANY OF THE MAPS DUKE BARMA USED THEN STILL HERE?
NO, NO...
OH, BUT...
KATSU (CLICK)
KATSU

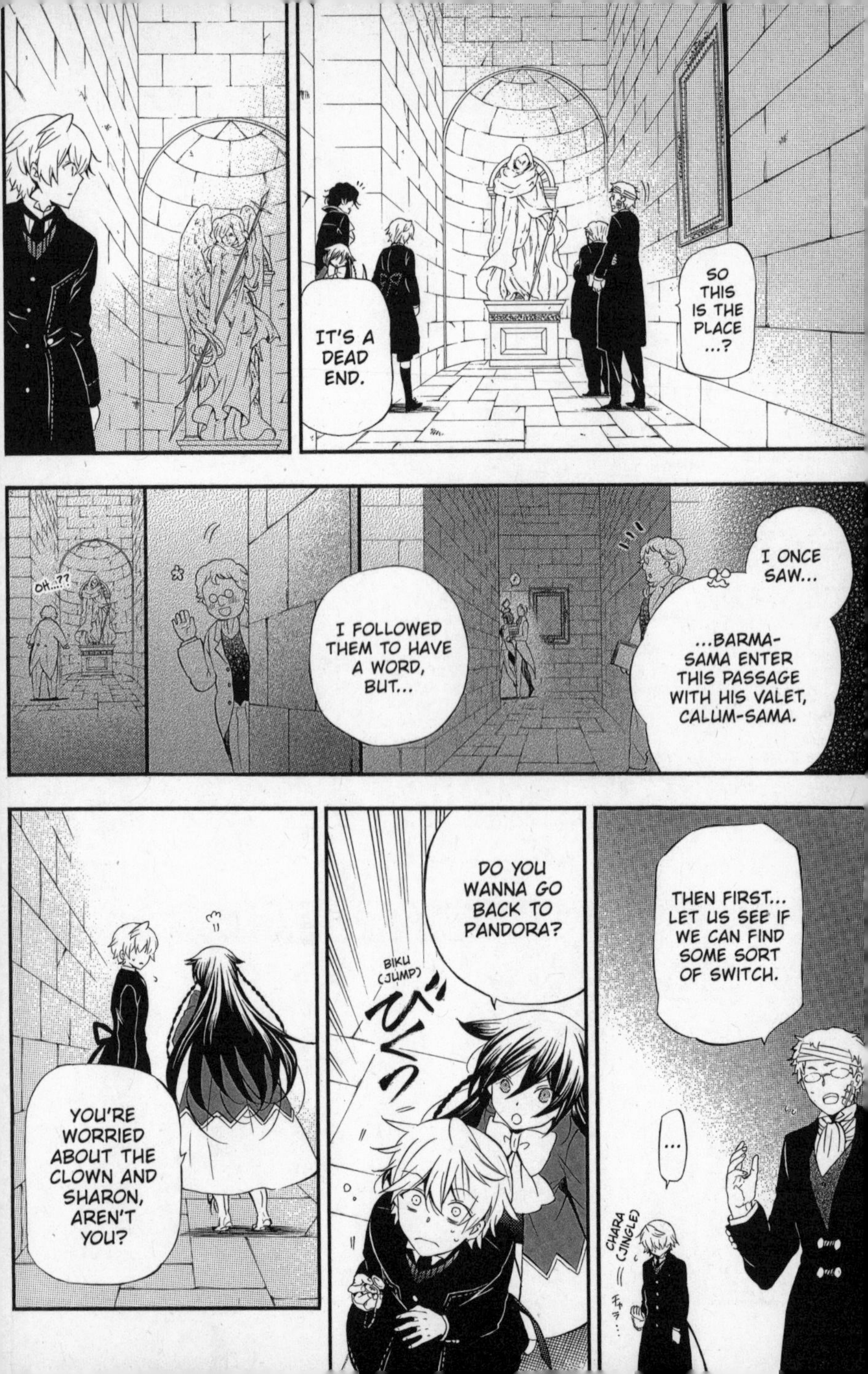
SO THIS IS THE PLACE ...?
IT'S A DEAD END.
I ONCE SAW...
...BARMA-SAMA ENTER THIS PASSAGE WITH HIS VALET, CALUM-SAMA.
I FOLLOWED THEM TO HAVE A WORD, BUT...
OH...??
THEN FIRST... LET US SEE IF WE CAN FIND SOME SORT OF SWITCH.
...
CHARA (JINGLE)
DO YOU WANNA GO BACK TO PANDORA?
BIKU (JUMP)
YOU'RE WORRIED ABOUT THE CLOWN AND SHARON, AREN'T YOU?

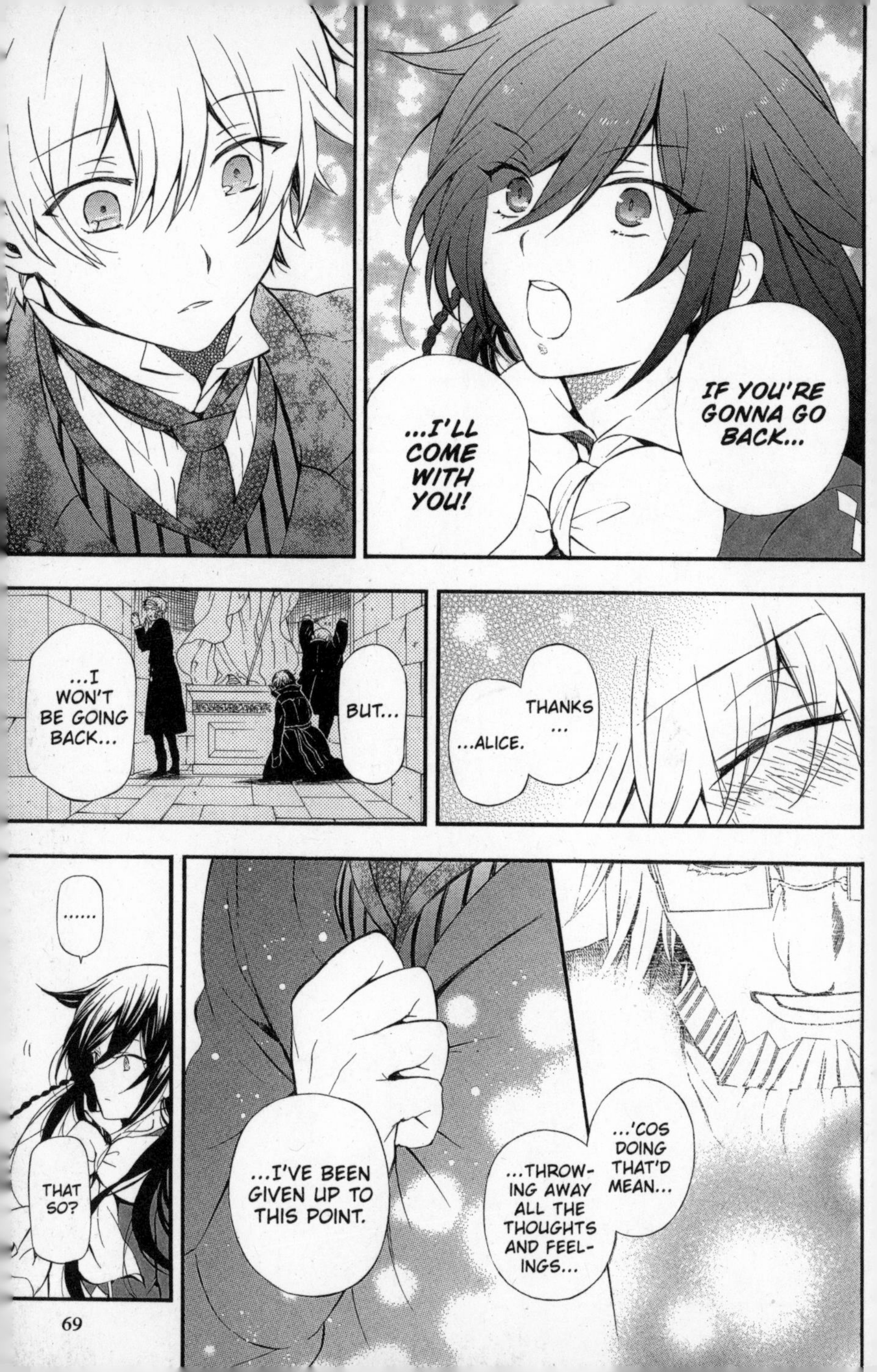
IF YOU'RE GONNA GO BACK...
...I'LL COME WITH YOU!
THANKS... ...ALICE.
BUT...
...I WON'T BE GOING BACK...
...'COS DOING THAT'D MEAN...
...THROW-ING AWAY ALL THE THOUGHTS AND FEEL-INGS...
...I'VE BEEN GIVEN UP TO THIS POINT.
......
THAT SO?

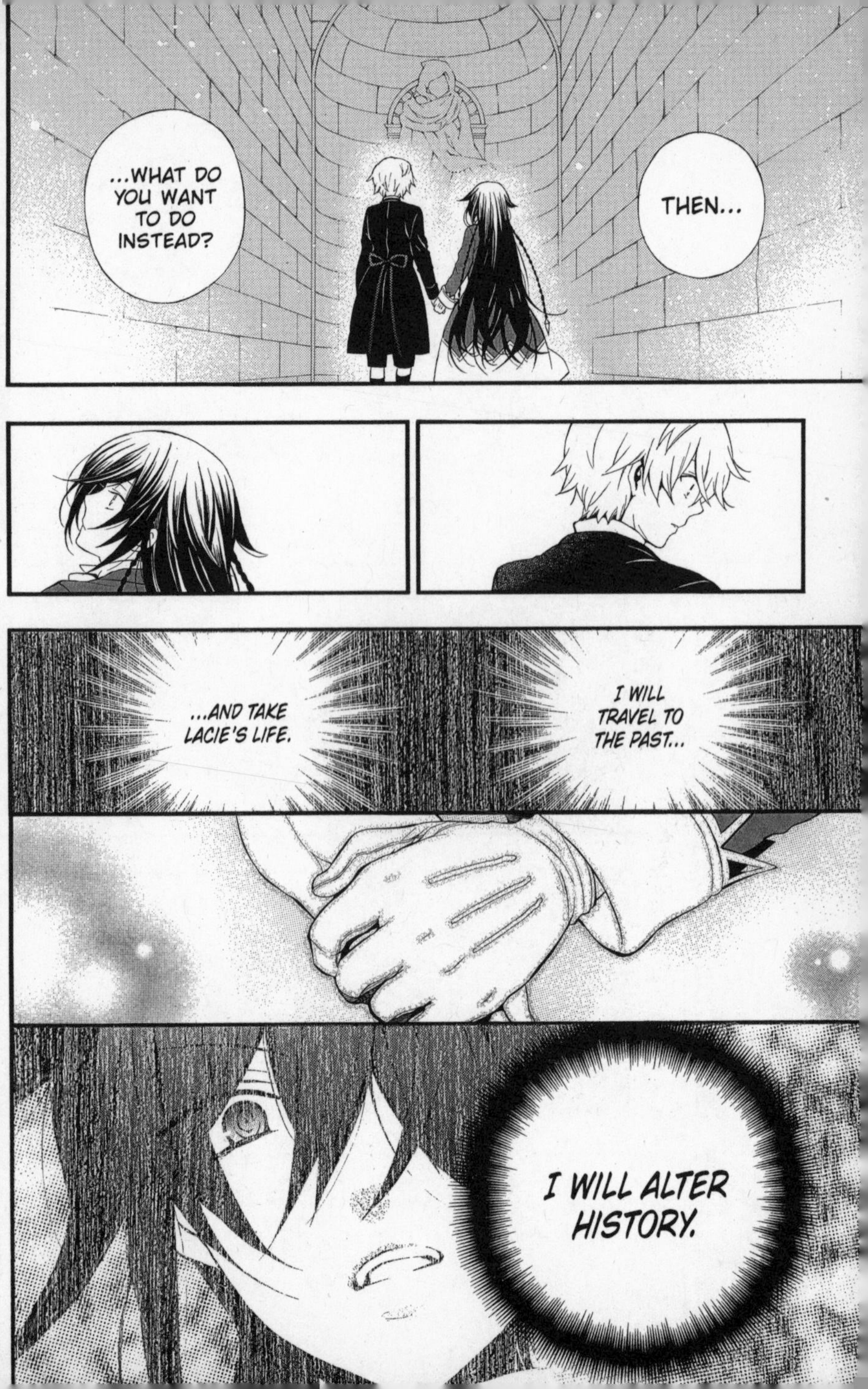
THEN...
...WHAT DO YOU WANT TO DO INSTEAD?
I WILL TRAVEL TO THE PAST...
...AND TAKE LACIE'S LIFE.
I WILL ALTER HISTORY.

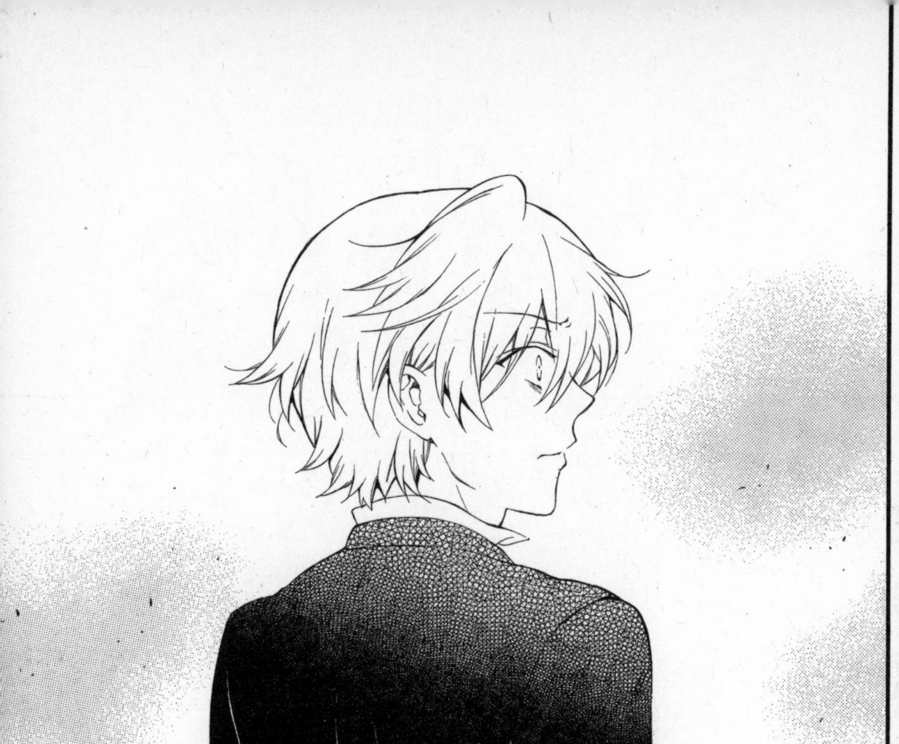

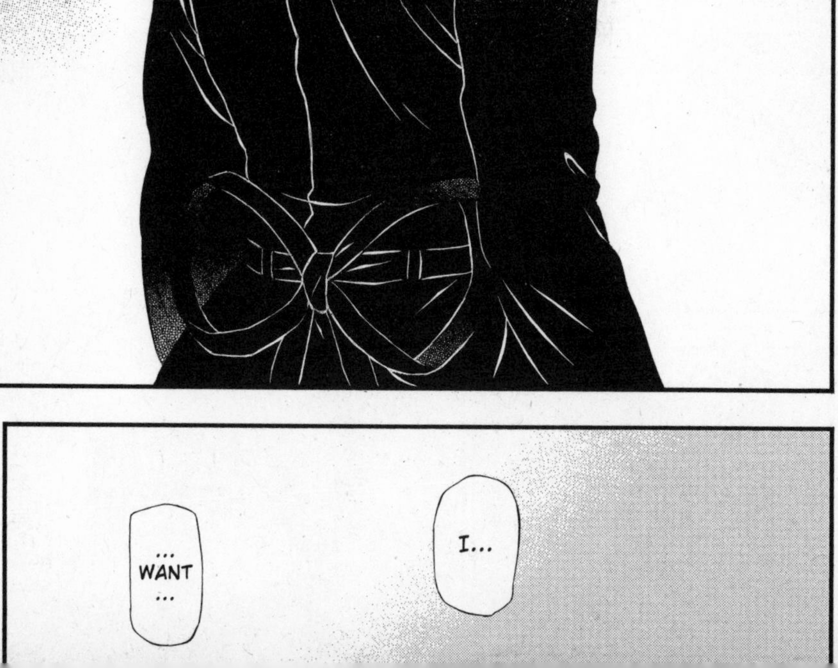
I...
...WANT...

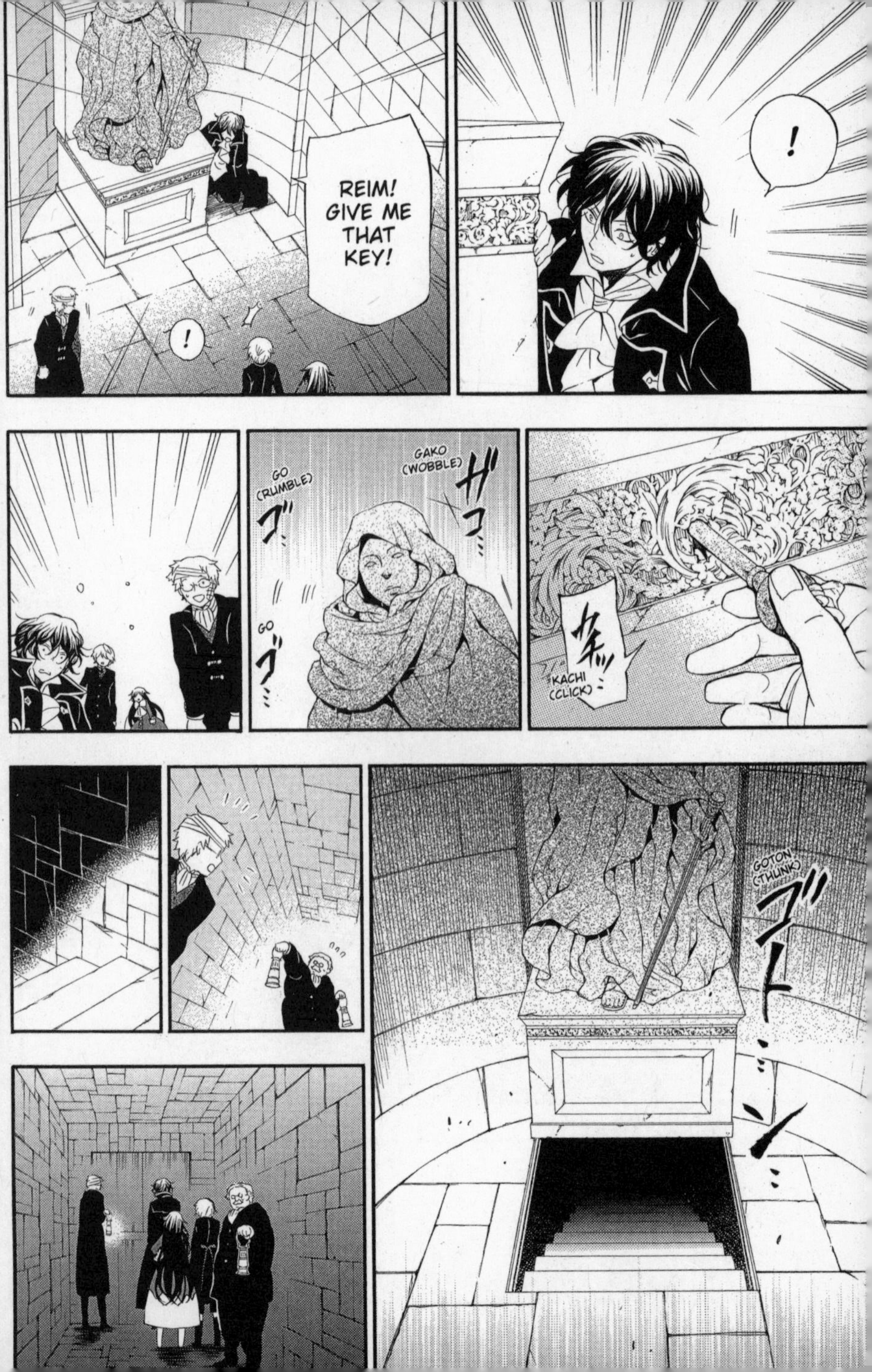
!
REIM! GIVE ME THAT KEY!
!
KACHI (CLICK)
GAKO (WOBBLE)
GO (RUMBLE)
GO
GOTON (THUNK)
!...

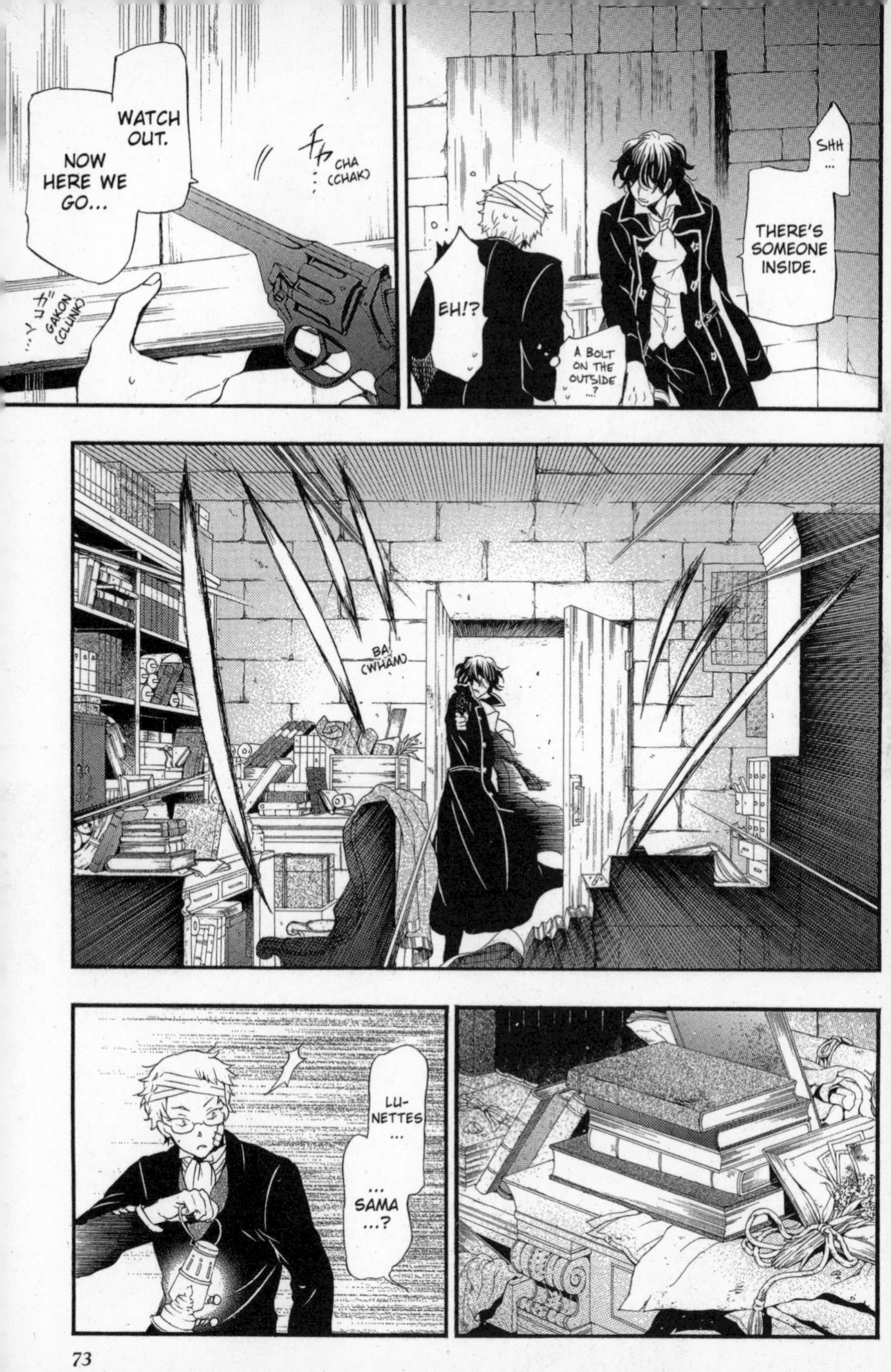
SHH ... THERE'S SOMEONE INSIDE.
EH!?
A BOLT ON THE OUTSIDE ...?
CHA (CHAK)
WATCH OUT. NOW HERE WE GO...
GAKON (CLUNK)
BA (WHAM)
LUNETTES ... ... SAMA ...?

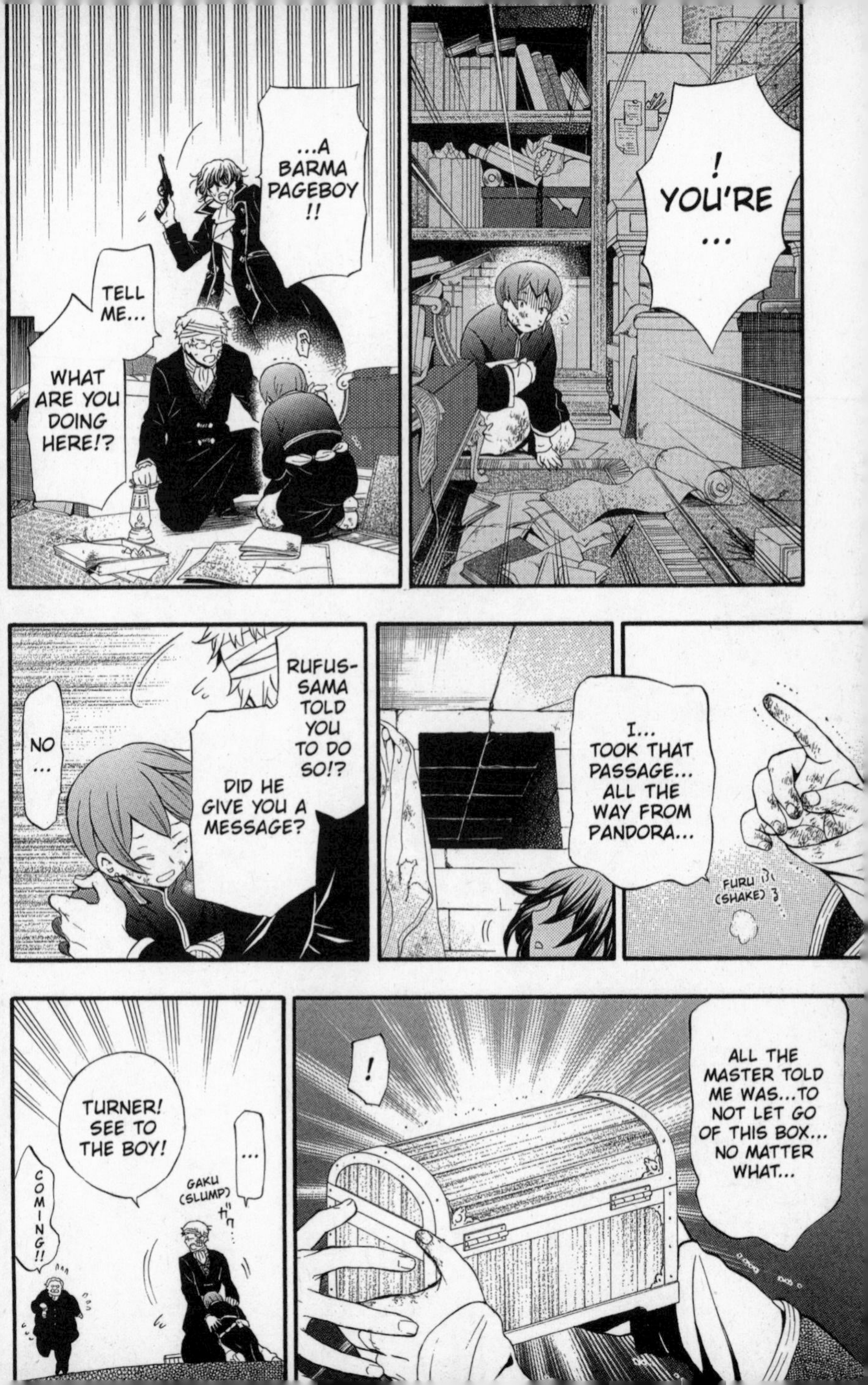
! YOU'RE ...
...A BARMA PAGEBOY !!
TELL ME...
WHAT ARE YOU DOING HERE!?
FURU (SHAKE)
I... TOOK THAT PASSAGE... ALL THE WAY FROM PANDORA...
RUFUS-SAMA TOLD YOU TO DO SO!?
DID HE GIVE YOU A MESSAGE?
NO ...
ALL THE MASTER TOLD ME WAS...TO NOT LET GO OF THIS BOX... NO MATTER WHAT...
!
...
GAKU (SLUMP)
TURNER! SEE TO THE BOY!
COMING!!

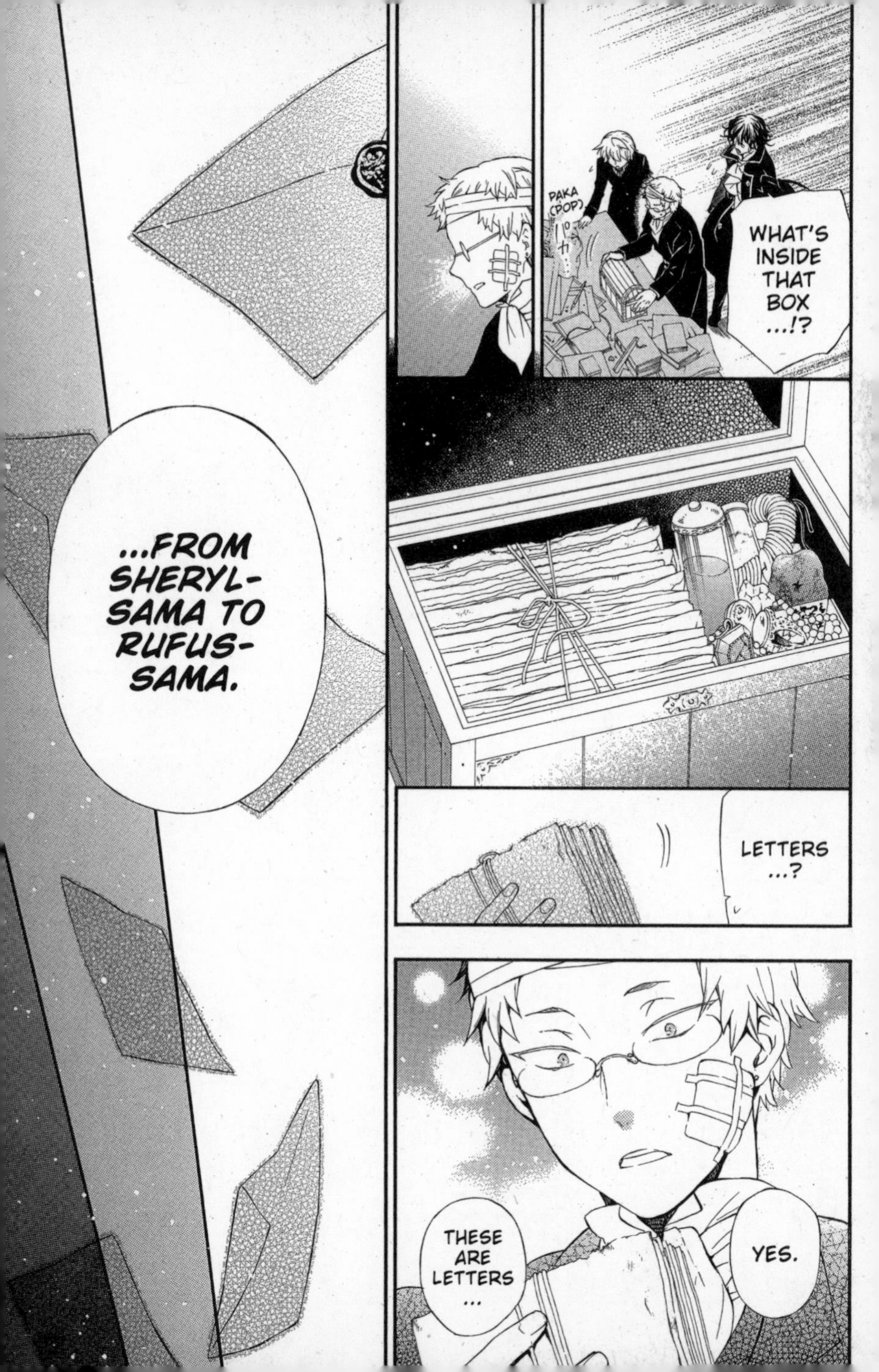
WHAT'S INSIDE THAT BOX ...!?
PAKA (POP)
LETTERS ...?
YES.
THESE ARE LETTERS ...
...FROM SHERYL-SAMA TO RUFUS-SAMA.

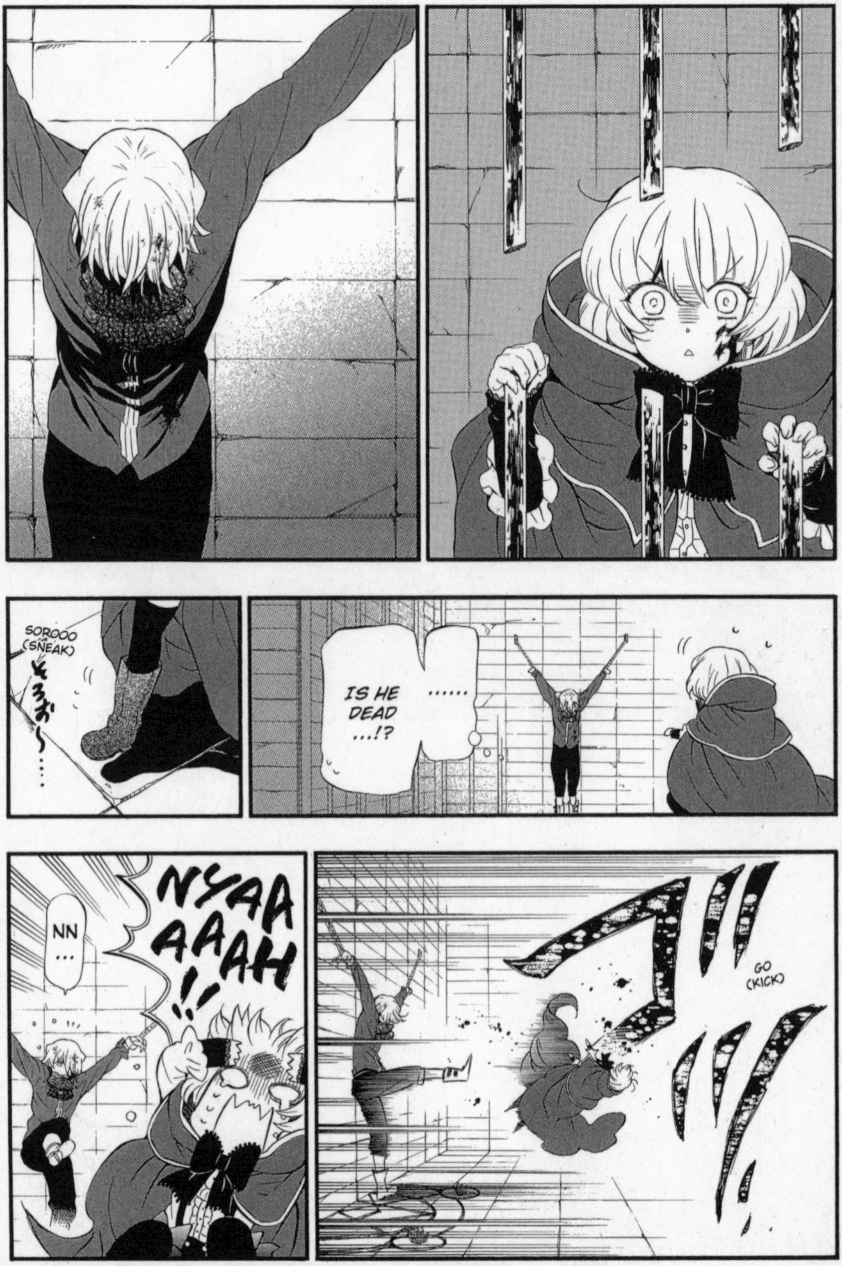
......
IS HE DEAD ...!?
SOROOO (SNEAK)
そろぉ～….
GO (KICK)
NYAAAAAH!!
NN ...

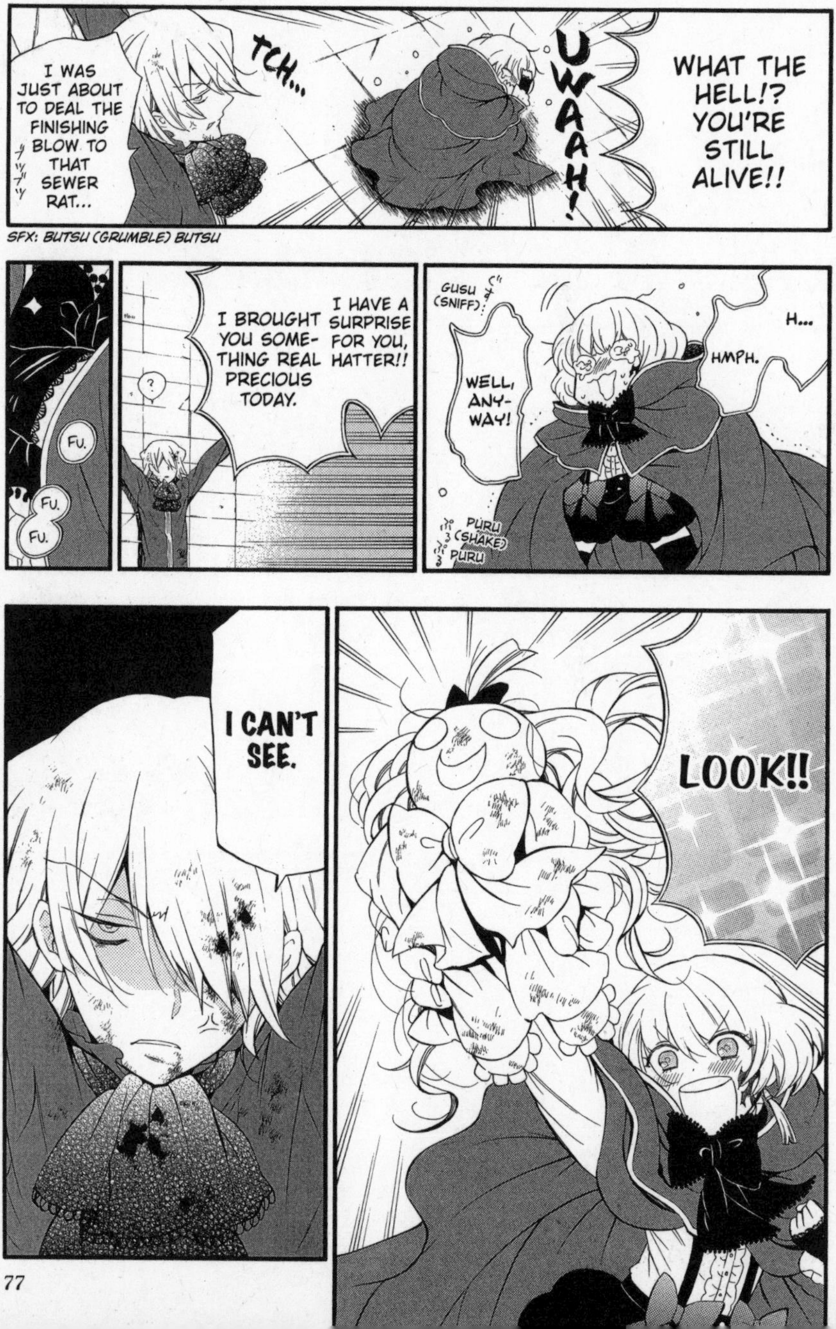
WHAT THE HELL!? YOU'RE STILL ALIVE!!
UWAAH!
TCH...
I WAS JUST ABOUT TO DEAL THE FINISHING BLOW TO THAT SEWER RAT...
SFX: BUTSU (GRUMBLE) BUTSU
H...
HMPH.
GUSU (SNIFF)
WELL, ANYWAY!
PURU (SHAKE) PURU
I HAVE A SURPRISE FOR YOU, HATTER!!
I BROUGHT YOU SOMETHING REAL PRECIOUS TODAY.
?
FU.
FU.
FU.
LOOK!!
I CAN'T SEE.

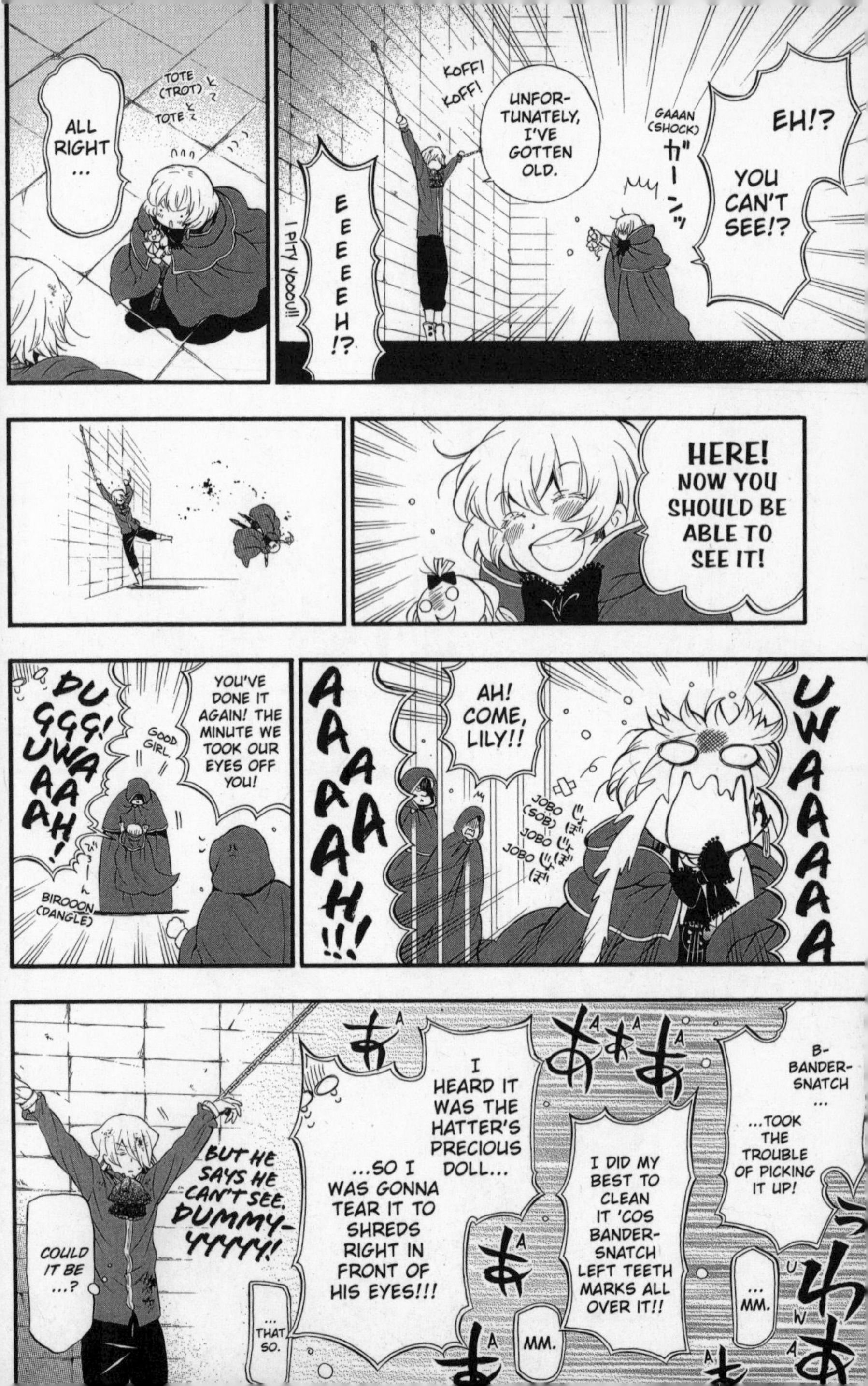

EH!?
YOU CAN'T SEE!?
GAAAN (SHOCK) ガーンッ
UNFORTUNATELY, I'VE GOTTEN OLD.
KOFF! KOFF!
EEEEEEH!?
I PITY YOOOU!!
ALL RIGHT...
TOTE (TROT) TOTE
HERE! NOW YOU SHOULD BE ABLE TO SEE IT!
UWAAAAAAA
AH! COME, LILY!!
JOBO (SOB) JOBO JOBO
AAAAAAH!!!
YOU'VE DONE IT AGAIN! THE MINUTE WE TOOK OUR EYES OFF YOU!
GOOD GIRL.
DUGGG! UWAAAAH!
BIROOON (DANGLE)
UWA
B-BANDERSNATCH...
...TOOK THE TROUBLE OF PICKING IT UP!
...MM.
AAA
I DID MY BEST TO CLEAN IT 'COS BANDERSNATCH LEFT TEETH MARKS ALL OVER IT!!
I HEARD IT WAS THE HATTER'S PRECIOUS DOLL...
...SO I WAS GONNA TEAR IT TO SHREDS RIGHT IN FRONT OF HIS EYES!!!
A
MM.
A
BUT HE SAYS HE CAN'T SEE. DUMMY-YYYYY!
...THAT SO.
COULD IT BE...?

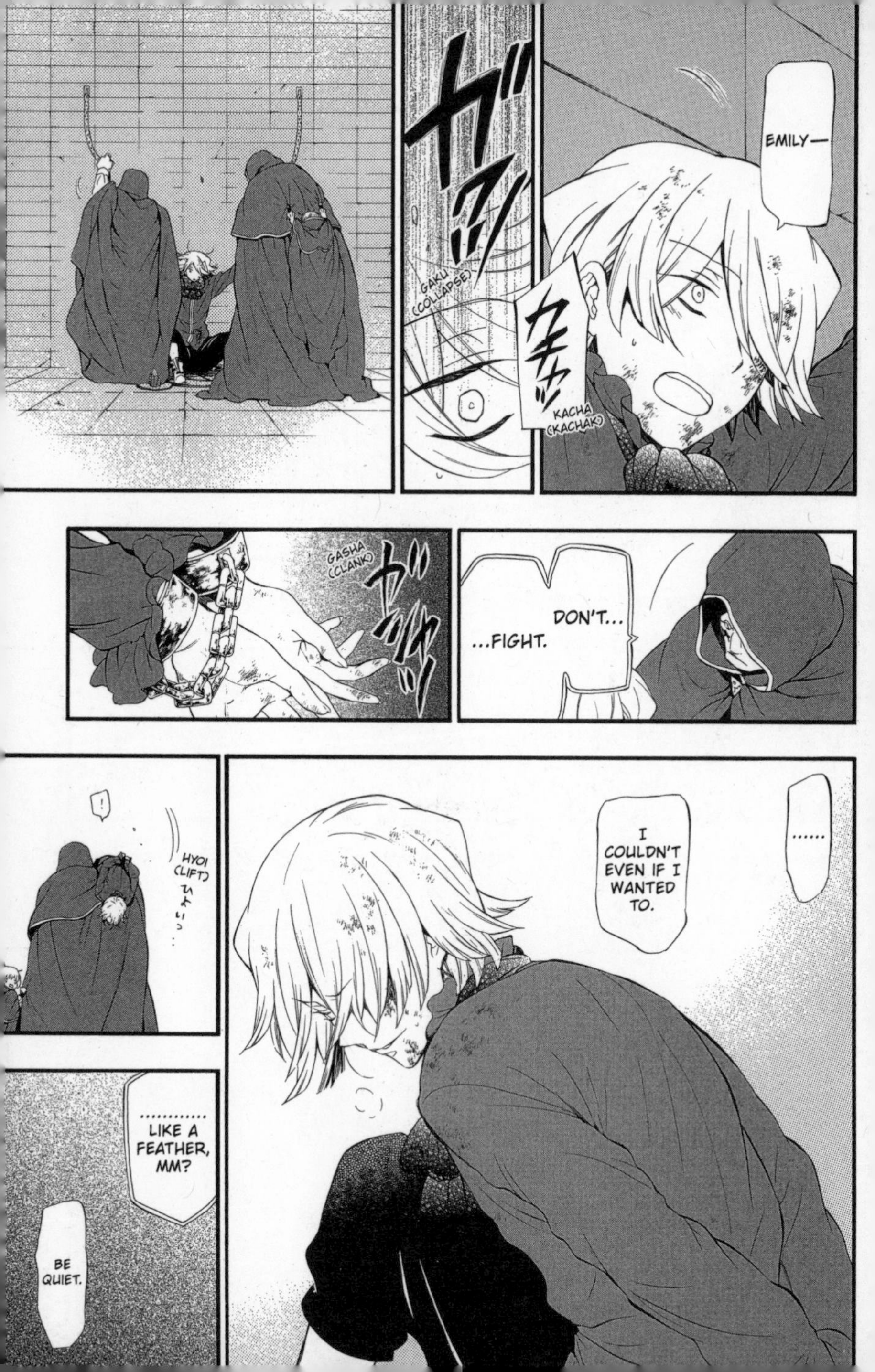
EMILY—
KACHA (KACHAK)
GAKU (COLLAPSE)
DON'T...
...FIGHT.
GASHA (CLANK)
......
I COULDN'T EVEN IF I WANTED TO.
!
HYOI (LIFT)
.... LIKE A FEATHER, MM?
BE QUIET.

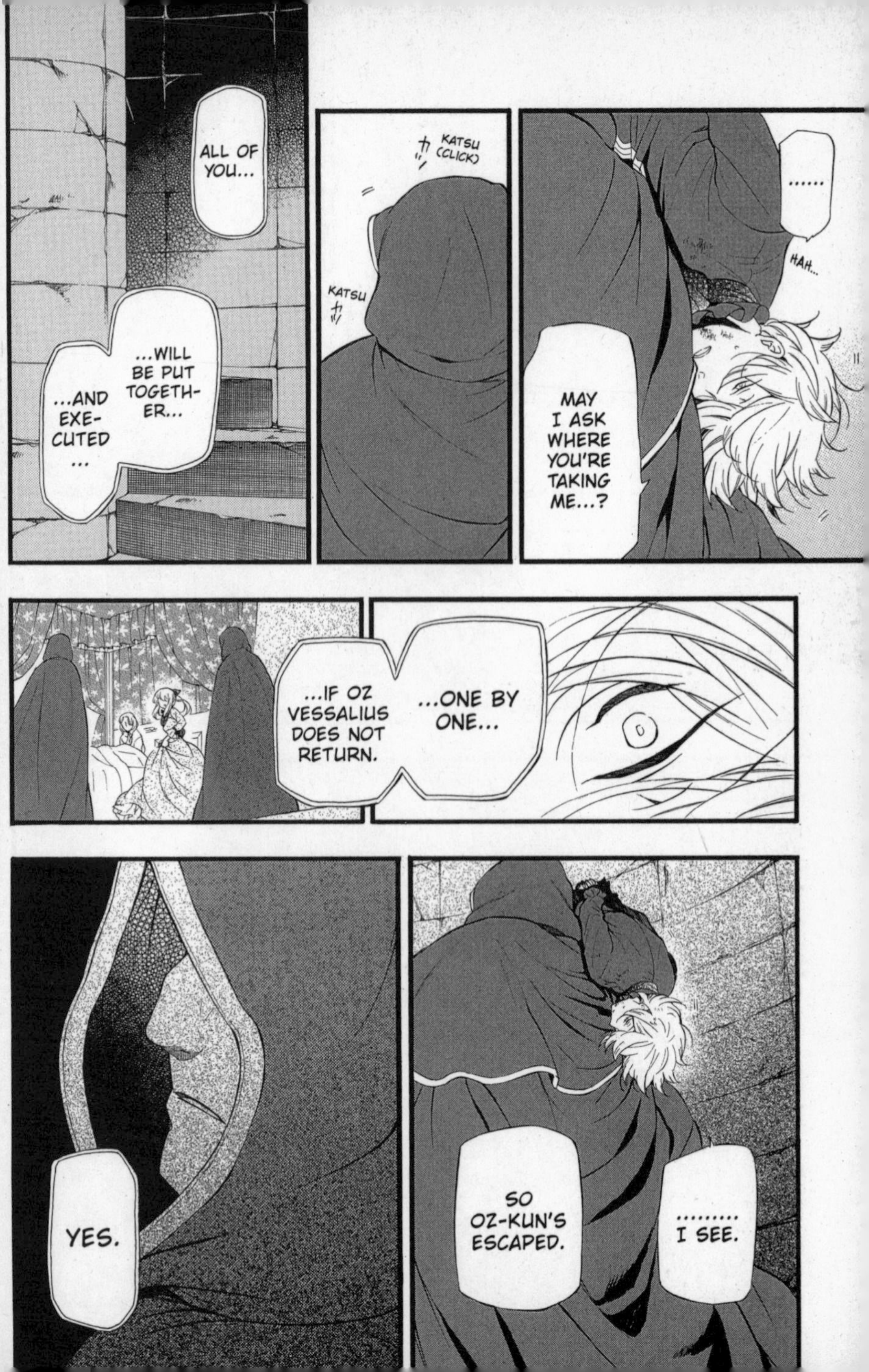
......
HAH...
MAY I ASK WHERE YOU'RE TAKING ME...?
KATSU (CLICK)
KATSU
ALL OF YOU...
...WILL BE PUT TOGETHER...
...AND EXECUTED...
...ONE BY ONE...
...IF OZ VESSALIUS DOES NOT RETURN.
.........I SEE.
SO OZ-KUN'S ESCAPED.
YES.

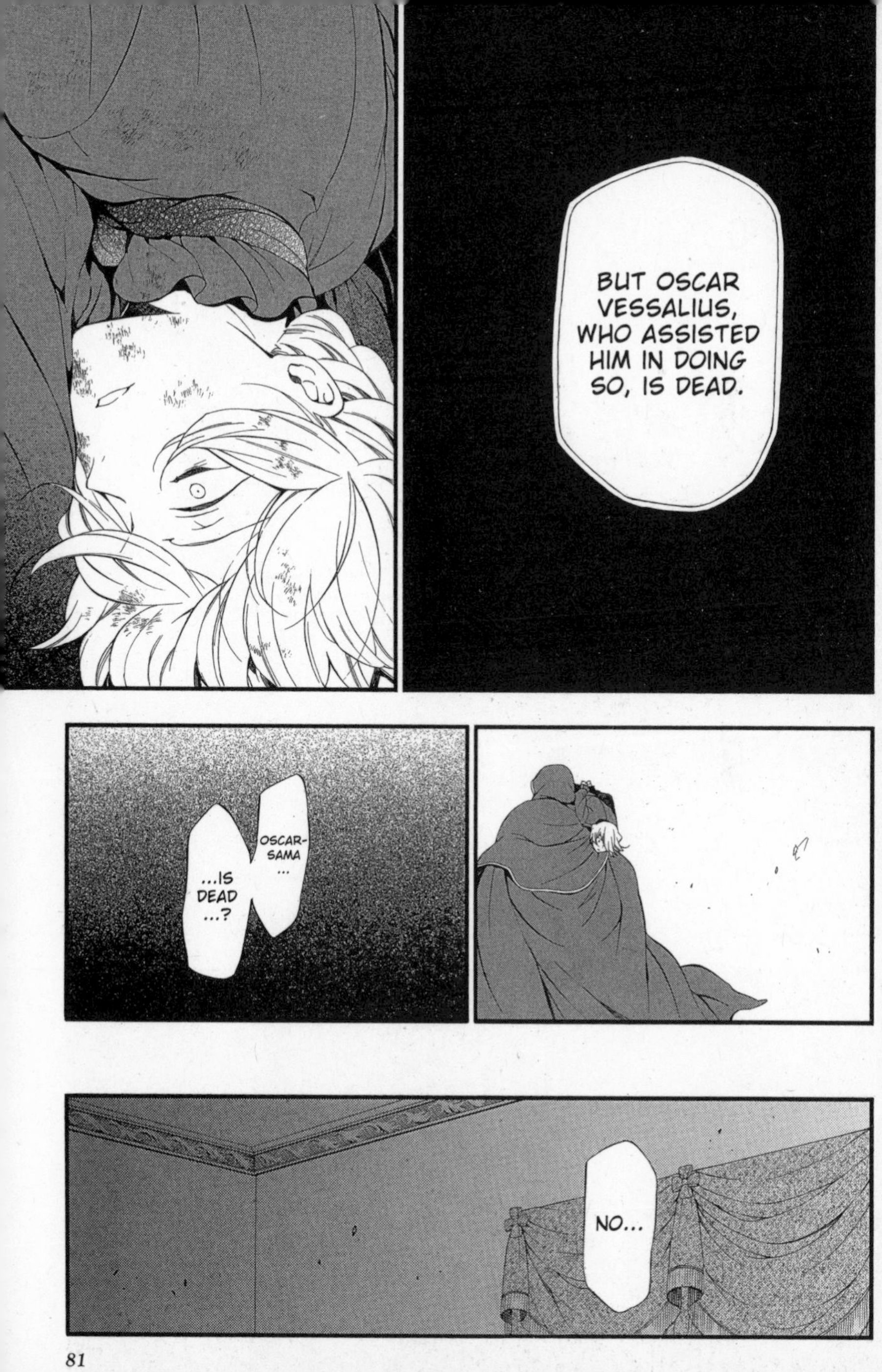
BUT OSCAR VESSALIUS, WHO ASSISTED HIM IN DOING SO, IS DEAD.
OSCAR-SAMA ...
...IS DEAD ...?
NO...

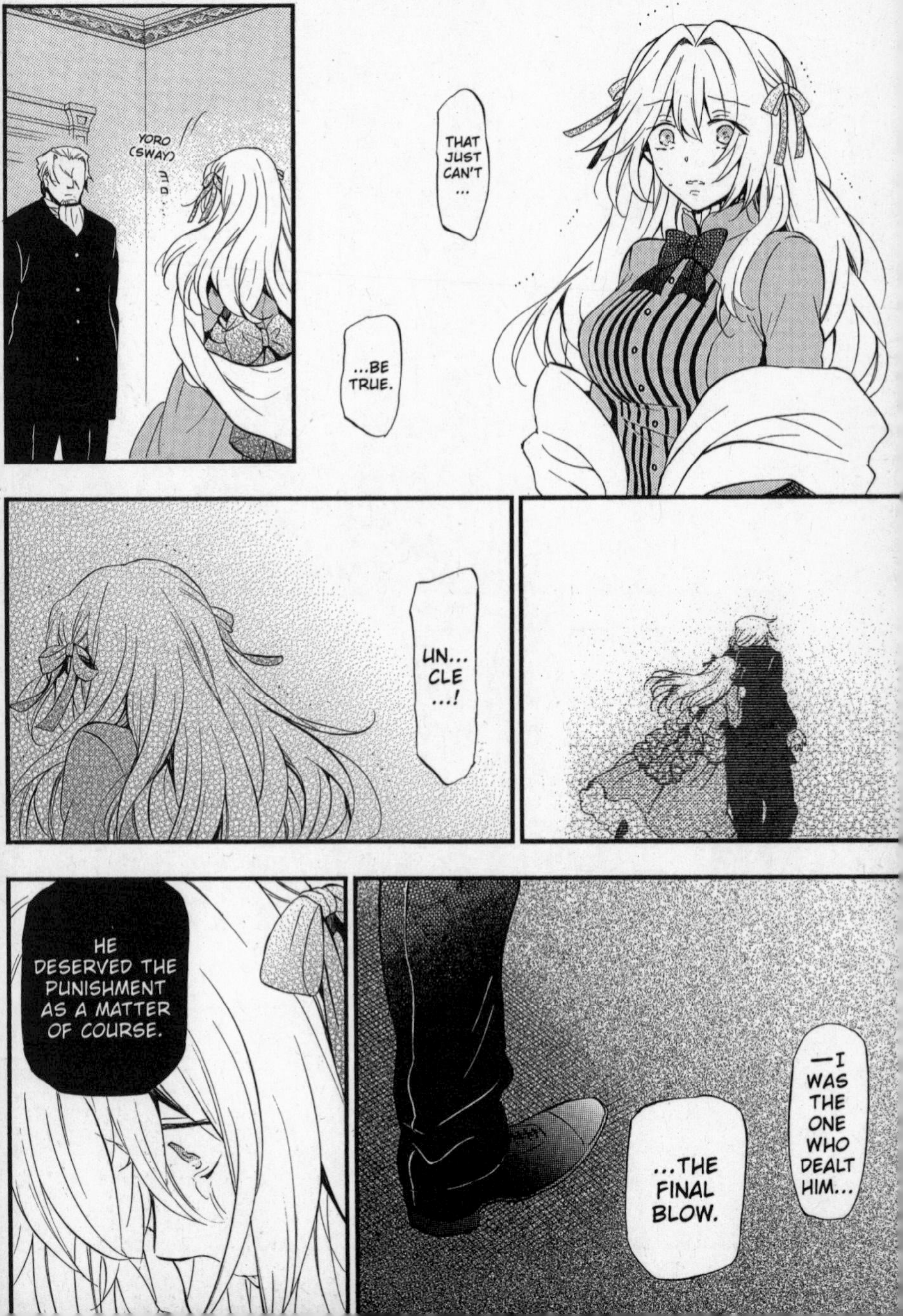
THAT JUST CAN'T ...
...BE TRUE.
YORO (SWAY)
UN... CLE ...!
—I WAS THE ONE WHO DEALT HIM...
...THE FINAL BLOW.
HE DESERVED THE PUNISHMENT AS A MATTER OF COURSE.

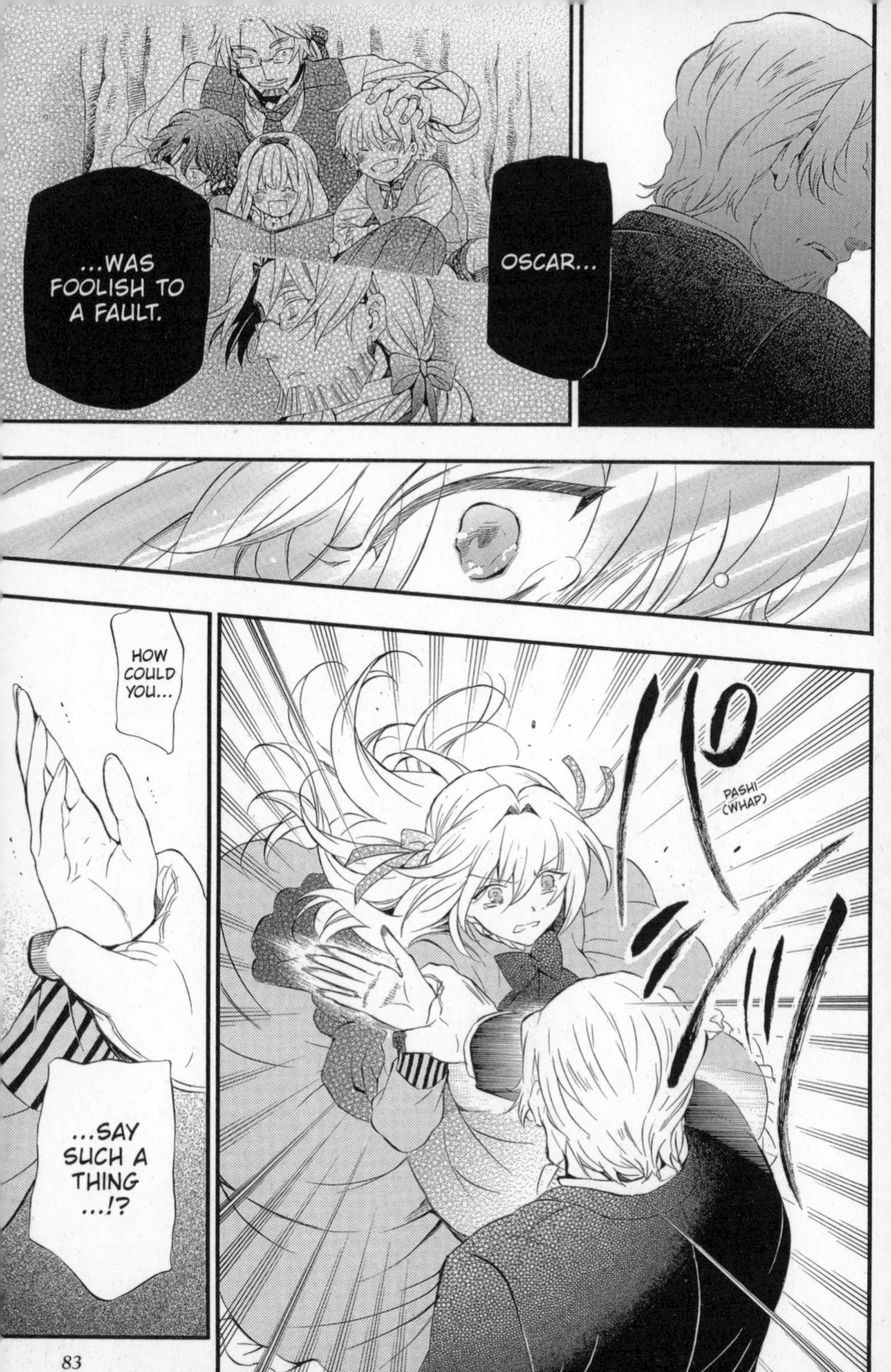
OSCAR...
...WAS FOOLISH TO A FAULT.
PASHI (WHAP)
HOW COULD YOU...
...SAY SUCH A THING ...!?

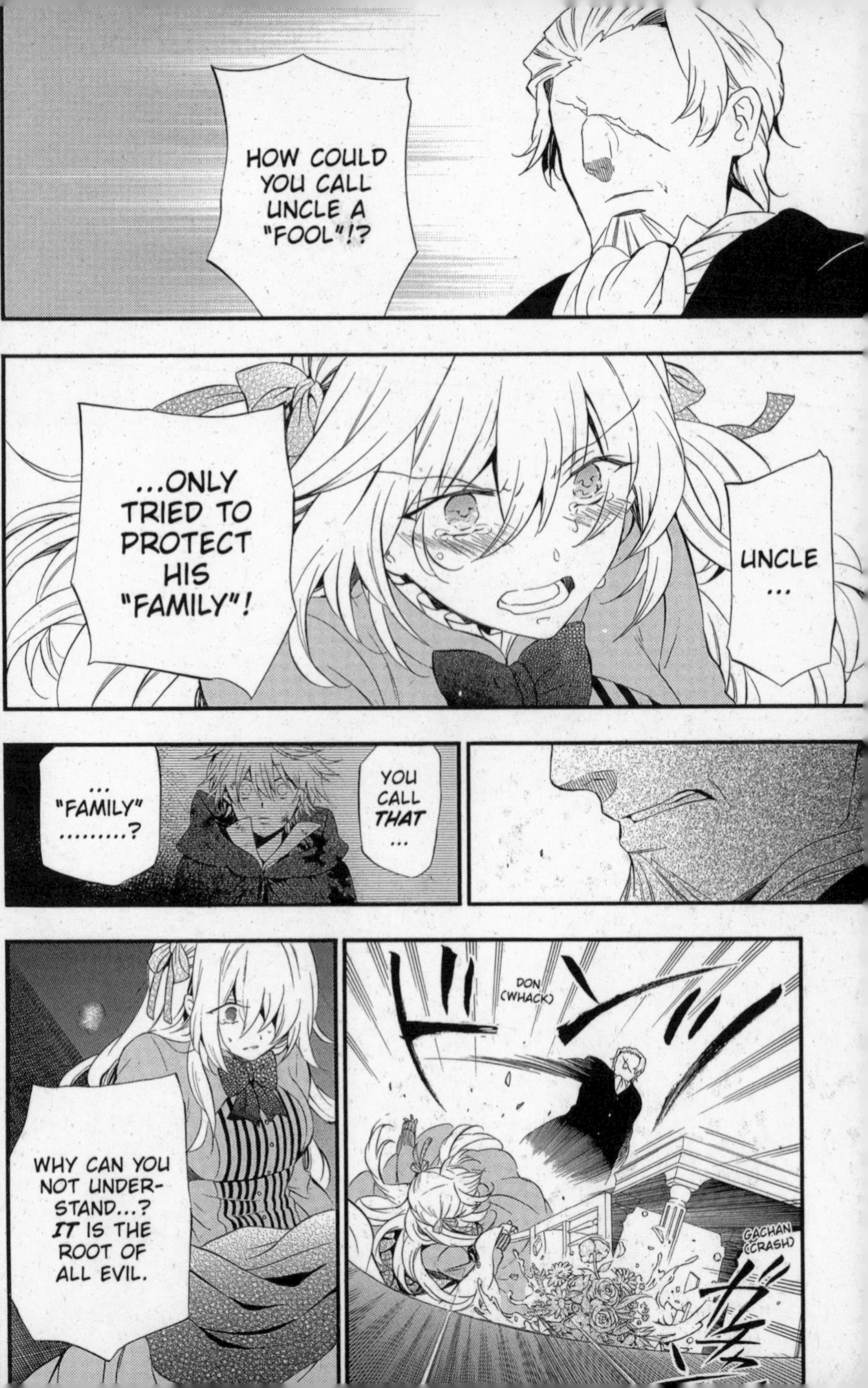
HOW COULD YOU CALL UNCLE A "FOOL"!?
UNCLE ...
...ONLY TRIED TO PROTECT HIS "FAMILY"!
YOU CALL *THAT* ...
... "FAMILY" ....?
DON (WHACK)
GACHAN (CRASH)
WHY CAN YOU NOT UNDER-STAND...? *IT* IS THE ROOT OF ALL EVIL.

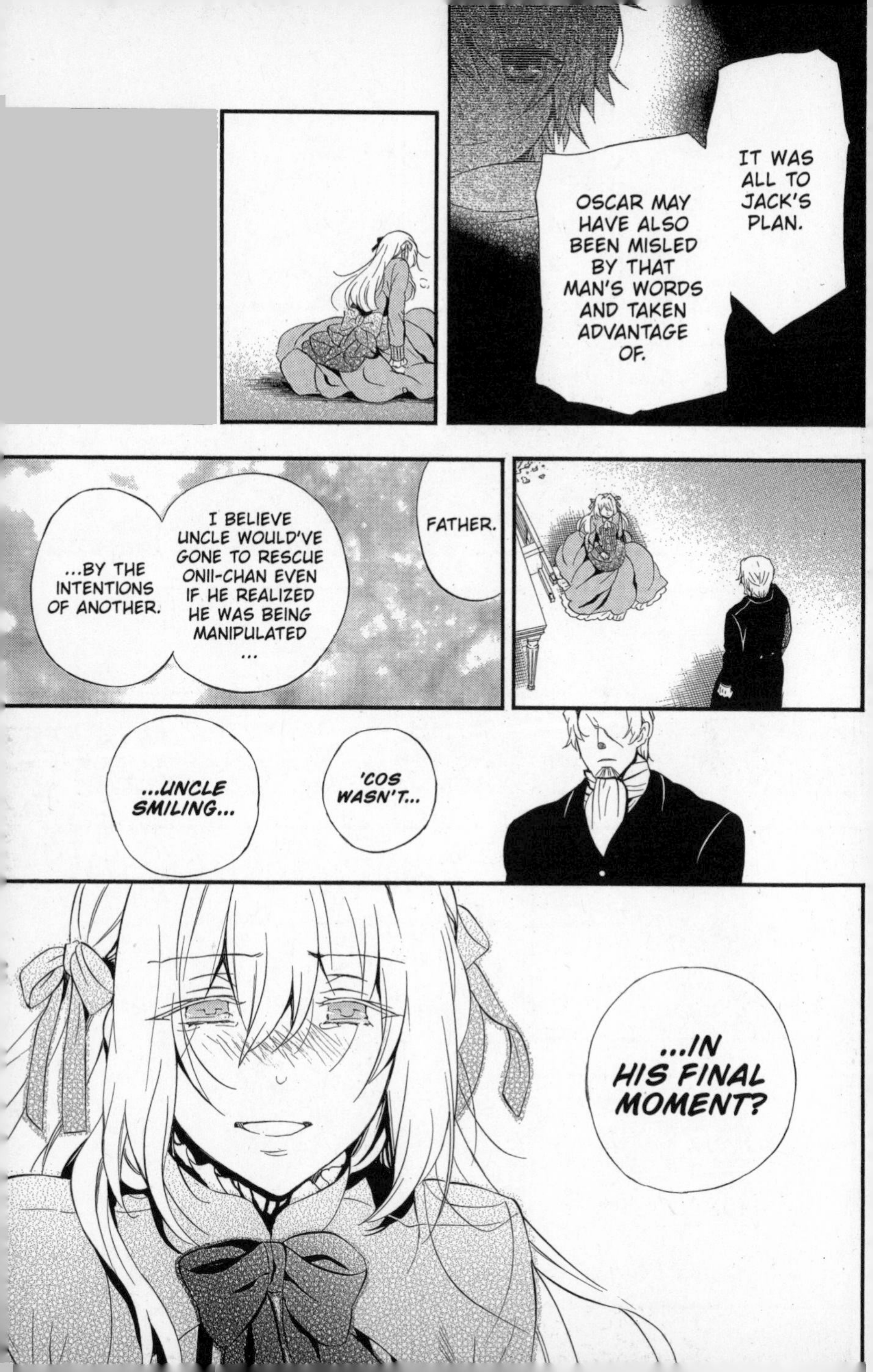
IT WAS ALL TO JACK'S PLAN.
OSCAR MAY HAVE ALSO BEEN MISLED BY THAT MAN'S WORDS AND TAKEN ADVANTAGE OF.
FATHER.
I BELIEVE UNCLE WOULD'VE GONE TO RESCUE ONII-CHAN EVEN IF HE REALIZED HE WAS BEING MANIPULATED ...
...BY THE INTENTIONS OF ANOTHER.
'COS WASN'T...
...UNCLE SMILING...
...IN HIS FINAL MOMENT?

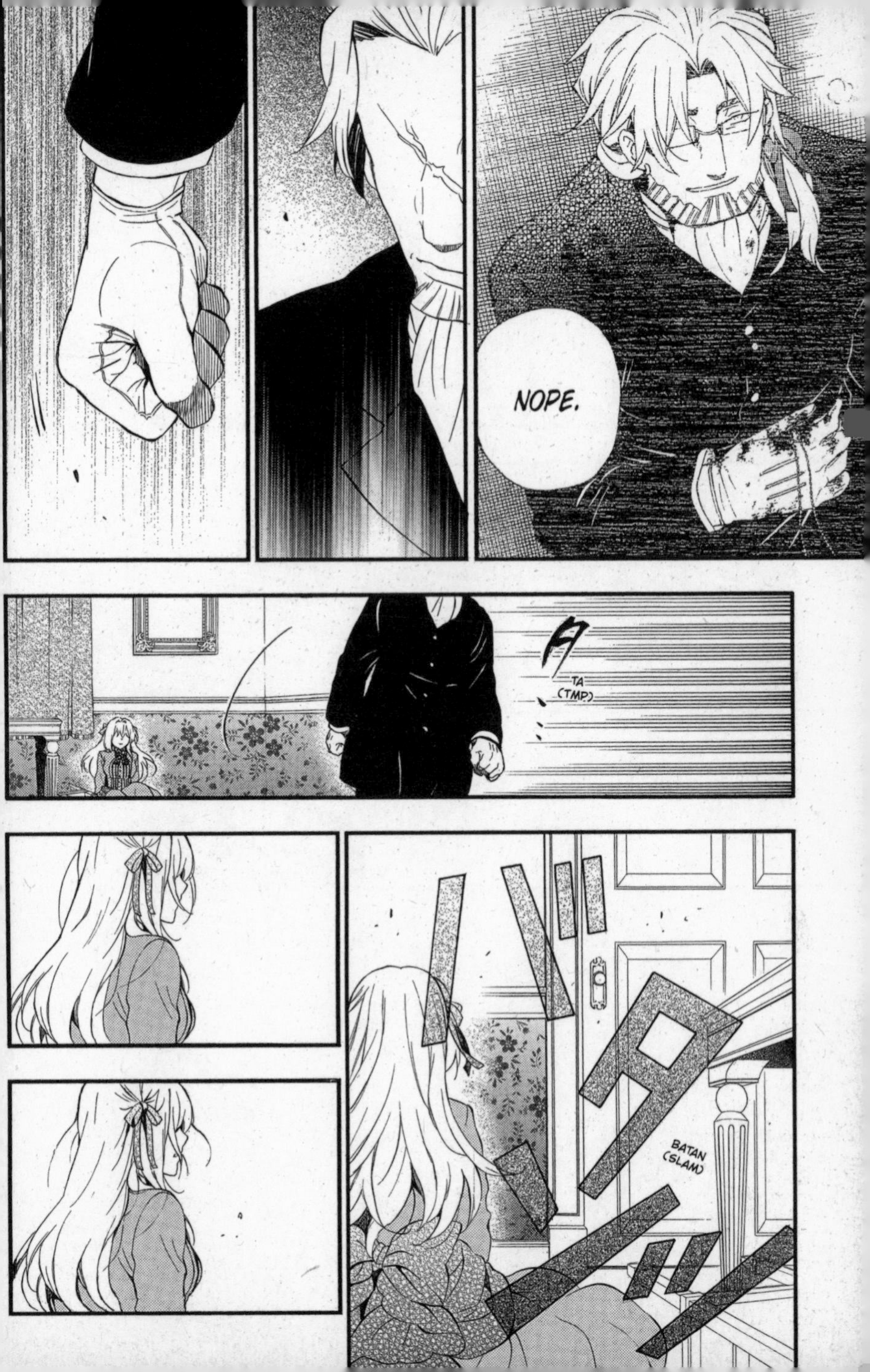
NOPE.
TA (TMP)
BATAN (SLAM)

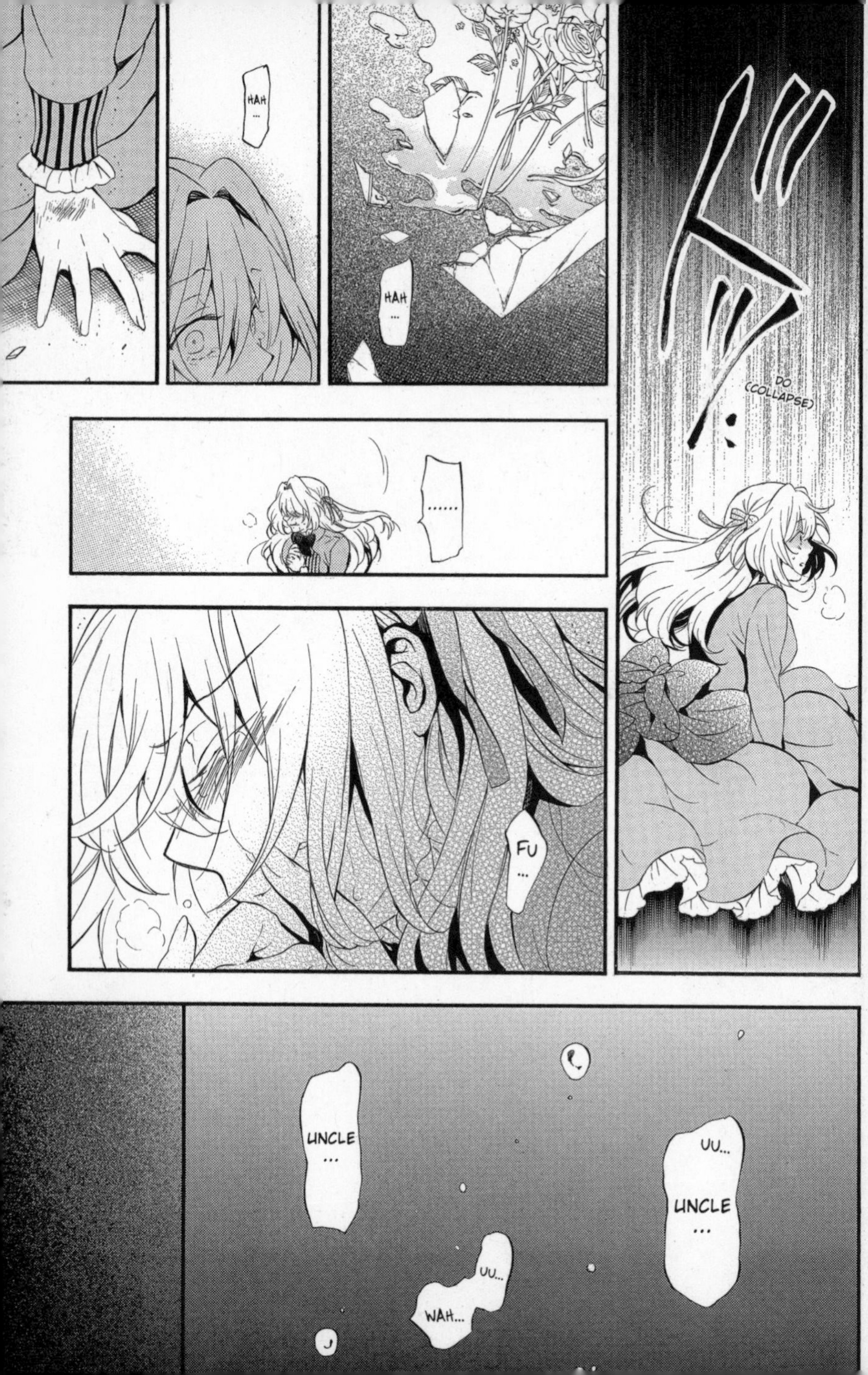
DO (COLLAPSE)
HAH ...
HAH ...
......
FU ...
UU... UNCLE ...
UNCLE ...
UU...
WAH...

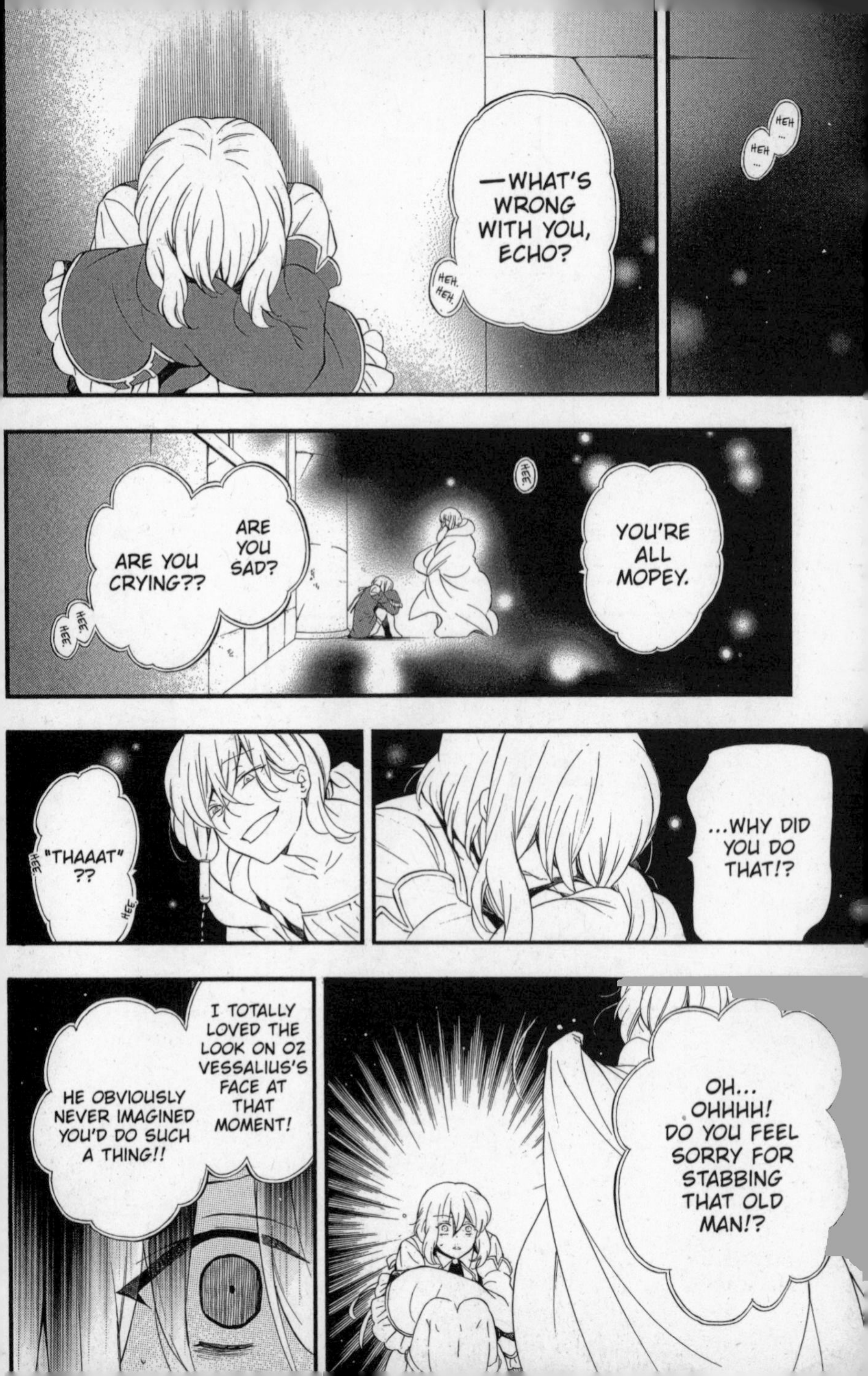
HEH... HEH...
—WHAT'S WRONG WITH YOU, ECHO?
HEH. HEH.
HEE.
YOU'RE ALL MOPEY.
ARE YOU SAD?
ARE YOU CRYING??
HEE. HEE.
...WHY DID YOU DO THAT!?
HEE.
"THAAAT"??
HEE.
OH... OHHHH! DO YOU FEEL SORRY FOR STABBING THAT OLD MAN!?
I TOTALLY LOVED THE LOOK ON OZ VESSALIUS'S FACE AT THAT MOMENT!
HE OBVIOUSLY NEVER IMAGINED YOU'D DO SUCH A THING!!

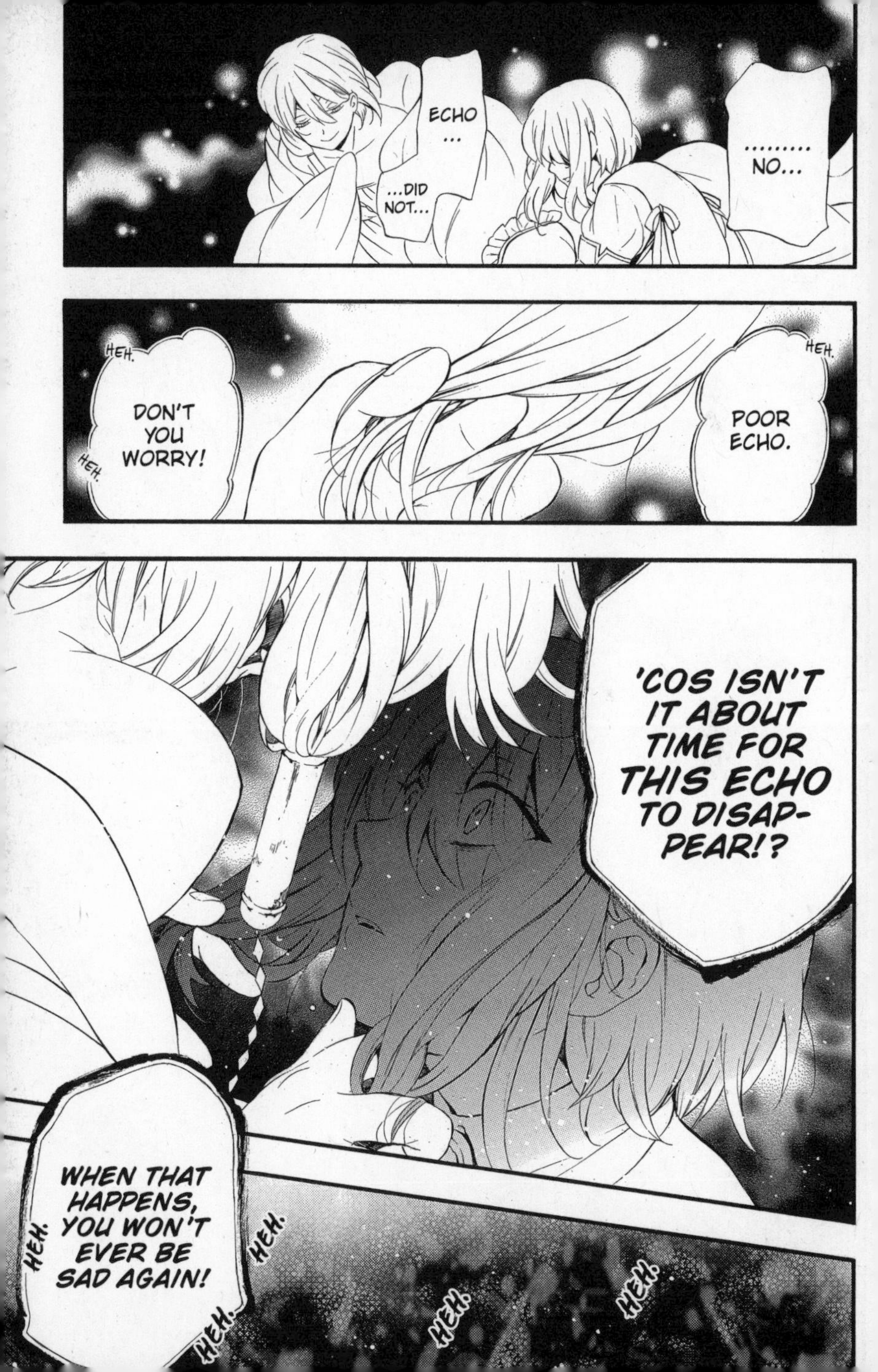
....
NO...
ECHO
...
...DID
NOT...
HEH.
POOR
ECHO.
HEH.
DON'T
YOU
WORRY!
HEH.
'COS ISN'T
IT ABOUT
TIME FOR
THIS ECHO
TO DISAP-
PEAR!?
WHEN THAT
HAPPENS,
YOU WON'T
EVER BE
SAD AGAIN!
HEH.
HEH.
HEH.
HEH.
HEH.

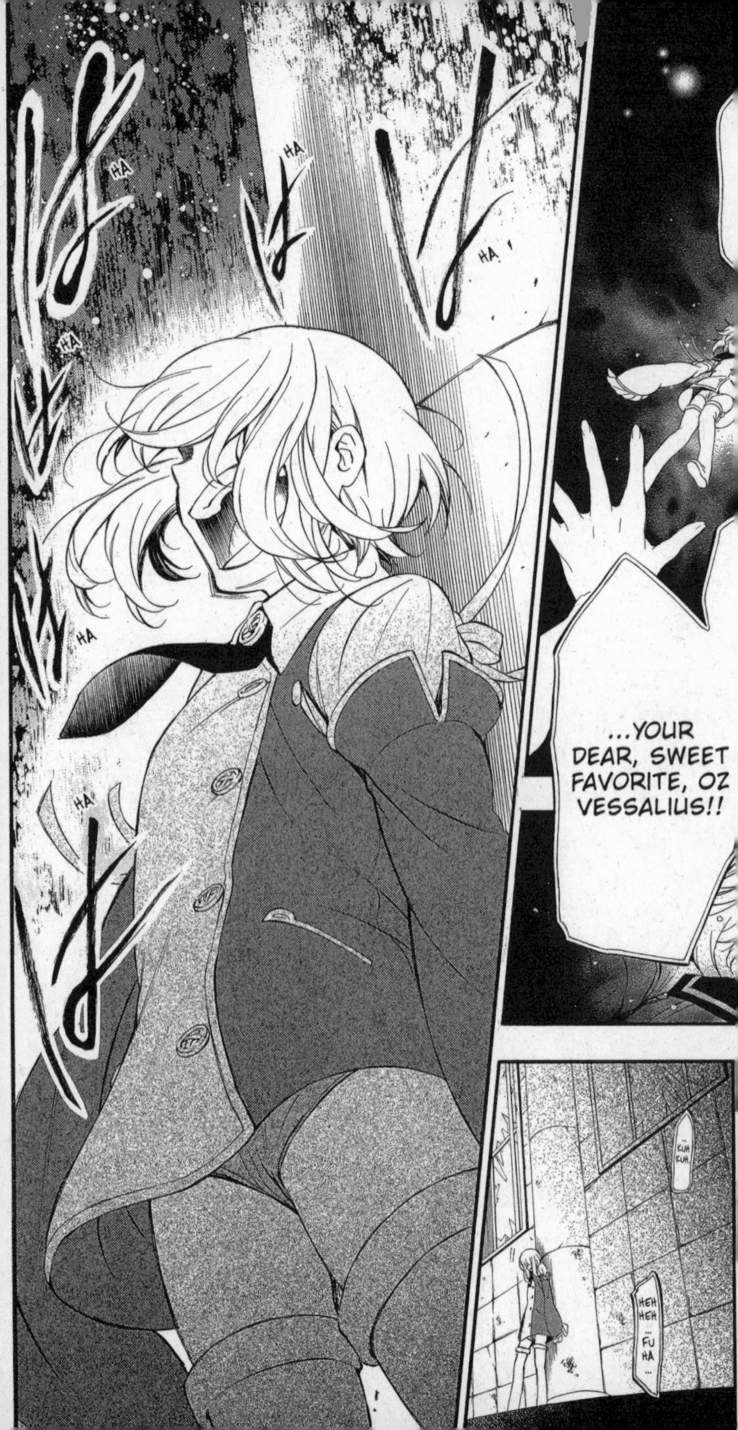
...YOUR DEAR, SWEET FAVORITE, OZ VESSALIUS!!
...KUH KUH.
HEH HEH ...FU HA ...
HA
HA
HA
HA
HA
HA

Retrace : LXXXV   Reverberate

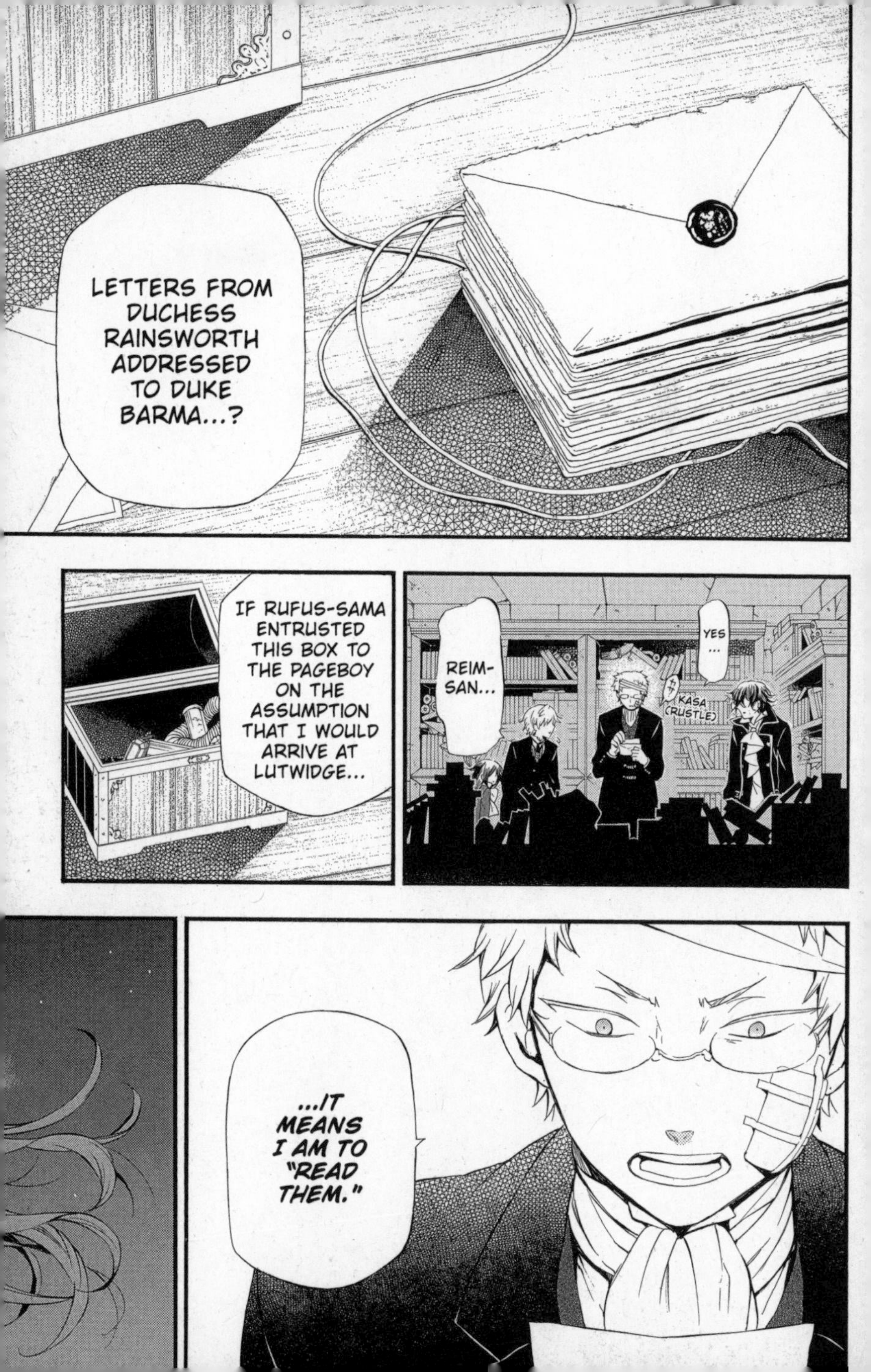
LETTERS FROM DUCHESS RAINSWORTH ADDRESSED TO DUKE BARMA...?
YES ...
KASA (RUSTLE)
REIM-SAN...
IF RUFUS-SAMA ENTRUSTED THIS BOX TO THE PAGEBOY ON THE ASSUMPTION THAT I WOULD ARRIVE AT LUTWIDGE...
...IT MEANS I AM TO "READ THEM."

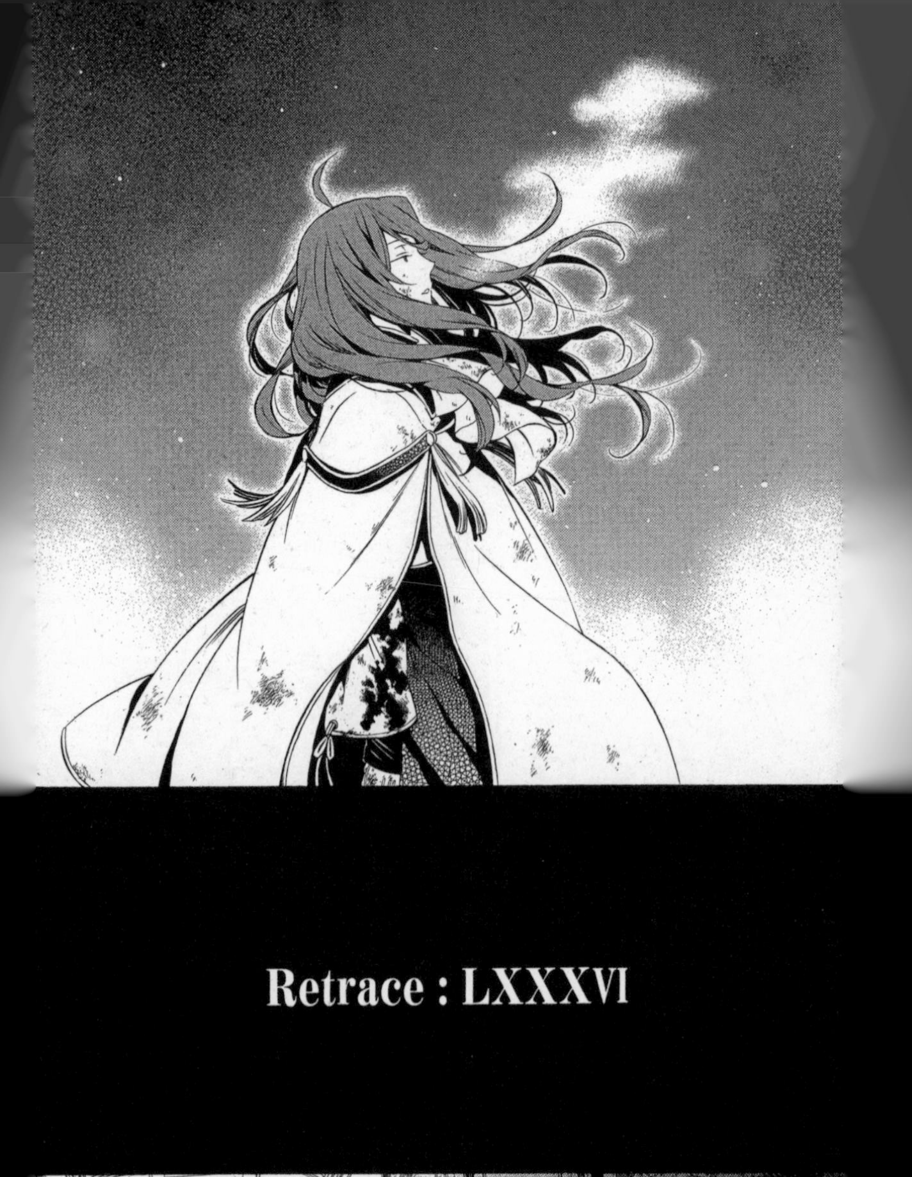

Retrace : LXXXVI

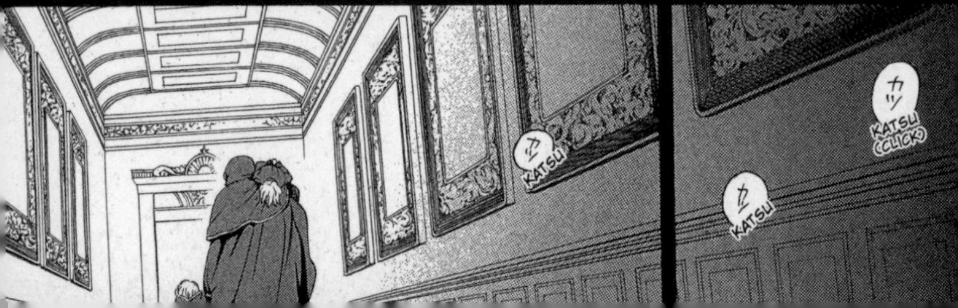
カッ
KATSU (CLICK)
KATSU
KATSU

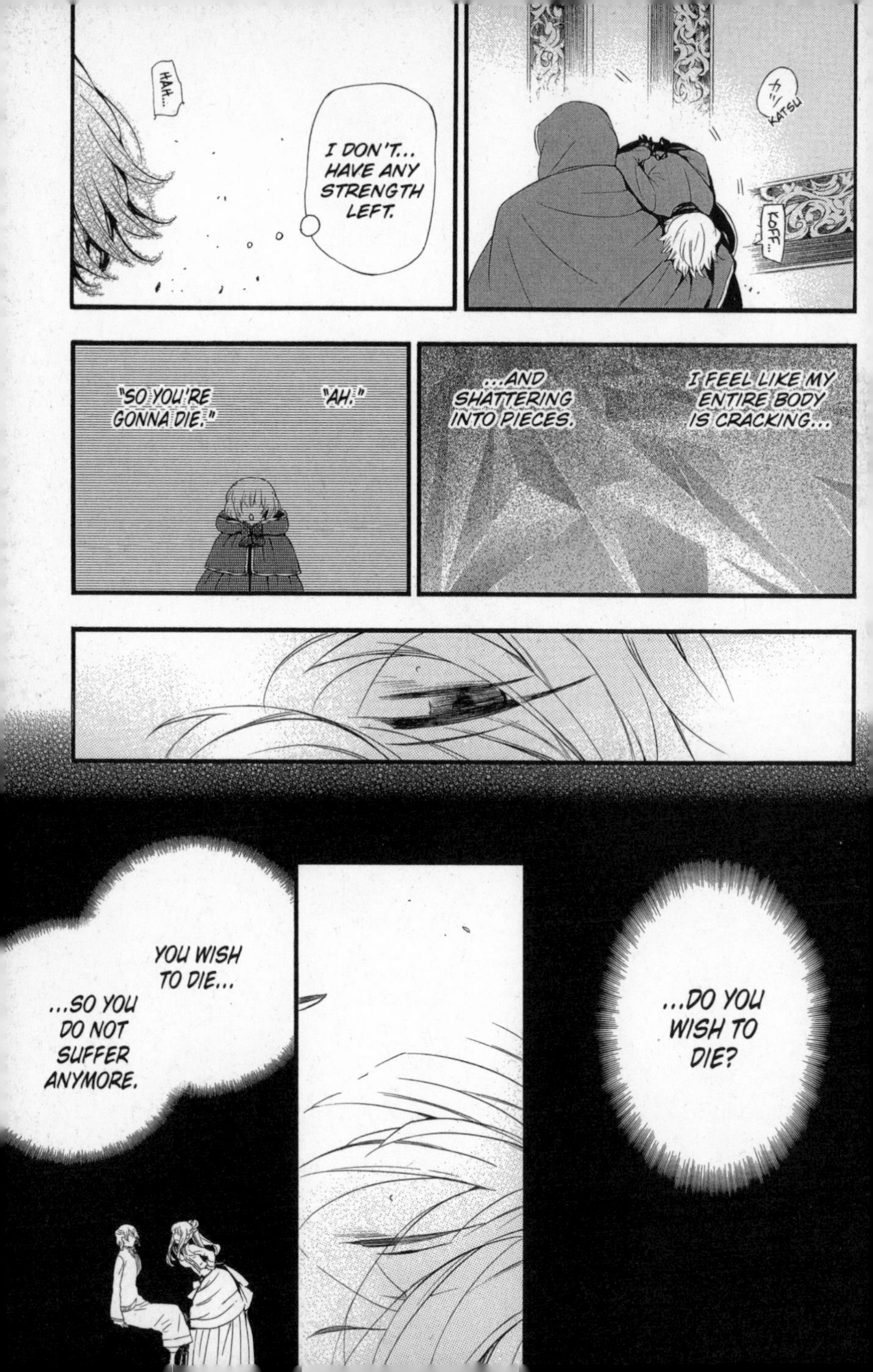
KATSU
KOFF...
I DON'T... HAVE ANY STRENGTH LEFT.
HAH...
I FEEL LIKE MY ENTIRE BODY IS CRACKING...
...AND SHATTERING INTO PIECES.
"AH."
"SO YOU'RE GONNA DIE."
...DO YOU WISH TO DIE?
YOU WISH TO DIE...
...SO YOU DO NOT SUFFER ANYMORE.

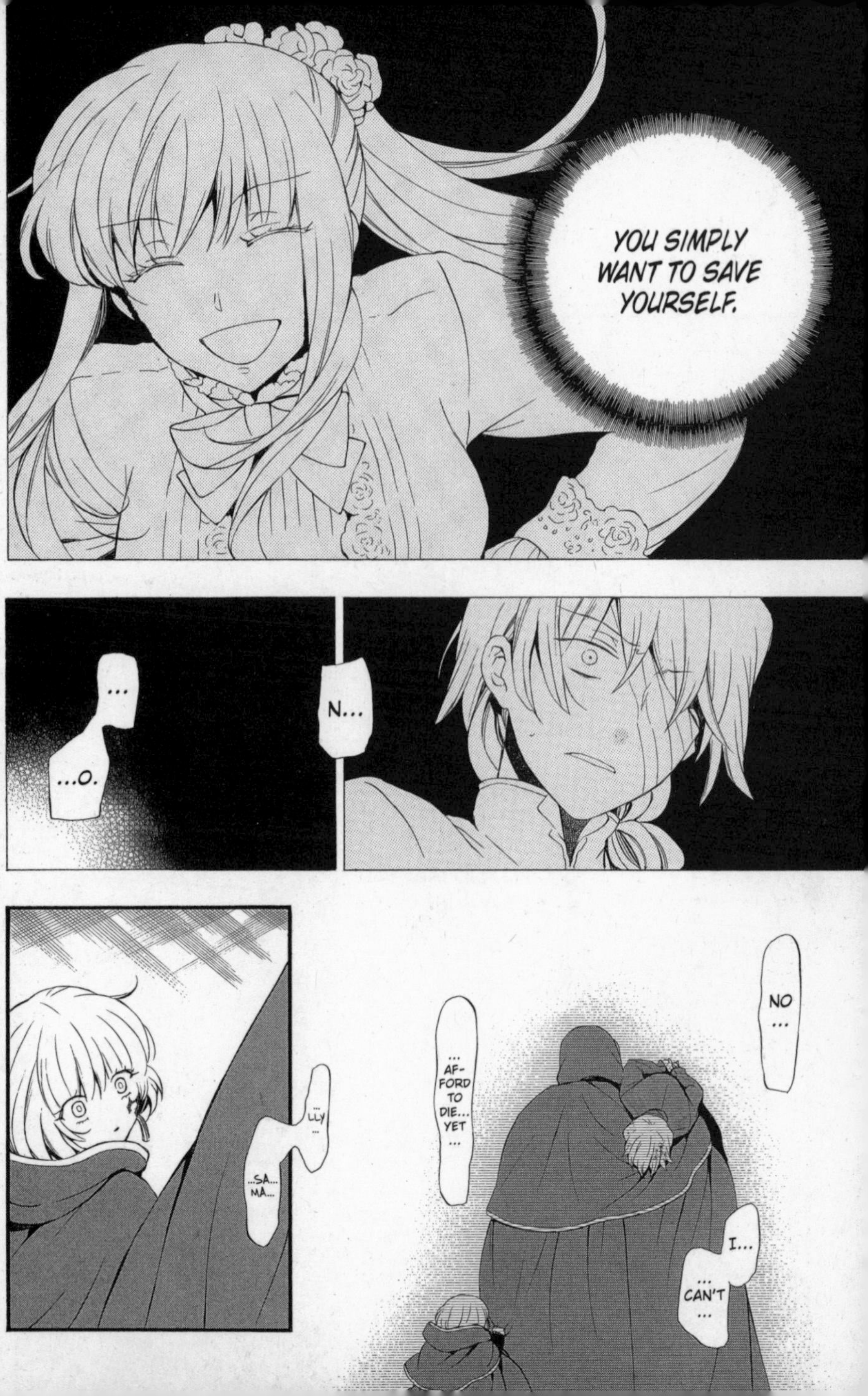
YOU SIMPLY WANT TO SAVE YOURSELF.
N...
...
...O.
NO ...
... AF-FORD TO DIE... YET ...
I...
... CAN'T ...
... LLY ...
...SA MA...

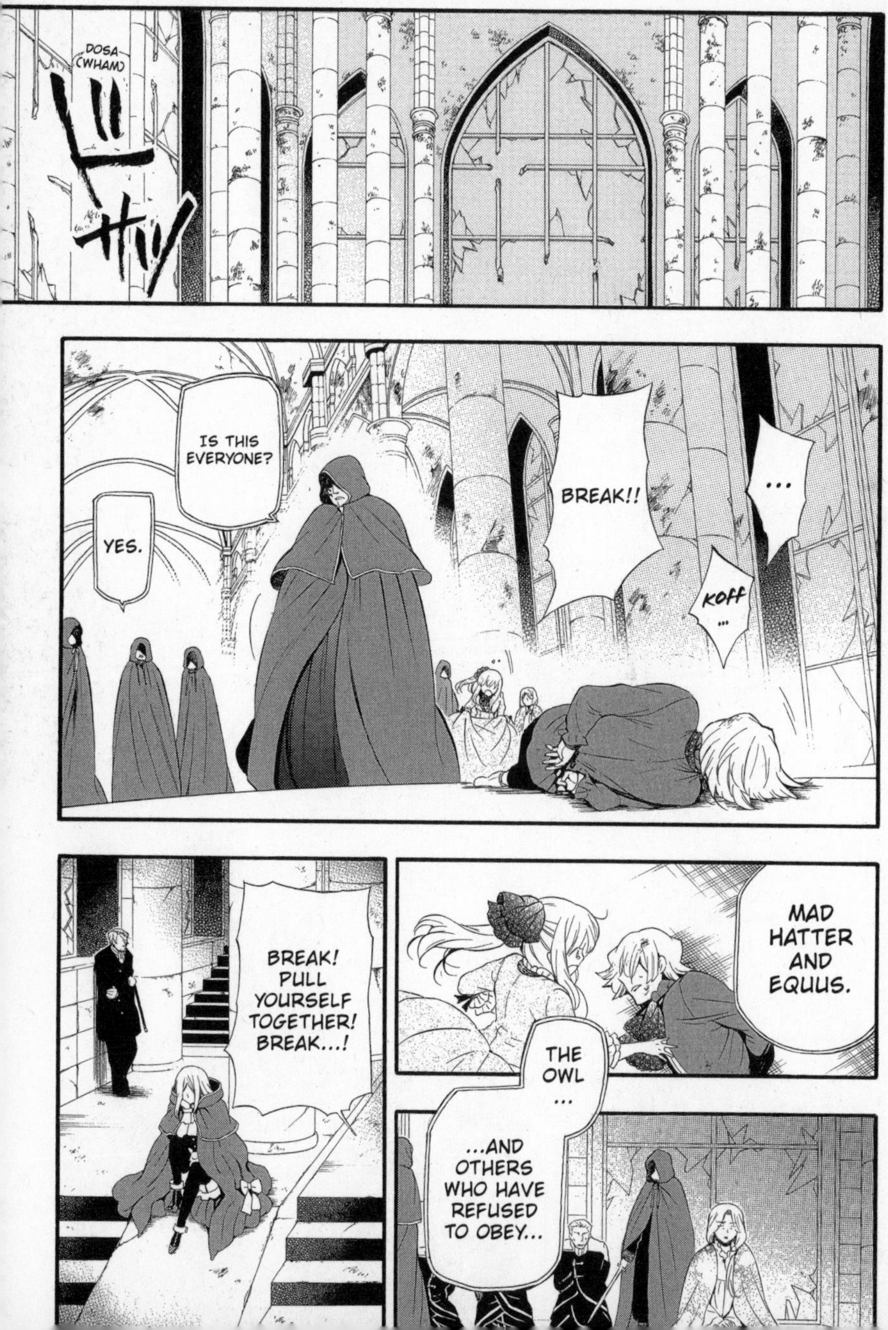

DOSA (WHAM)
ドサッ
...
KOFF ...
BREAK!!
IS THIS EVERYONE?
YES.
MAD HATTER AND EQUUS.
THE OWL ...
...AND OTHERS WHO HAVE REFUSED TO OBEY...
BREAK! PULL YOURSELF TOGETHER! BREAK...!

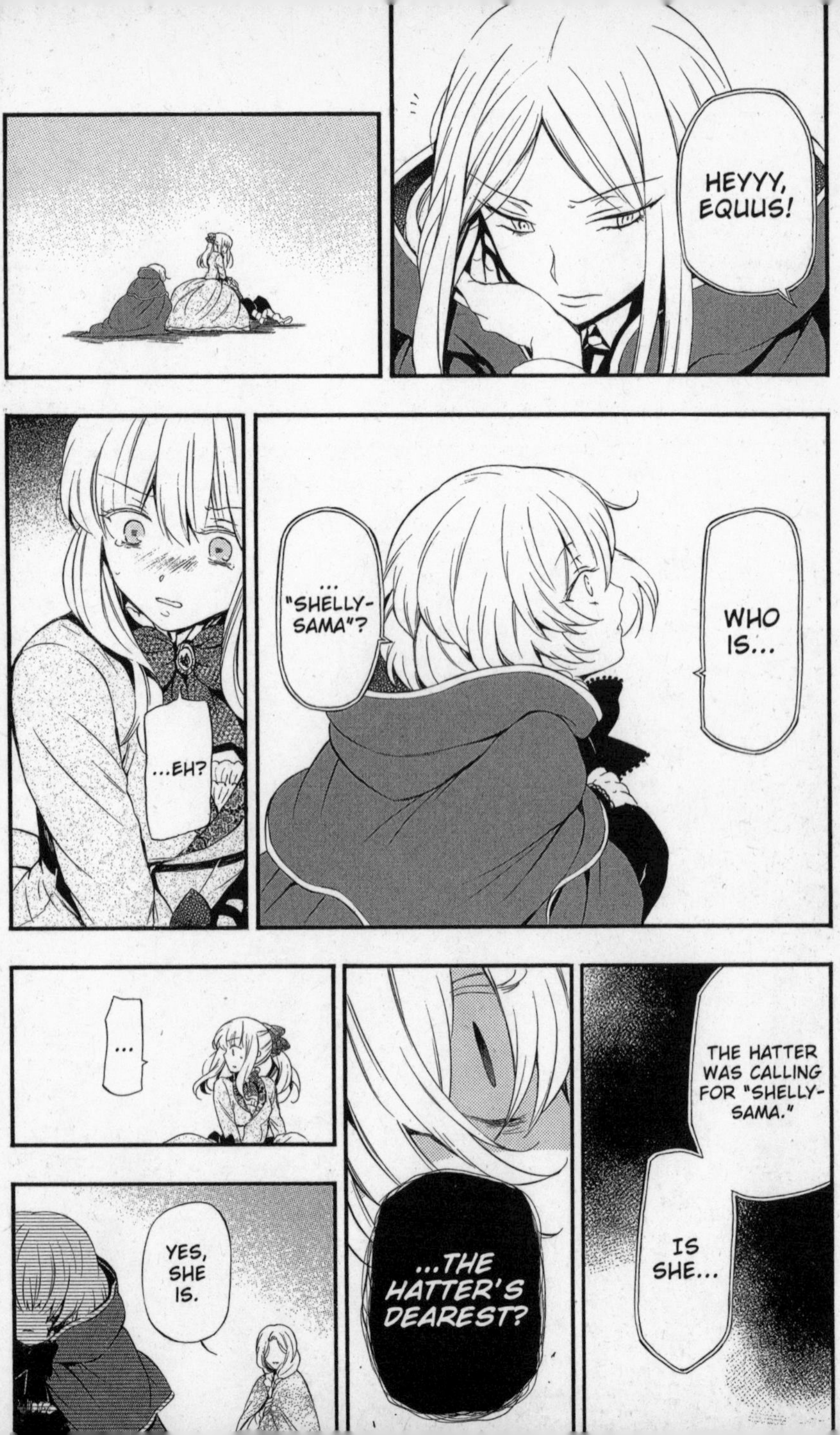
HEYYY, EQUUS!
WHO IS...
... "SHELLY-SAMA"?
...EH?
THE HATTER WAS CALLING FOR "SHELLY-SAMA."
IS SHE...
...THE HATTER'S DEAREST?
...
YES, SHE IS.

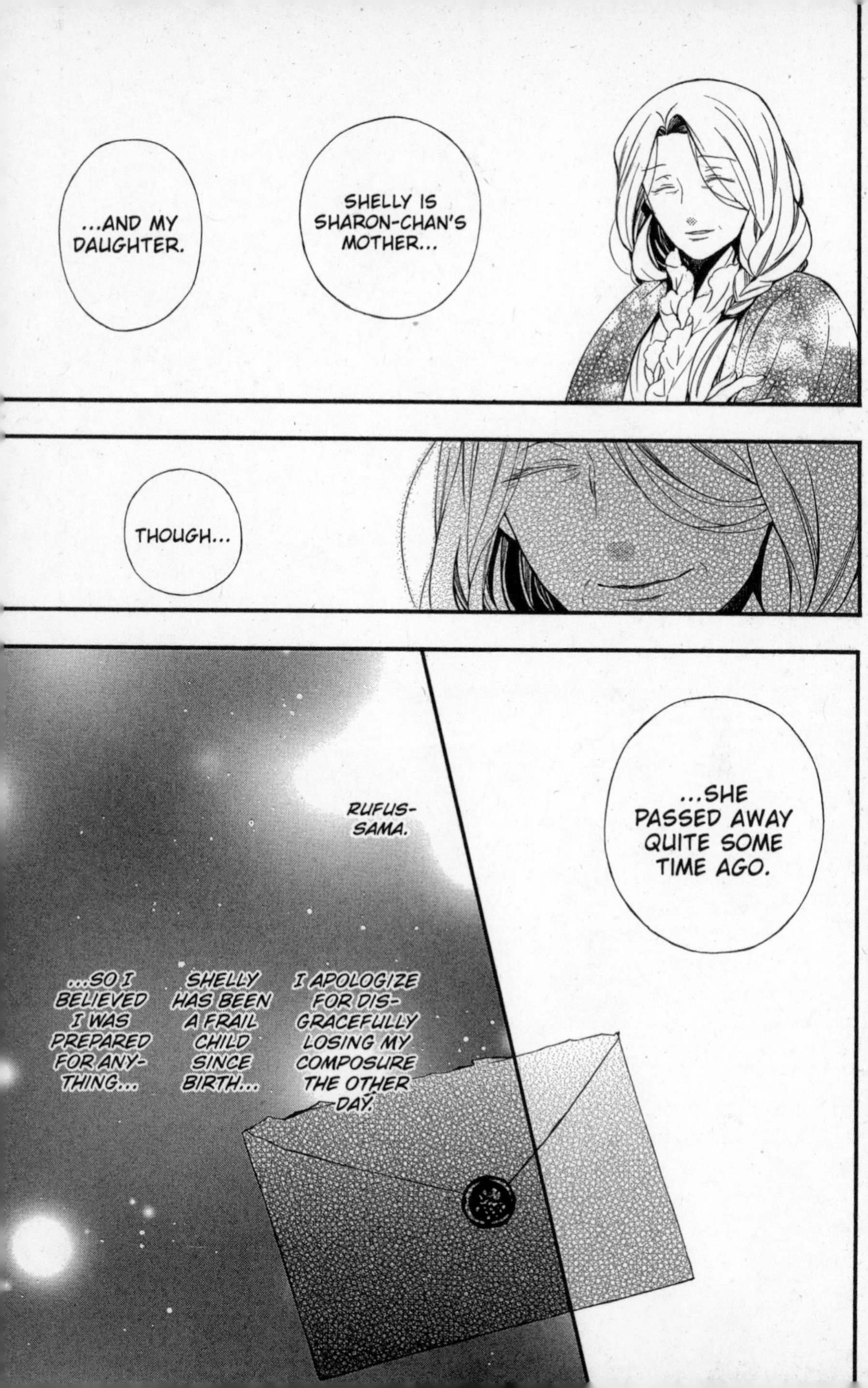
SHELLY IS SHARON-CHAN'S MOTHER...
...AND MY DAUGHTER.
THOUGH...
...SHE PASSED AWAY QUITE SOME TIME AGO.
RUFUS-SAMA.
I APOLOGIZE FOR DIS-GRACEFULLY LOSING MY COMPOSURE THE OTHER DAY.
SHELLY HAS BEEN A FRAIL CHILD SINCE BIRTH...
...SO I BELIEVED I WAS PREPARED FOR ANY-THING...

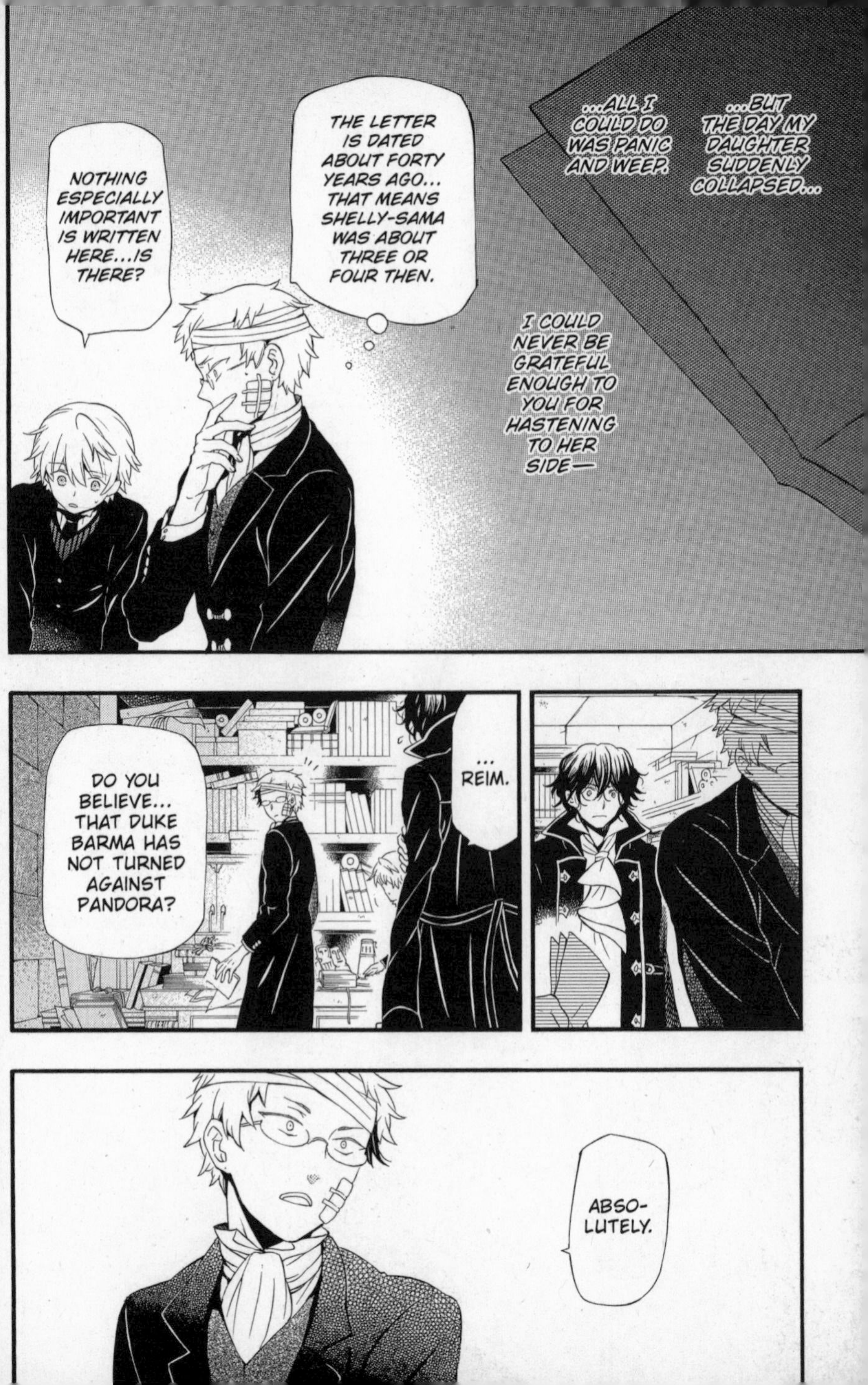
...BUT THE DAY MY DAUGHTER SUDDENLY COLLAPSED...
...ALL I COULD DO WAS PANIC AND WEEP.
I COULD NEVER BE GRATEFUL ENOUGH TO YOU FOR HASTENING TO HER SIDE—
THE LETTER IS DATED ABOUT FORTY YEARS AGO... THAT MEANS SHELLY-SAMA WAS ABOUT THREE OR FOUR THEN.
NOTHING ESPECIALLY IMPORTANT IS WRITTEN HERE...IS THERE?
... REIM.
DO YOU BELIEVE... THAT DUKE BARMA HAS NOT TURNED AGAINST PANDORA?
ABSO-LUTELY.

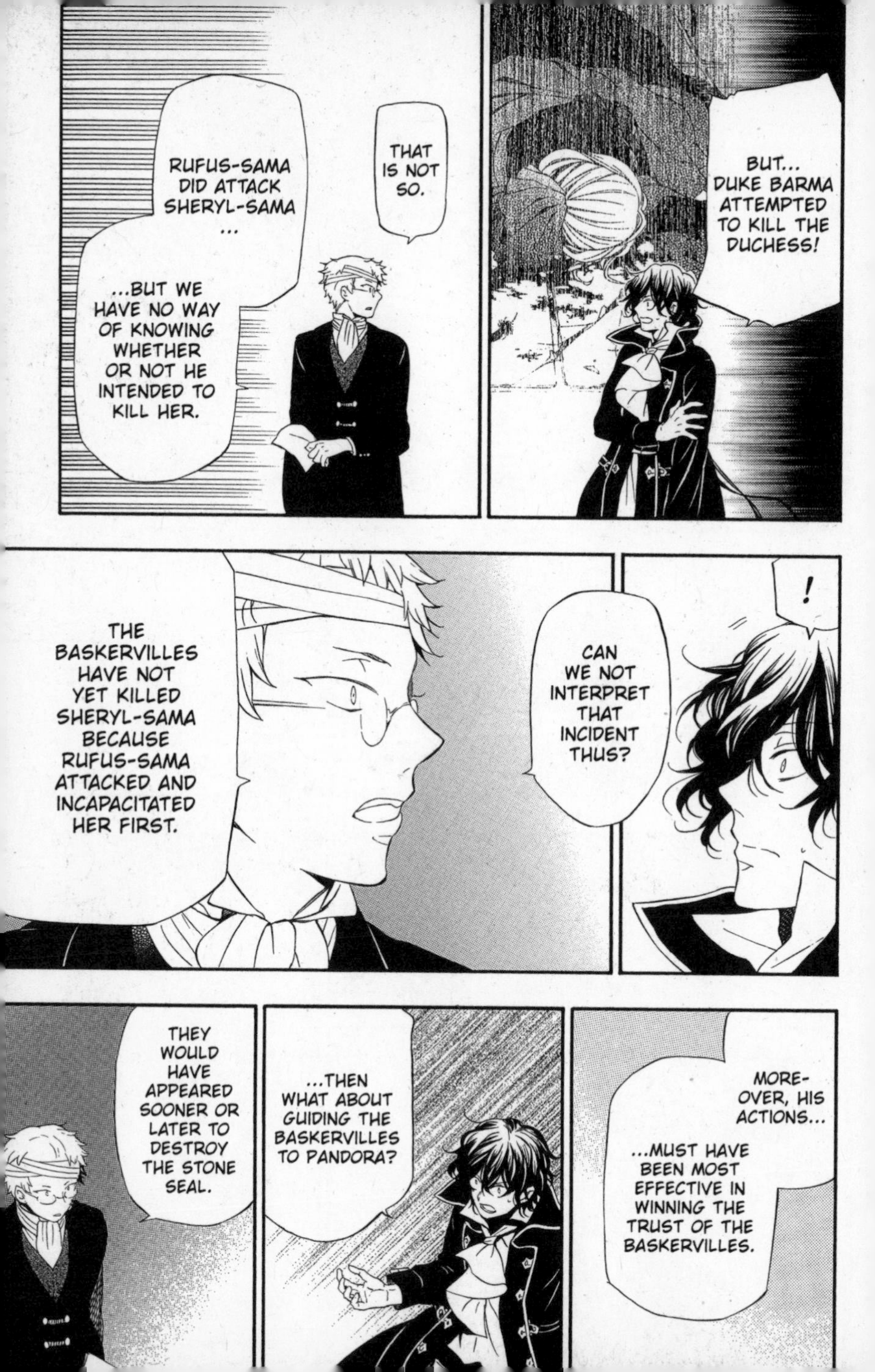
BUT... DUKE BARMA ATTEMPTED TO KILL THE DUCHESS!
THAT IS NOT SO.
RUFUS-SAMA DID ATTACK SHERYL-SAMA ...
...BUT WE HAVE NO WAY OF KNOWING WHETHER OR NOT HE INTENDED TO KILL HER.
!
CAN WE NOT INTERPRET THAT INCIDENT THUS?
THE BASKERVILLES HAVE NOT YET KILLED SHERYL-SAMA BECAUSE RUFUS-SAMA ATTACKED AND INCAPACITATED HER FIRST.
MORE-OVER, HIS ACTIONS...
...MUST HAVE BEEN MOST EFFECTIVE IN WINNING THE TRUST OF THE BASKERVILLES.
...THEN WHAT ABOUT GUIDING THE BASKERVILLES TO PANDORA?
THEY WOULD HAVE APPEARED SOONER OR LATER TO DESTROY THE STONE SEAL.

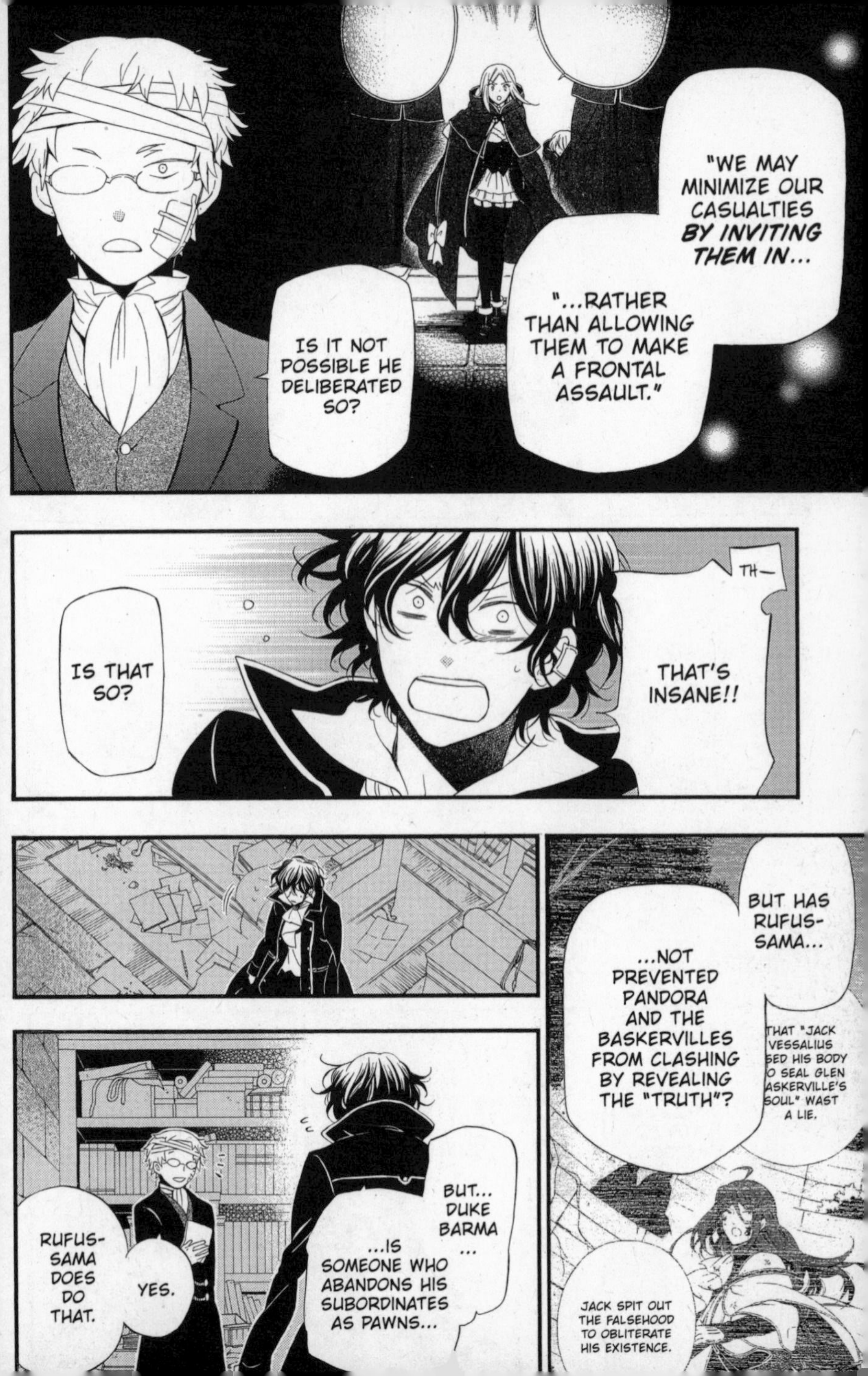
"WE MAY MINIMIZE OUR CASUALTIES BY INVITING THEM IN...
"...RATHER THAN ALLOWING THEM TO MAKE A FRONTAL ASSAULT."
IS IT NOT POSSIBLE HE DELIBERATED SO?
TH—
THAT'S INSANE!!
IS THAT SO?
BUT HAS RUFUS-SAMA...
...NOT PREVENTED PANDORA AND THE BASKERVILLES FROM CLASHING BY REVEALING THE "TRUTH"?
THAT "JACK VESSALIUS SED HIS BODY O SEAL GLEN ASKERVILLE'S SOUL" WAST A LIE.
JACK SPIT OUT THE FALSEHOOD TO OBLITERATE HIS EXISTENCE.
BUT... DUKE BARMA ...
...IS SOMEONE WHO ABANDONS HIS SUBORDINATES AS PAWNS...
YES.
RUFUS-SAMA DOES DO THAT.

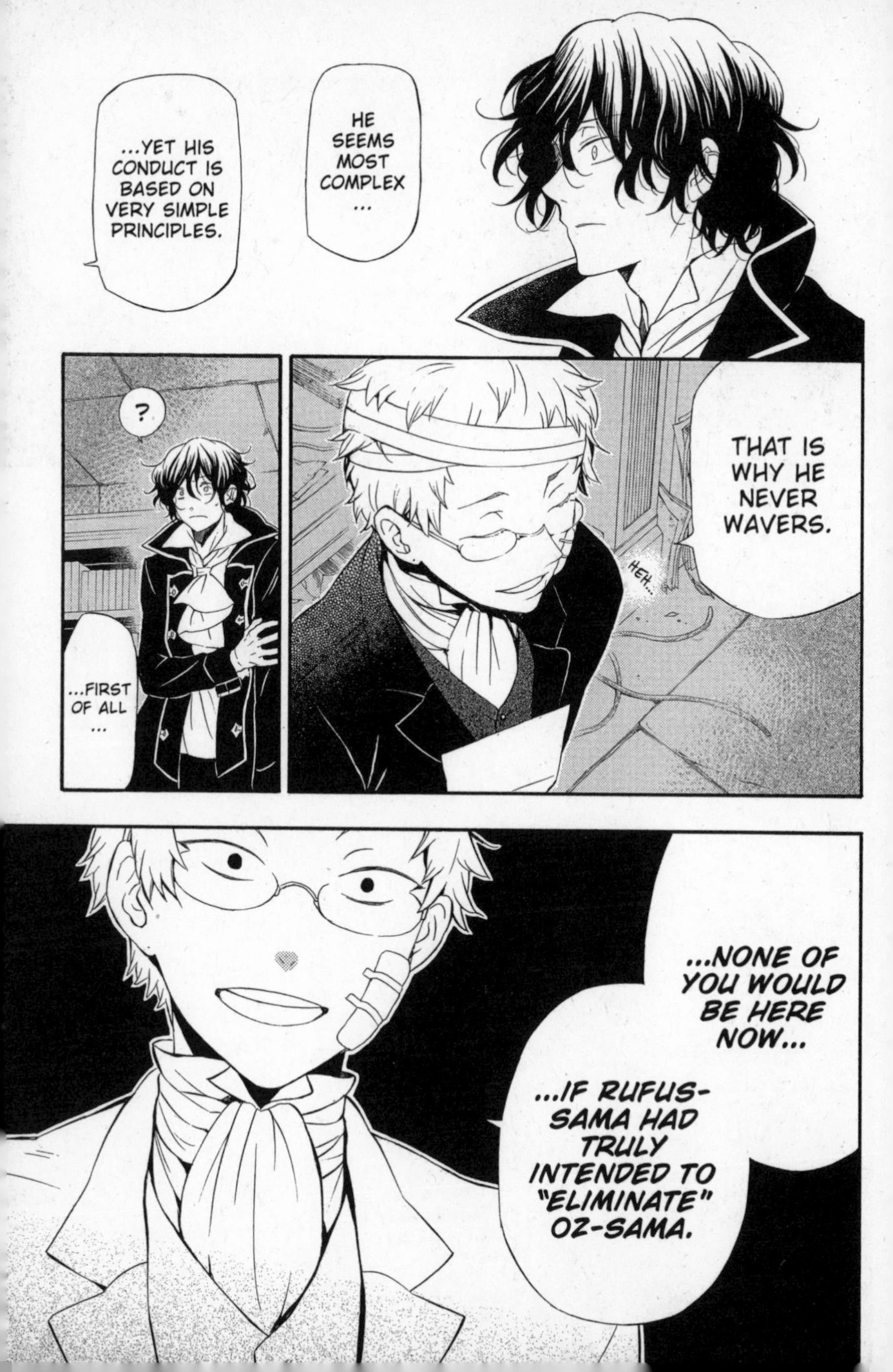
HE SEEMS MOST COMPLEX ...
...YET HIS CONDUCT IS BASED ON VERY SIMPLE PRINCIPLES.
THAT IS WHY HE NEVER WAVERS.
HEH...
?
...FIRST OF ALL ...
...NONE OF YOU WOULD BE HERE NOW...
...IF RUFUS-SAMA HAD TRULY INTENDED TO "ELIMINATE" OZ-SAMA.

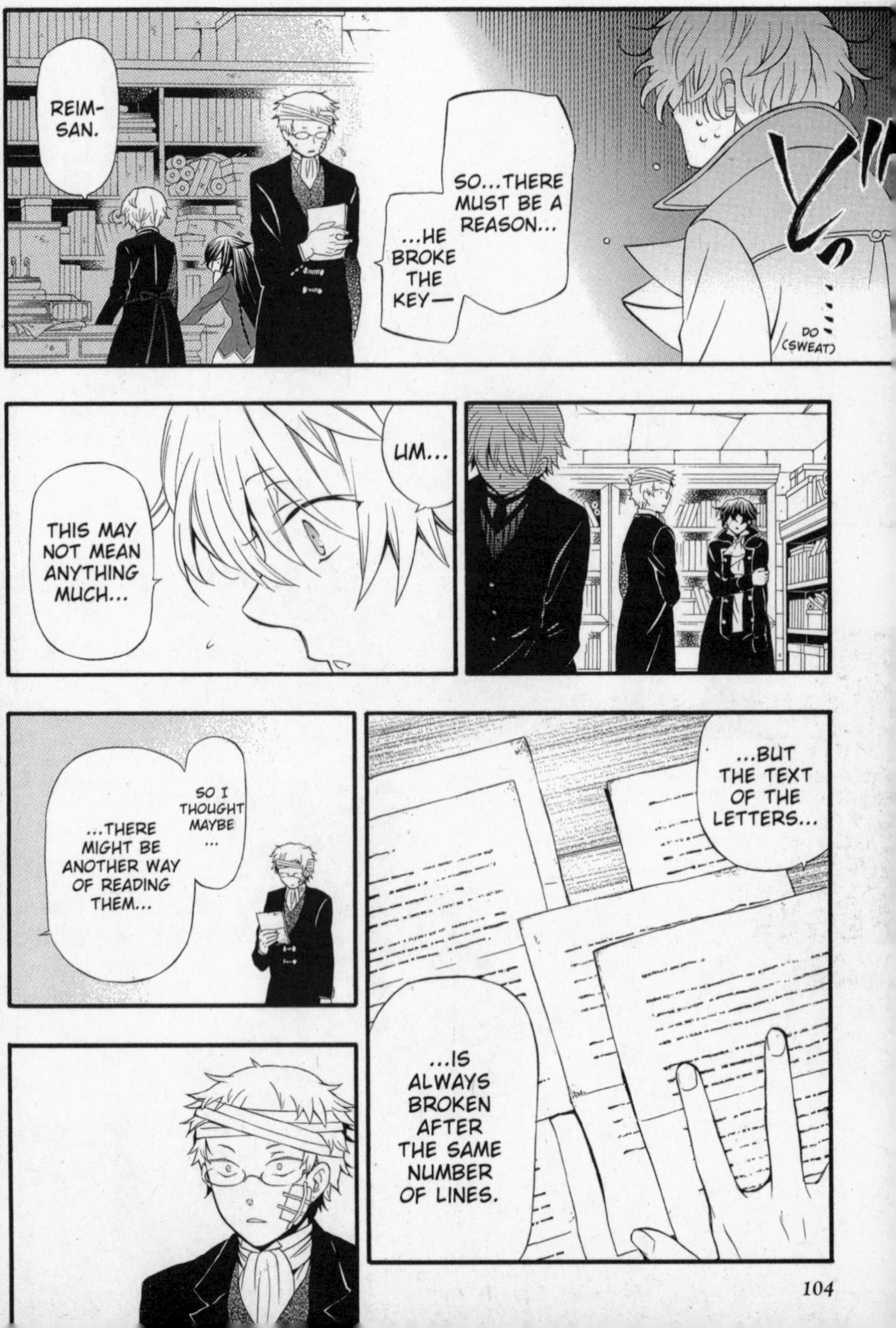
DO (SWEAT)
SO...THERE MUST BE A REASON...
...HE BROKE THE KEY—
REIM-SAN.
UM...
THIS MAY NOT MEAN ANYTHING MUCH...
...BUT THE TEXT OF THE LETTERS...
...IS ALWAYS BROKEN AFTER THE SAME NUMBER OF LINES.
SO I THOUGHT MAYBE ...
...THERE MIGHT BE ANOTHER WAY OF READING THEM...

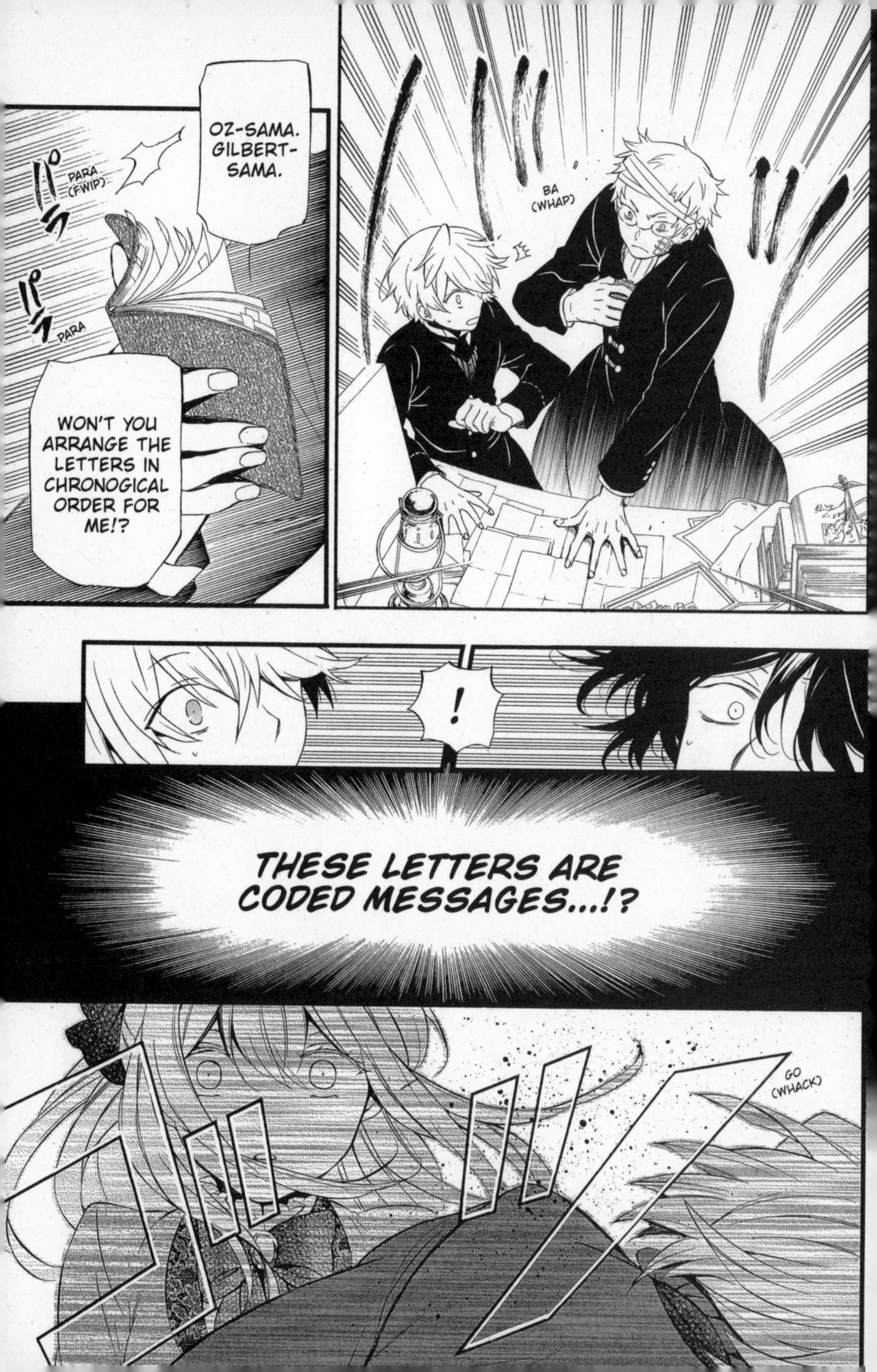
BA (WHAP)
OZ-SAMA. GILBERT-SAMA.
パラ PARA (FWIP)
パラ PARA
WON'T YOU ARRANGE THE LETTERS IN CHRONOGICAL ORDER FOR ME!?
!
THESE LETTERS ARE CODED MESSAGES...!?
GO (WHACK)

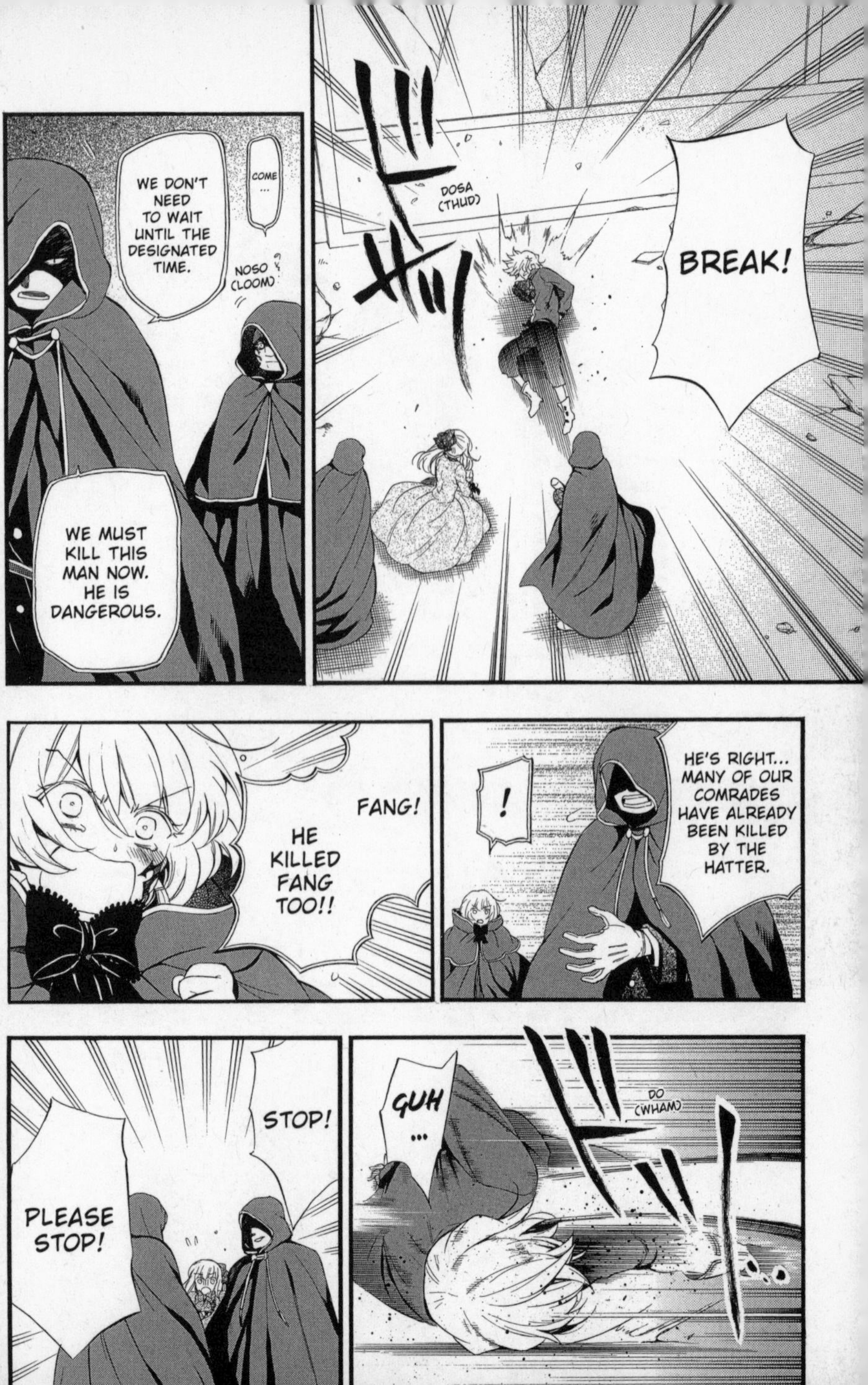
BREAK!
DOSA (THUD)
COME...
WE DON'T NEED TO WAIT UNTIL THE DESIGNATED TIME.
NOSO (LOOM)
WE MUST KILL THIS MAN NOW. HE IS DANGEROUS.
HE'S RIGHT... MANY OF OUR COMRADES HAVE ALREADY BEEN KILLED BY THE HATTER.
!
FANG!
HE KILLED FANG TOO!!
DO (WHAM)
GUH...
STOP!
PLEASE STOP!

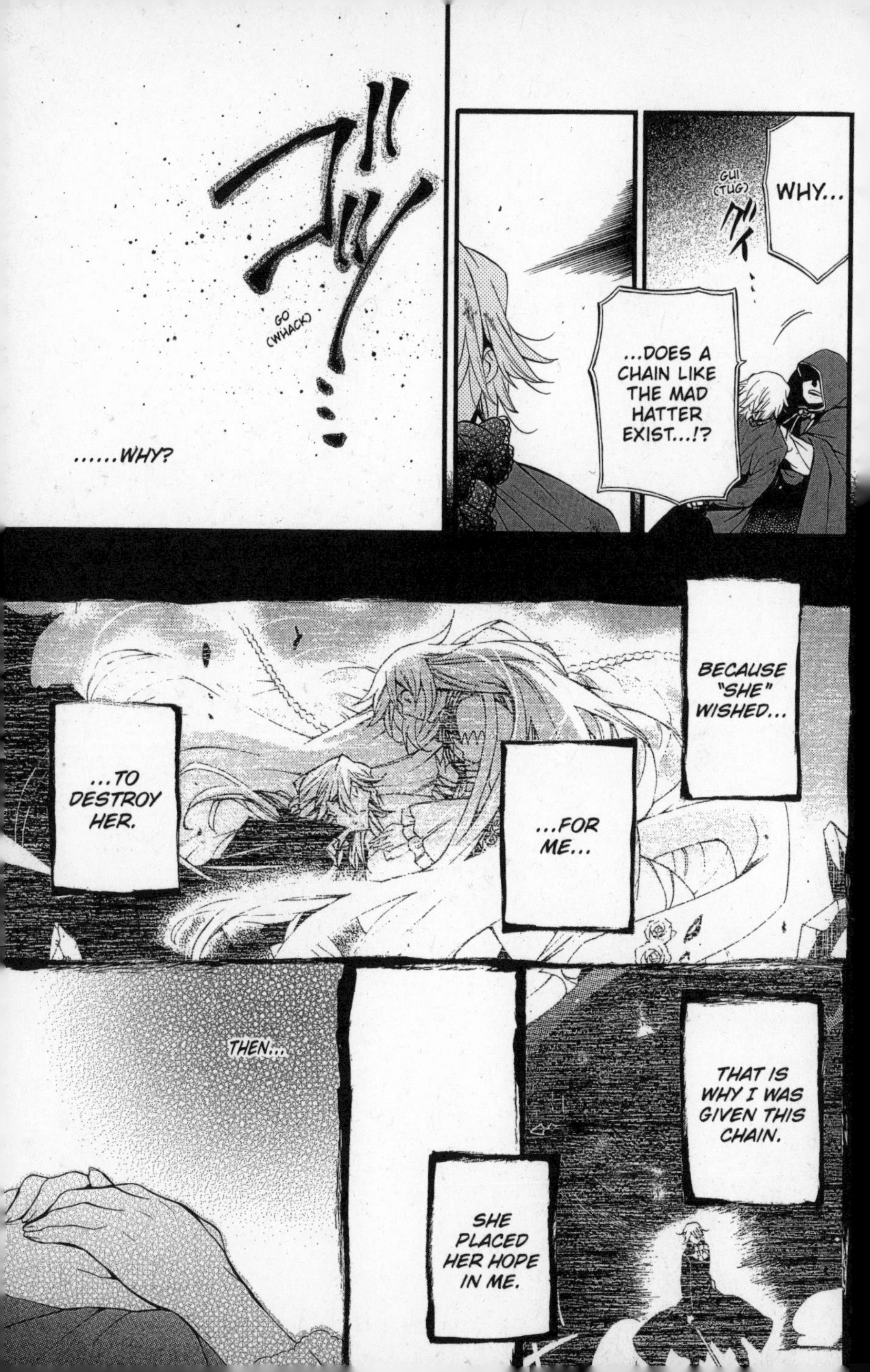
WHY...
GUI (TUG)
グイ
...DOES A CHAIN LIKE THE MAD HATTER EXIST...!?
ゴッ
GO (WHACK)
......WHY?
BECAUSE "SHE" WISHED...
...FOR ME...
...TO DESTROY HER.
THAT IS WHY I WAS GIVEN THIS CHAIN.
SHE PLACED HER HOPE IN ME.
THEN...

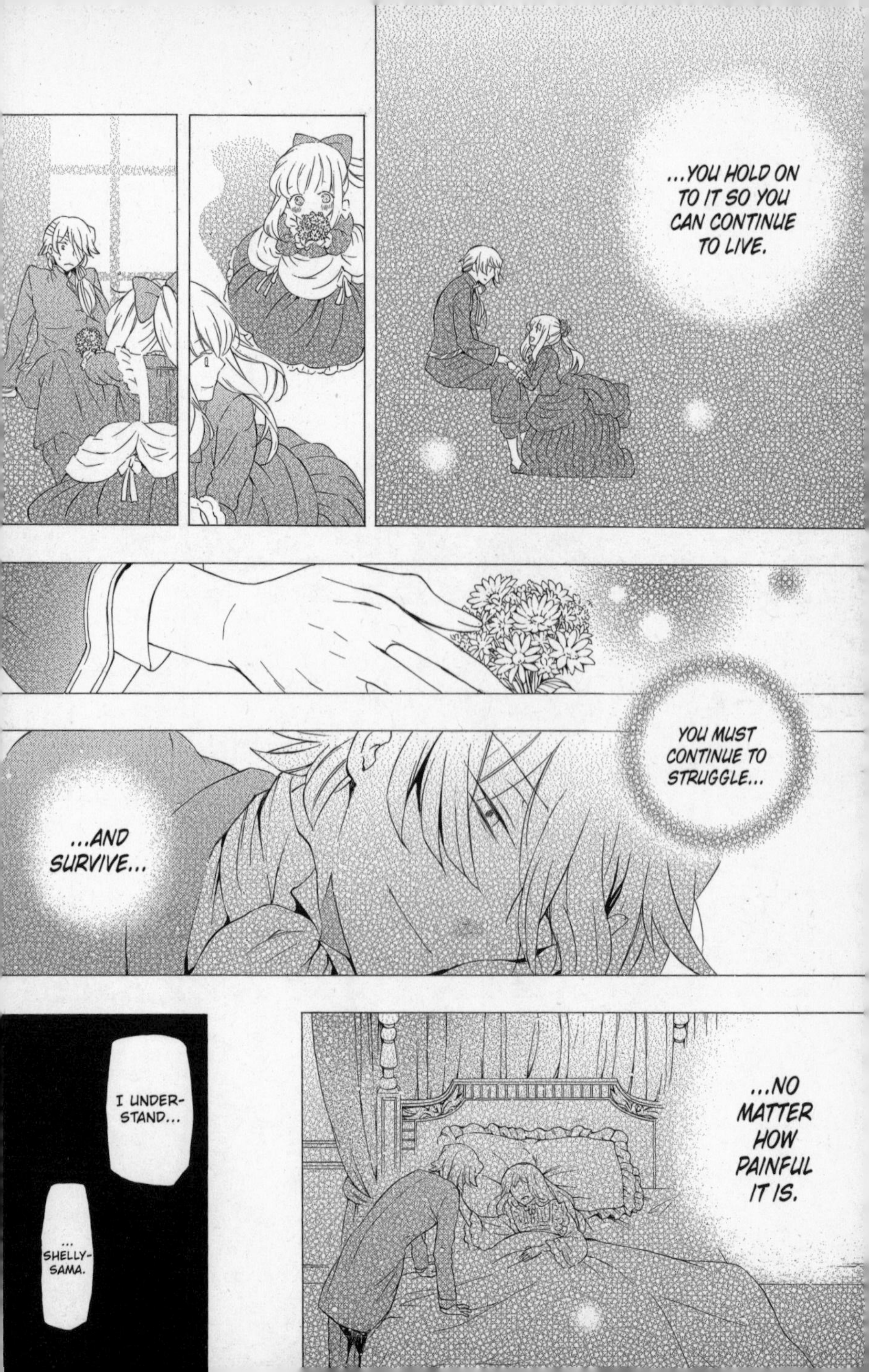
...YOU HOLD ON TO IT SO YOU CAN CONTINUE TO LIVE.
YOU MUST CONTINUE TO STRUGGLE...
...AND SURVIVE...
...NO MATTER HOW PAINFUL IT IS.
I UNDER-STAND...
... SHELLY-SAMA.

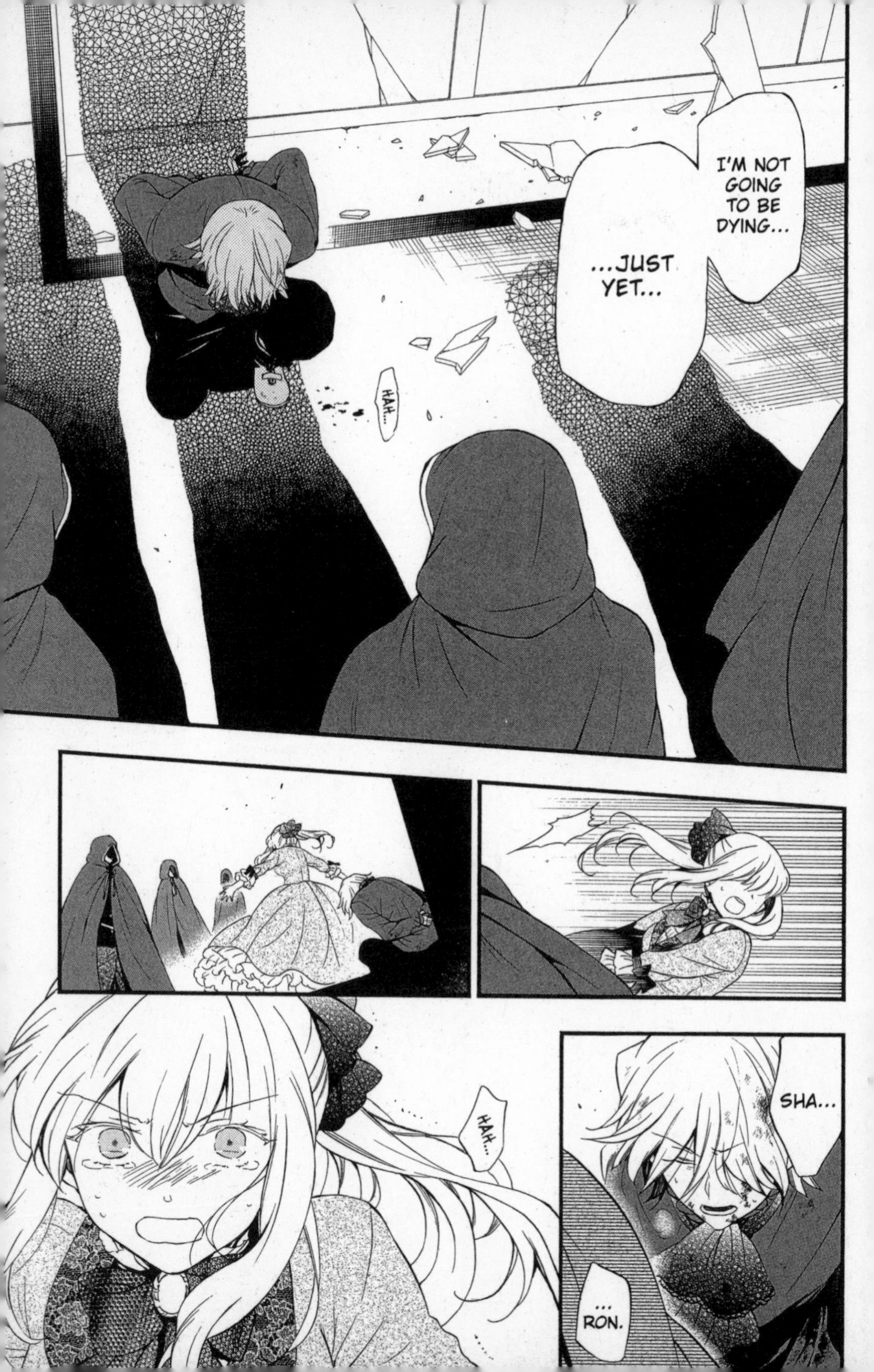
I'M NOT GOING TO BE DYING...
...JUST YET...
HAH...
SHA...
...RON.
HAH...

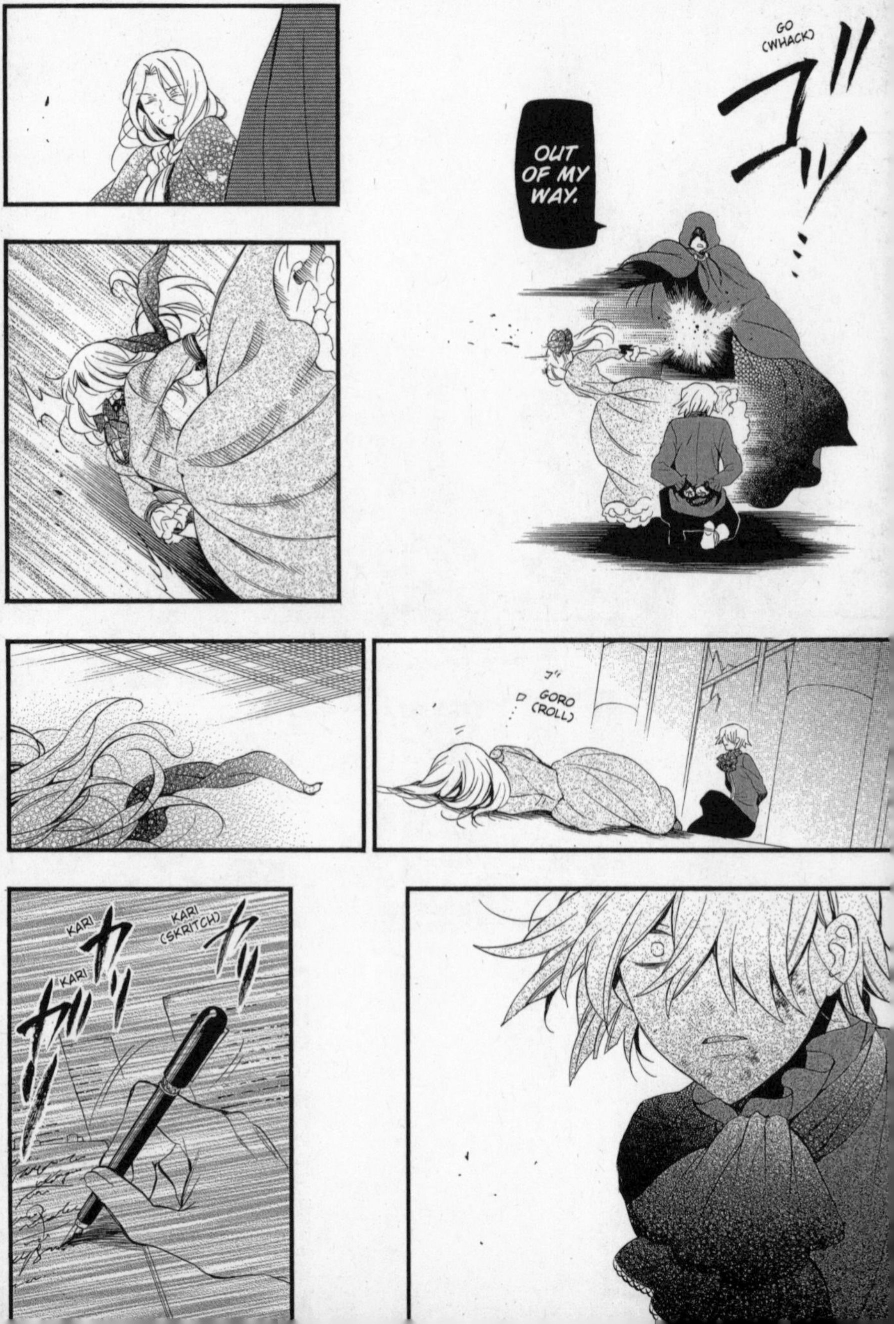
GO (WHACK)
OUT OF MY WAY.
GORO (ROLL)
KARI (SKRITCH)
KARI
KARI

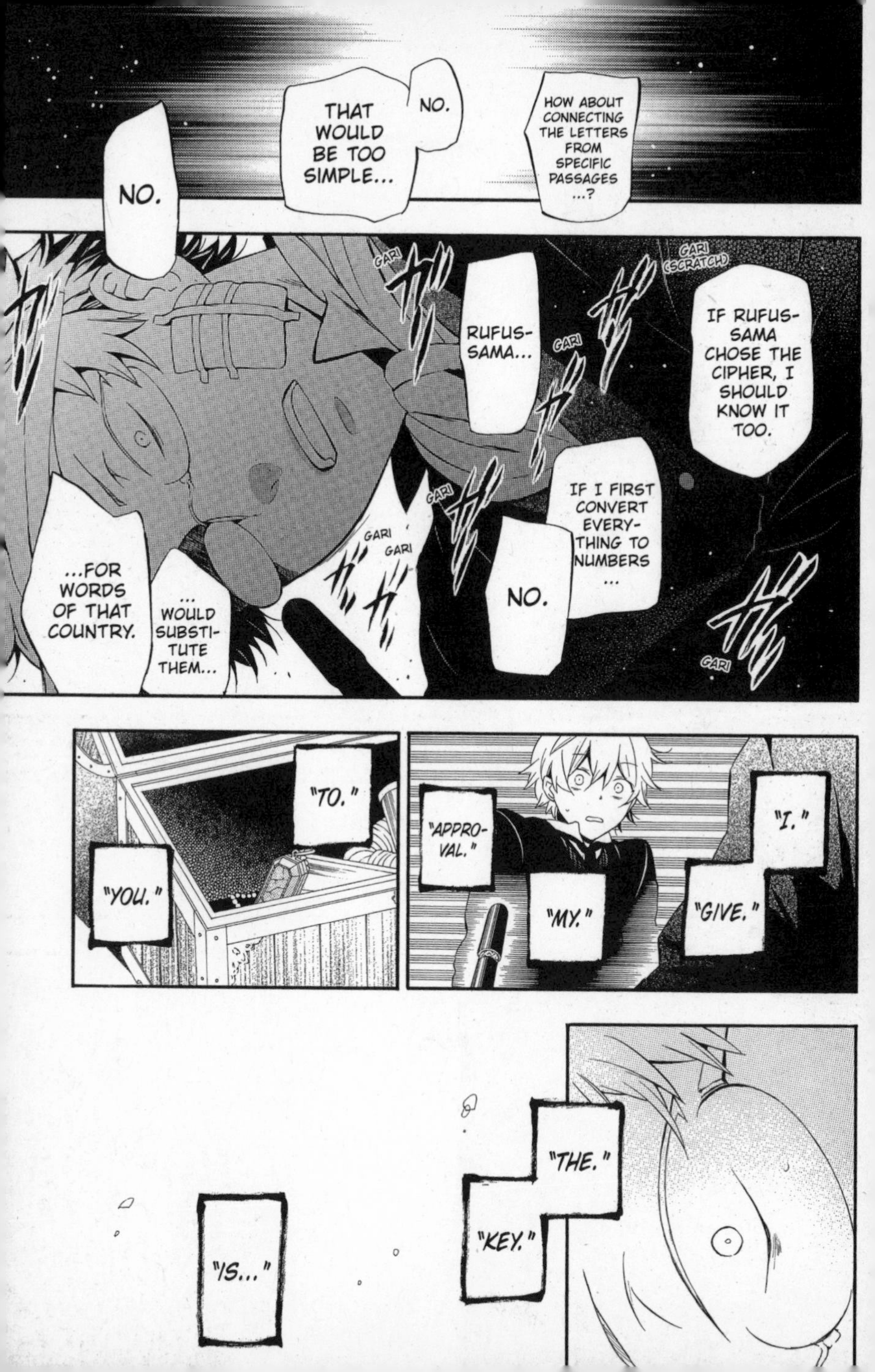
HOW ABOUT CONNECTING THE LETTERS FROM SPECIFIC PASSAGES ...?
NO.
THAT WOULD BE TOO SIMPLE...
NO.
GARI (SCRATCH)
IF RUFUS-SAMA CHOSE THE CIPHER, I SHOULD KNOW IT TOO.
GARI
RUFUS-SAMA...
GARI
GARI
IF I FIRST CONVERT EVERYTHING TO NUMBERS...
NO.
GARI
GARI GARI
...WOULD SUBSTITUTE THEM...
...FOR WORDS OF THAT COUNTRY.
"I."
"GIVE."
"MY."
"APPROVAL."
"TO."
"YOU."
"THE."
"KEY."
"IS..."

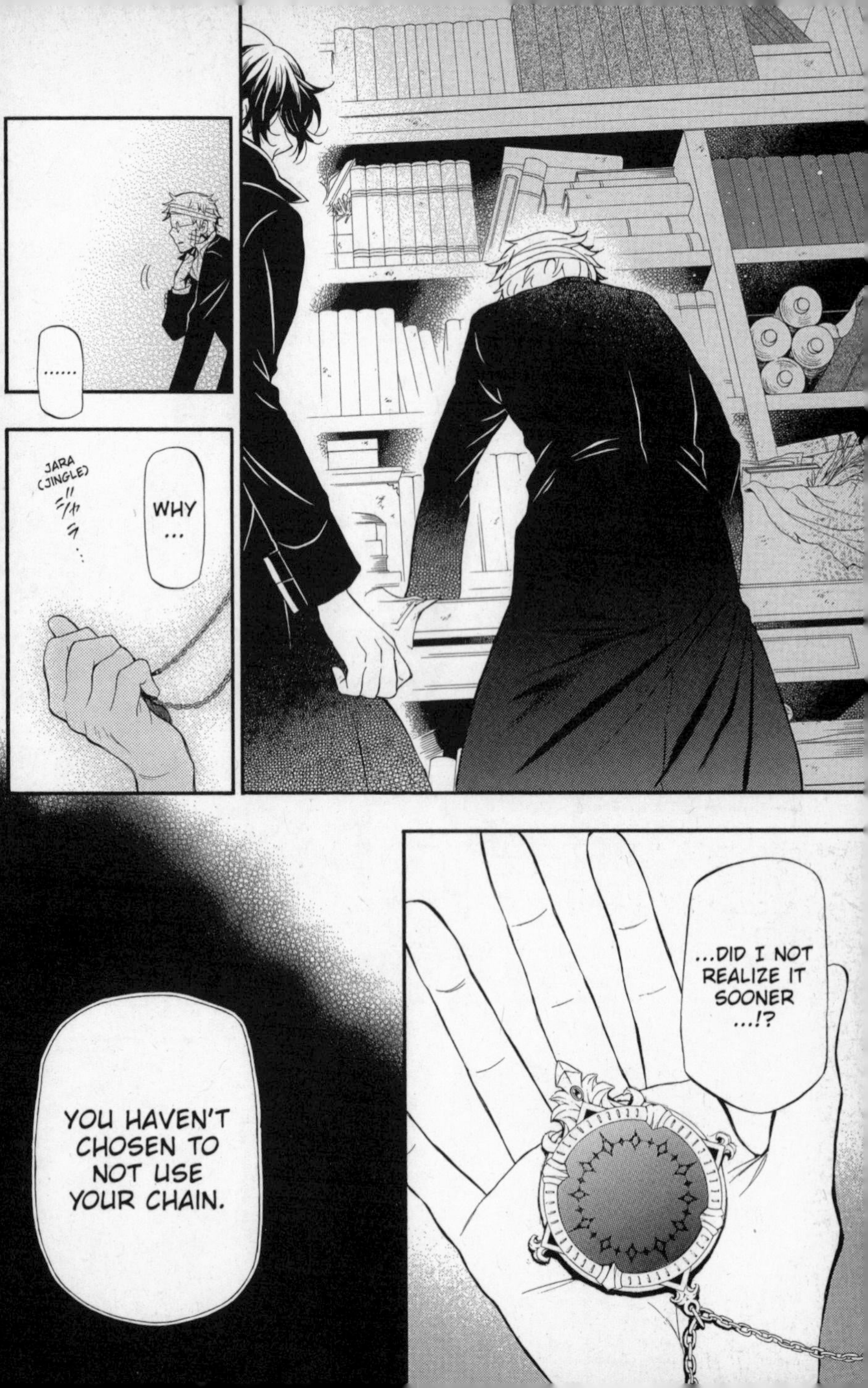
......
JARA (JINGLE)
WHY...
...DID I NOT REALIZE IT SOONER ...!?
YOU HAVEN'T CHOSEN TO NOT USE YOUR CHAIN.

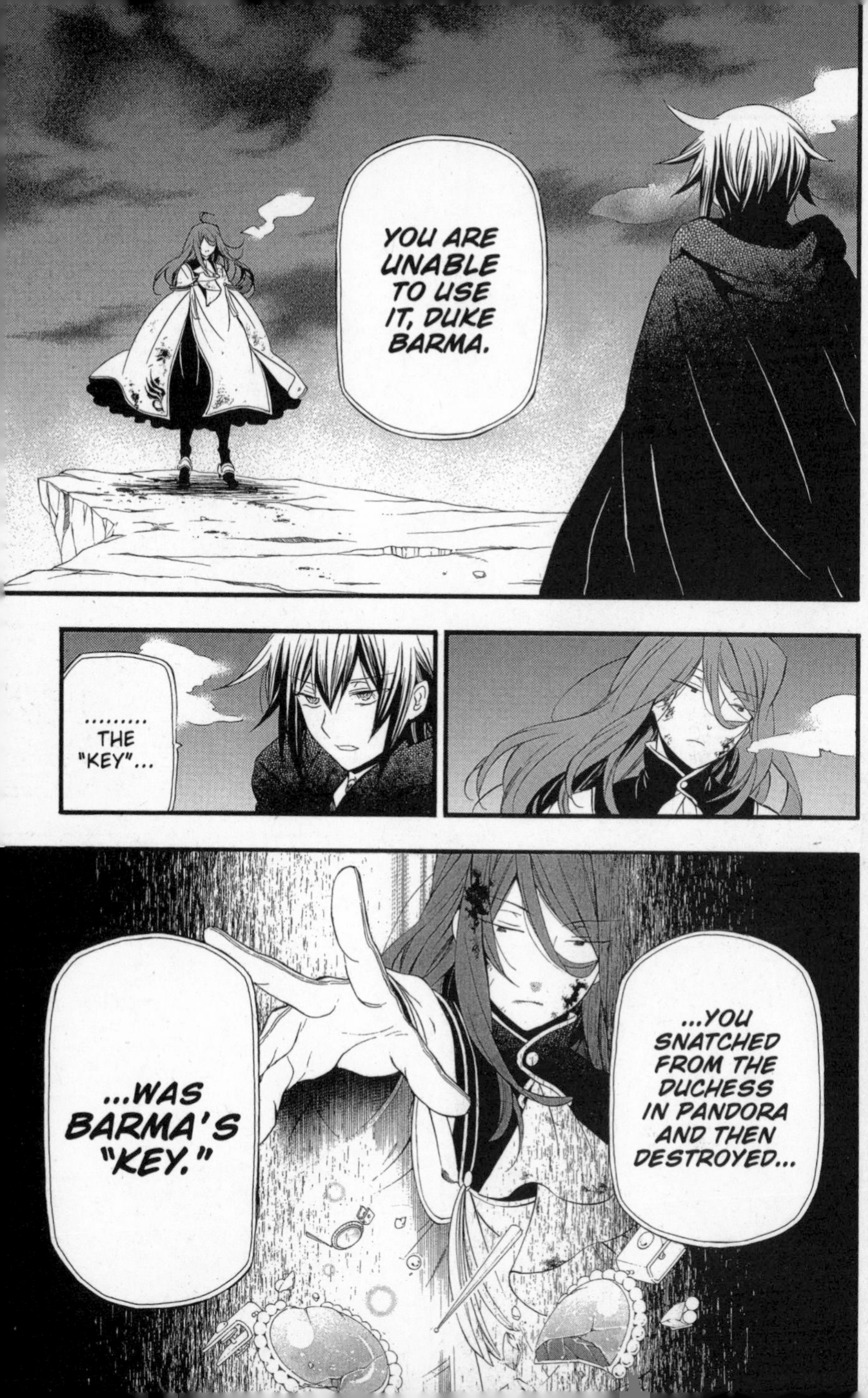
YOU ARE UNABLE TO USE IT, DUKE BARMA.
.... THE "KEY"...
...YOU SNATCHED FROM THE DUCHESS IN PANDORA AND THEN DESTROYED...
...WAS BARMA'S "KEY."

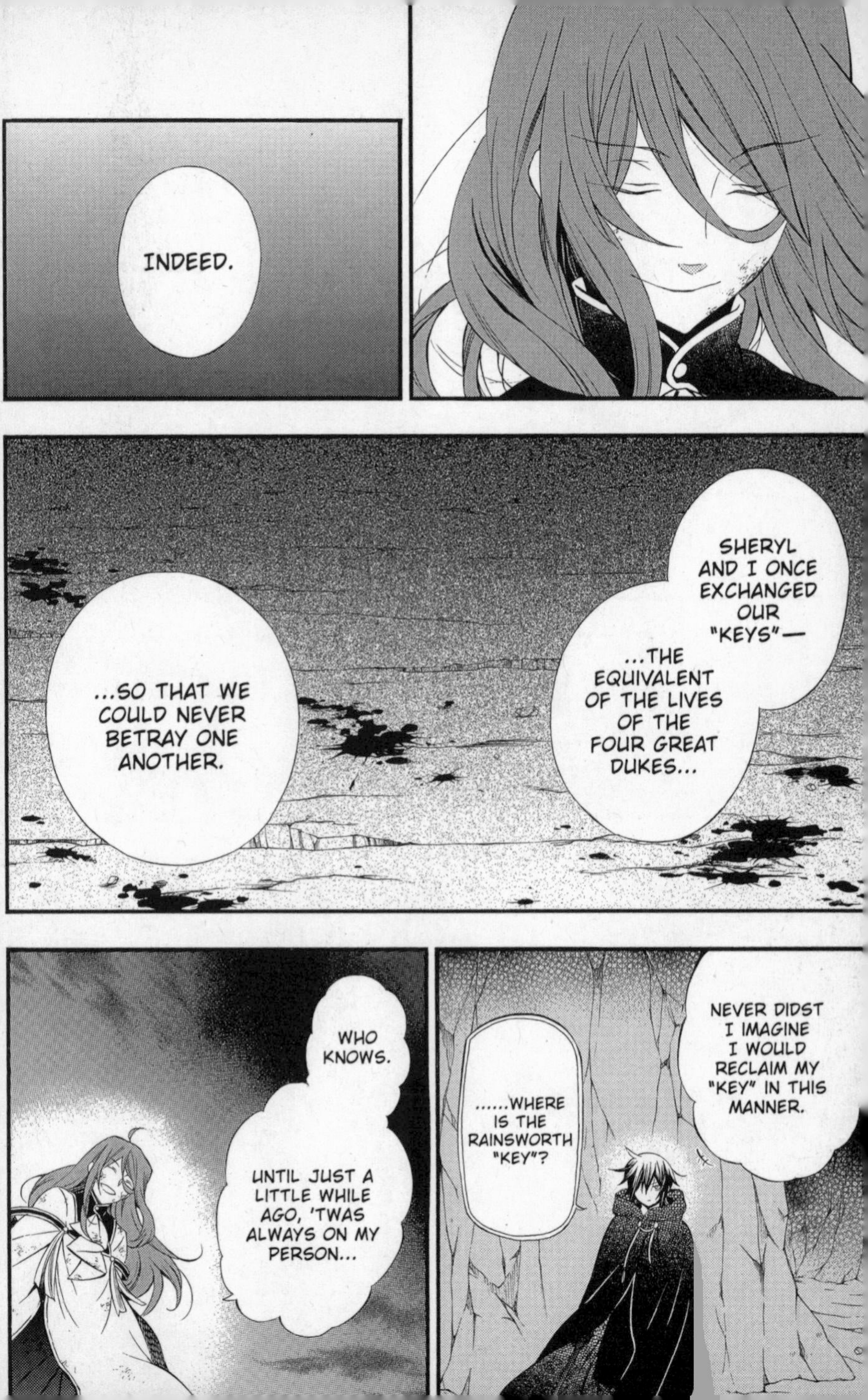
INDEED.
SHERYL AND I ONCE EXCHANGED OUR "KEYS"—
...THE EQUIVALENT OF THE LIVES OF THE FOUR GREAT DUKES...
...SO THAT WE COULD NEVER BETRAY ONE ANOTHER.
NEVER DIDST I IMAGINE I WOULD RECLAIM MY "KEY" IN THIS MANNER.
......WHERE IS THE RAINSWORTH "KEY"?
WHO KNOWS.
UNTIL JUST A LITTLE WHILE AGO, 'TWAS ALWAYS ON MY PERSON...

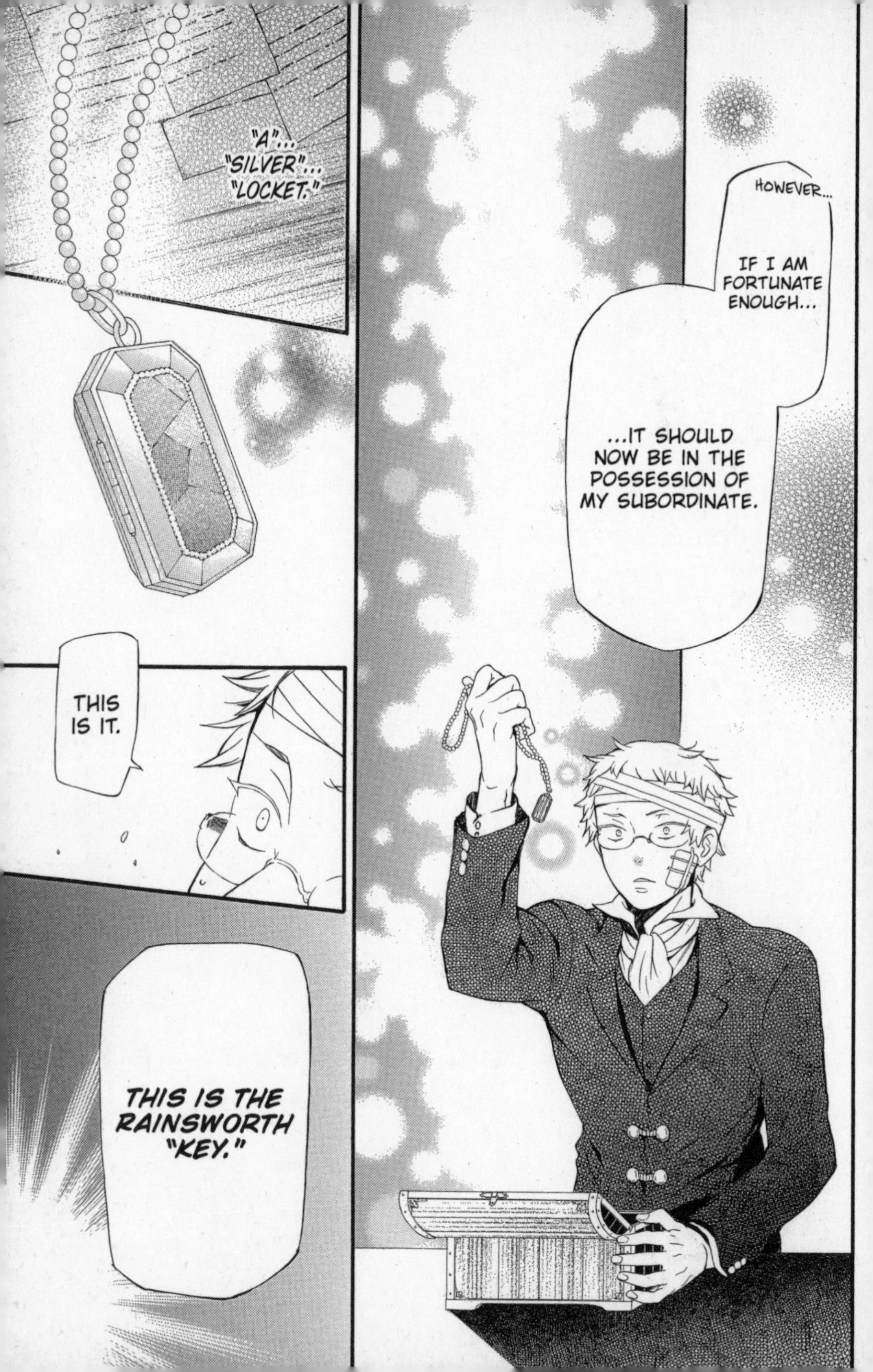
HOWEVER...
IF I AM FORTUNATE ENOUGH...
...IT SHOULD NOW BE IN THE POSSESSION OF MY SUBORDINATE.
"A"... "SILVER"... "LOCKET."
THIS IS IT.
THIS IS THE RAINSWORTH "KEY."

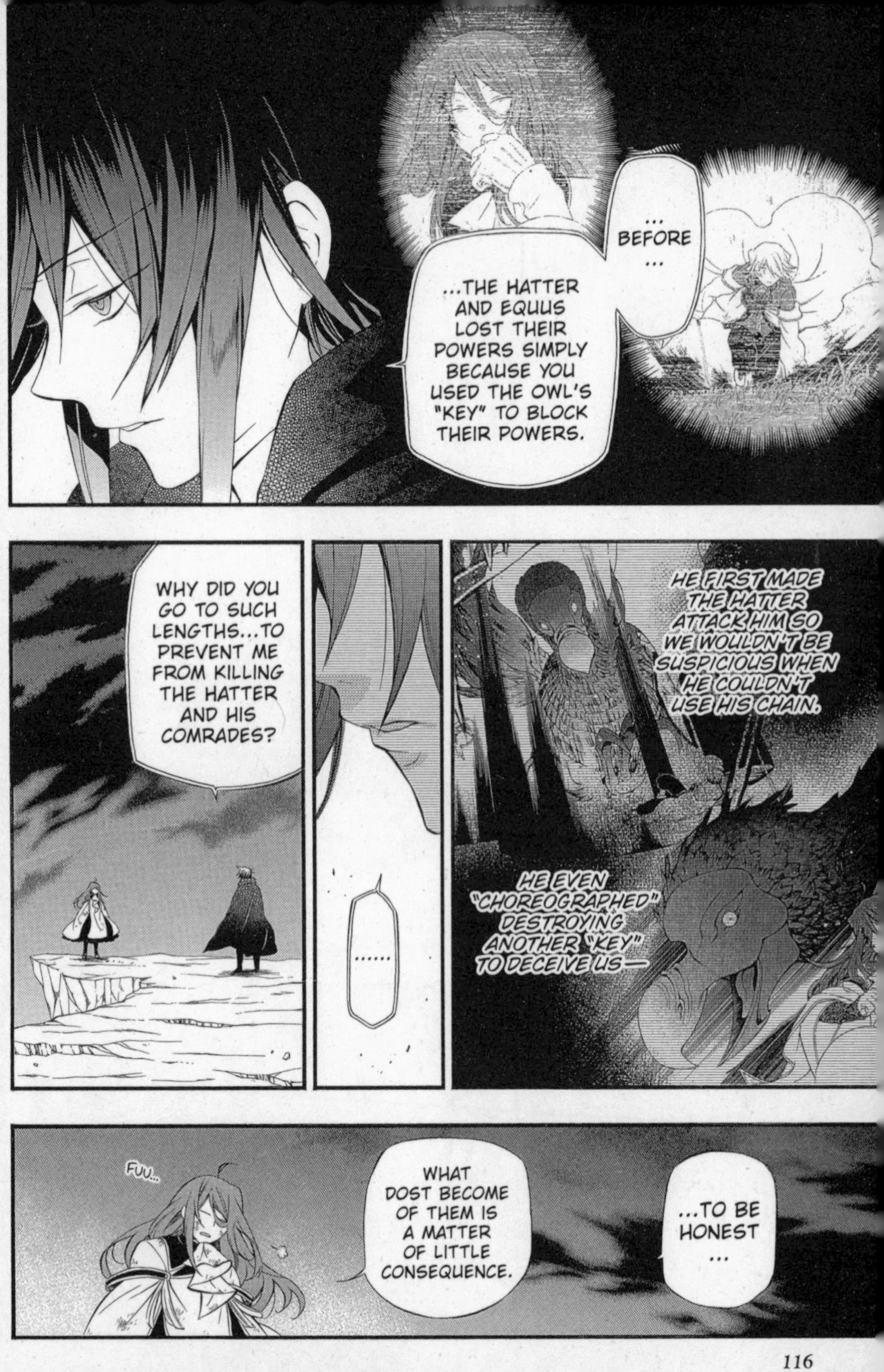
... BEFORE ...
...THE HATTER AND EQUUS LOST THEIR POWERS SIMPLY BECAUSE YOU USED THE OWL'S "KEY" TO BLOCK THEIR POWERS.
HE FIRST MADE THE HATTER ATTACK HIM SO WE WOULDN'T BE SUSPICIOUS WHEN HE COULDN'T USE HIS CHAIN.
HE EVEN "CHOREOGRAPHED" DESTROYING ANOTHER "KEY" TO DECEIVE US—
......
WHY DID YOU GO TO SUCH LENGTHS...TO PREVENT ME FROM KILLING THE HATTER AND HIS COMRADES?
...TO BE HONEST ...
WHAT DOST BECOME OF THEM IS A MATTER OF LITTLE CONSEQUENCE.
FUU...

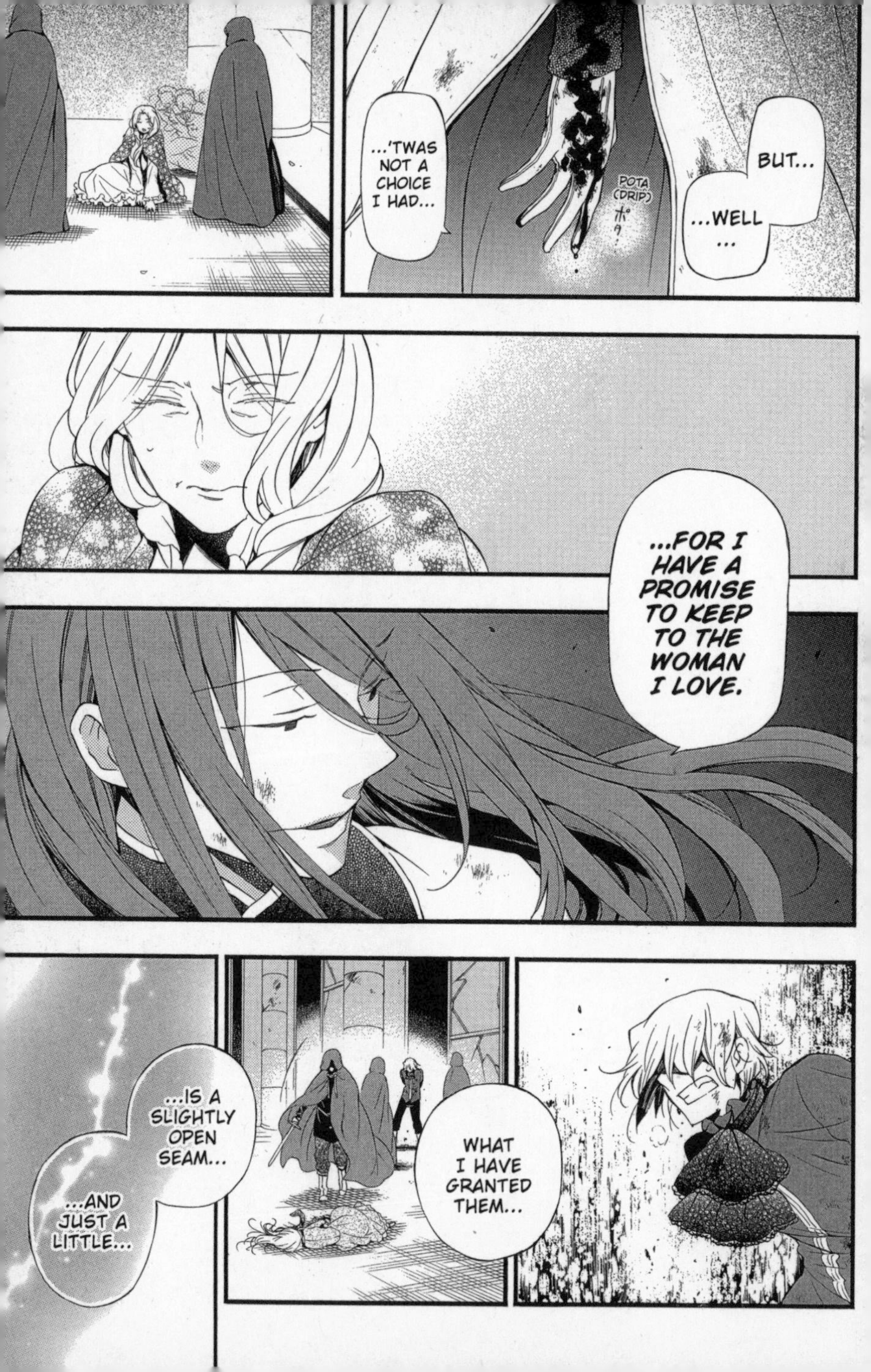
BUT...
...WELL ...
POTA (DRIP) ポタ
...'TWAS NOT A CHOICE I HAD...
...FOR I HAVE A PROMISE TO KEEP TO THE WOMAN I LOVE.
WHAT I HAVE GRANTED THEM...
...IS A SLIGHTLY OPEN SEAM...
...AND JUST A LITTLE...

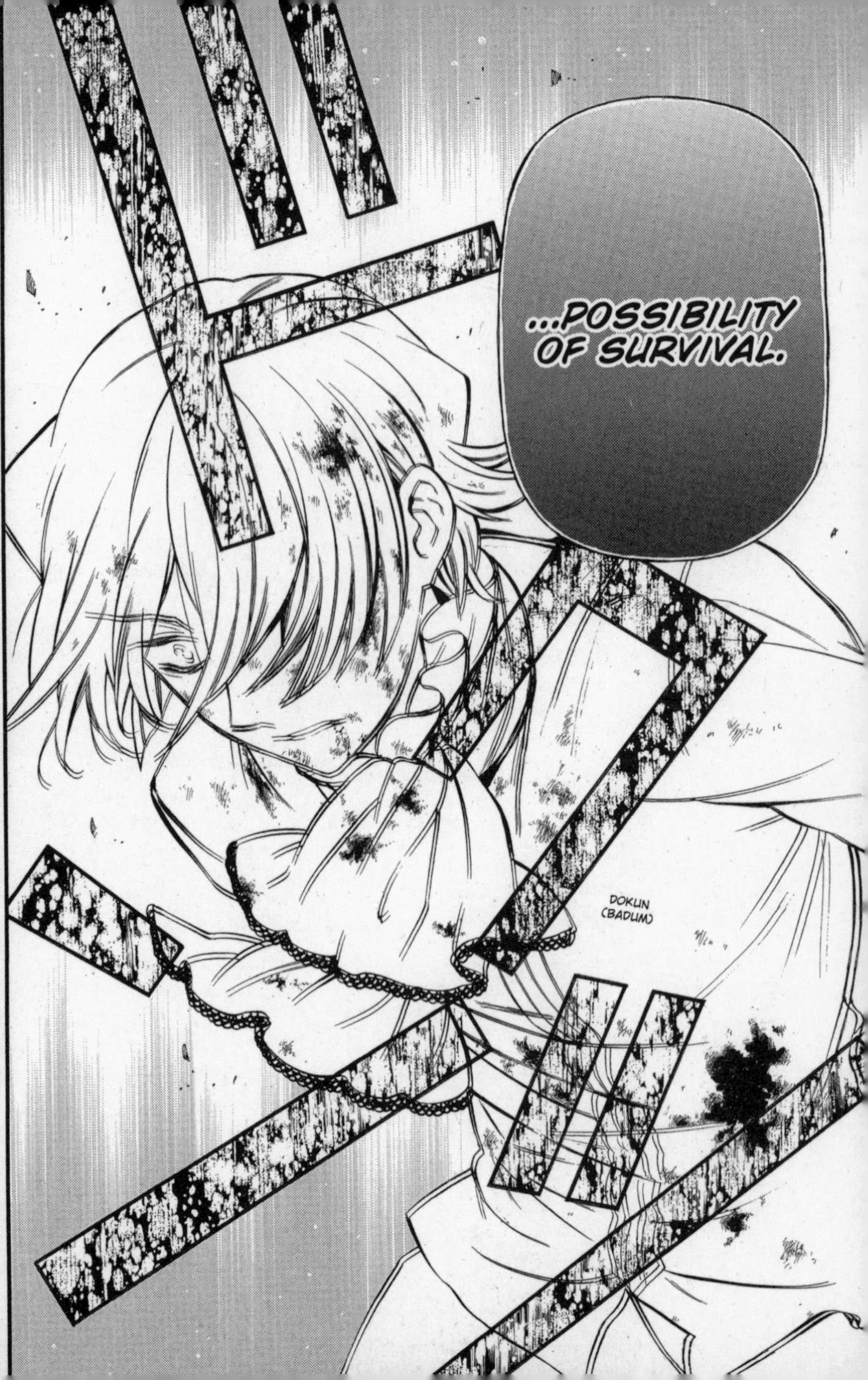
...POSSIBILITY OF SURVIVAL.
DOKUN (BADUM)

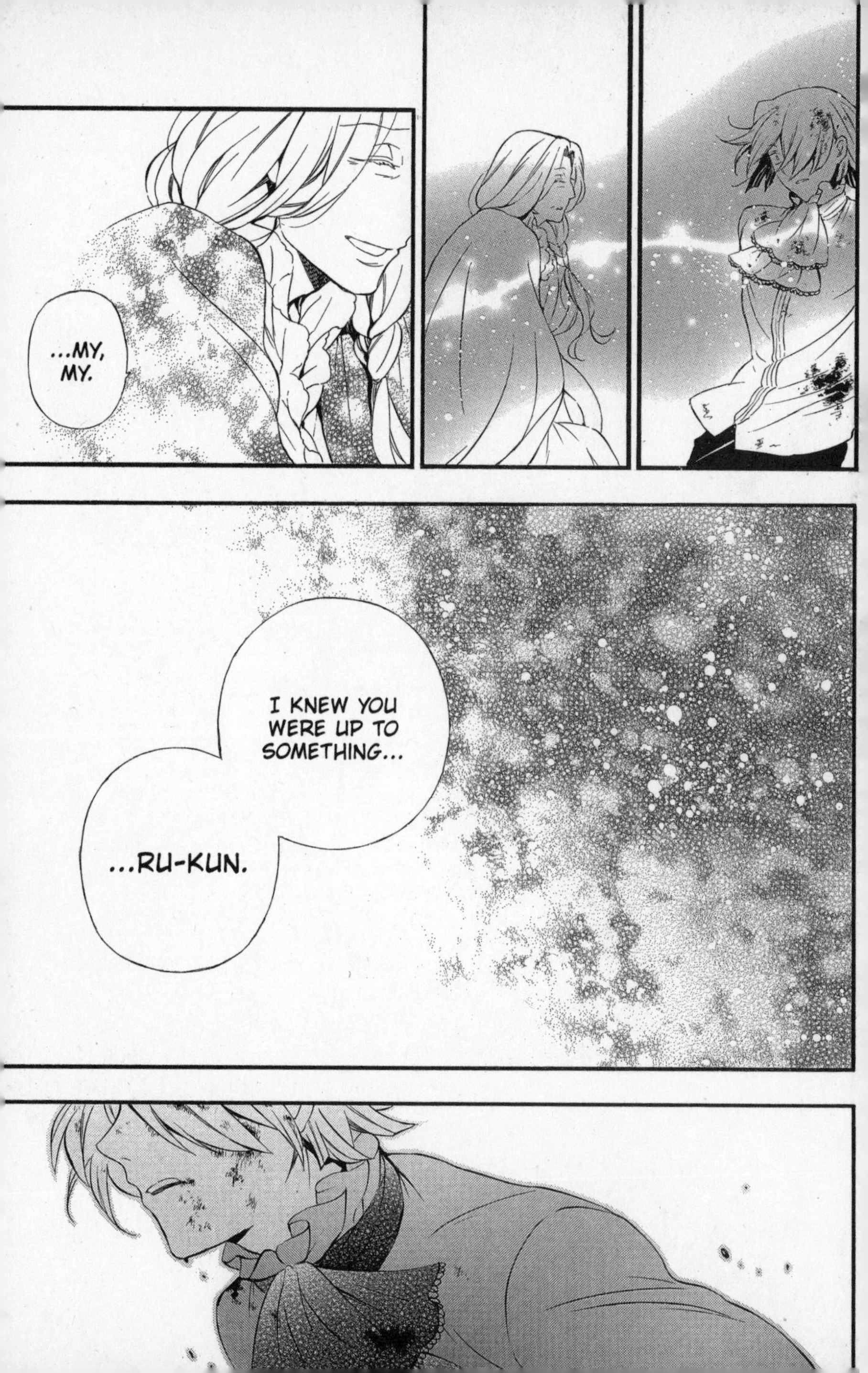
...MY, MY.
I KNEW YOU WERE UP TO SOMETHING...
...RU-KUN.

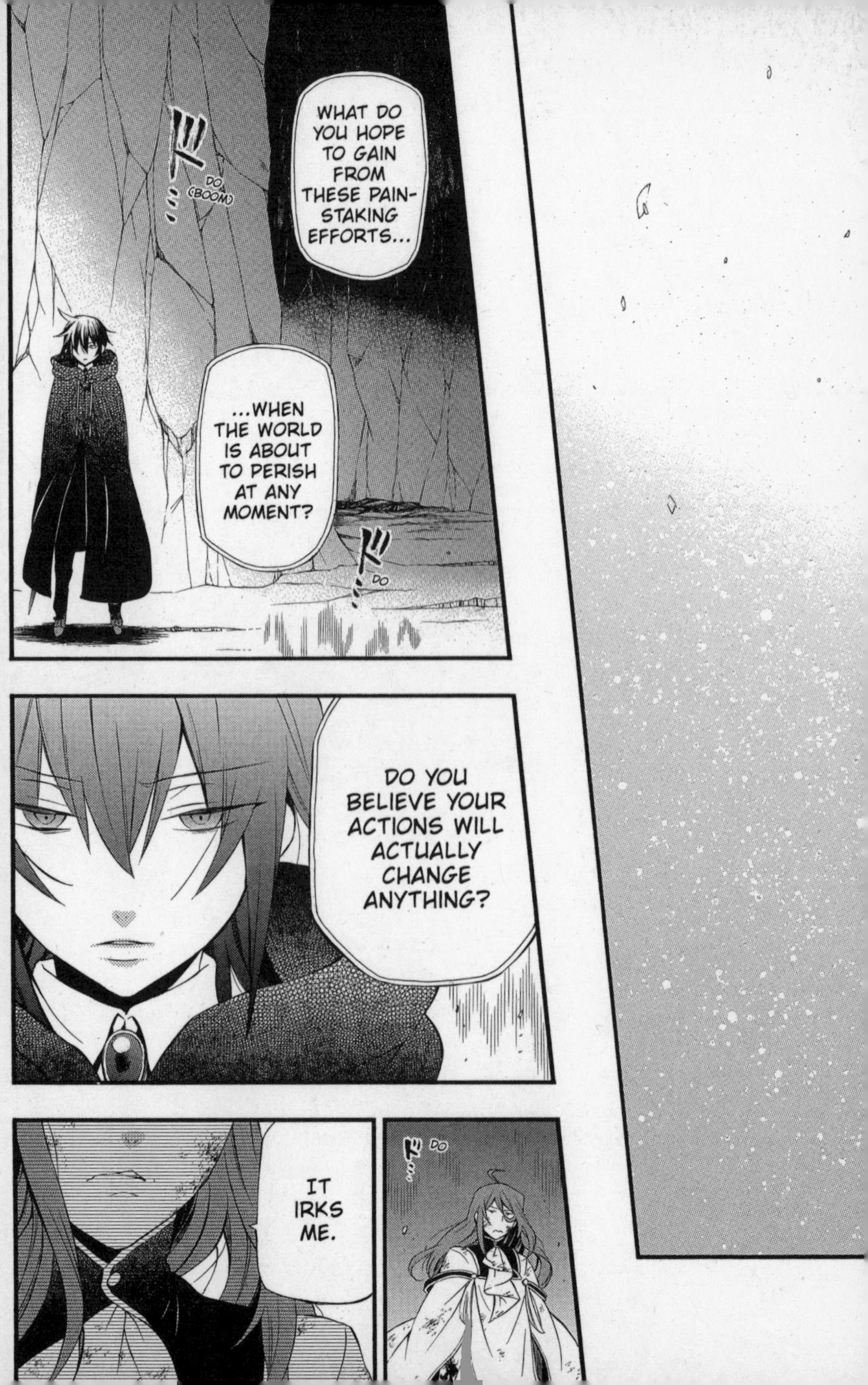
WHAT DO YOU HOPE TO GAIN FROM THESE PAIN-STAKING EFFORTS...
DO (BOOM)
...WHEN THE WORLD IS ABOUT TO PERISH AT ANY MOMENT?
DO
DO YOU BELIEVE YOUR ACTIONS WILL ACTUALLY CHANGE ANYTHING?
DO
IT IRKS ME.

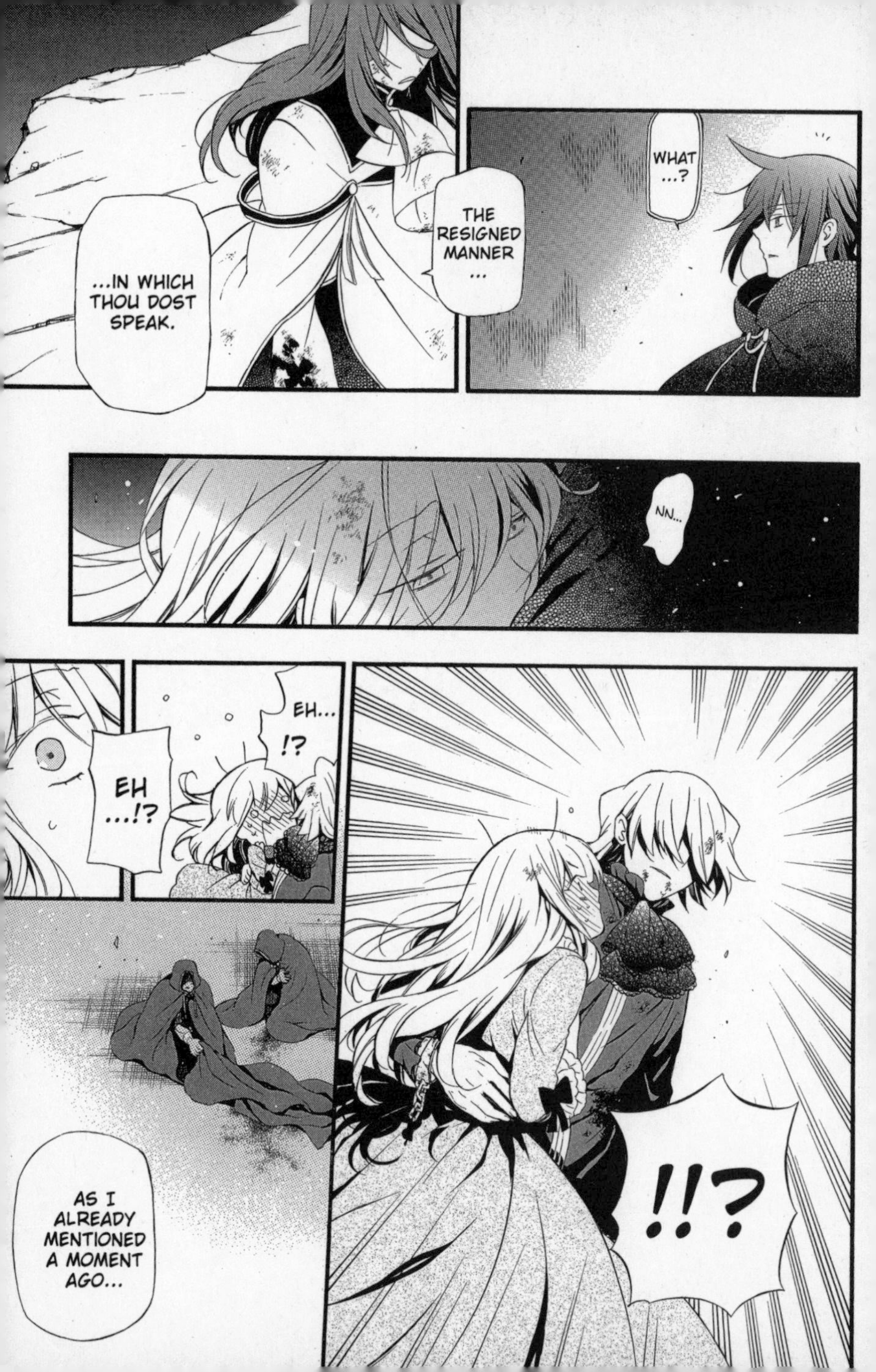
WHAT ...?
THE RESIGNED MANNER ...
...IN WHICH THOU DOST SPEAK.
NN...
!!?
EH... !?
EH ...!?
AS I ALREADY MENTIONED A MOMENT AGO...

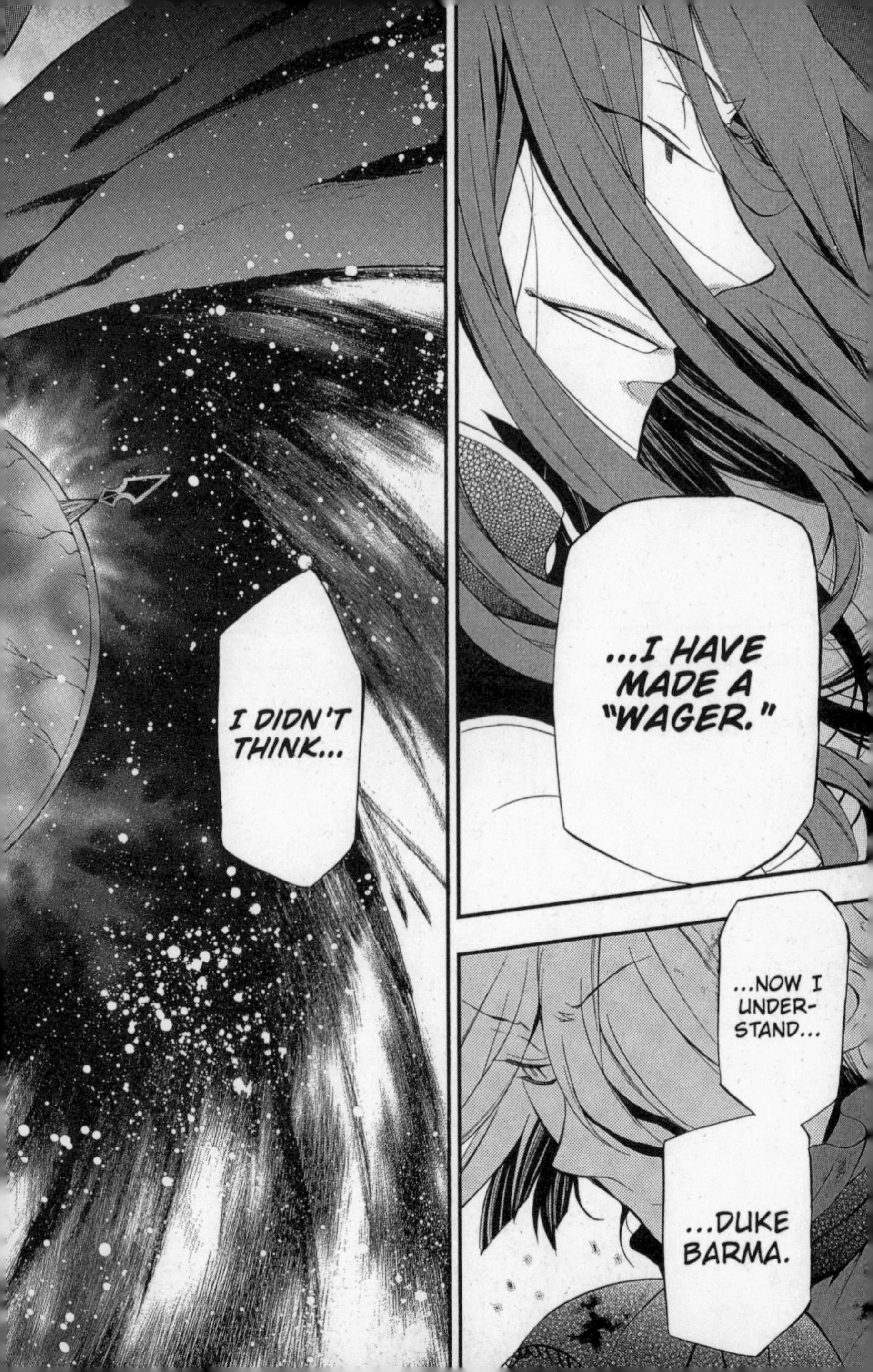
...I HAVE MADE A "WAGER."
...NOW I UNDER-STAND...
...DUKE BARMA.
I DIDN'T THINK...

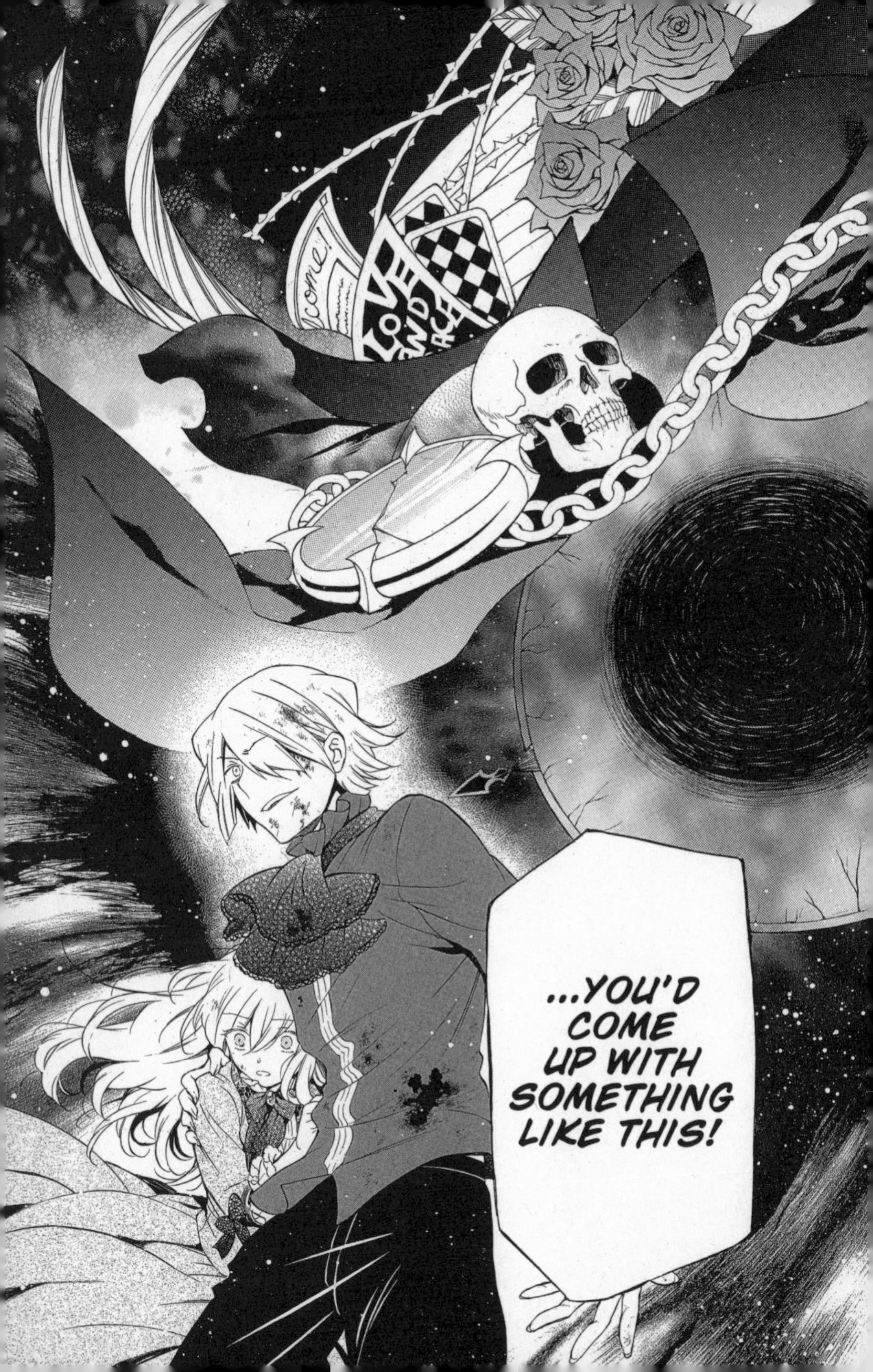
...YOU'D COME UP WITH SOMETHING LIKE THIS!

Retrace : LXXXVI Wager

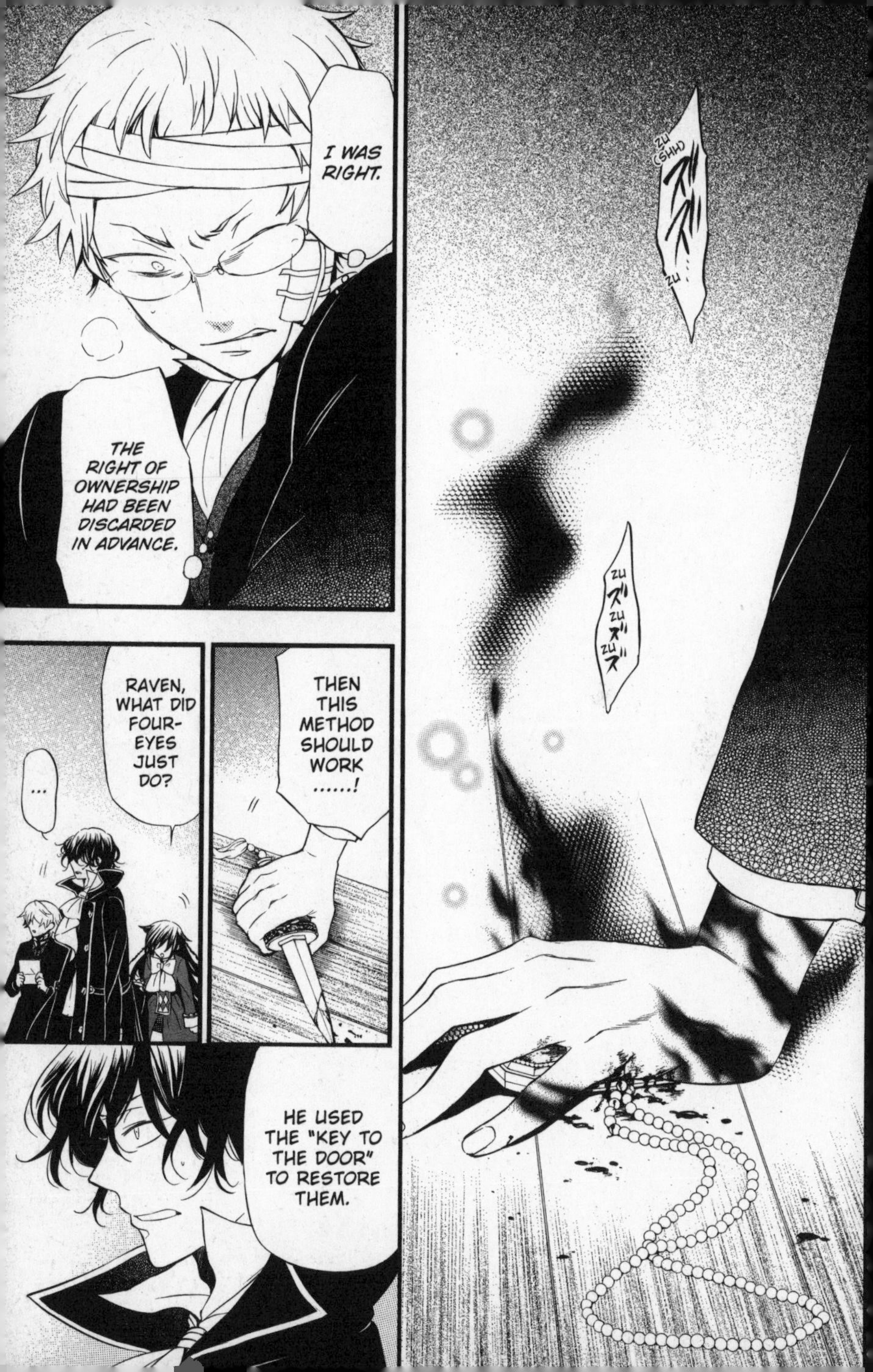
ZU (SHH)
ズズズ…
ZU
ZU ズ ZU ズ ZU ズ
I WAS RIGHT.
THE RIGHT OF OWNERSHIP HAD BEEN DISCARDED IN ADVANCE.
THEN THIS METHOD SHOULD WORK ......!
RAVEN, WHAT DID FOUR-EYES JUST DO?
...
HE USED THE "KEY TO THE DOOR" TO RESTORE THEM.

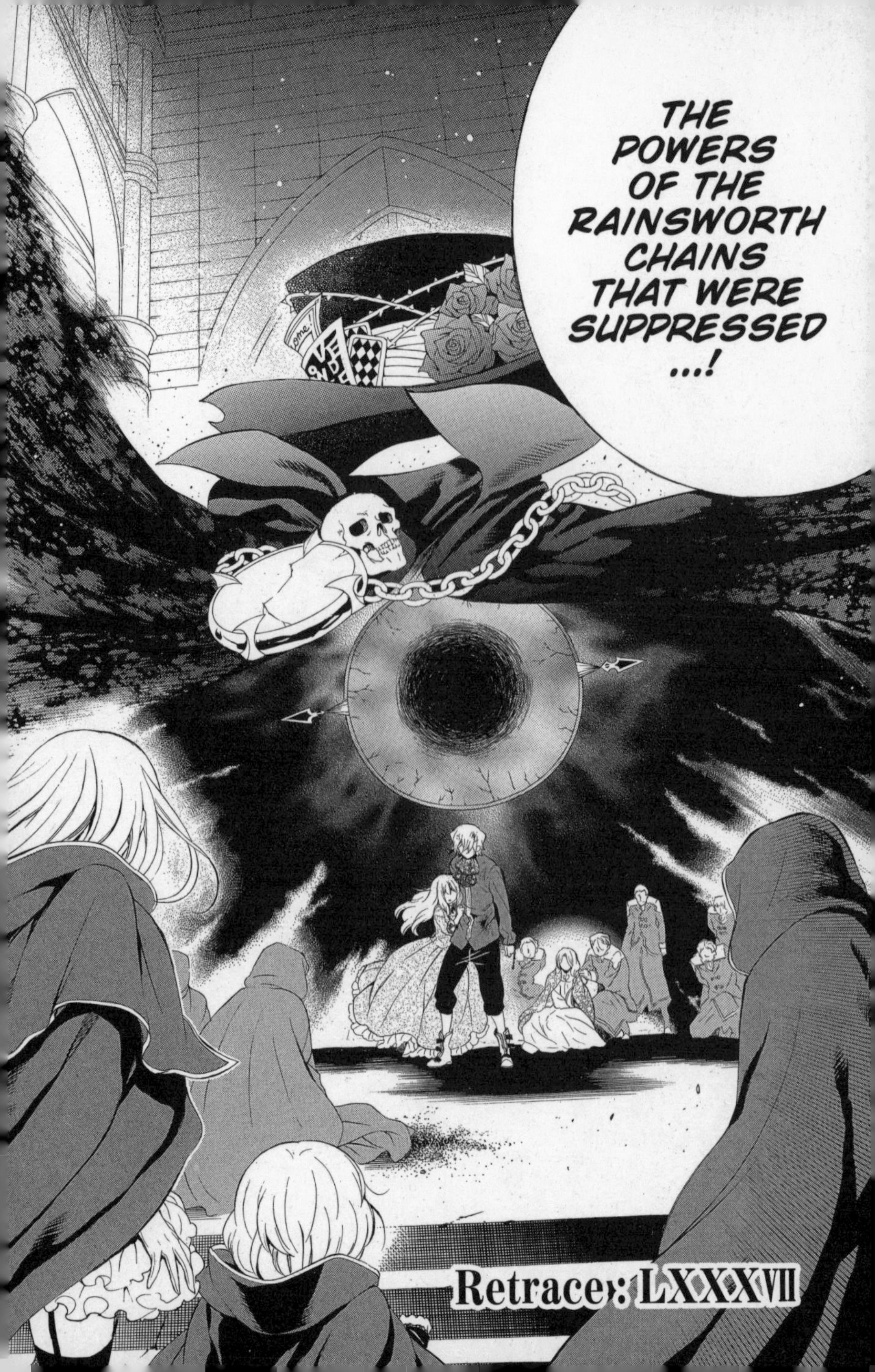
THE POWERS OF THE RAINSWORTH CHAINS THAT WERE SUPPRESSED ...!
Retrace: LXXXVII

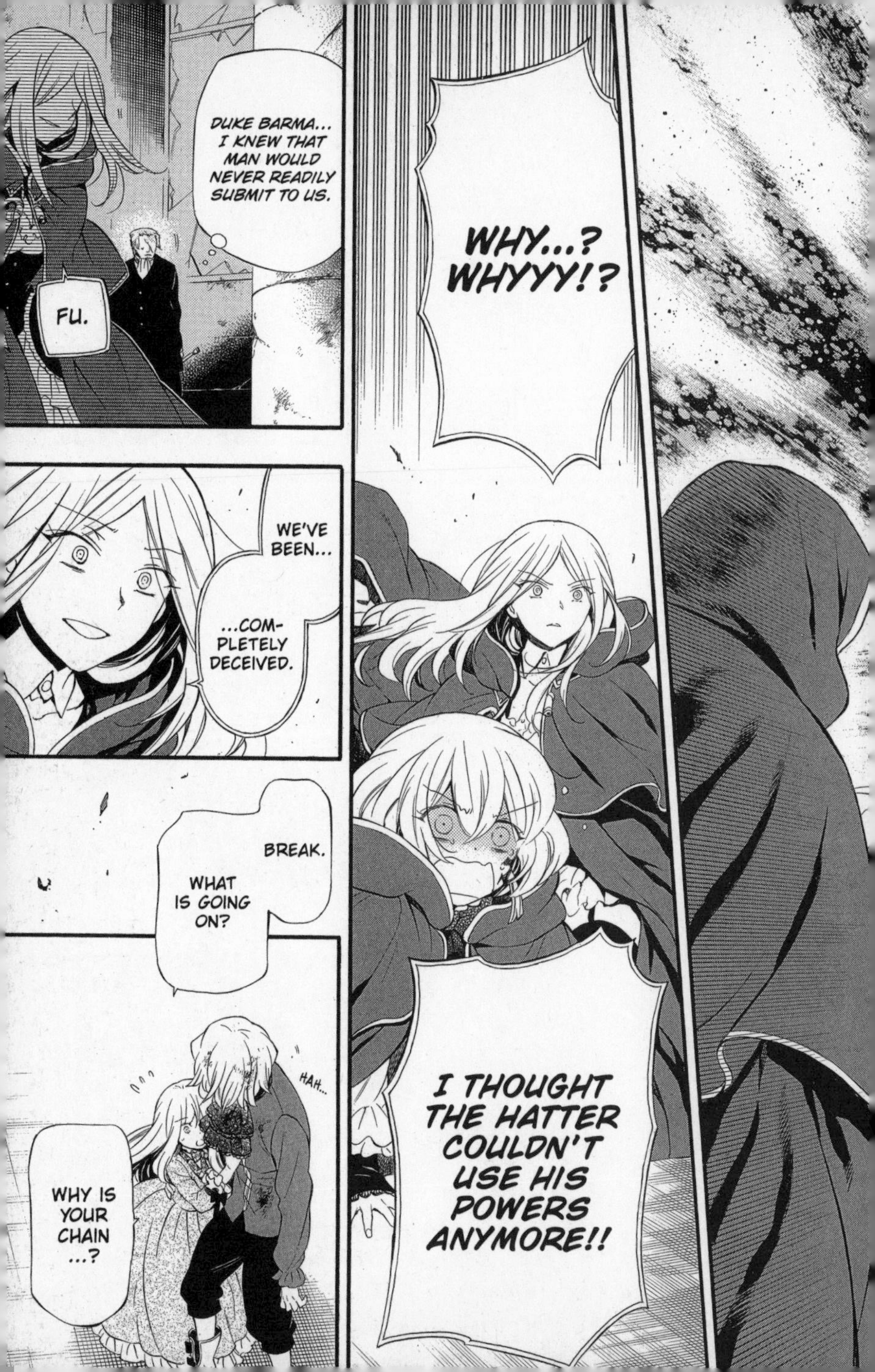
WHY...? WHYYY!?
I THOUGHT THE HATTER COULDN'T USE HIS POWERS ANYMORE!!
DUKE BARMA... I KNEW THAT MAN WOULD NEVER READILY SUBMIT TO US.
FU.
WE'VE BEEN...
...COM-PLETELY DECEIVED.
BREAK.
WHAT IS GOING ON?
HAH...
WHY IS YOUR CHAIN ...?

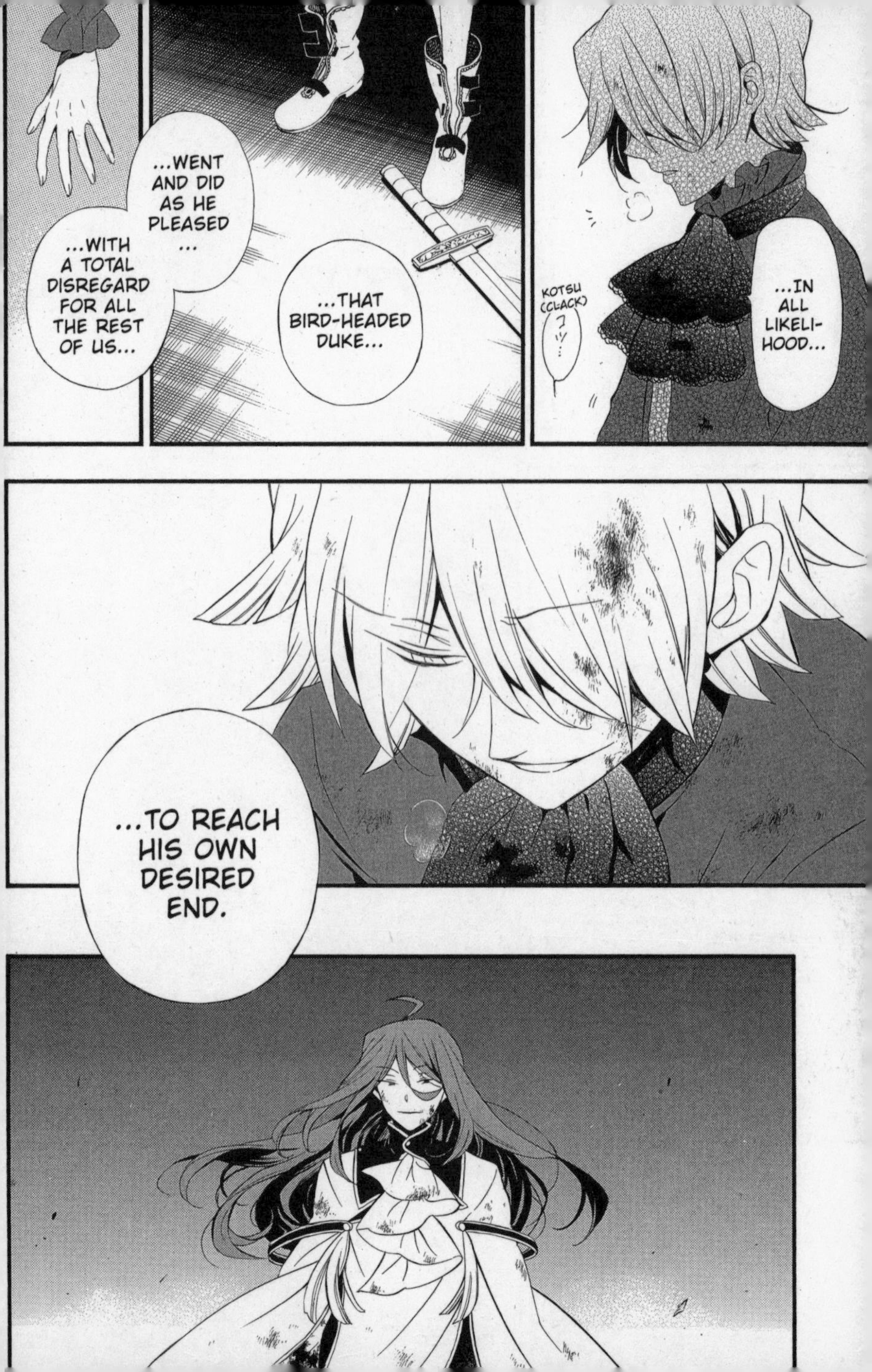
...IN ALL LIKELI-HOOD...
KOTSU (CLACK)
コツ…
...THAT BIRD-HEADED DUKE...
...WENT AND DID AS HE PLEASED...
...WITH A TOTAL DISREGARD FOR ALL THE REST OF US...
...TO REACH HIS OWN DESIRED END.

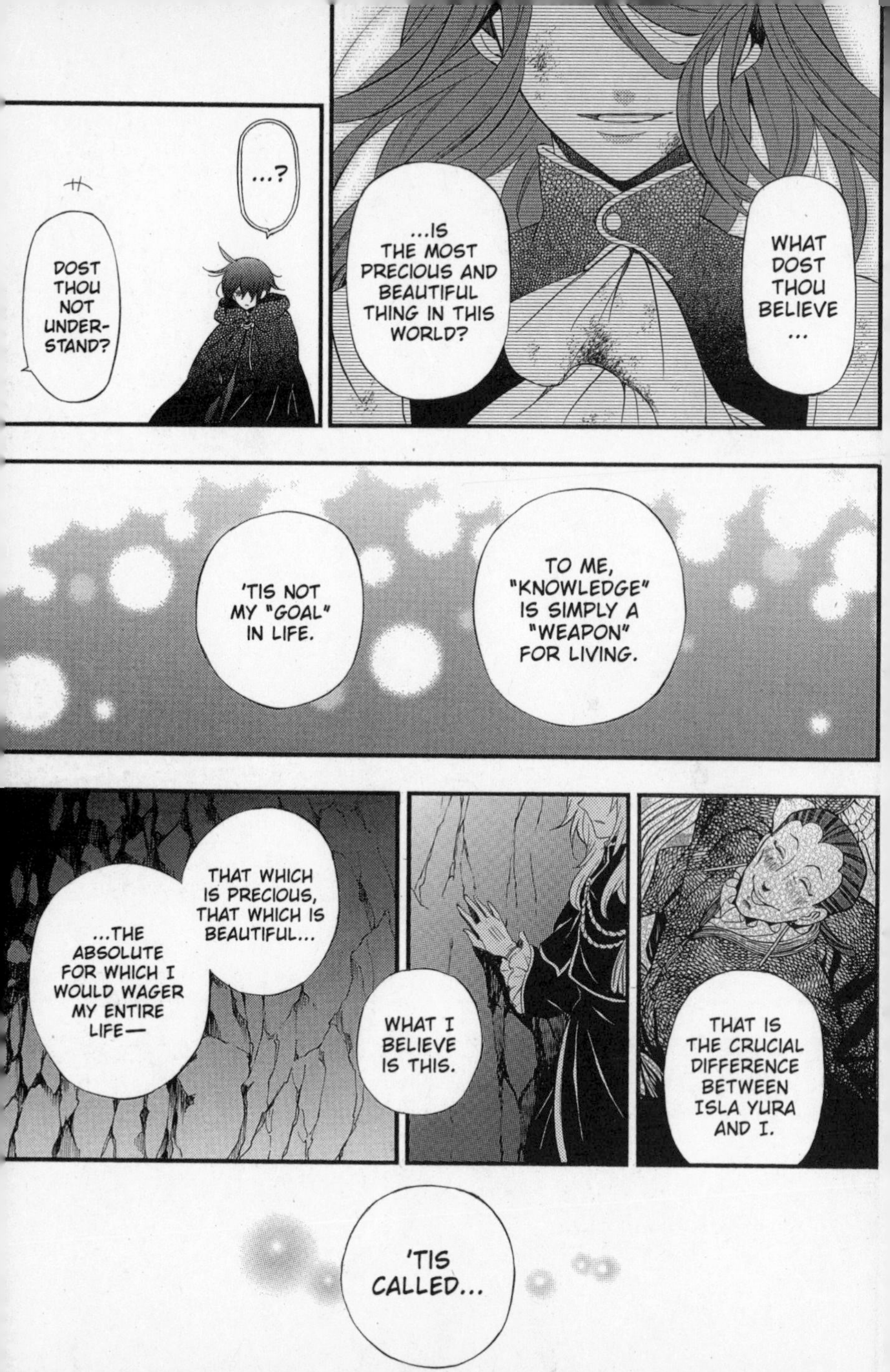
WHAT DOST THOU BELIEVE ...
...IS THE MOST PRECIOUS AND BEAUTIFUL THING IN THIS WORLD?
...?
DOST THOU NOT UNDERSTAND?
TO ME, "KNOWLEDGE" IS SIMPLY A "WEAPON" FOR LIVING.
'TIS NOT MY "GOAL" IN LIFE.
THAT IS THE CRUCIAL DIFFERENCE BETWEEN ISLA YURA AND I.
WHAT I BELIEVE IS THIS.
THAT WHICH IS PRECIOUS, THAT WHICH IS BEAUTIFUL...
...THE ABSOLUTE FOR WHICH I WOULD WAGER MY ENTIRE LIFE—
'TIS CALLED...

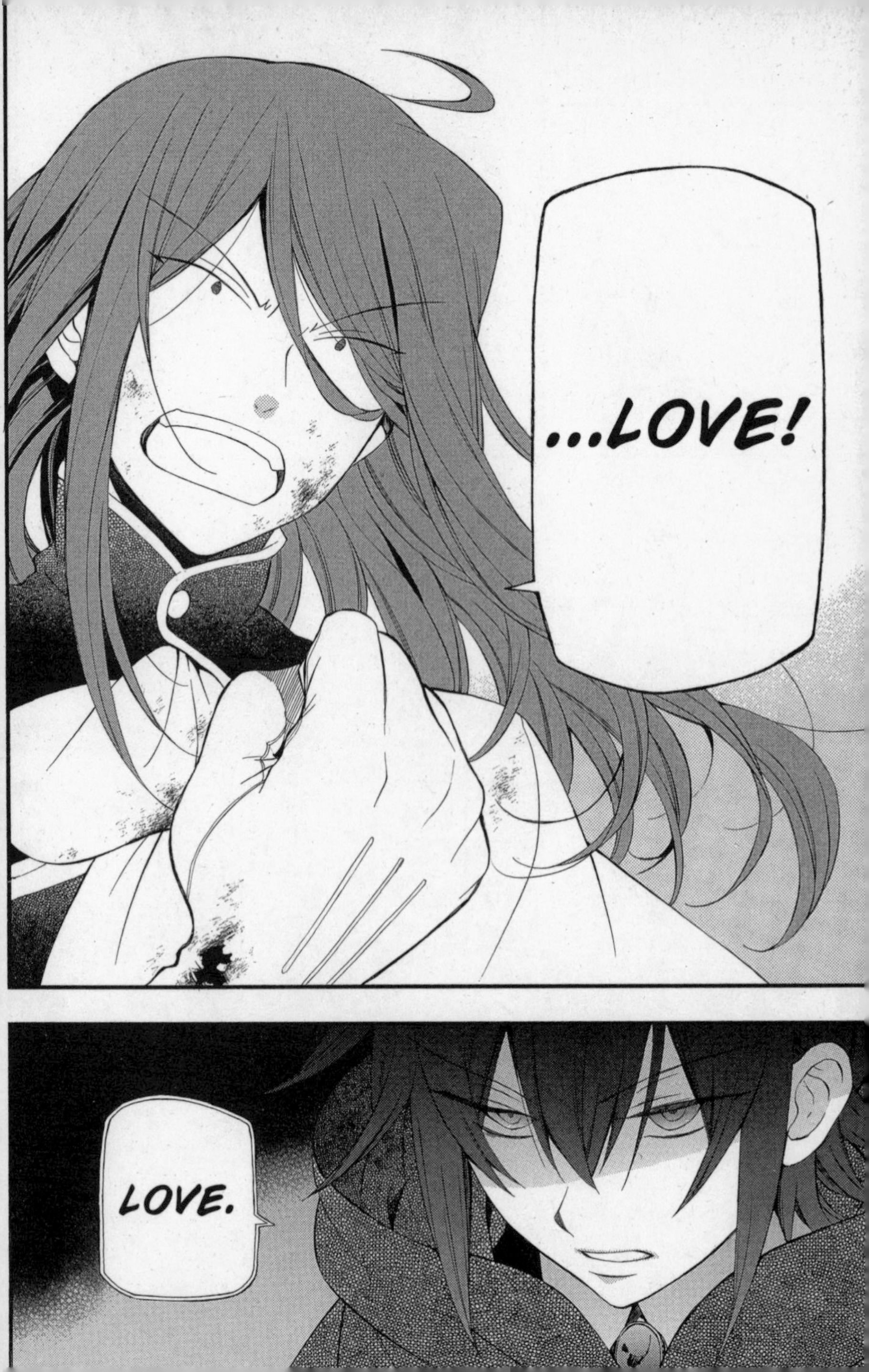
...LOVE!
LOVE.

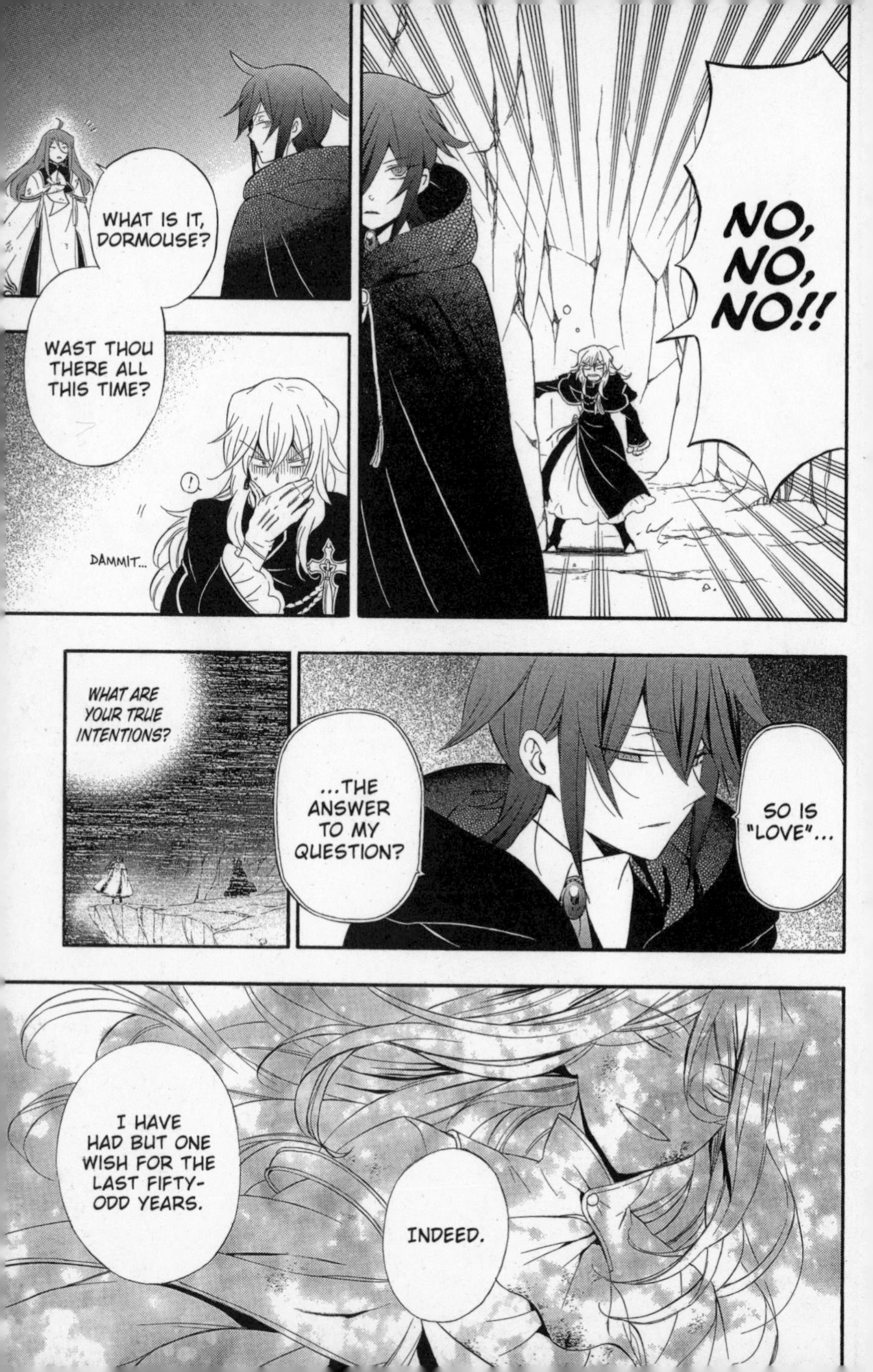
NO, NO, NO!!
WHAT IS IT, DORMOUSE?
WAST THOU THERE ALL THIS TIME?
DAMMIT...
SO IS "LOVE"...
...THE ANSWER TO MY QUESTION?
WHAT ARE YOUR TRUE INTENTIONS?
INDEED.
I HAVE HAD BUT ONE WISH FOR THE LAST FIFTY-ODD YEARS.

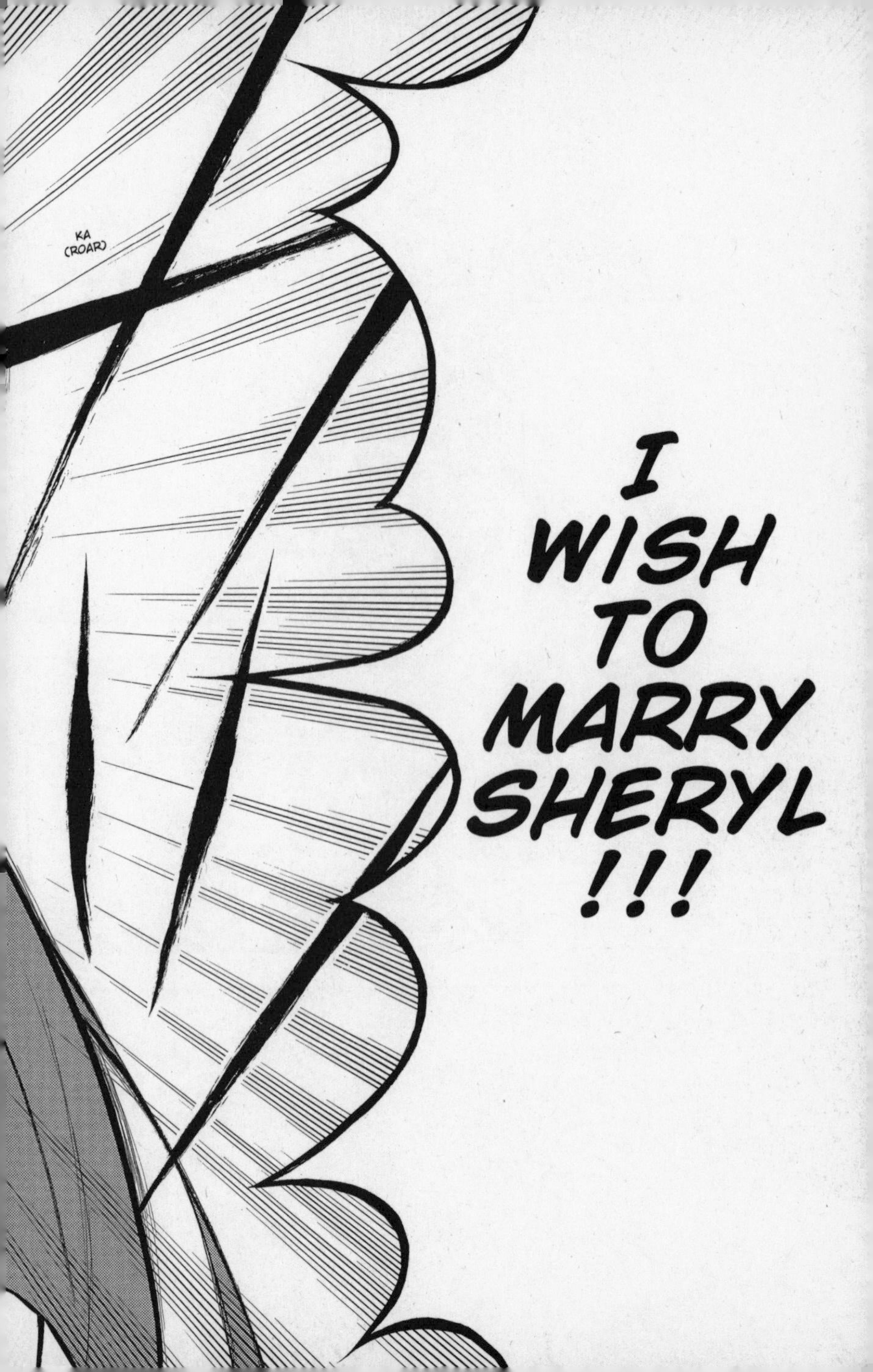
I WISH TO MARRY SHERYL!!!
KA (ROAR)

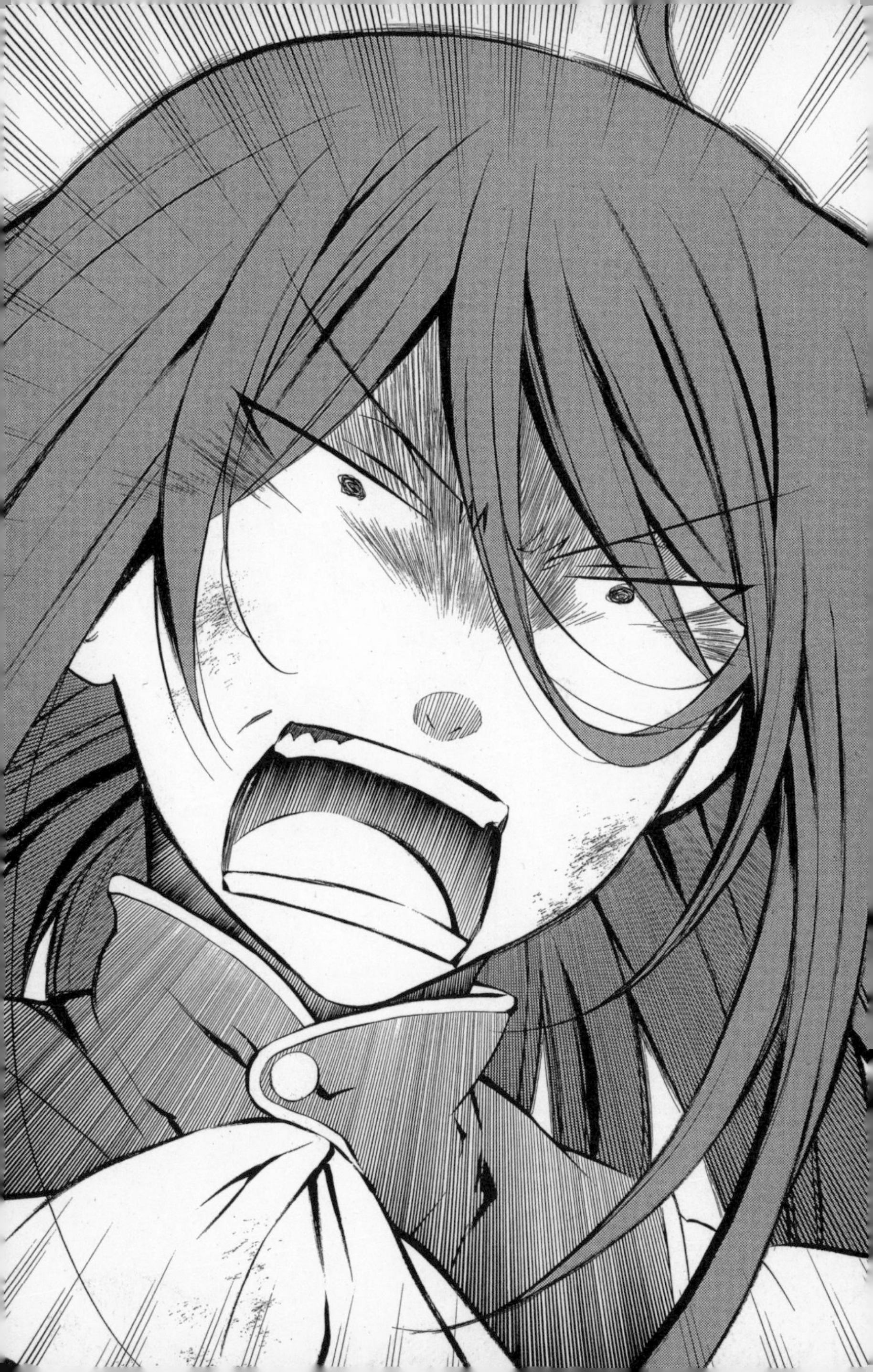

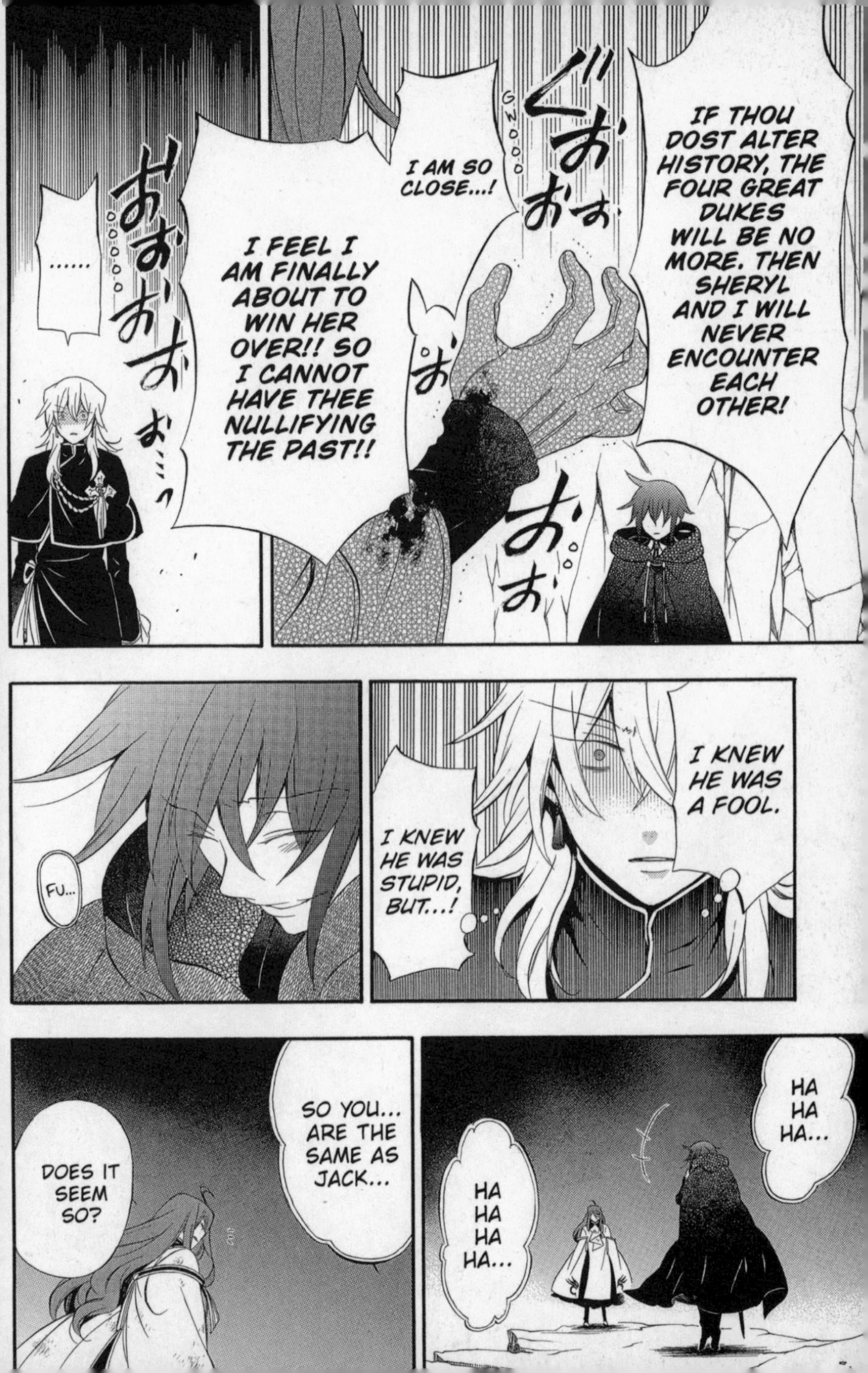

IF THOU DOST ALTER HISTORY, THE FOUR GREAT DUKES WILL BE NO MORE. THEN SHERYL AND I WILL NEVER ENCOUNTER EACH OTHER!
GWOOOO
I AM SO CLOSE...!
I FEEL I AM FINALLY ABOUT TO WIN HER OVER!! SO I CANNOT HAVE THEE NULLIFYING THE PAST!!
......
I KNEW HE WAS A FOOL.
I KNEW HE WAS STUPID, BUT...!
FU...
HA HA HA...
HA HA HA HA...
SO YOU... ARE THE SAME AS JACK...
DOES IT SEEM SO?

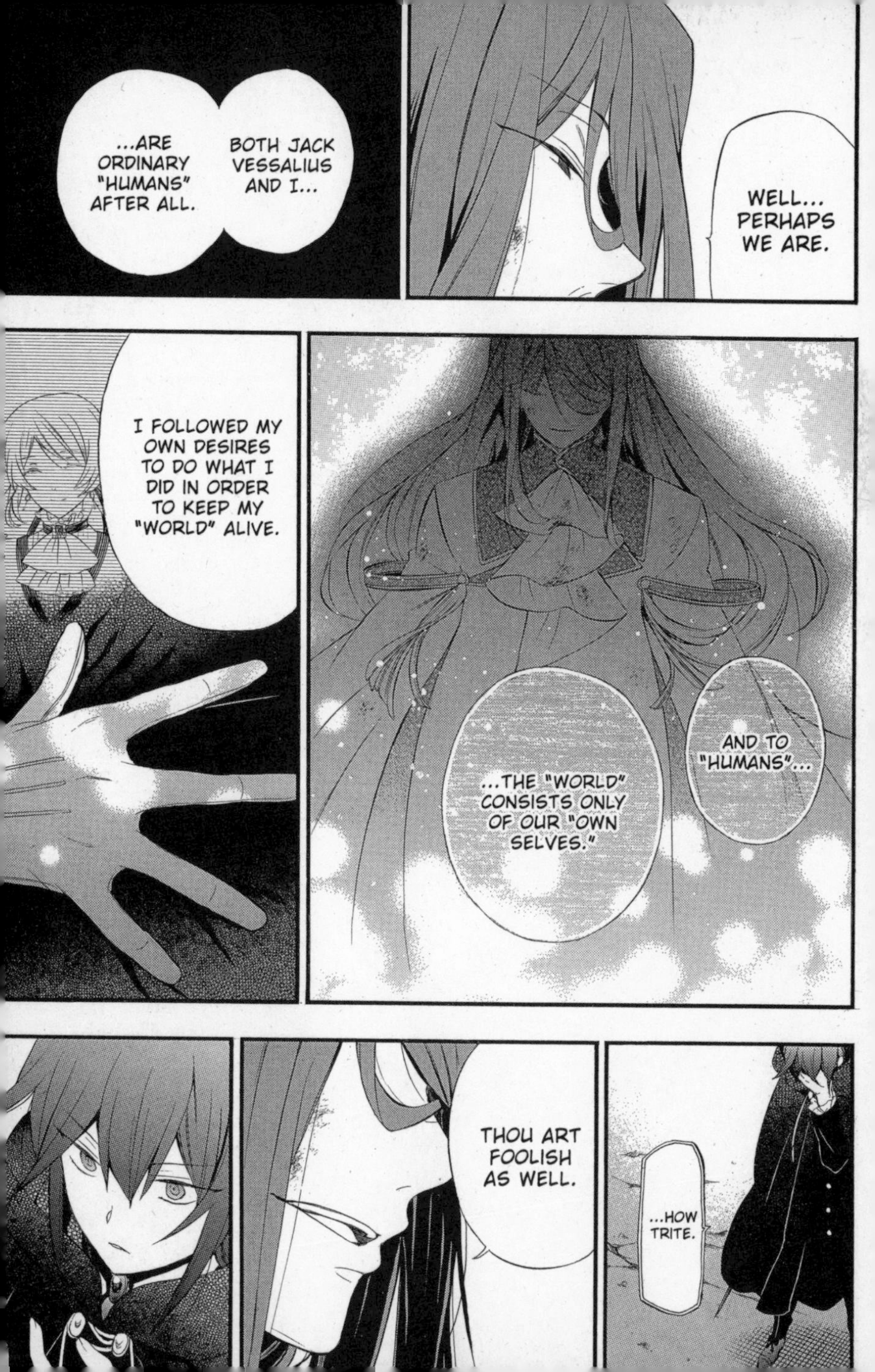
WELL... PERHAPS WE ARE.
BOTH JACK VESSALIUS AND I...
...ARE ORDINARY "HUMANS" AFTER ALL.
AND TO "HUMANS"...
...THE "WORLD" CONSISTS ONLY OF OUR "OWN SELVES."
I FOLLOWED MY OWN DESIRES TO DO WHAT I DID IN ORDER TO KEEP MY "WORLD" ALIVE.
...HOW TRITE.
THOU ART FOOLISH AS WELL.

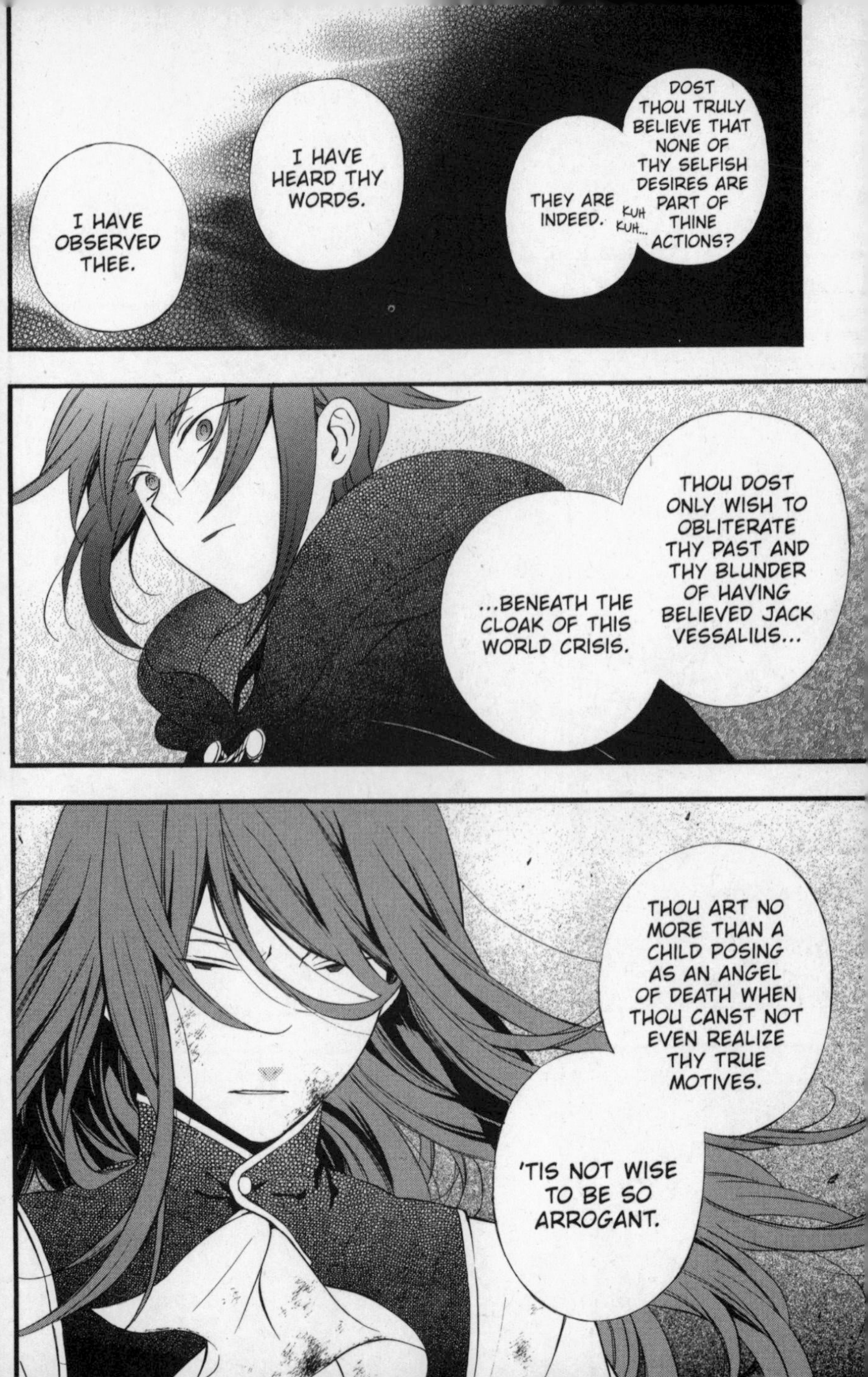
DOST THOU TRULY BELIEVE THAT NONE OF THY SELFISH DESIRES ARE PART OF THINE ACTIONS?
KUH KUH...
THEY ARE INDEED.
I HAVE HEARD THY WORDS.
I HAVE OBSERVED THEE.
THOU DOST ONLY WISH TO OBLITERATE THY PAST AND THY BLUNDER OF HAVING BELIEVED JACK VESSALIUS...
...BENEATH THE CLOAK OF THIS WORLD CRISIS.
THOU ART NO MORE THAN A CHILD POSING AS AN ANGEL OF DEATH WHEN THOU CANST NOT EVEN REALIZE THY TRUE MOTIVES.
'TIS NOT WISE TO BE SO ARROGANT.

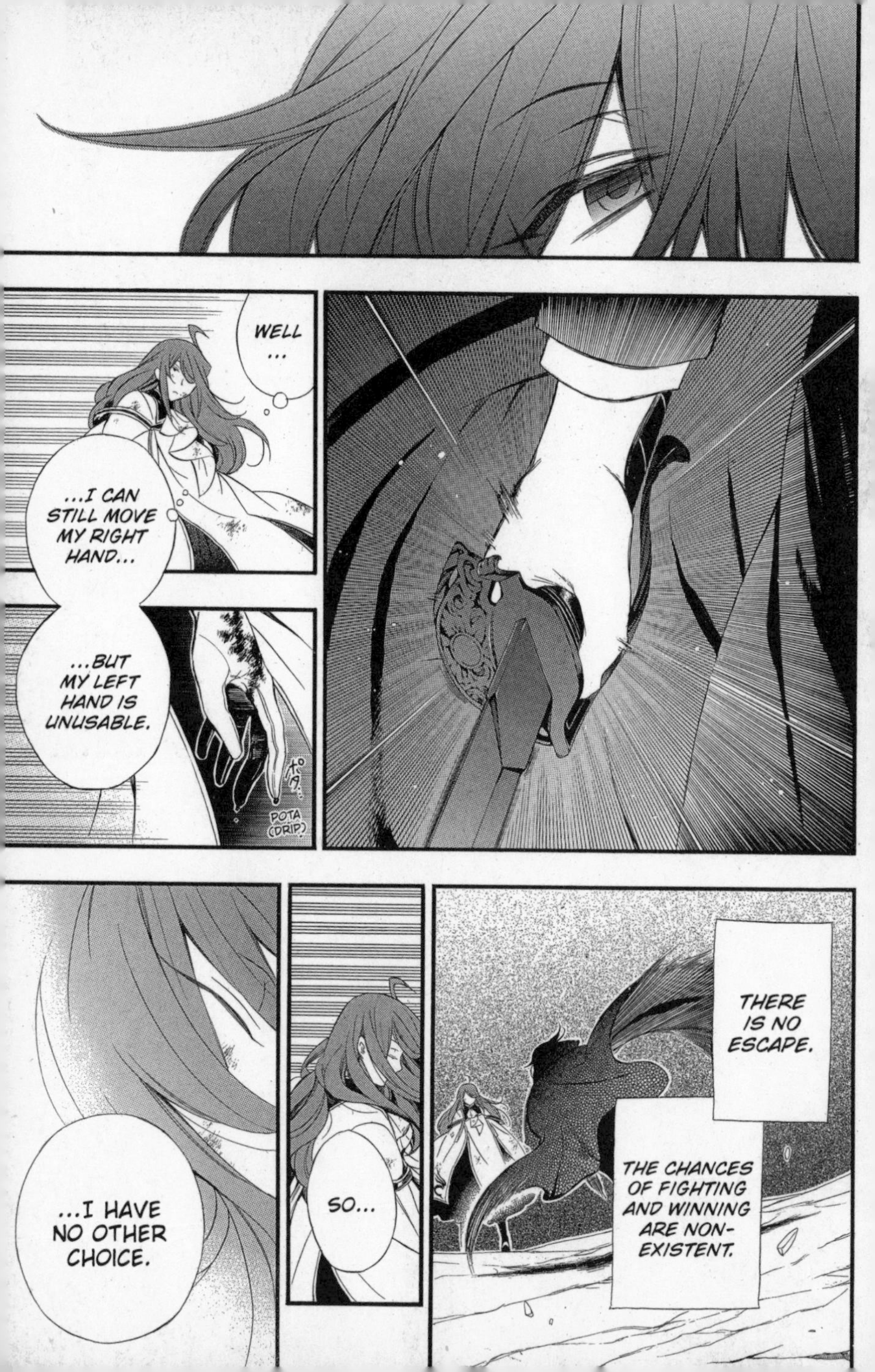
WELL...
...I CAN STILL MOVE MY RIGHT HAND...
...BUT MY LEFT HAND IS UNUSABLE.
POTA (DRIP)
THERE IS NO ESCAPE.
THE CHANCES OF FIGHTING AND WINNING ARE NON-EXISTENT.
SO...
...I HAVE NO OTHER CHOICE.

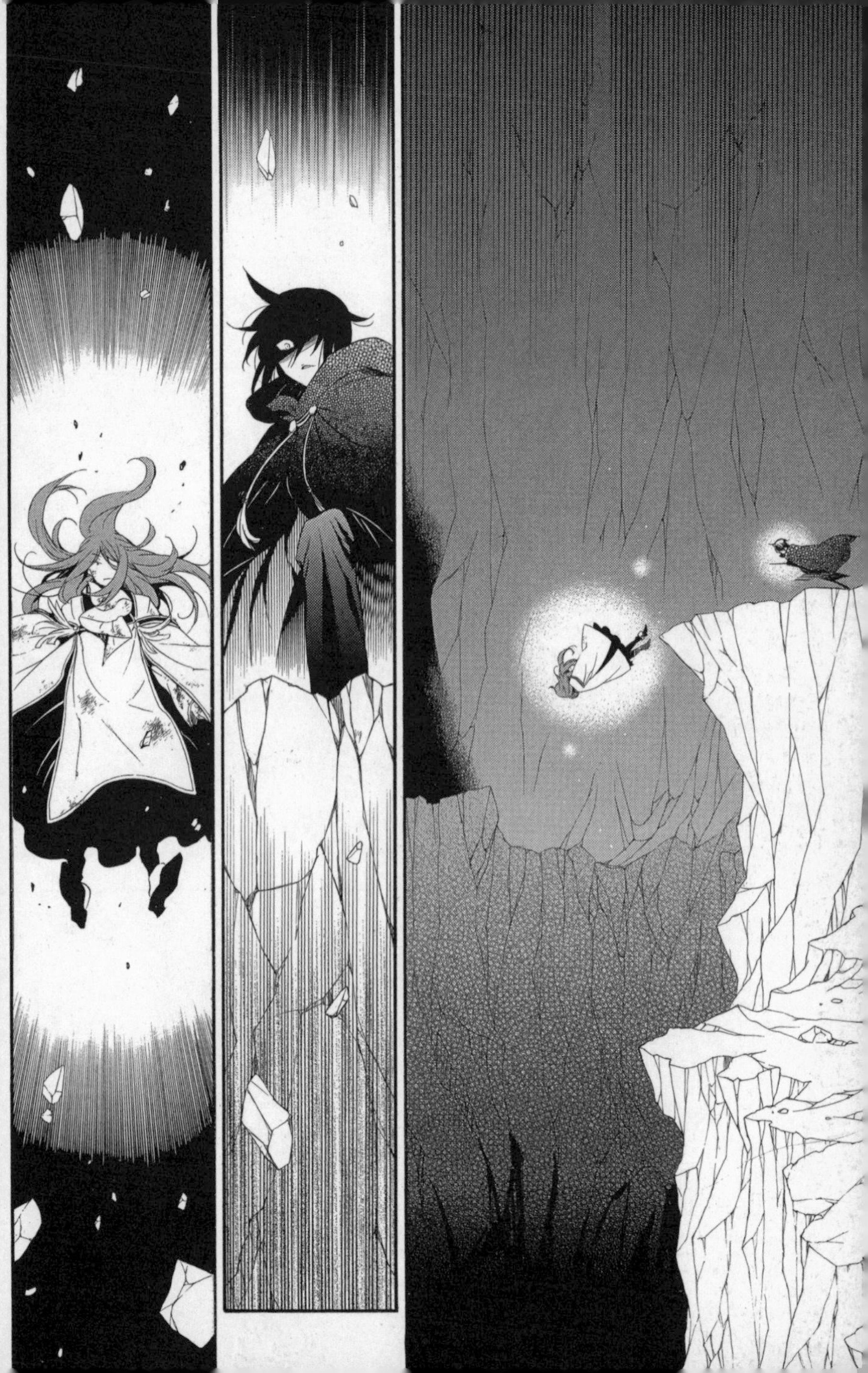

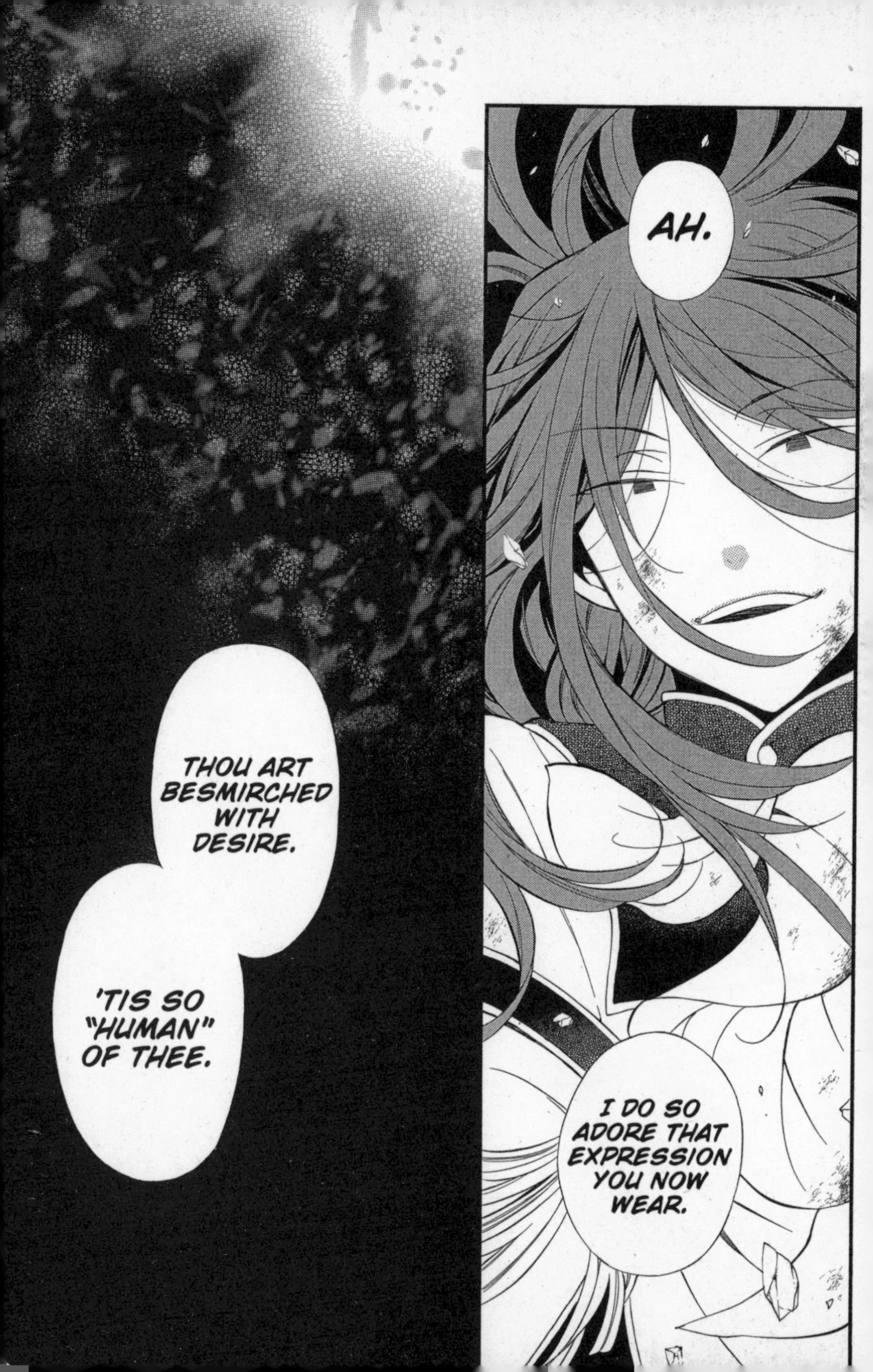
AH.
I DO SO ADORE THAT EXPRESSION YOU NOW WEAR.
THOU ART BESMIRCHED WITH DESIRE.
'TIS SO "HUMAN" OF THEE.

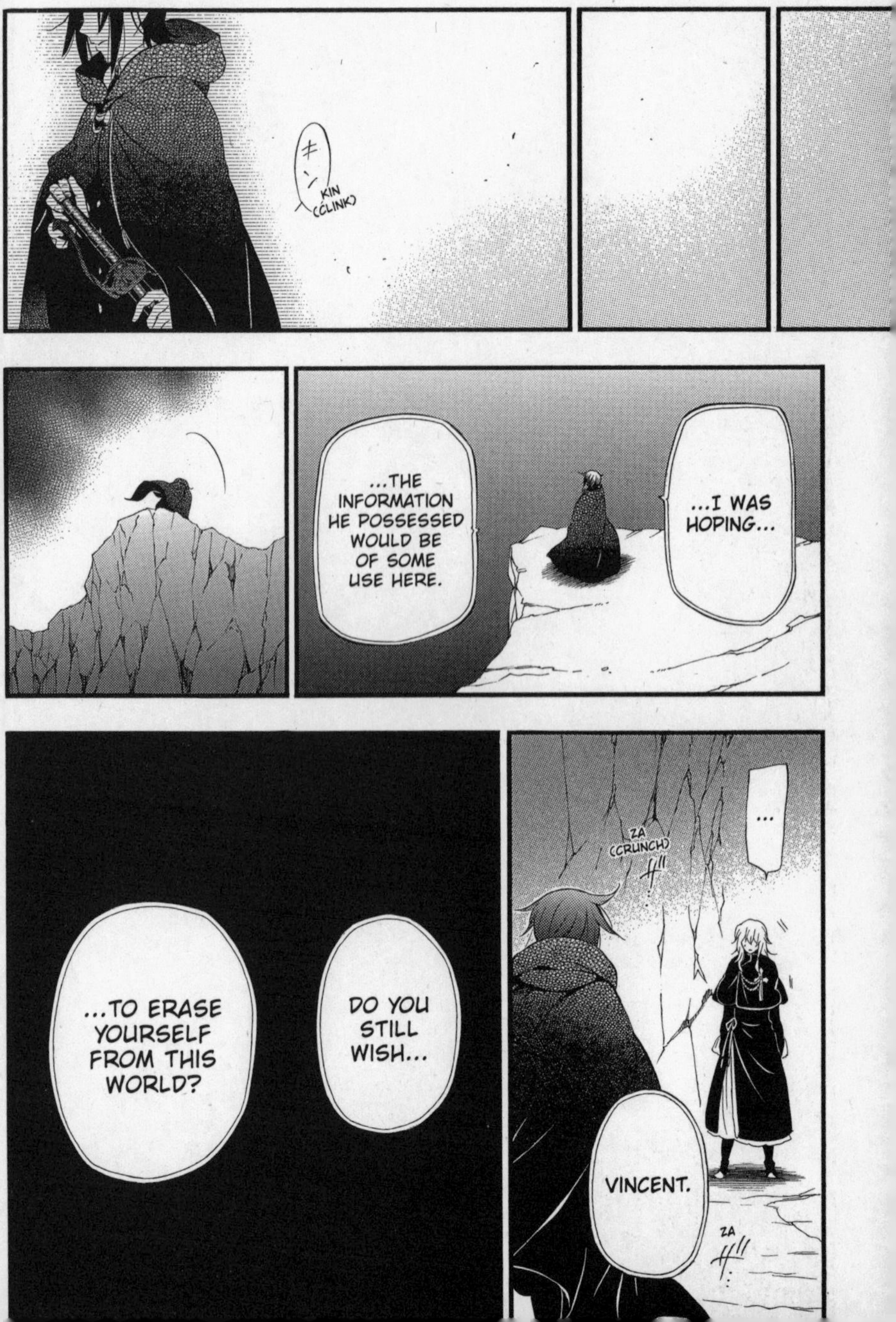
キン
KIN (CLINK)
...I WAS HOPING...
...THE INFORMATION HE POSSESSED WOULD BE OF SOME USE HERE.
...
ZA (CRUNCH)
VINCENT.
ZA
DO YOU STILL WISH...
...TO ERASE YOURSELF FROM THIS WORLD?

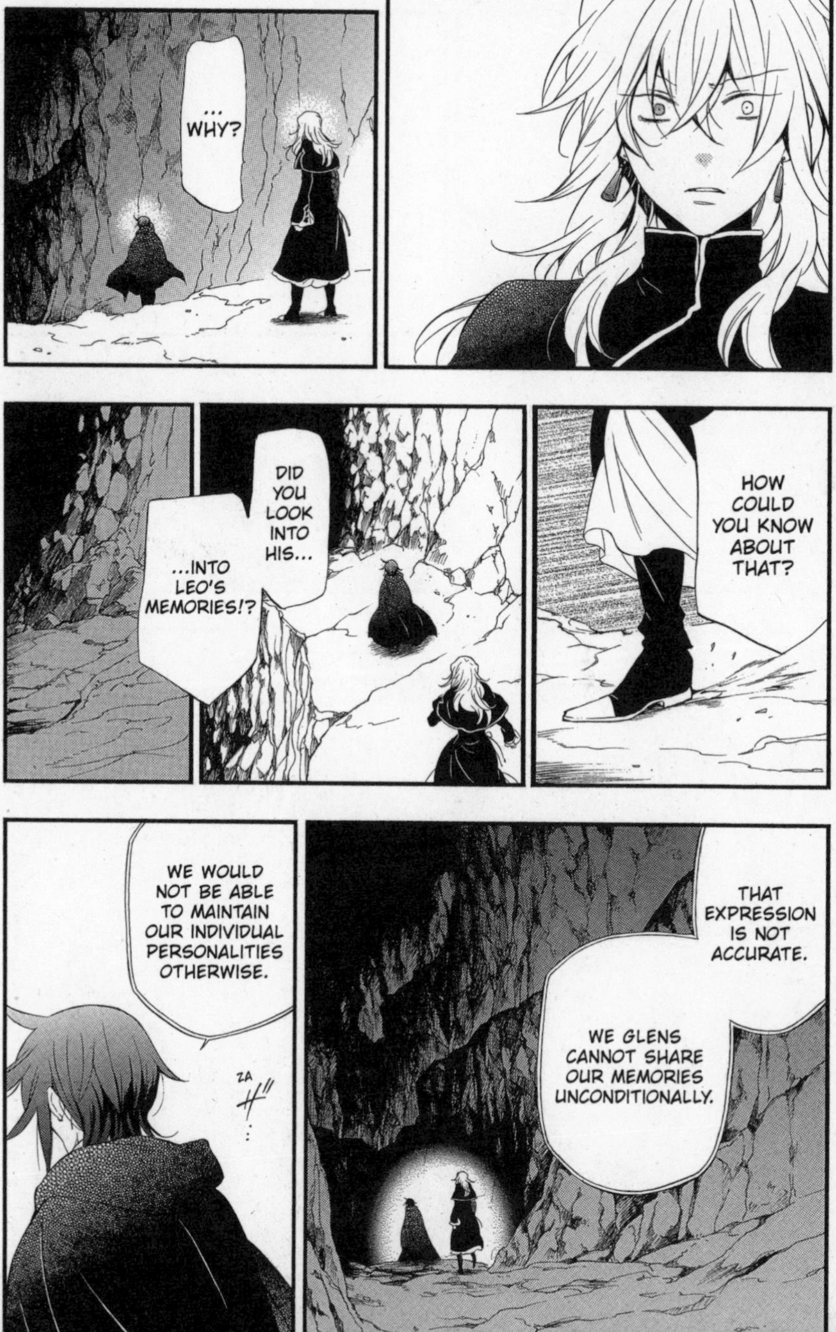
...WHY?
HOW COULD YOU KNOW ABOUT THAT?
DID YOU LOOK INTO HIS...
...INTO LEO'S MEMORIES!?
THAT EXPRESSION IS NOT ACCURATE.
WE GLENS CANNOT SHARE OUR MEMORIES UNCONDITIONALLY.
WE WOULD NOT BE ABLE TO MAINTAIN OUR INDIVIDUAL PERSONALITIES OTHERWISE.
ZA

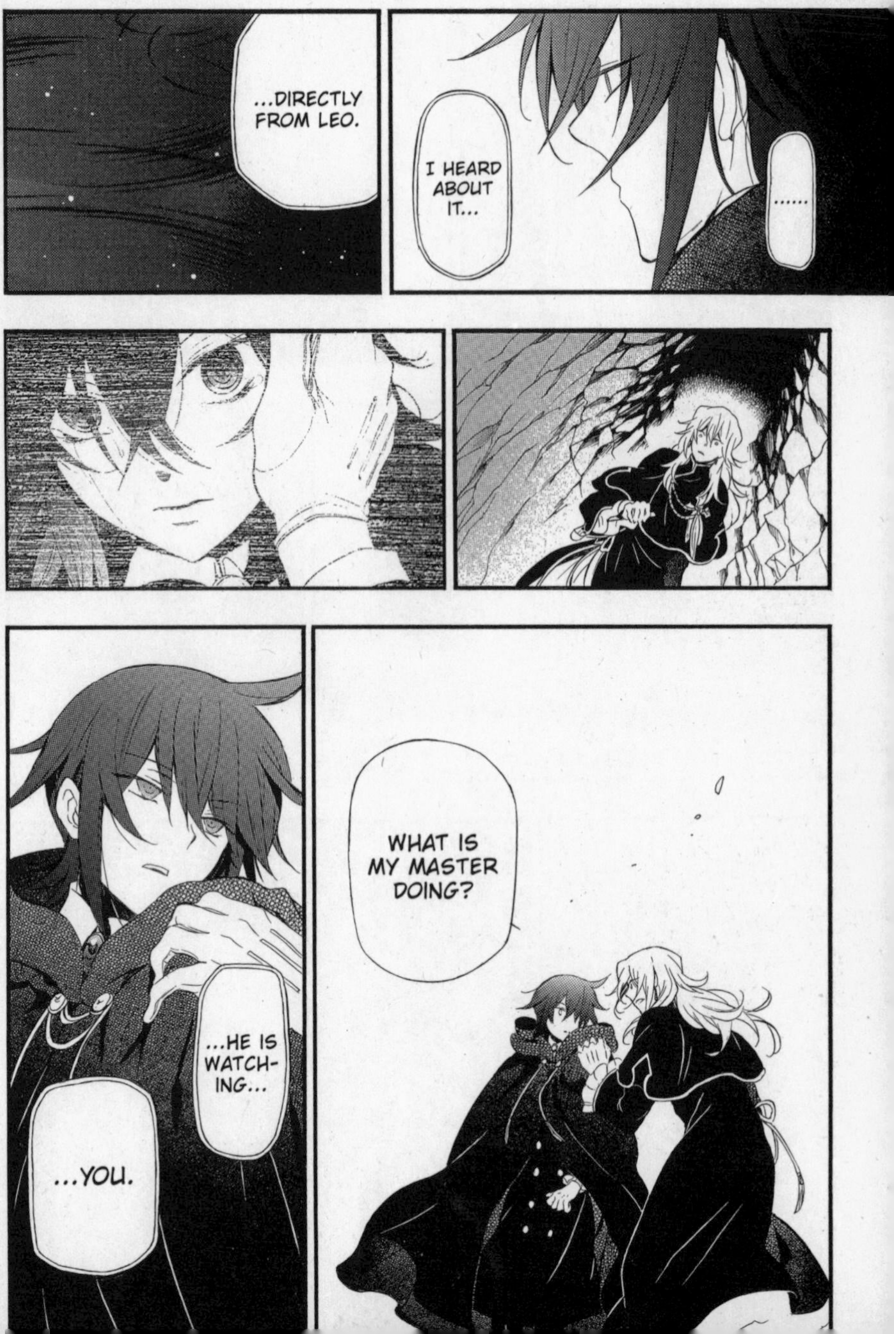
......
I HEARD ABOUT IT...
...DIRECTLY FROM LEO.
WHAT IS MY MASTER DOING?
...HE IS WATCHING...
...YOU.

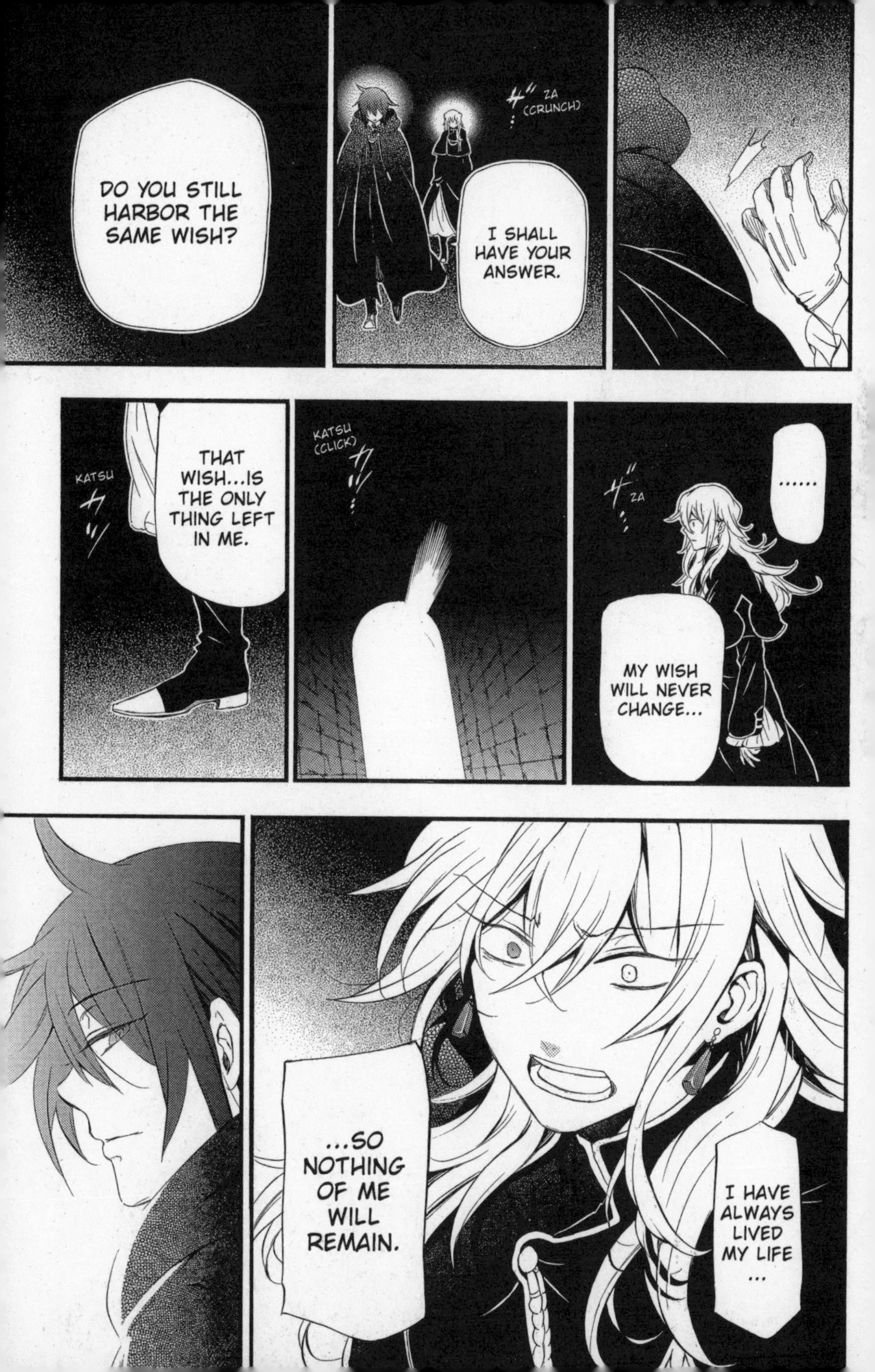
ZA (CRUNCH)
I SHALL HAVE YOUR ANSWER.
DO YOU STILL HARBOR THE SAME WISH?
......
ZA
MY WISH WILL NEVER CHANGE...
KATSU (CLICK)
KATSU
THAT WISH...IS THE ONLY THING LEFT IN ME.
I HAVE ALWAYS LIVED MY LIFE ...
...SO NOTHING OF ME WILL REMAIN.

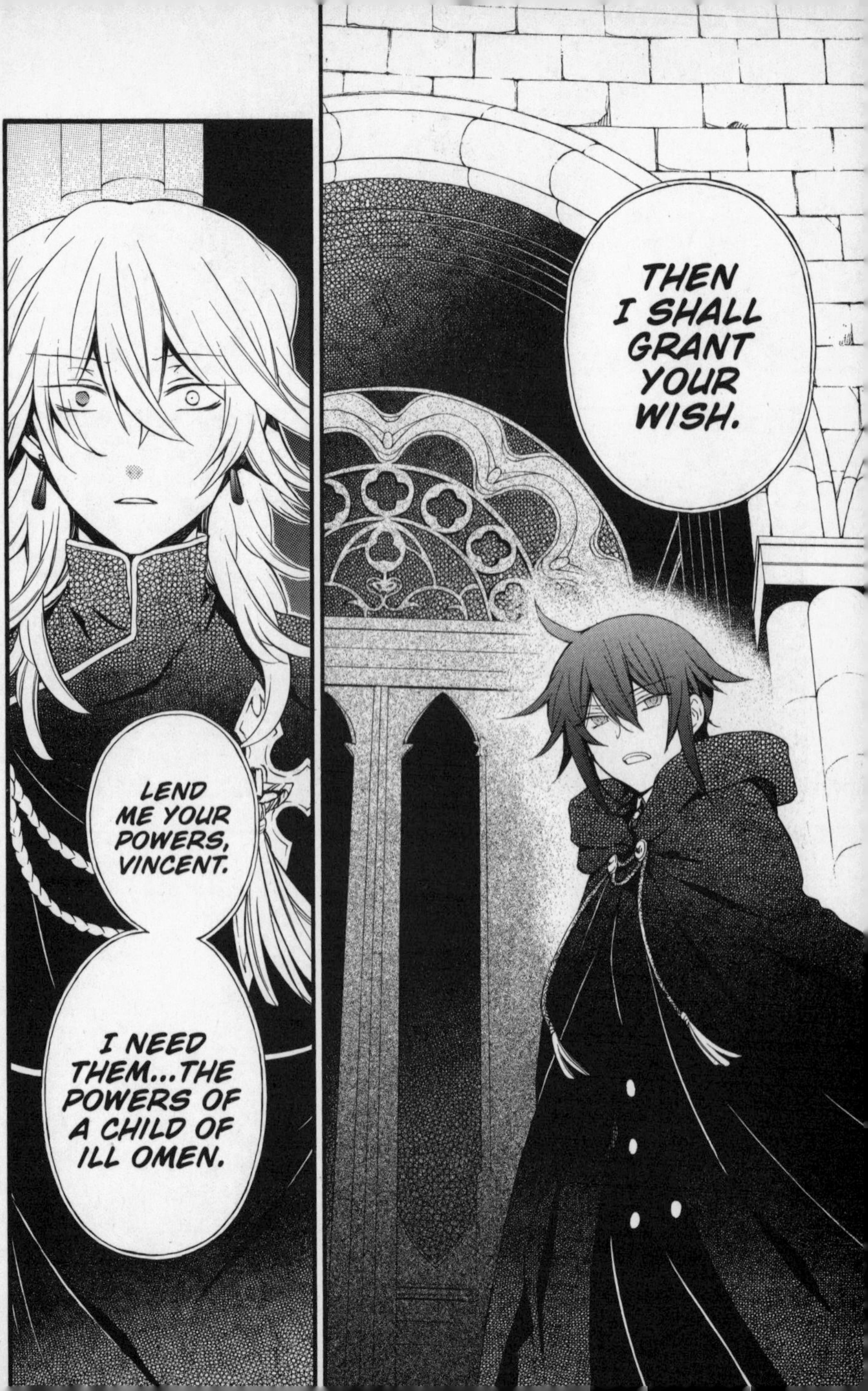
THEN I SHALL GRANT YOUR WISH.
LEND ME YOUR POWERS, VINCENT.
I NEED THEM...THE POWERS OF A CHILD OF ILL OMEN.

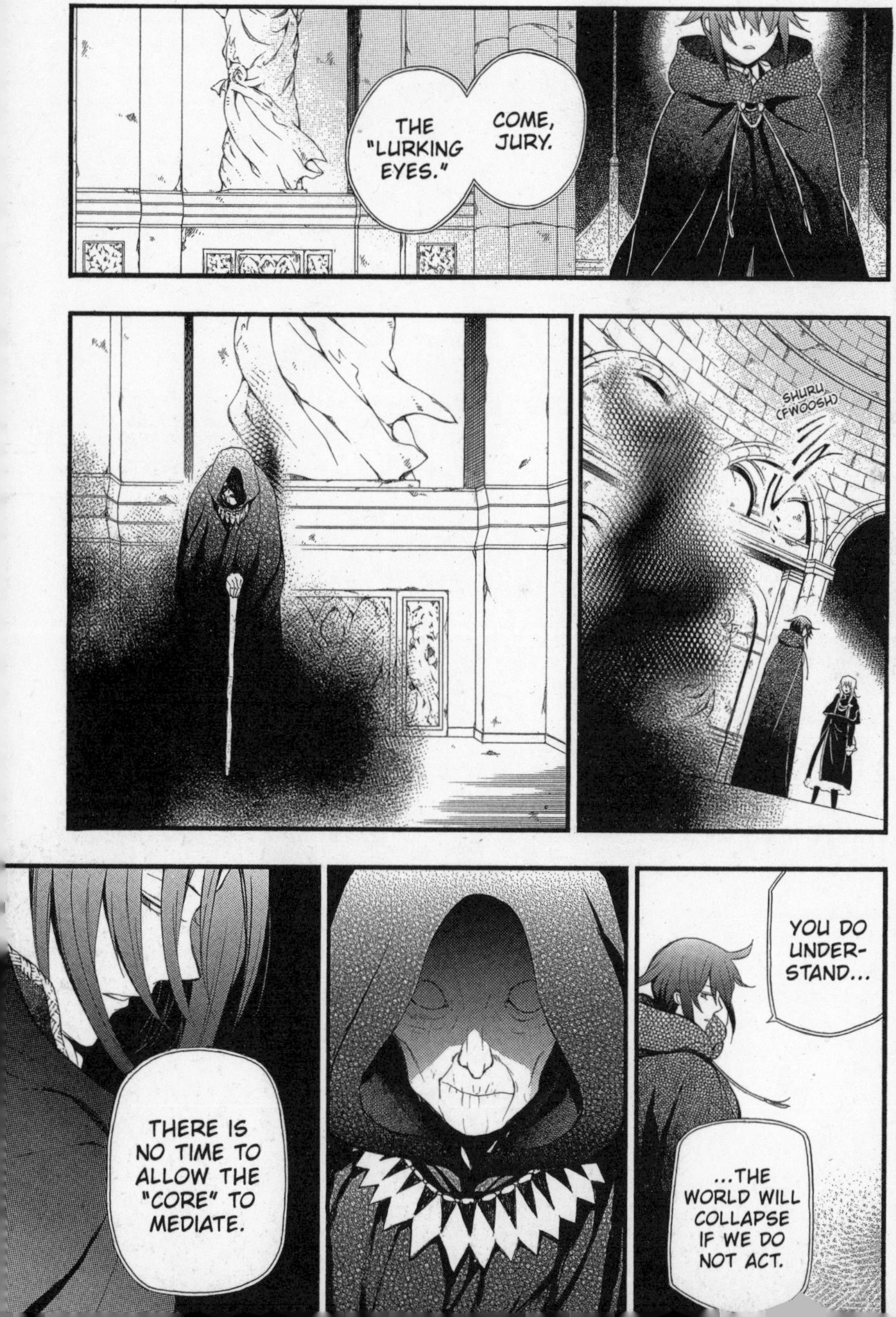
COME, JURY.
THE "LURKING EYES."
SHURU (FWOOSH)
YOU DO UNDER-STAND...
...THE WORLD WILL COLLAPSE IF WE DO NOT ACT.
THERE IS NO TIME TO ALLOW THE "CORE" TO MEDIATE.

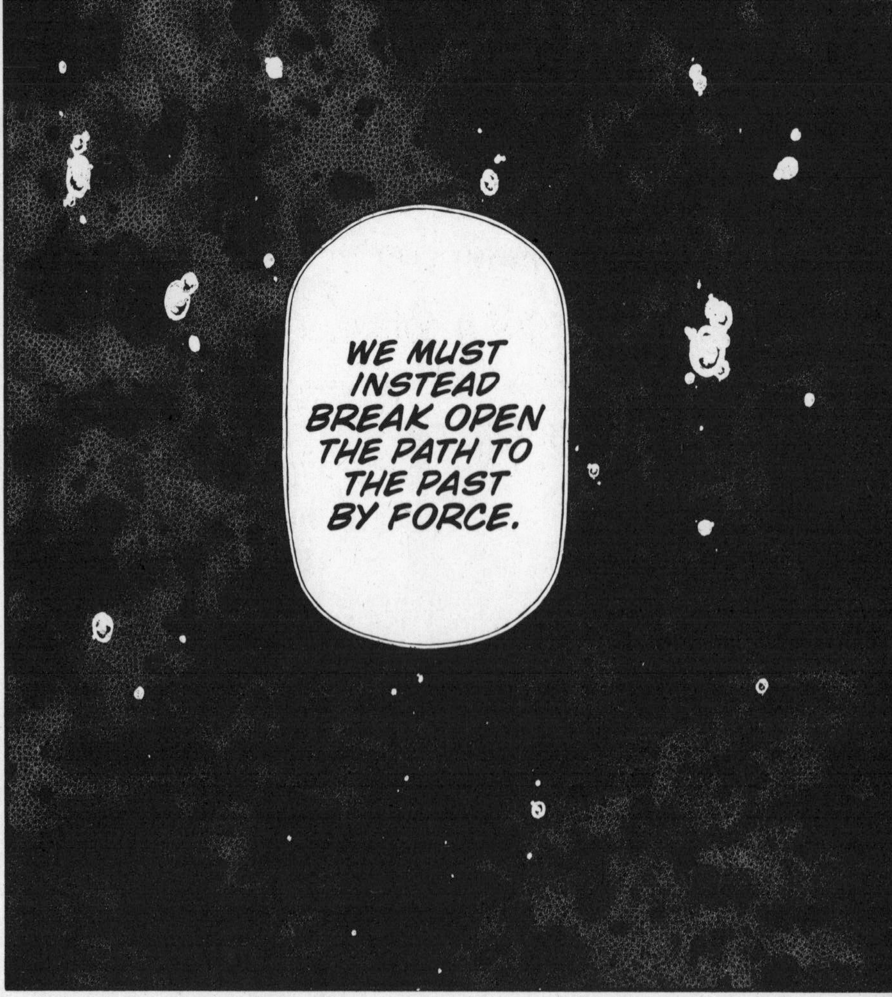
WE MUST INSTEAD BREAK OPEN THE PATH TO THE PAST BY FORCE.
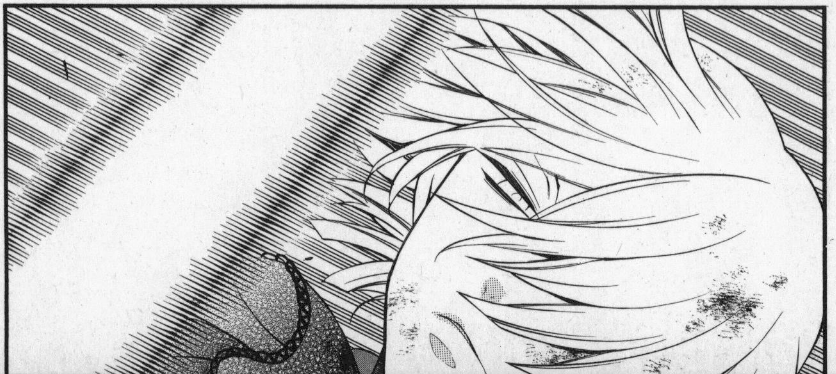

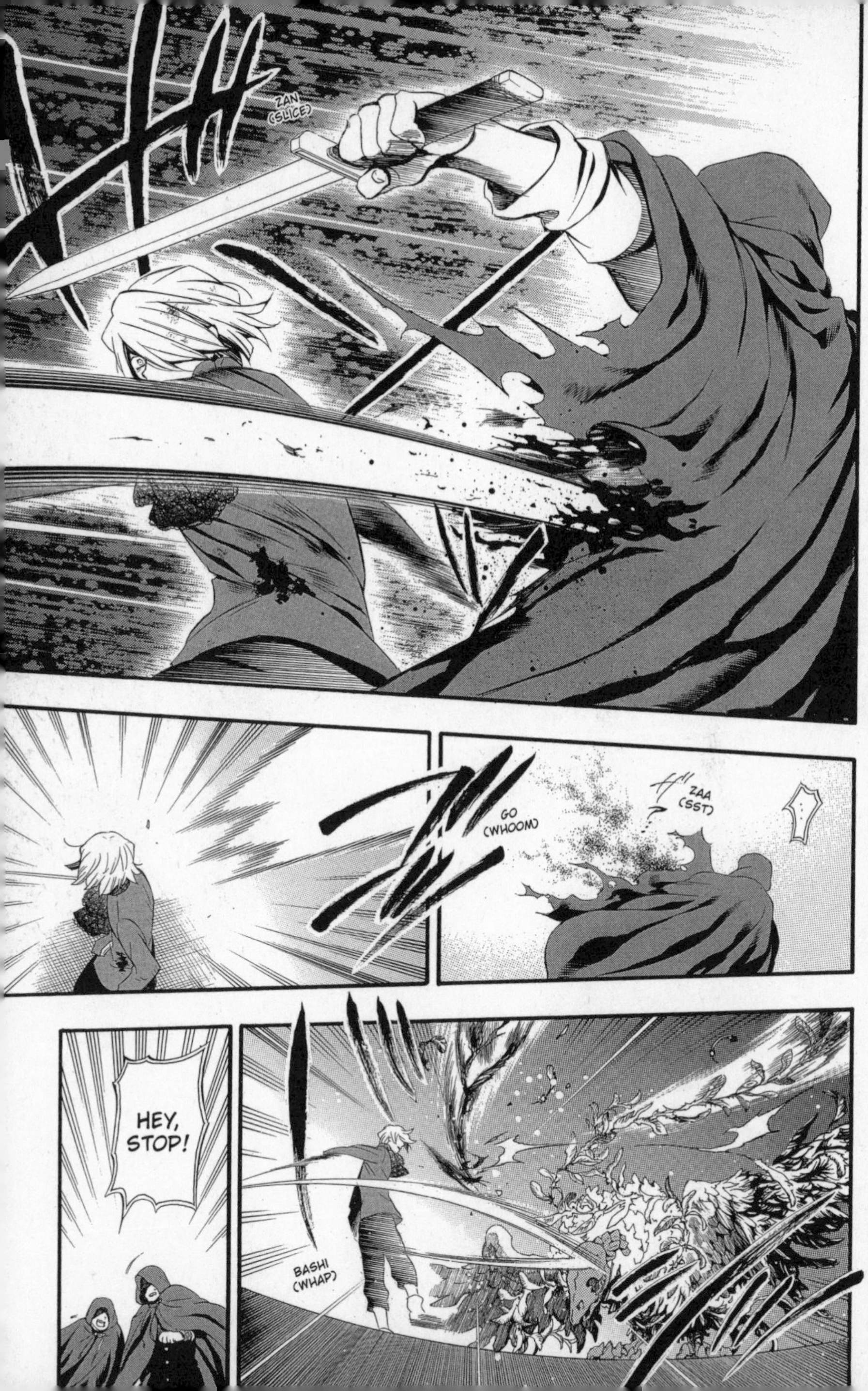
ZAN
(SLICE)
!
ZAA
(SST)
GO
(WHOOM)
BASHI
(WHAP)
HEY, STOP!

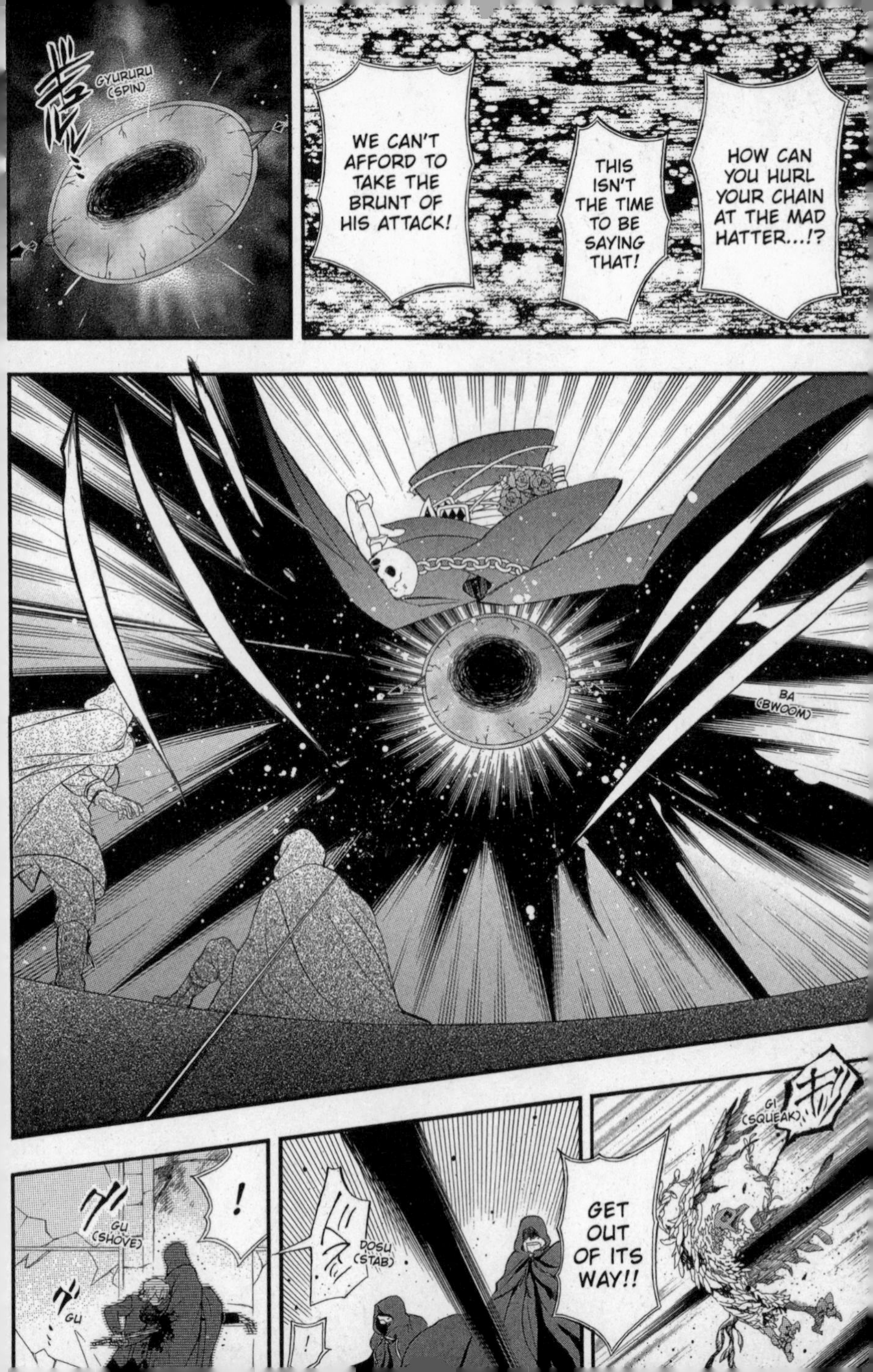
HOW CAN YOU HURL YOUR CHAIN AT THE MAD HATTER...!?
THIS ISN'T THE TIME TO BE SAYING THAT!
WE CAN'T AFFORD TO TAKE THE BRUNT OF HIS ATTACK!
GYURURU (SPIN)
BA (BWOOM)
GI (SQUEAK)
GET OUT OF ITS WAY!!
DOSU (STAB)
!
GU (SHOVE)
GU

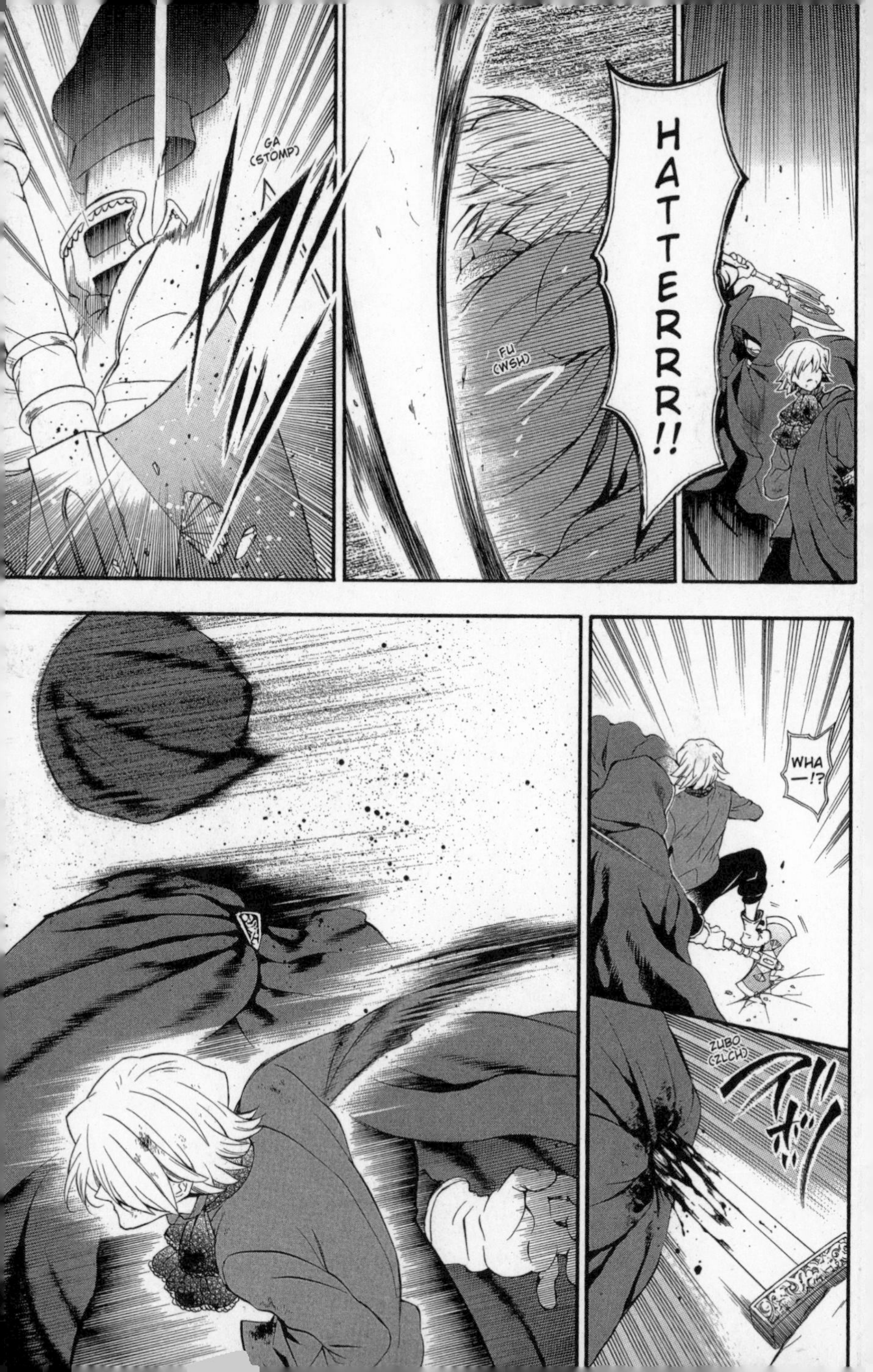
HATTERRR!!
FU (WSH)
GA (STOMP)
WHA—!?
ZUBO (ZLCH)

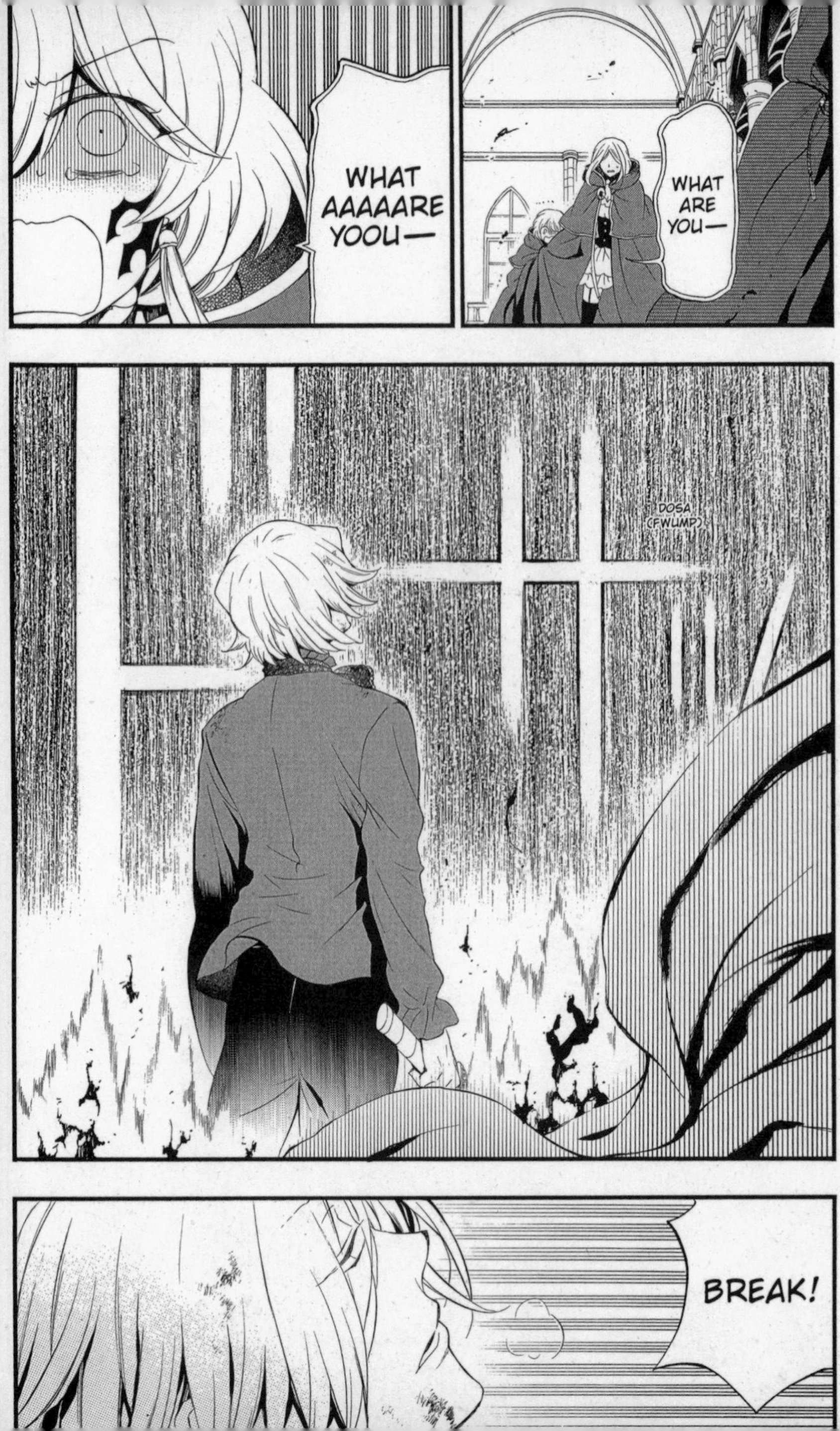
WHAT ARE YOU—
WHAT AAAAARE YOOU—
DOSA (FWUMP)
BREAK!

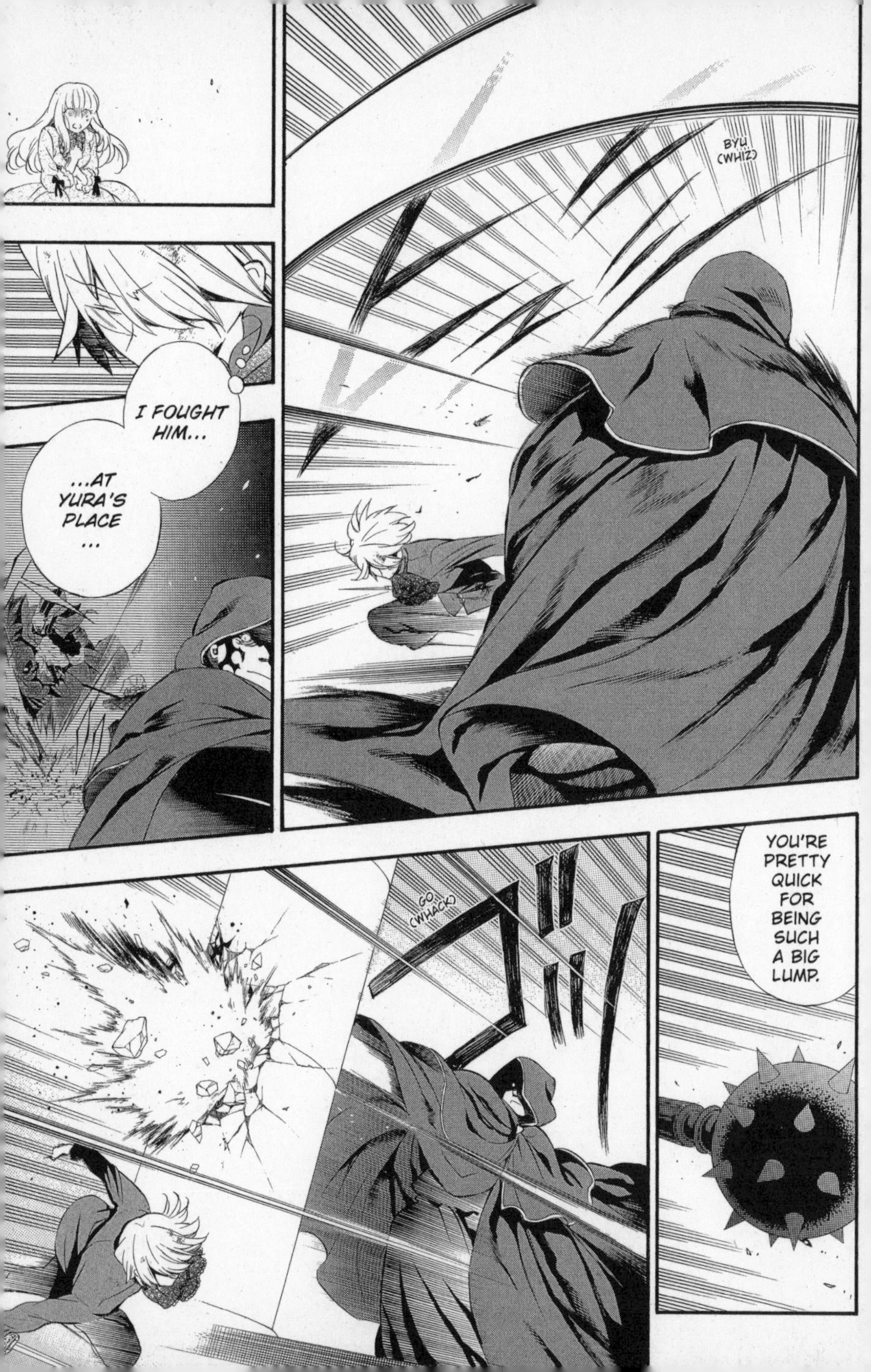
BYU
(WHIZ)
I FOUGHT HIM...
...AT YURA'S PLACE ...
YOU'RE PRETTY QUICK FOR BEING SUCH A BIG LUMP.
GO
(WHACK)

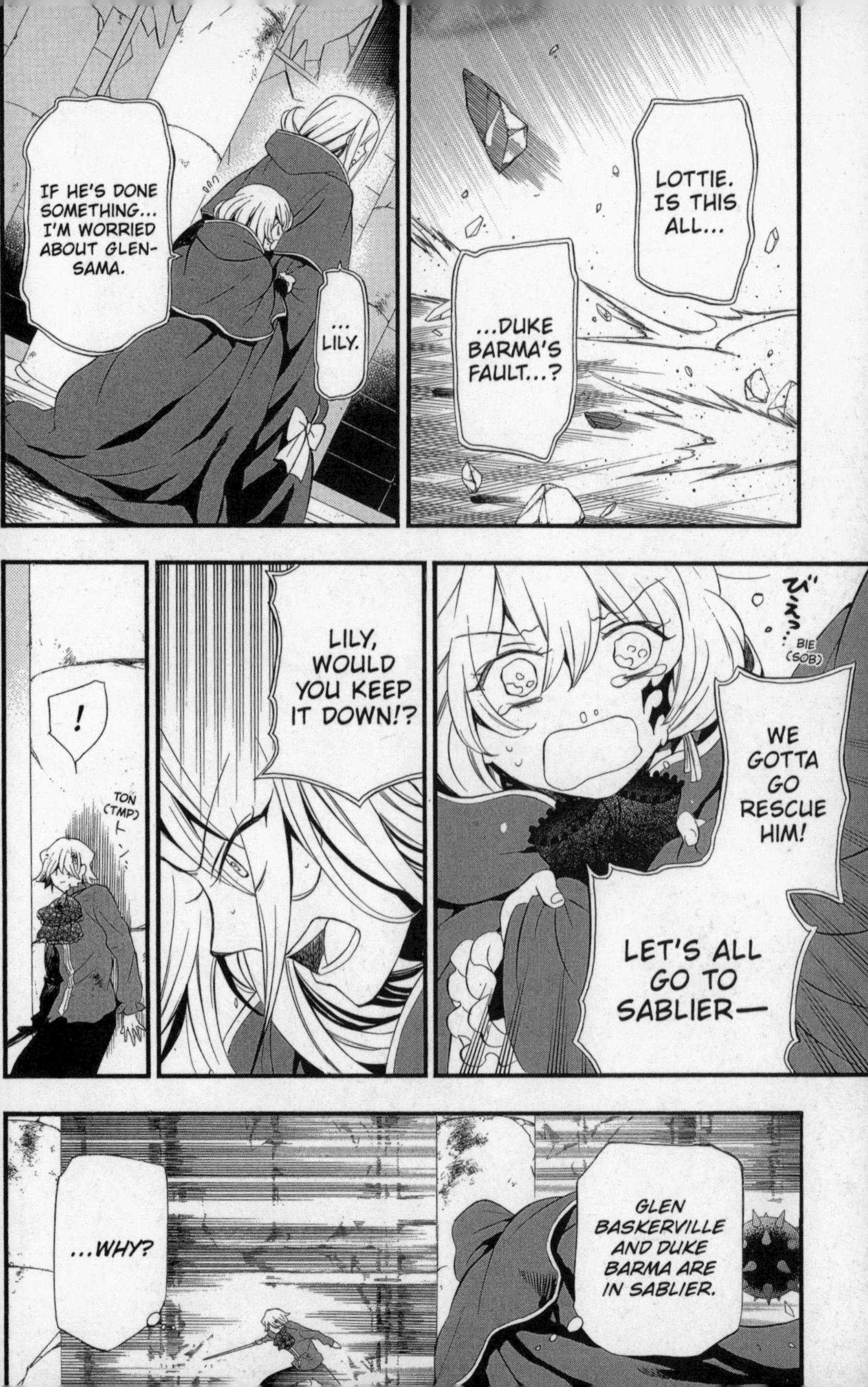
LOTTIE. IS THIS ALL...
...DUKE BARMA'S FAULT...?
IF HE'S DONE SOMETHING... I'M WORRIED ABOUT GLEN-SAMA.
... LILY.
びえっ
BIE (SOB)
WE GOTTA GO RESCUE HIM!
LET'S ALL GO TO SABLIER—
LILY, WOULD YOU KEEP IT DOWN!?
!
TON (TMP)
GLEN BASKERVILLE AND DUKE BARMA ARE IN SABLIER.
...WHY?

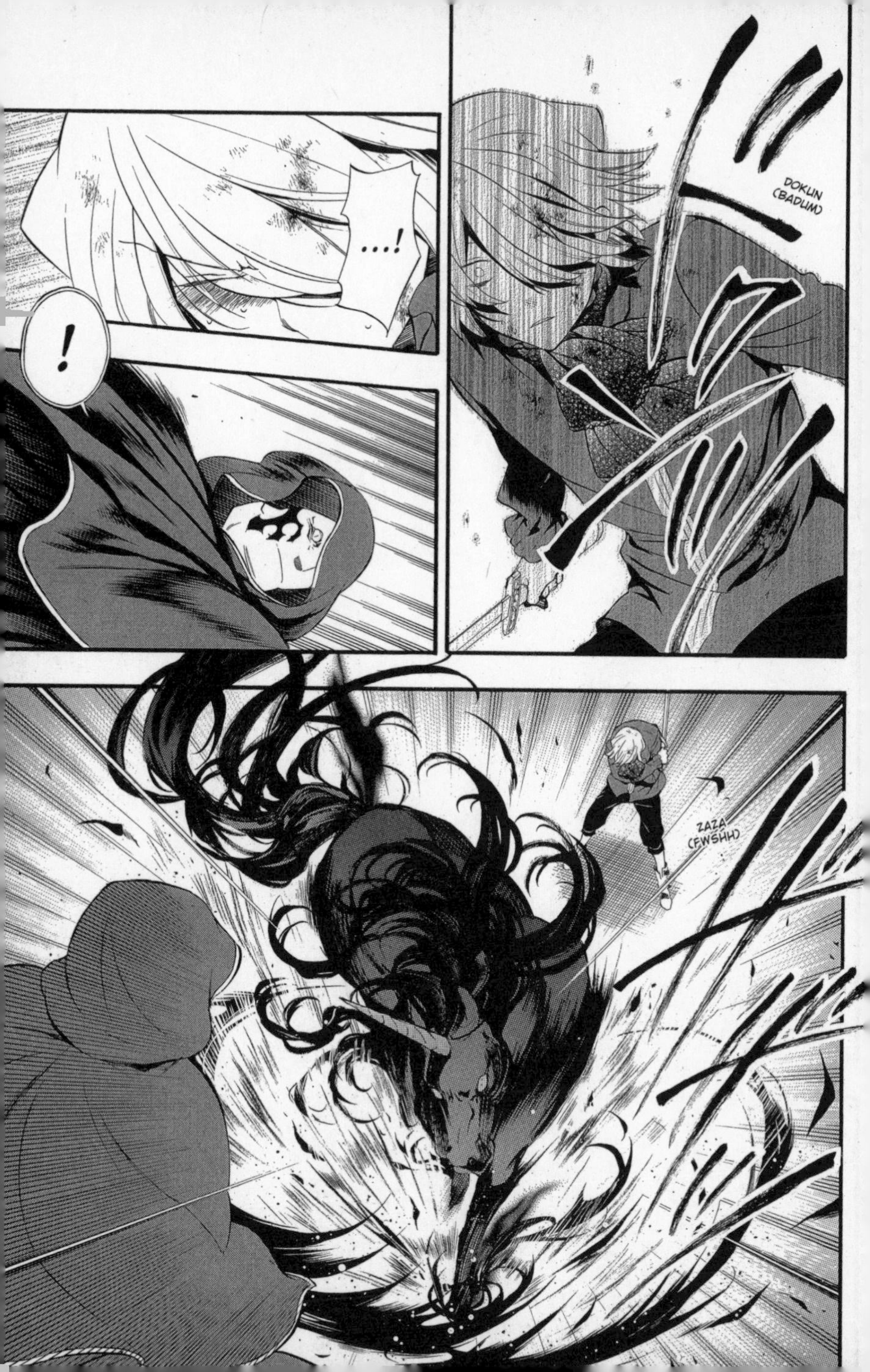
DOKUN
(BADUM)
...!
!
ZAZA
(FWSHH)

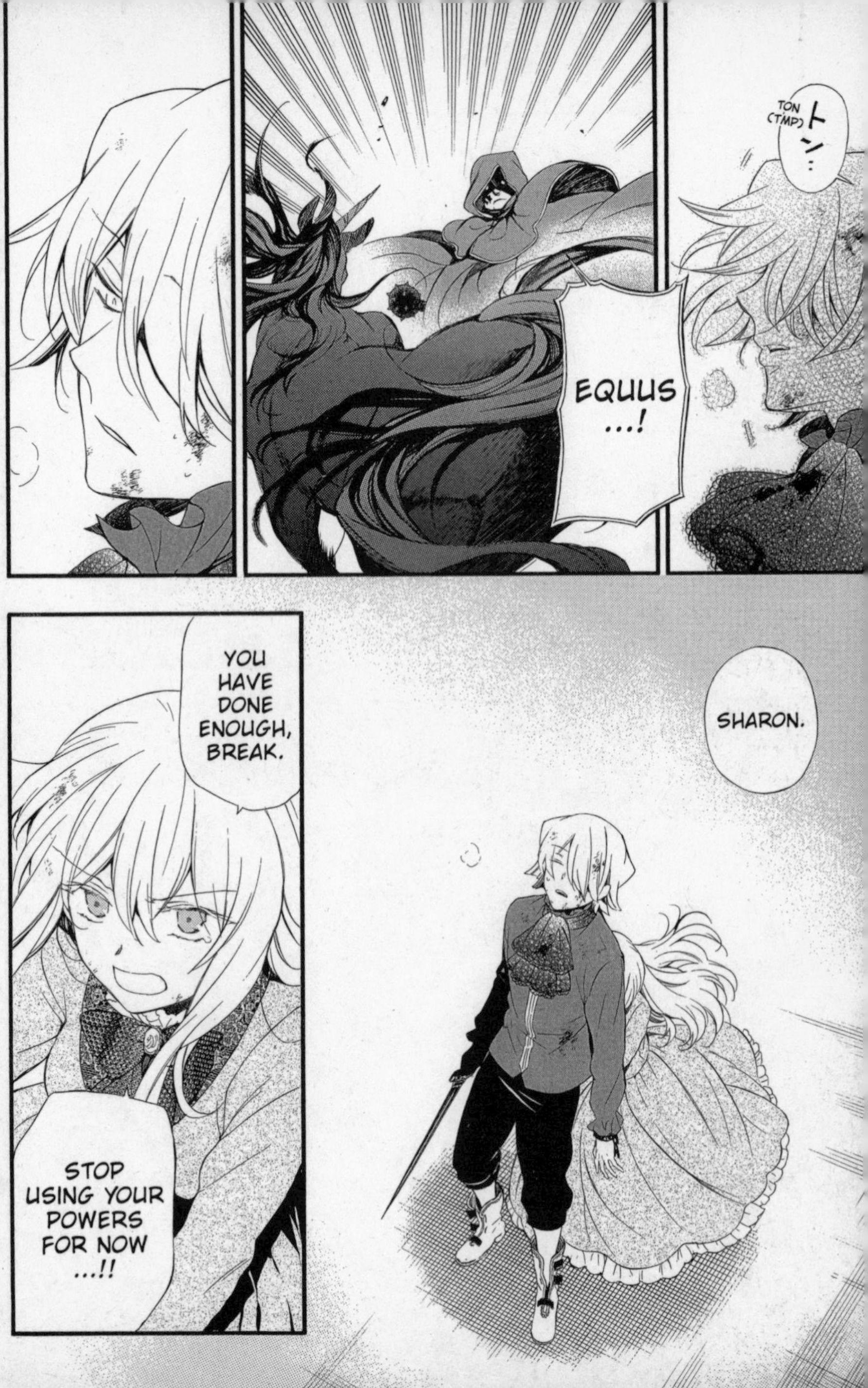
TON (TMP)
トン…
EQUUS …!
SHARON.
YOU HAVE DONE ENOUGH, BREAK.
STOP USING YOUR POWERS FOR NOW …!!

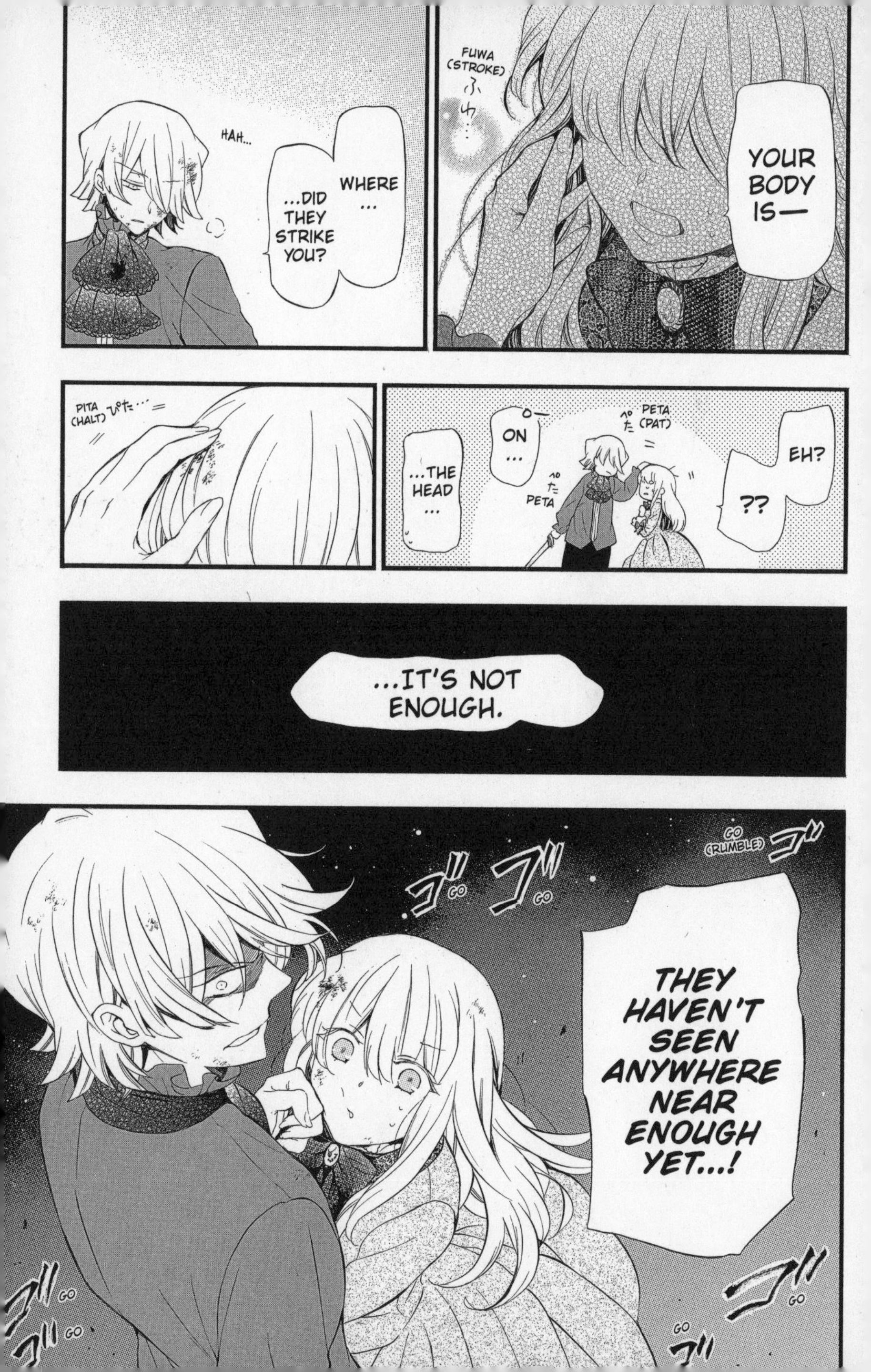
FUWA (STROKE) ふわ…
YOUR BODY IS—
HAH…
WHERE …
…DID THEY STRIKE YOU?
EH?
??
PETA (PAT)
ON …
…THE HEAD …
PETA
PITA (HALT) ぴた…
…IT'S NOT ENOUGH.
GO (RUMBLE)
GO
GO
THEY HAVEN'T SEEN ANYWHERE NEAR ENOUGH YET…!
GO
GO
GO
GO

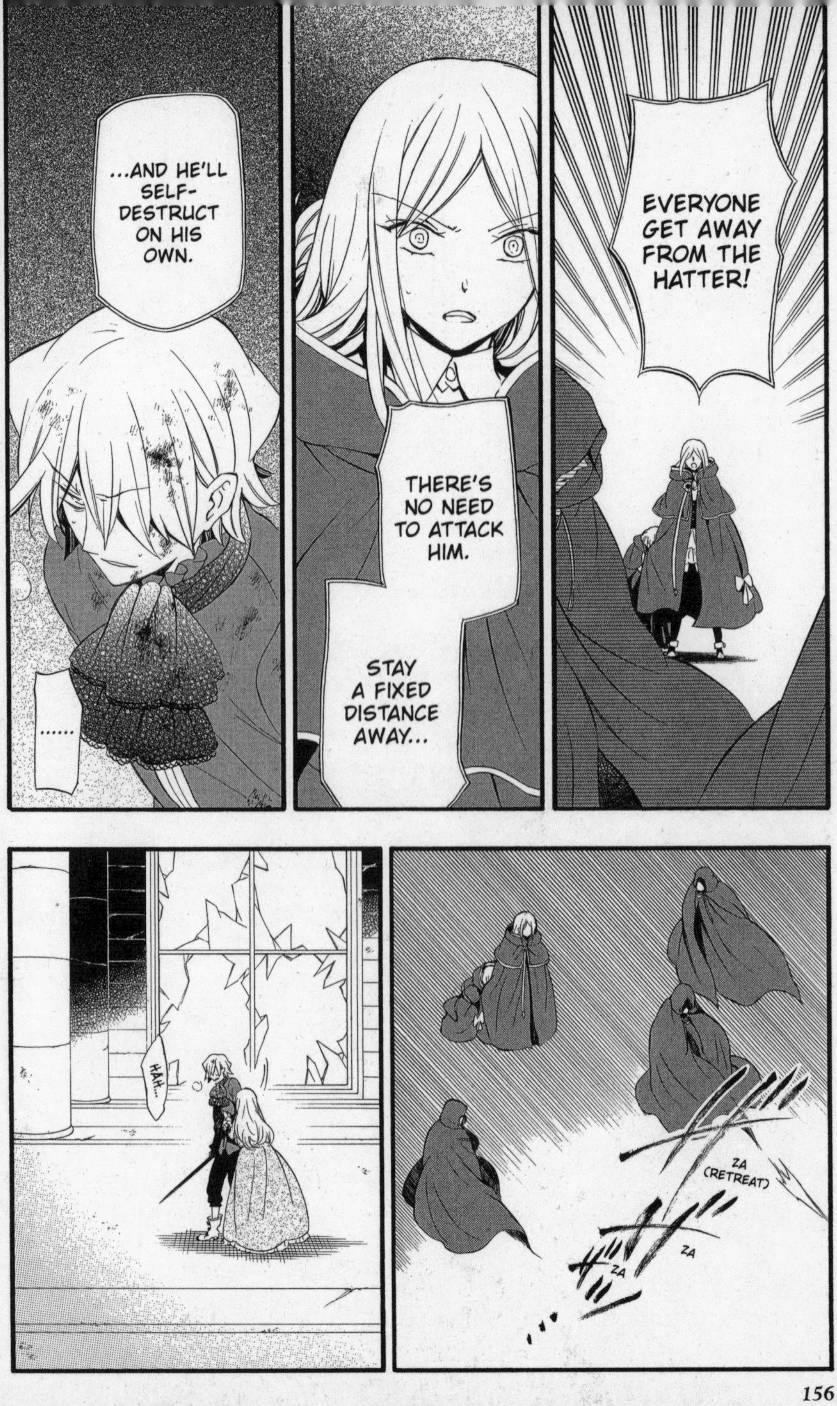
EVERYONE GET AWAY FROM THE HATTER!
THERE'S NO NEED TO ATTACK HIM.
STAY A FIXED DISTANCE AWAY...
...AND HE'LL SELF-DESTRUCT ON HIS OWN.
......
ZA (RETREAT)
ZA
ZA
HAH...

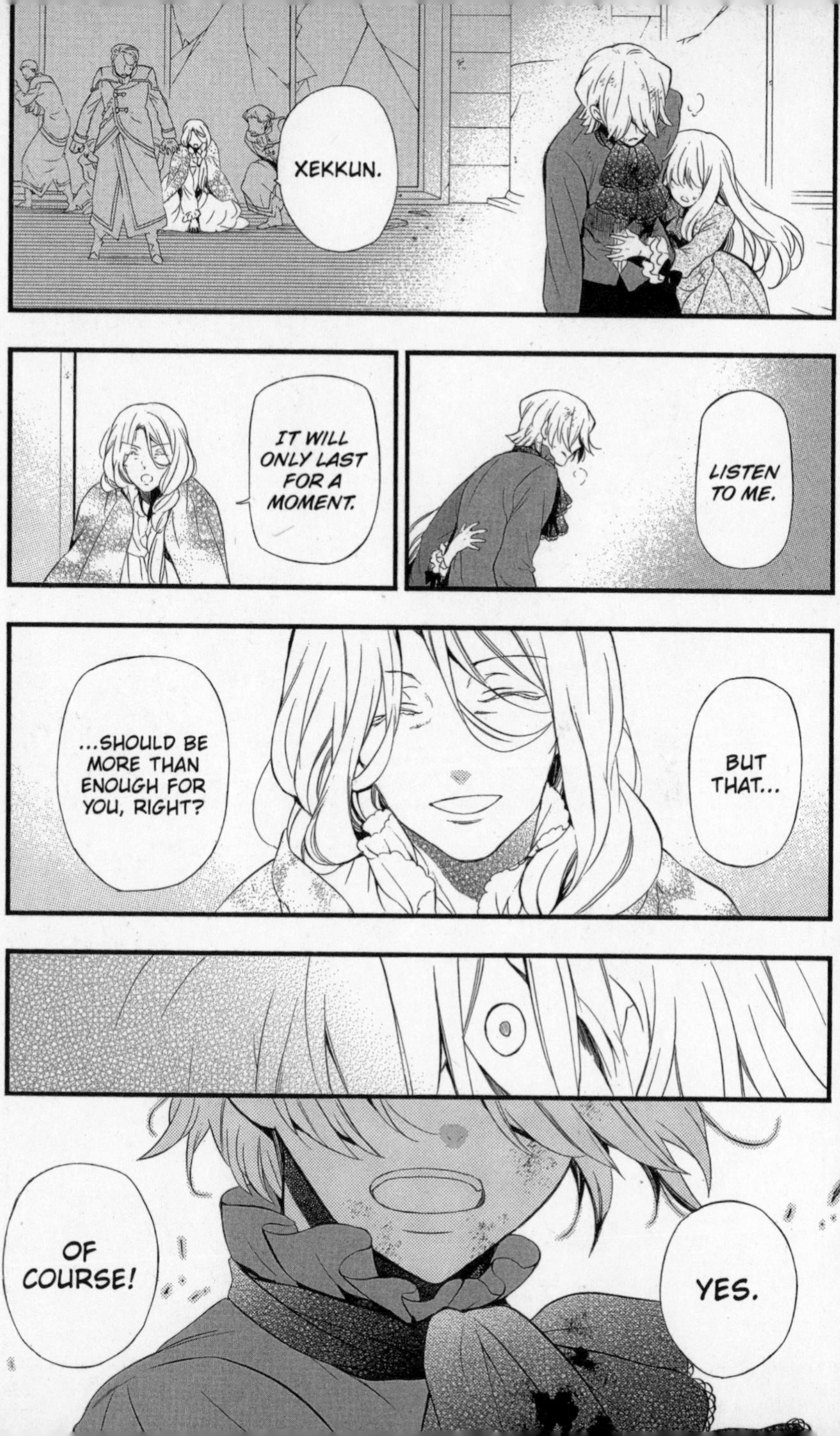
XEKKUN.
LISTEN TO ME.
IT WILL ONLY LAST FOR A MOMENT.
BUT THAT...
...SHOULD BE MORE THAN ENOUGH FOR YOU, RIGHT?
YES.
OF COURSE!

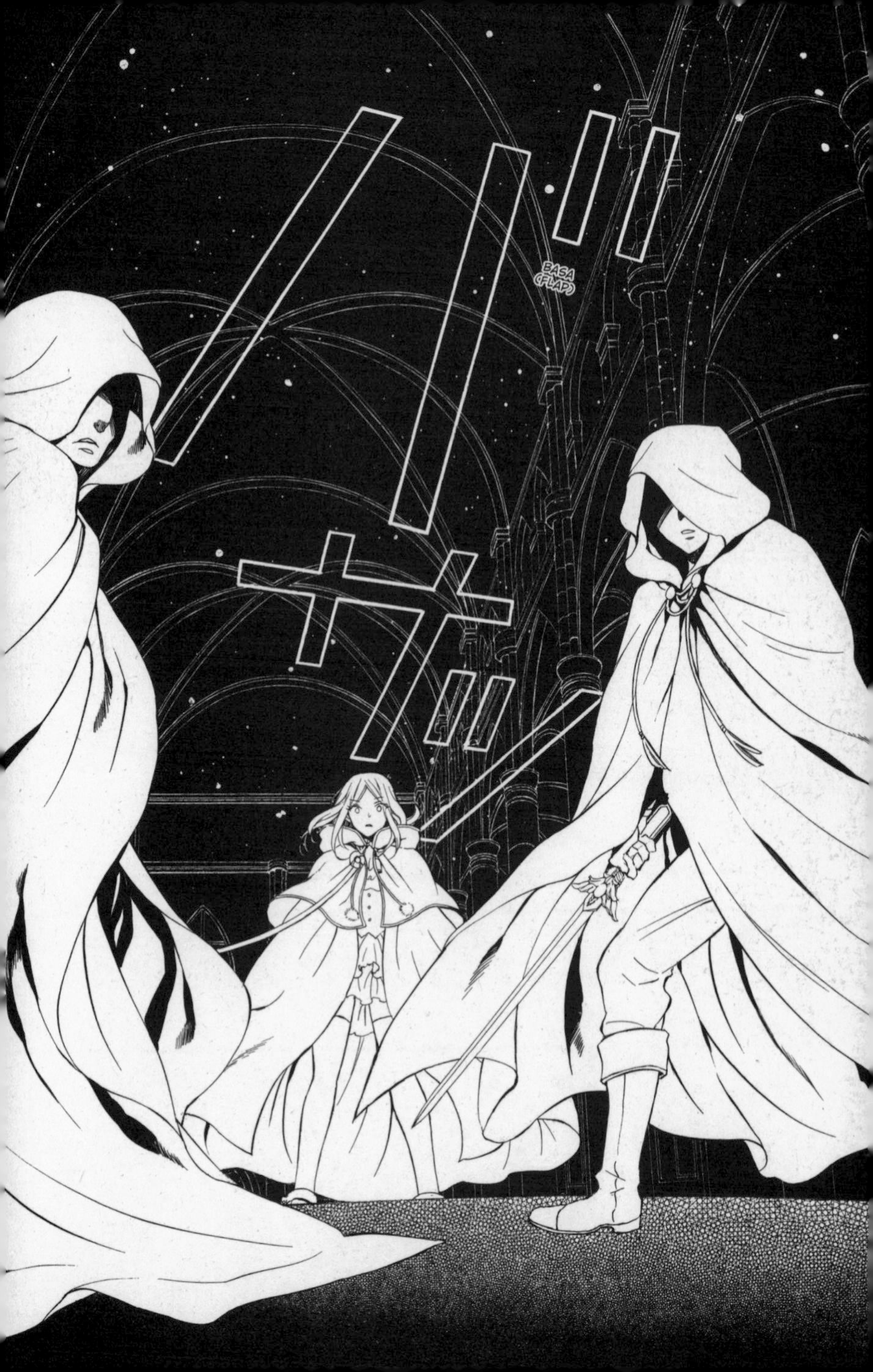
BASA (FLAP)

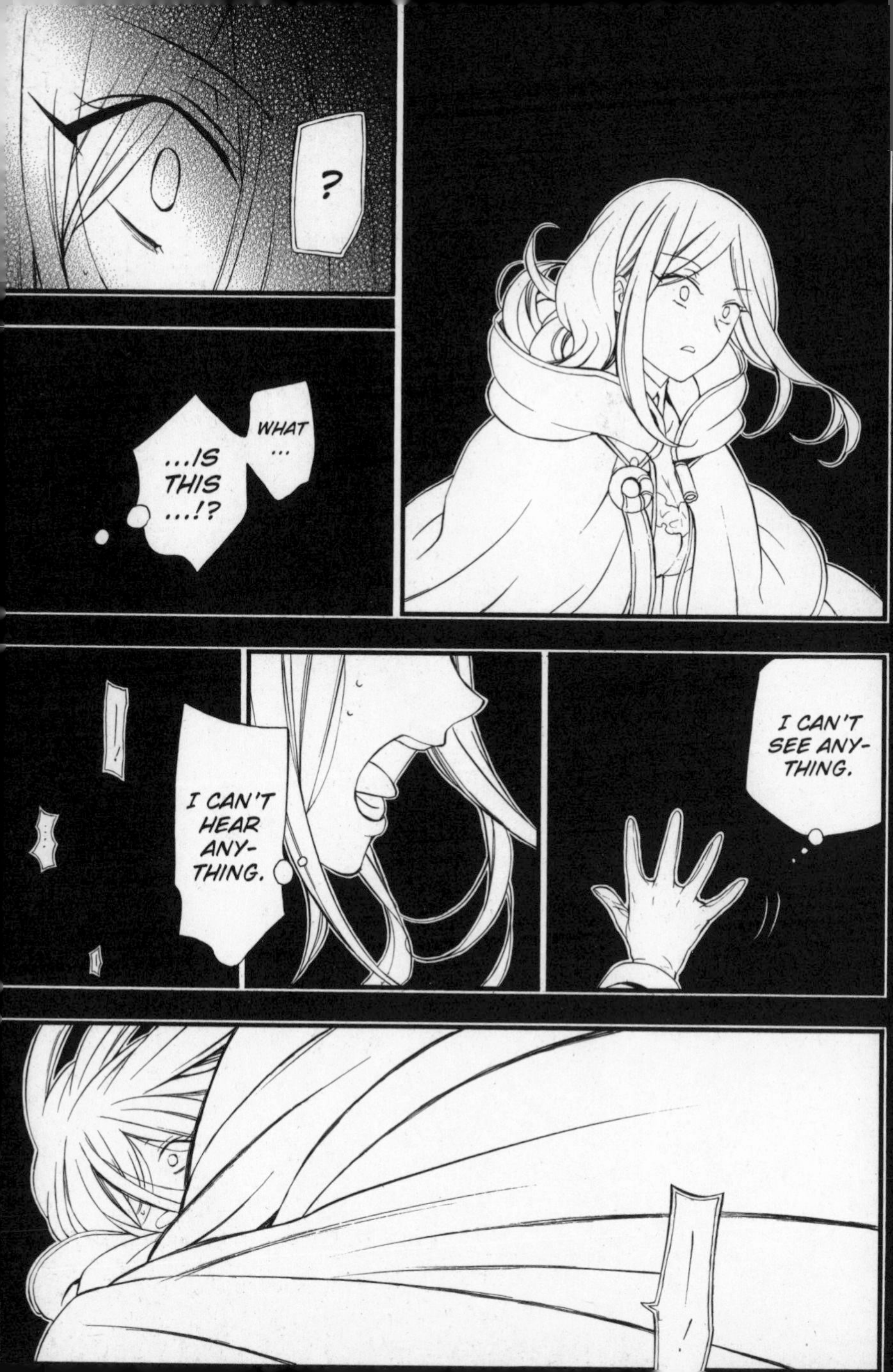
?
WHAT ...
...IS THIS ...!?
I CAN'T SEE ANY-THING.
I CAN'T HEAR ANY-THING.
!
...
!

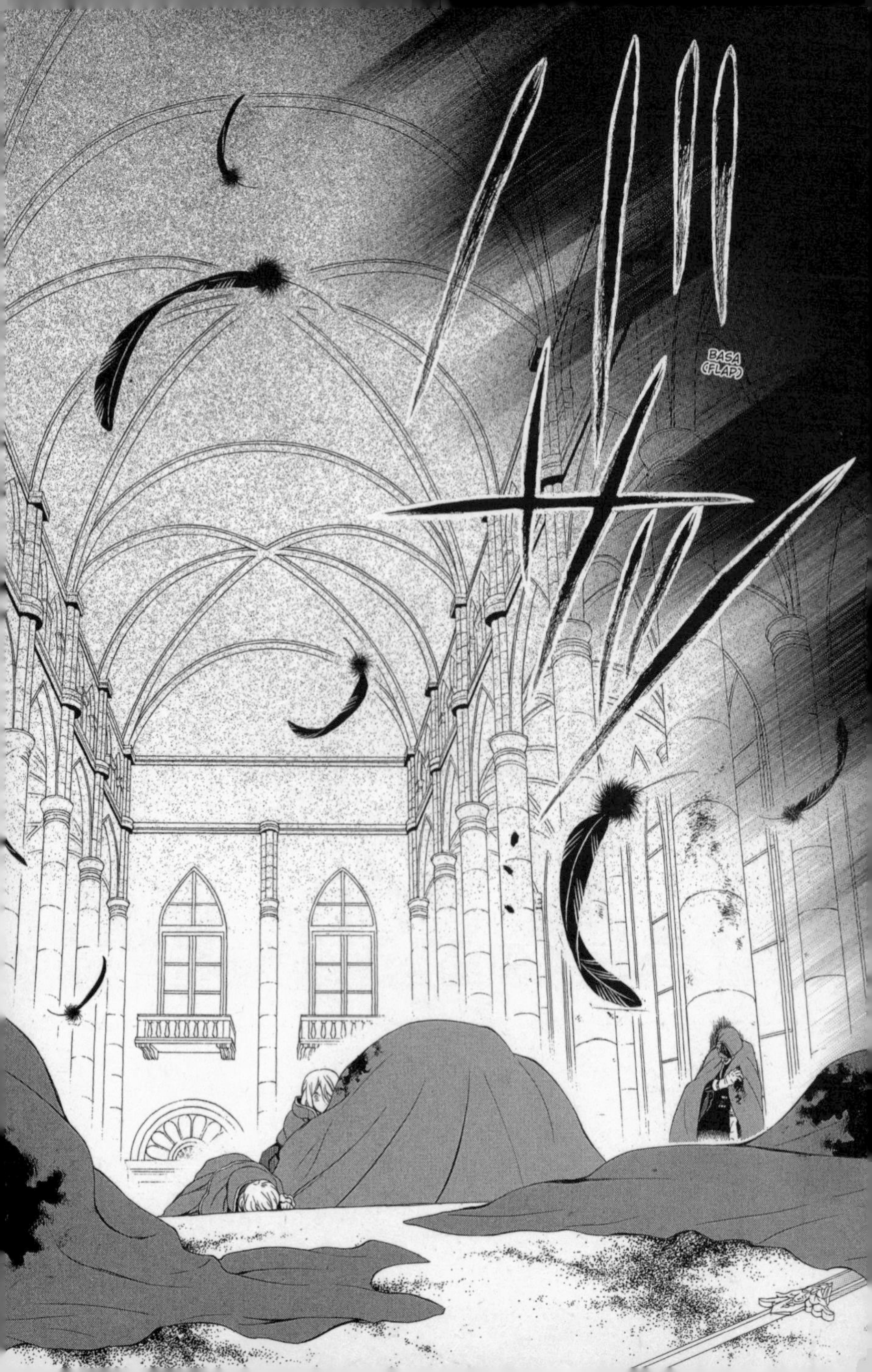
BASA
(FLAP)

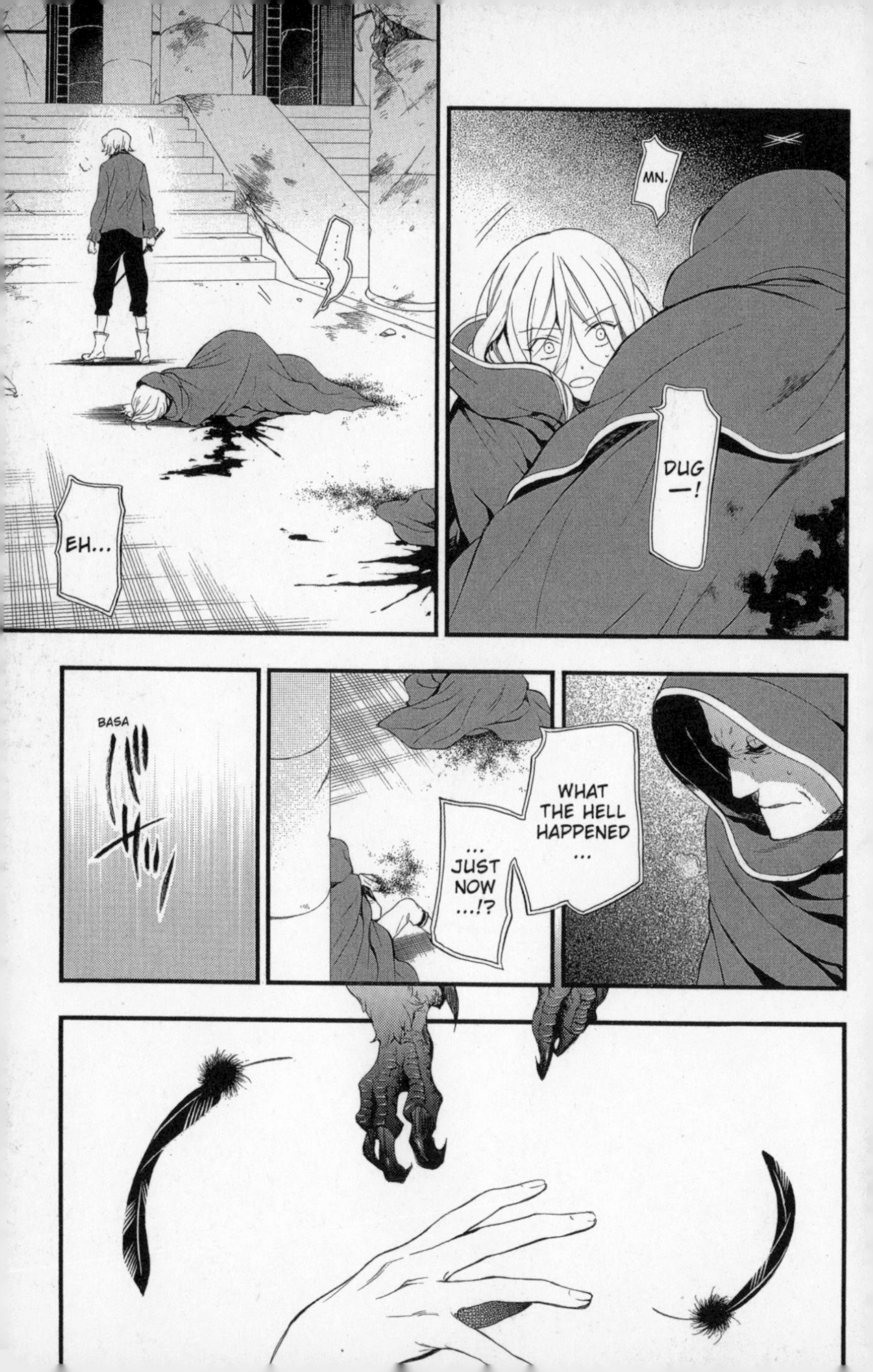
MN.
DUG—!
...
EH...
WHAT THE HELL HAPPENED ...
... JUST NOW ...!?
BASA

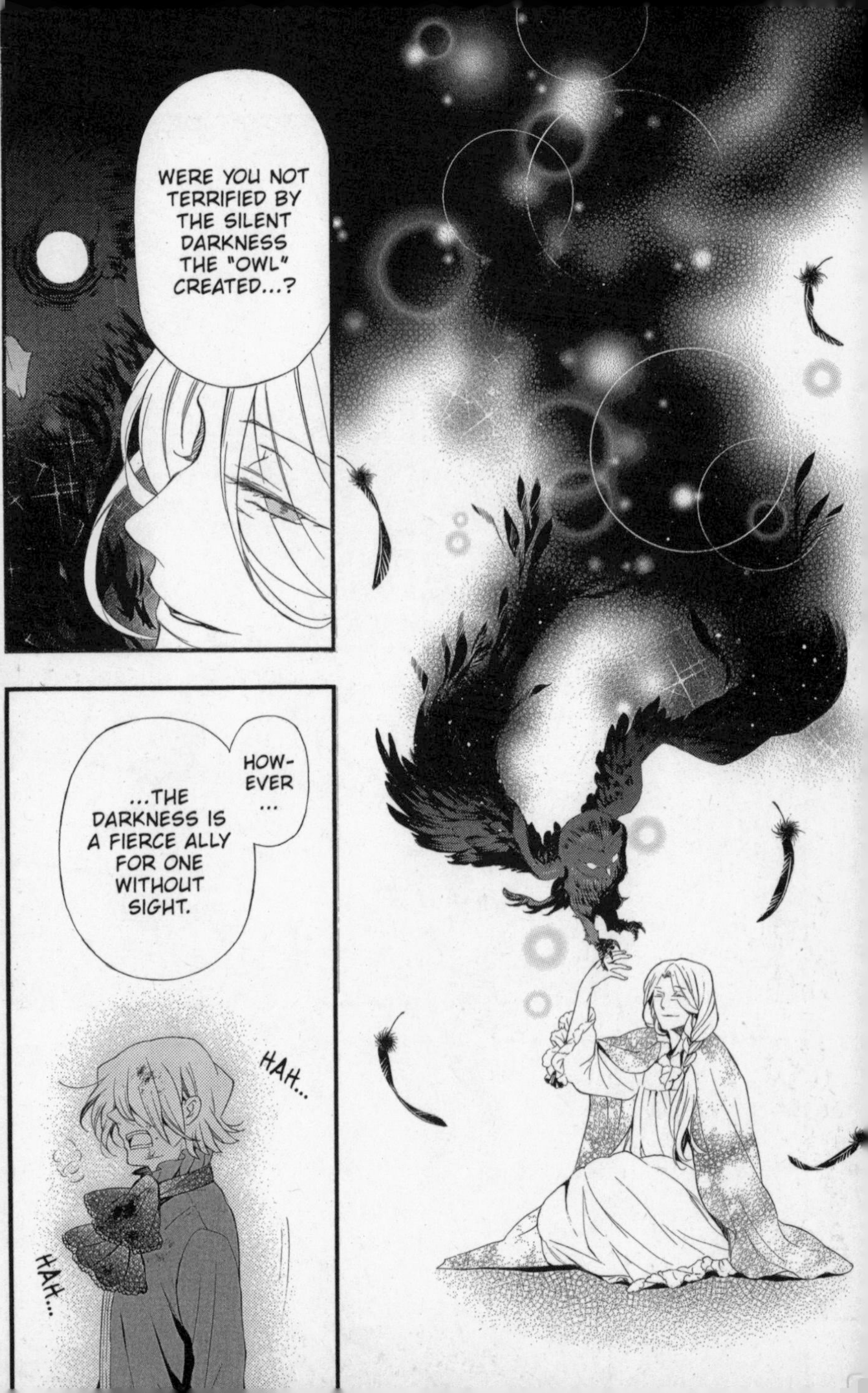
WERE YOU NOT TERRIFIED BY THE SILENT DARKNESS THE "OWL" CREATED...?
HOW-EVER...
...THE DARKNESS IS A FIERCE ALLY FOR ONE WITHOUT SIGHT.
HAH...
HAH...

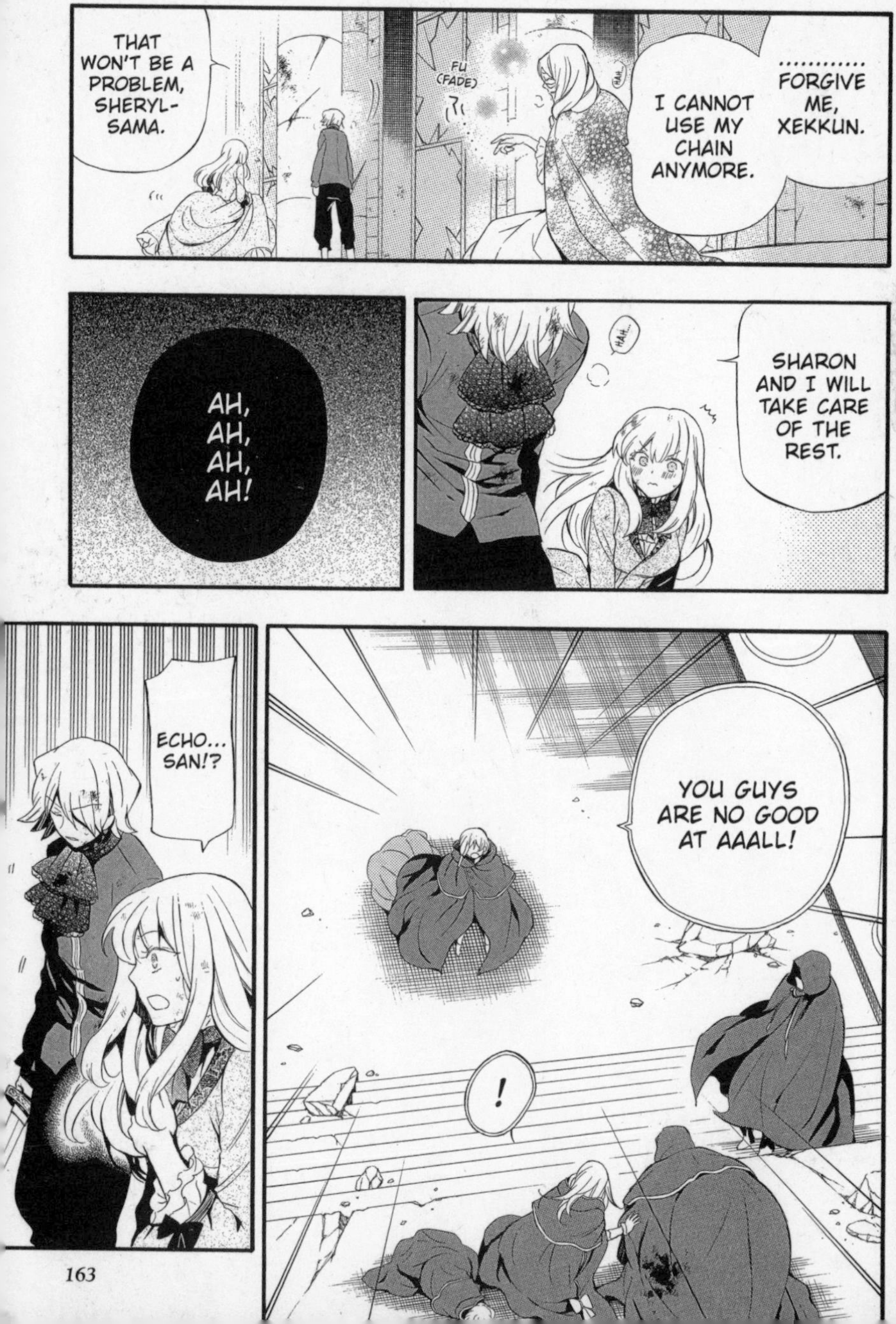
.... FORGIVE ME, XEKKUN.
I CANNOT USE MY CHAIN ANYMORE.
HAH...
FU (FADE)
THAT WON'T BE A PROBLEM, SHERYL-SAMA.
SHARON AND I WILL TAKE CARE OF THE REST.
HAH...
AH, AH, AH, AH!
YOU GUYS ARE NO GOOD AT AAALL!
!
ECHO... SAN!?

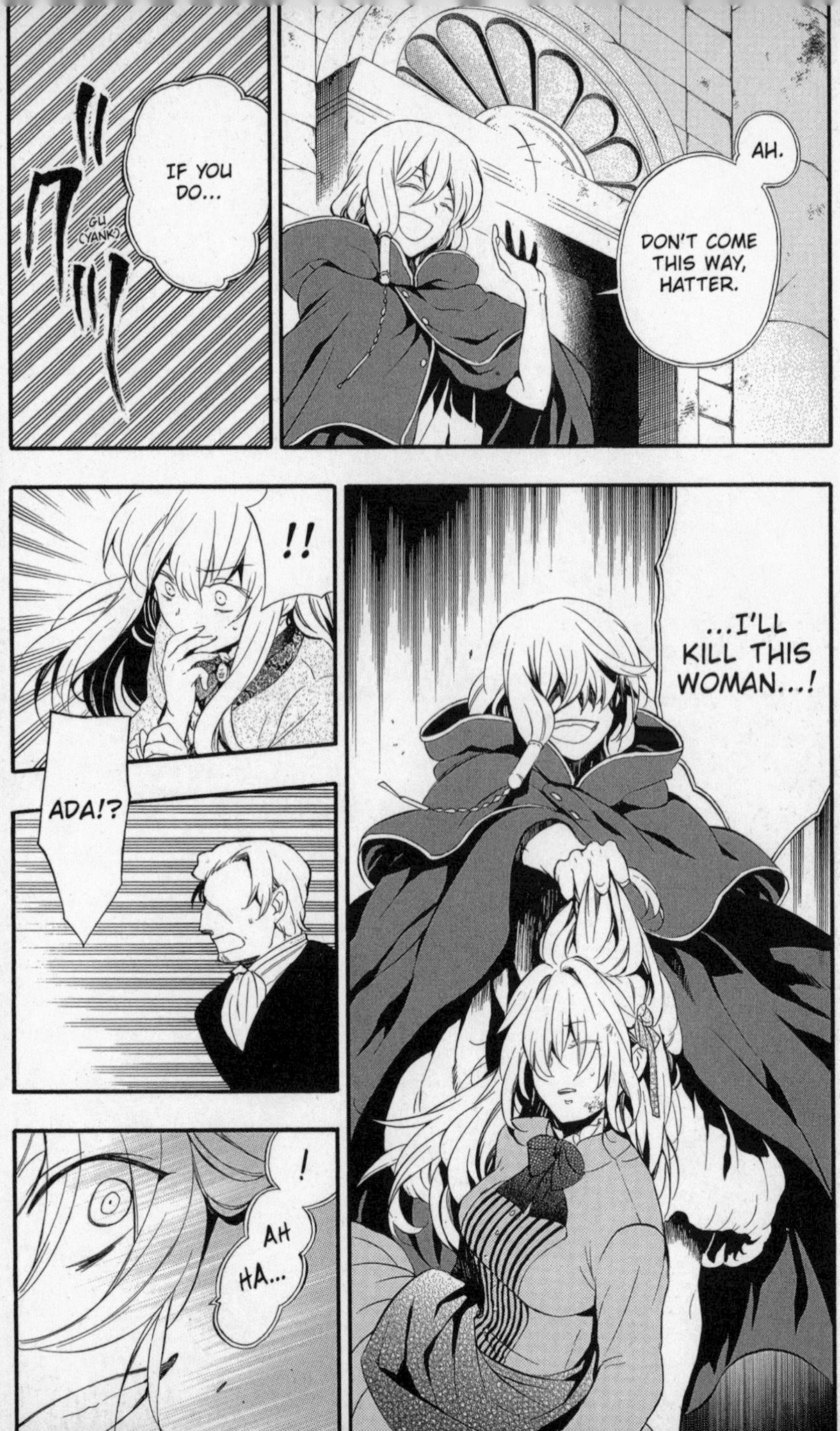
AH.
DON'T COME THIS WAY, HATTER.
IF YOU DO...
GU (YANK)
...I'LL KILL THIS WOMAN...!
!!
ADA!?
!
AH HA...

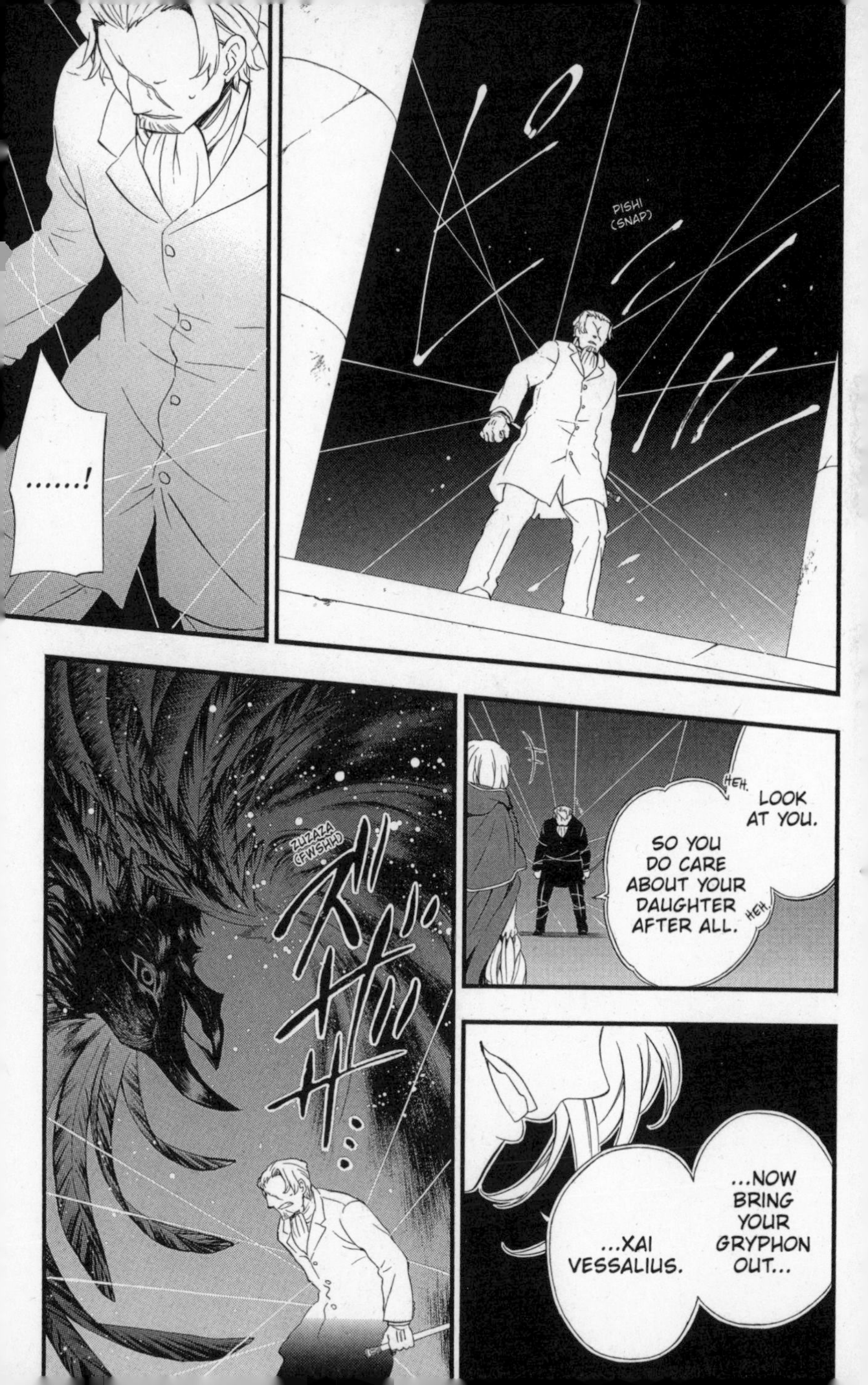
PISHI (SNAP)
......!
HEH.
LOOK AT YOU.
SO YOU DO CARE ABOUT YOUR DAUGHTER AFTER ALL.
HEH.
...NOW BRING YOUR GRYPHON OUT...
...XAI VESSALIUS.
ZUZAZA (FWSHH)

I'M GOING TO SABLIER...

...'COS I WANNA SEE VINCENT RIGHT AWAY.

ZWEI!?

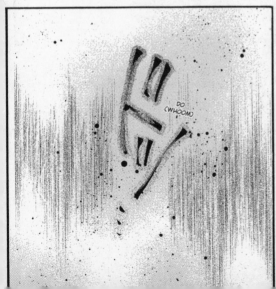

DUG...

BA
(DASH)

WAIT—

DO
(WHOOM)

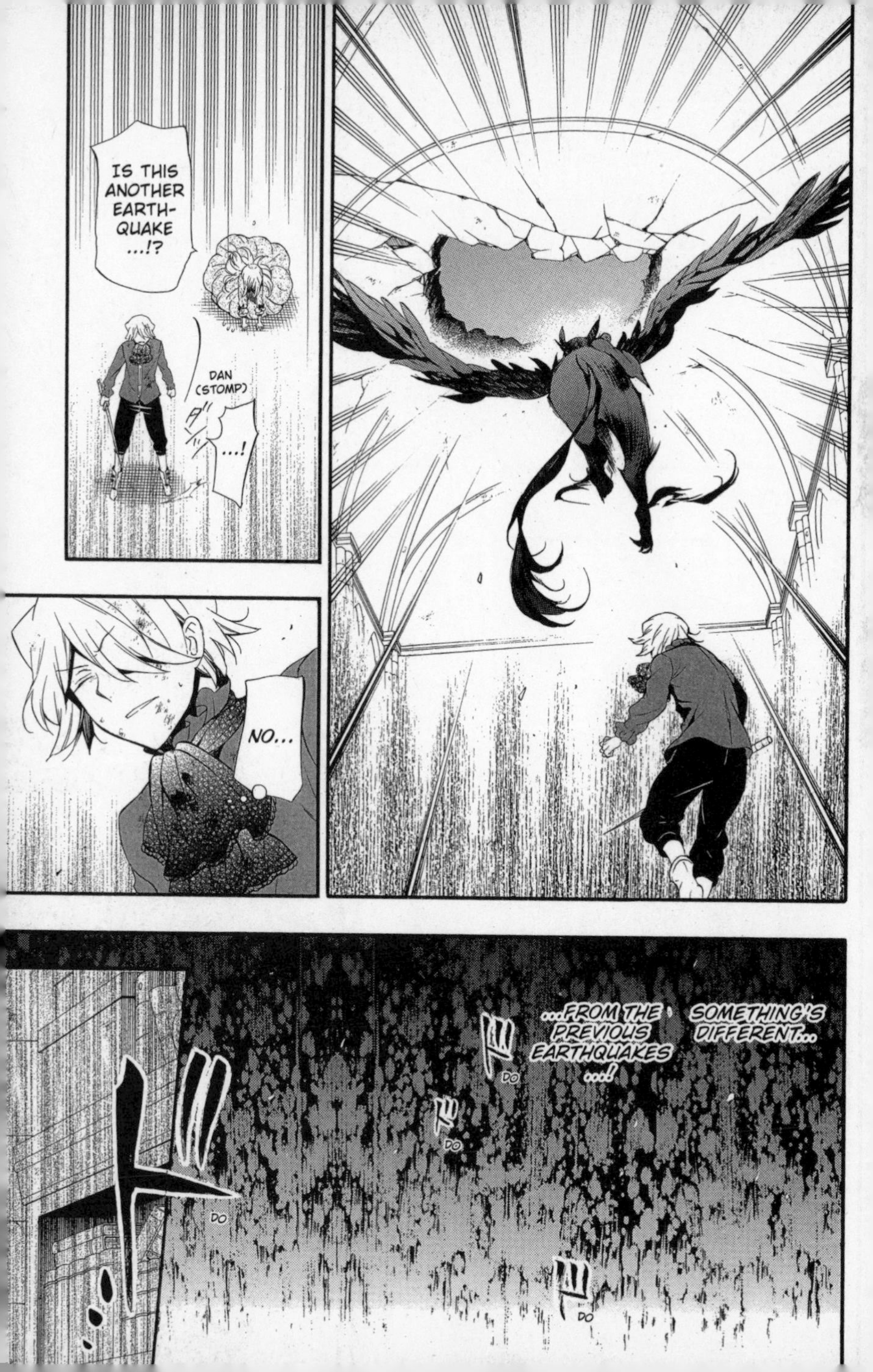
IS THIS ANOTHER EARTH-QUAKE ...!?
DAN (STOMP)
...!
NO...
SOMETHING'S DIFFERENT...
...FROM THE PREVIOUS EARTHQUAKES ...!
DO
DO
DO
DO

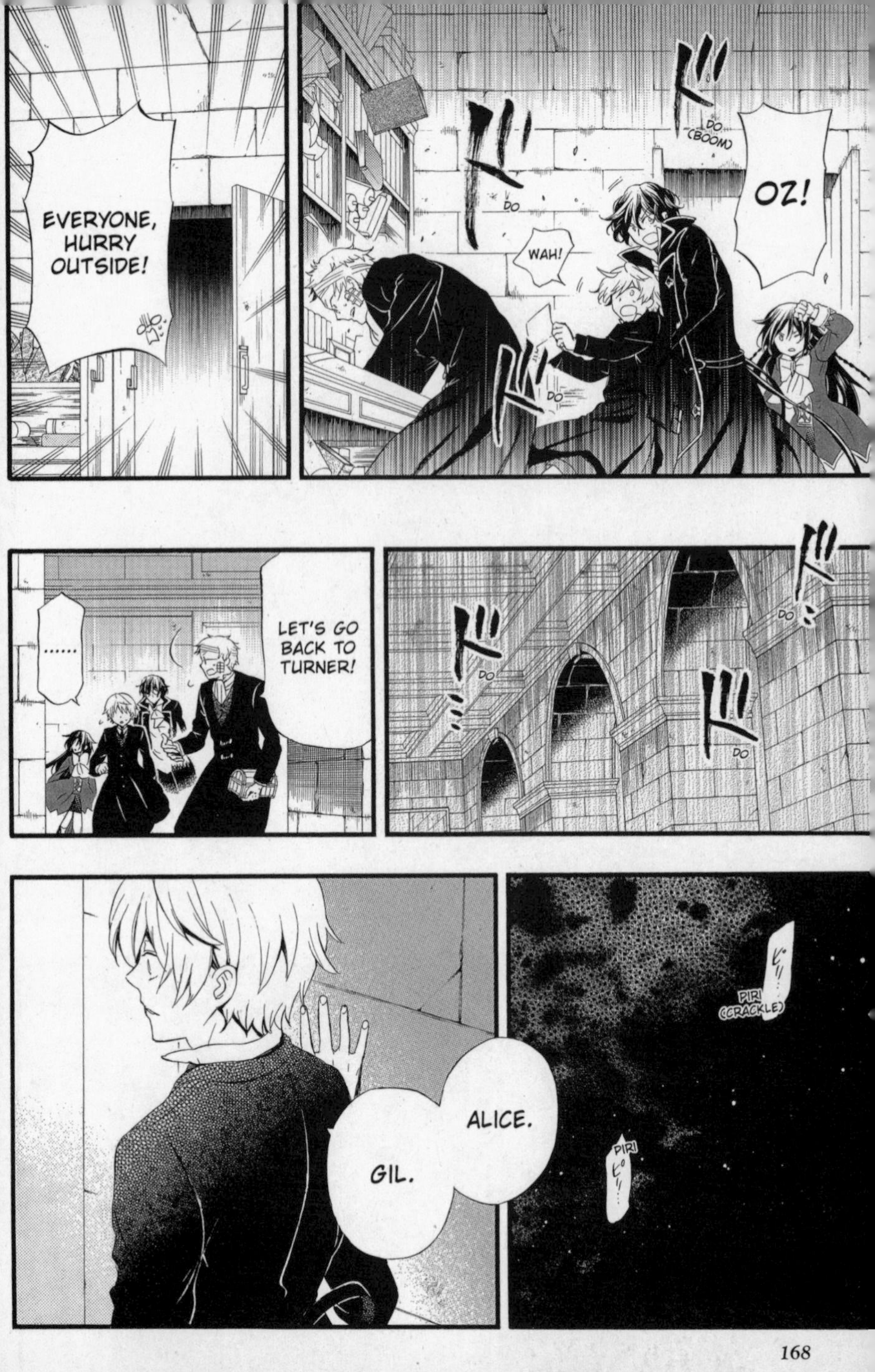
DO (BOOM)
OZ!
DO
WAH!
DO
EVERYONE, HURRY OUTSIDE!
DO
DO
DO
LET'S GO BACK TO TURNER!
......
PIRI (CRACKLE)
PIRI
ALICE.
GIL.

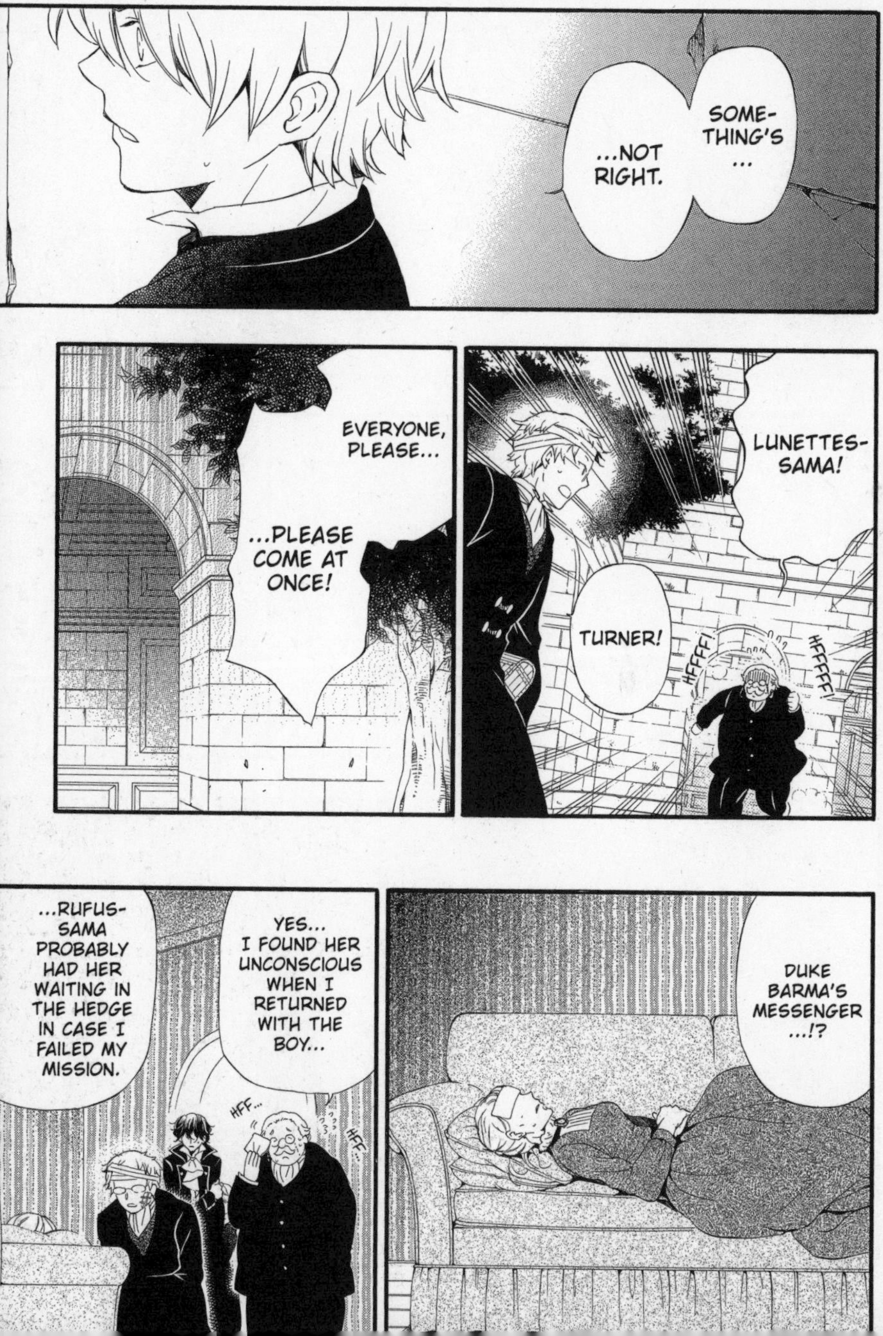
SOME-THING'S ...
...NOT RIGHT.
LUNETTES-SAMA!
TURNER!
HFFFF!
HFFFFF!
EVERYONE, PLEASE...
...PLEASE COME AT ONCE!
DUKE BARMA'S MESSENGER ...!?
YES... I FOUND HER UNCONSCIOUS WHEN I RETURNED WITH THE BOY...
...RUFUS-SAMA PROBABLY HAD HER WAITING IN THE HEDGE IN CASE I FAILED MY MISSION.
HFF...
HFF...

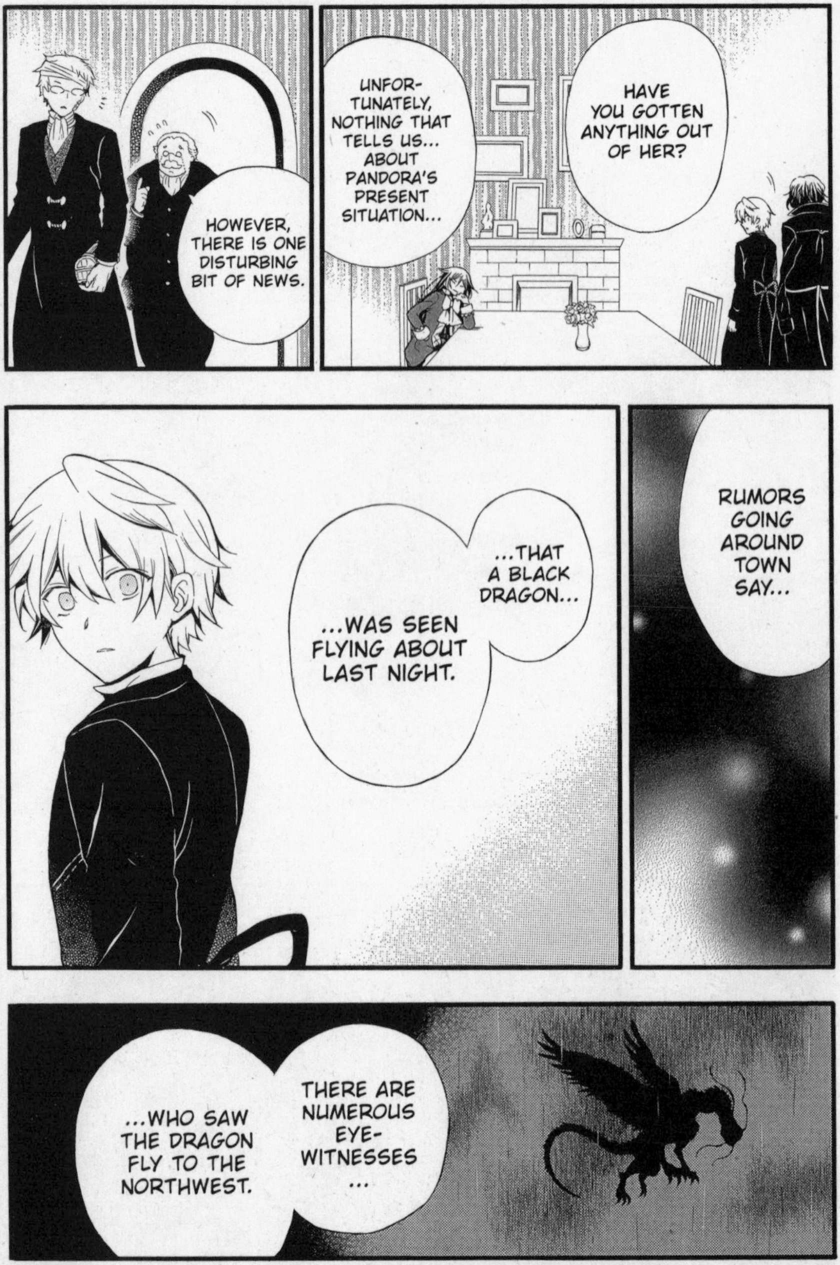
HAVE YOU GOTTEN ANYTHING OUT OF HER?
UNFORTUNATELY, NOTHING THAT TELLS US... ABOUT PANDORA'S PRESENT SITUATION...
HOWEVER, THERE IS ONE DISTURBING BIT OF NEWS.
RUMORS GOING AROUND TOWN SAY...
...THAT A BLACK DRAGON...
...WAS SEEN FLYING ABOUT LAST NIGHT.
THERE ARE NUMEROUS EYE-WITNESSES ...
...WHO SAW THE DRAGON FLY TO THE NORTHWEST.

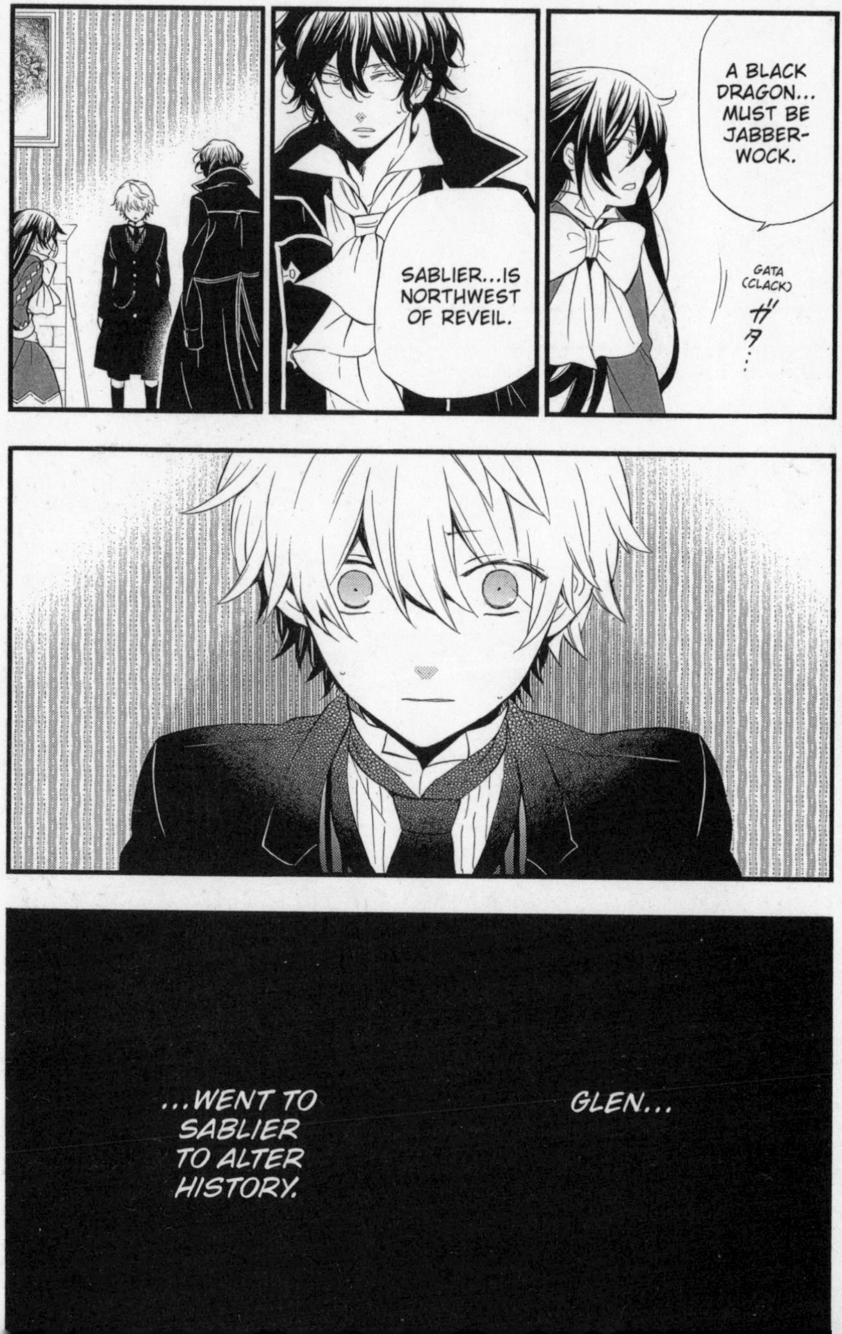
A BLACK DRAGON... MUST BE JABBER-WOCK.
GATA (CLACK)
ガタ…
SABLIER...IS NORTHWEST OF REVEIL.
GLEN...
...WENT TO SABLIER TO ALTER HISTORY.

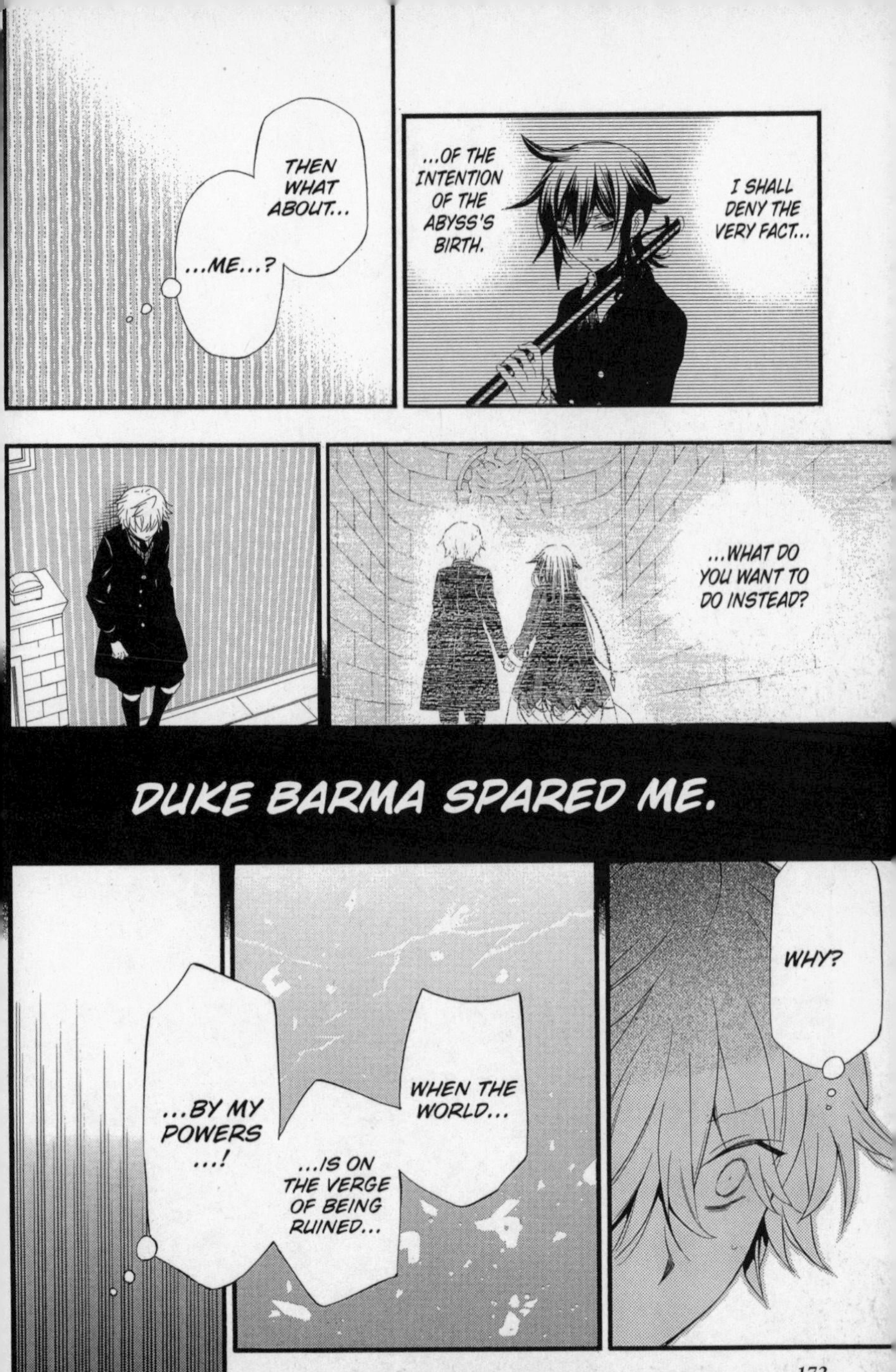
I SHALL DENY THE VERY FACT...
...OF THE INTENTION OF THE ABYSS'S BIRTH.
THEN WHAT ABOUT...
...ME...?
...WHAT DO YOU WANT TO DO INSTEAD?
DUKE BARMA SPARED ME.
WHY?
WHEN THE WORLD...
...IS ON THE VERGE OF BEING RUINED...
...BY MY POWERS ...!

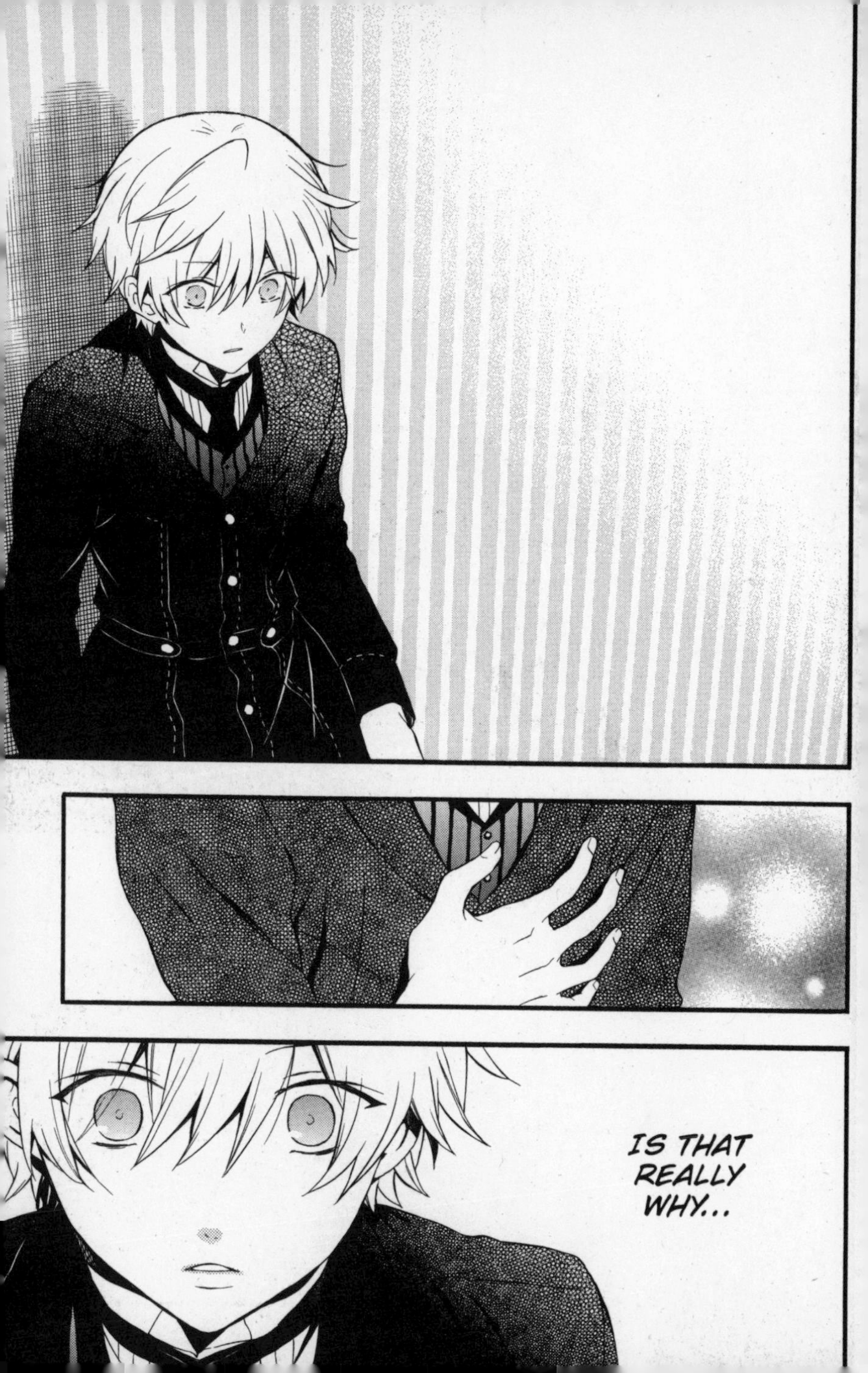
IS THAT REALLY WHY...

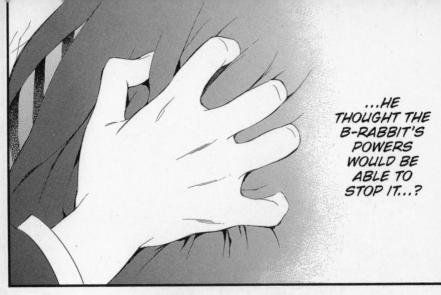

...HE THOUGHT THE B-RABBIT'S POWERS WOULD BE ABLE TO STOP IT...?

GIL.

ALICE.

I KNOW I SHOULDN'T SAY THIS.

I KNOW I SHOULDN'T...

...BUT...

I HAVE TO...

...GO.

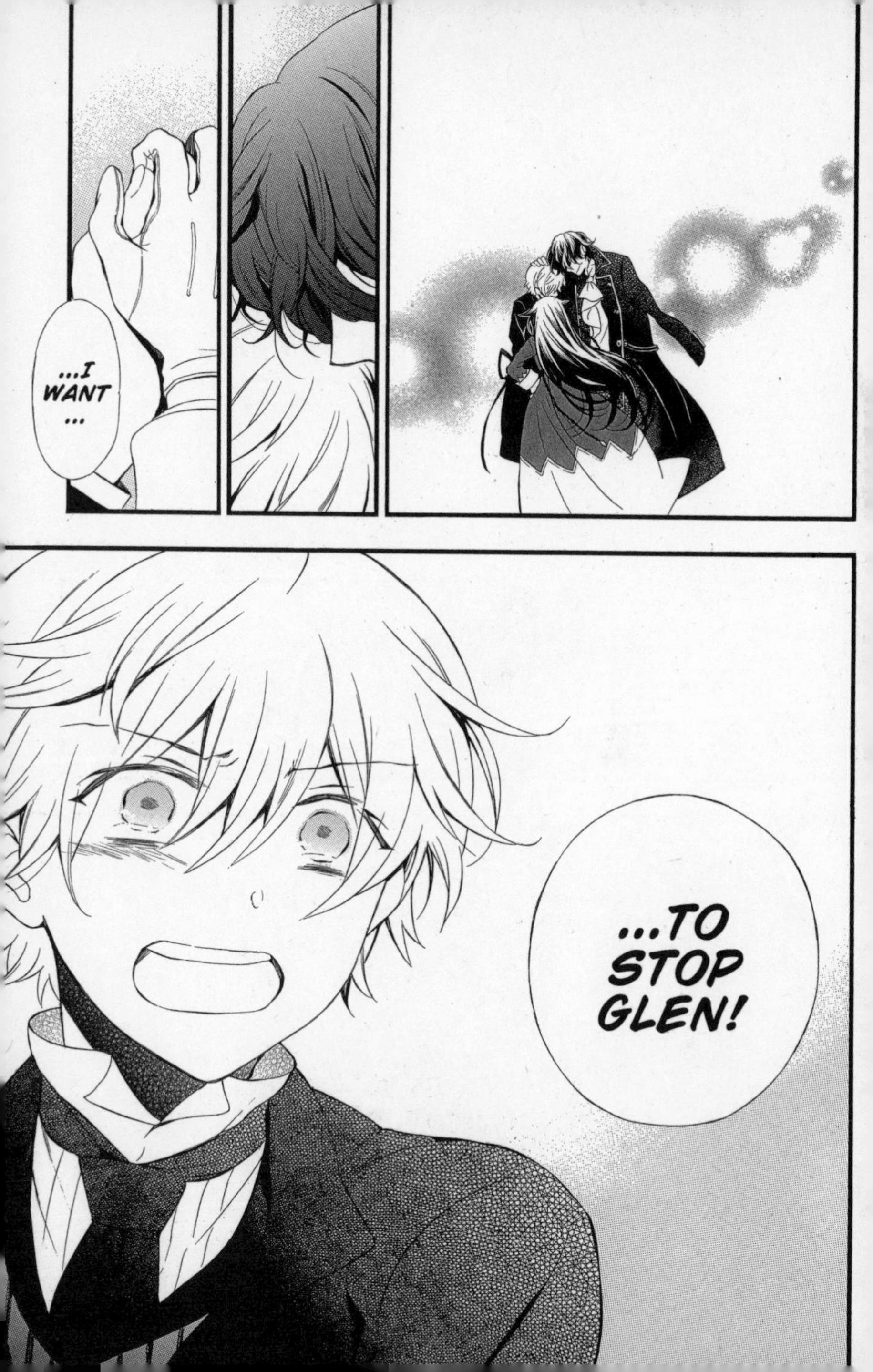
...I WANT ...
...TO STOP GLEN!

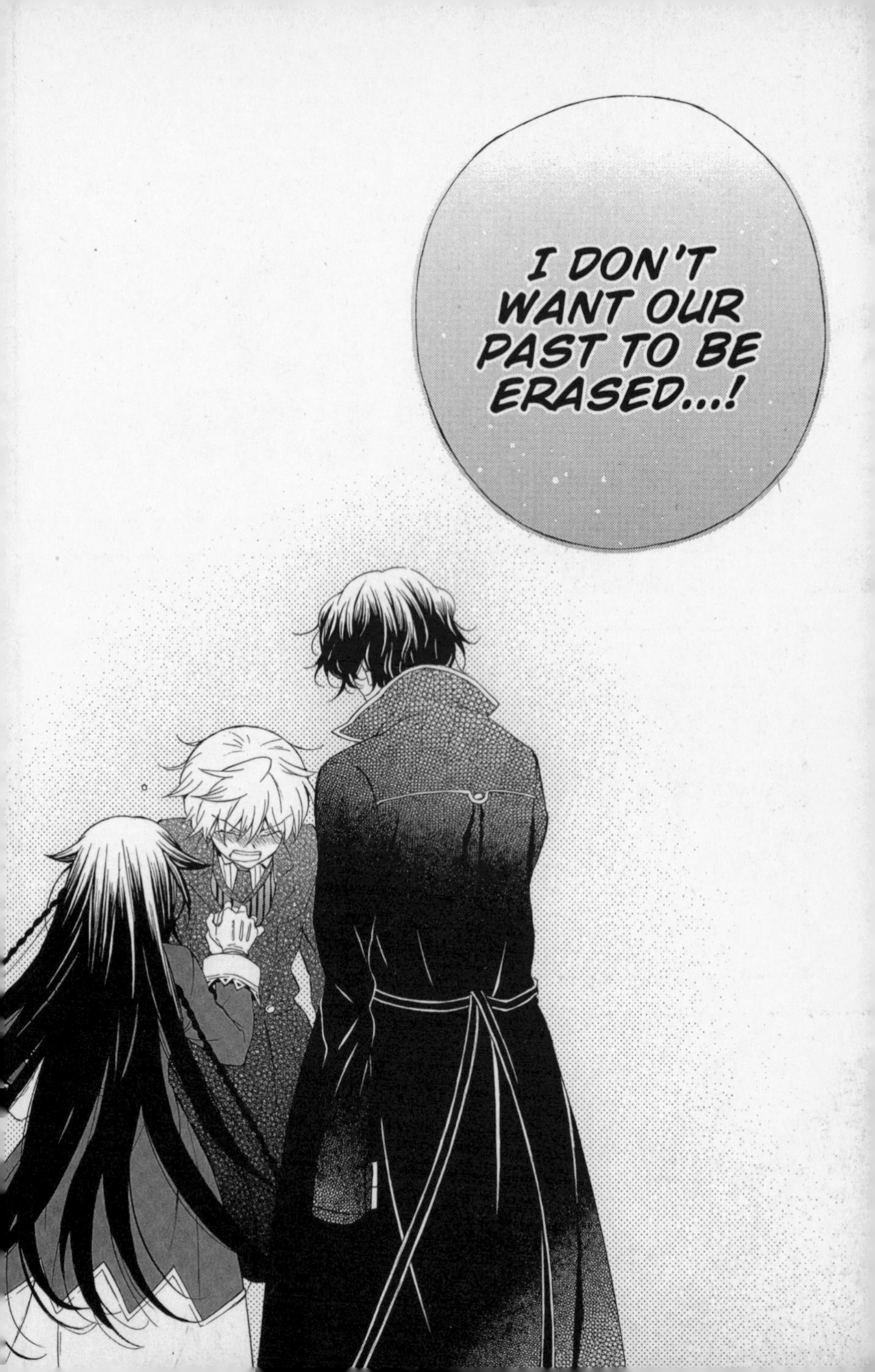
I DON'T WANT OUR PAST TO BE ERASED...!

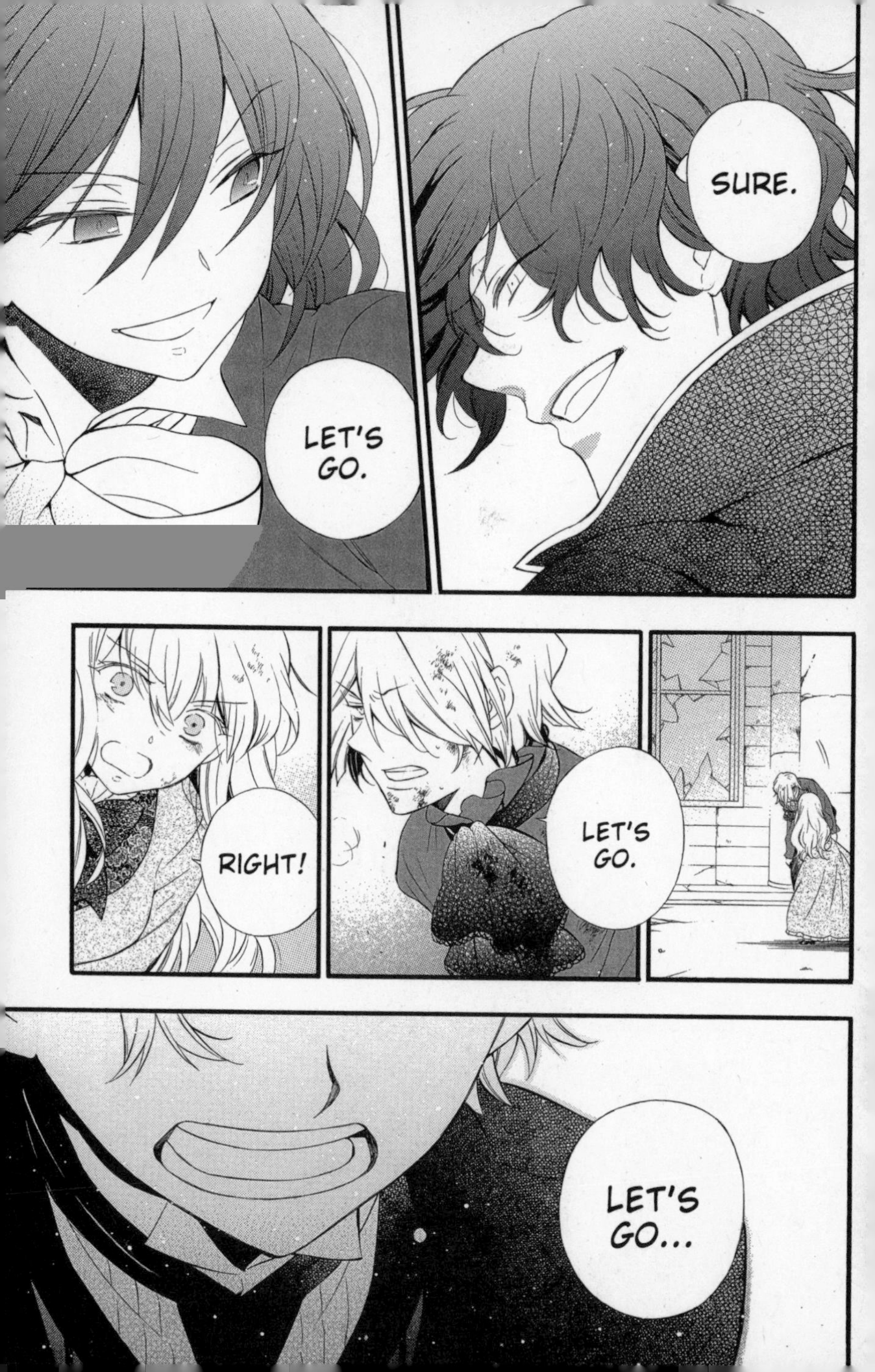
SURE.
LET'S GO.
LET'S GO.
RIGHT!
LET'S GO...

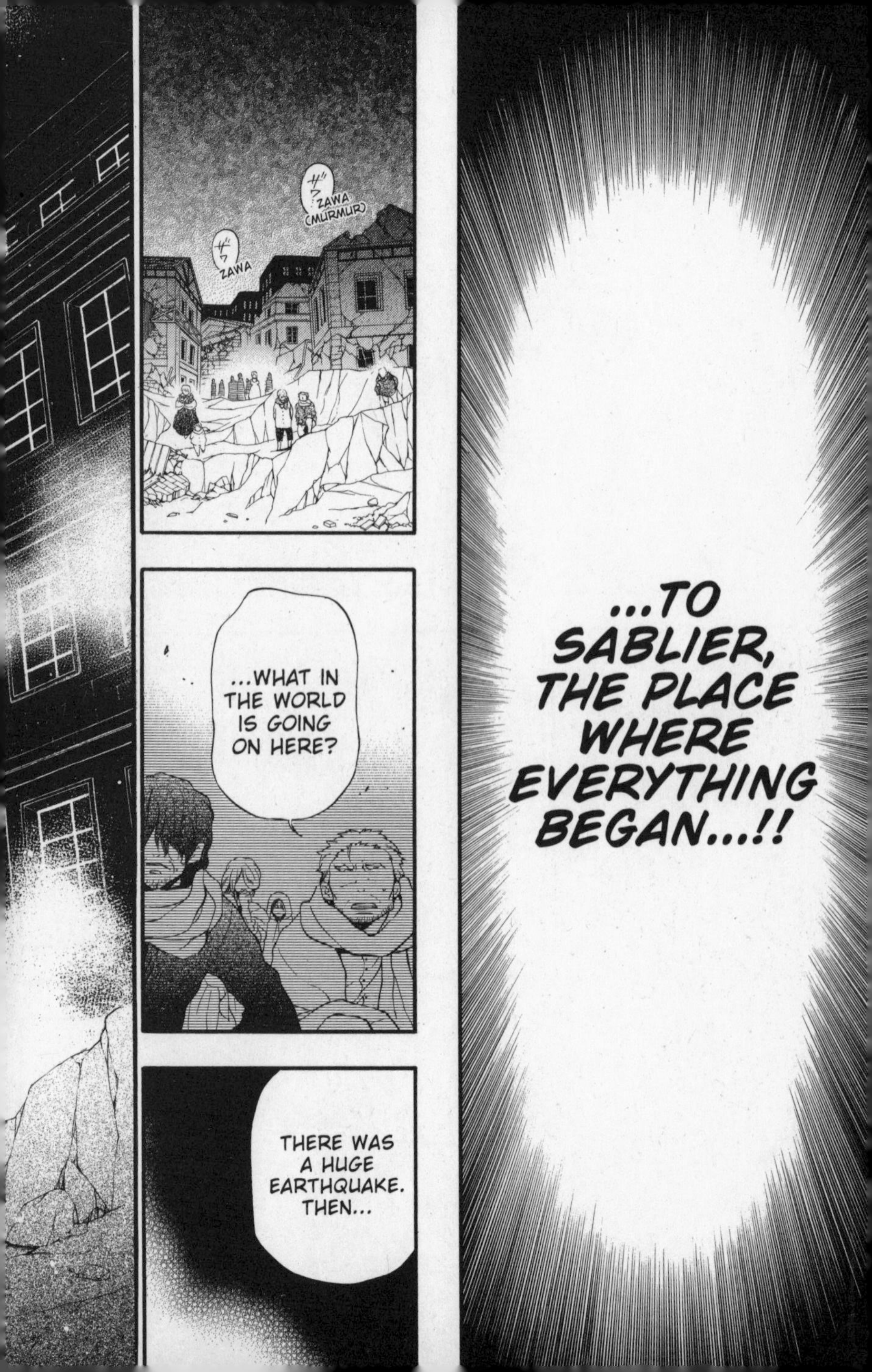
...TO SABLIER, THE PLACE WHERE EVERYTHING BEGAN...!!
ザワ ZAWA (MURMUR)
ザワ ZAWA
...WHAT IN THE WORLD IS GOING ON HERE?
THERE WAS A HUGE EARTHQUAKE. THEN...

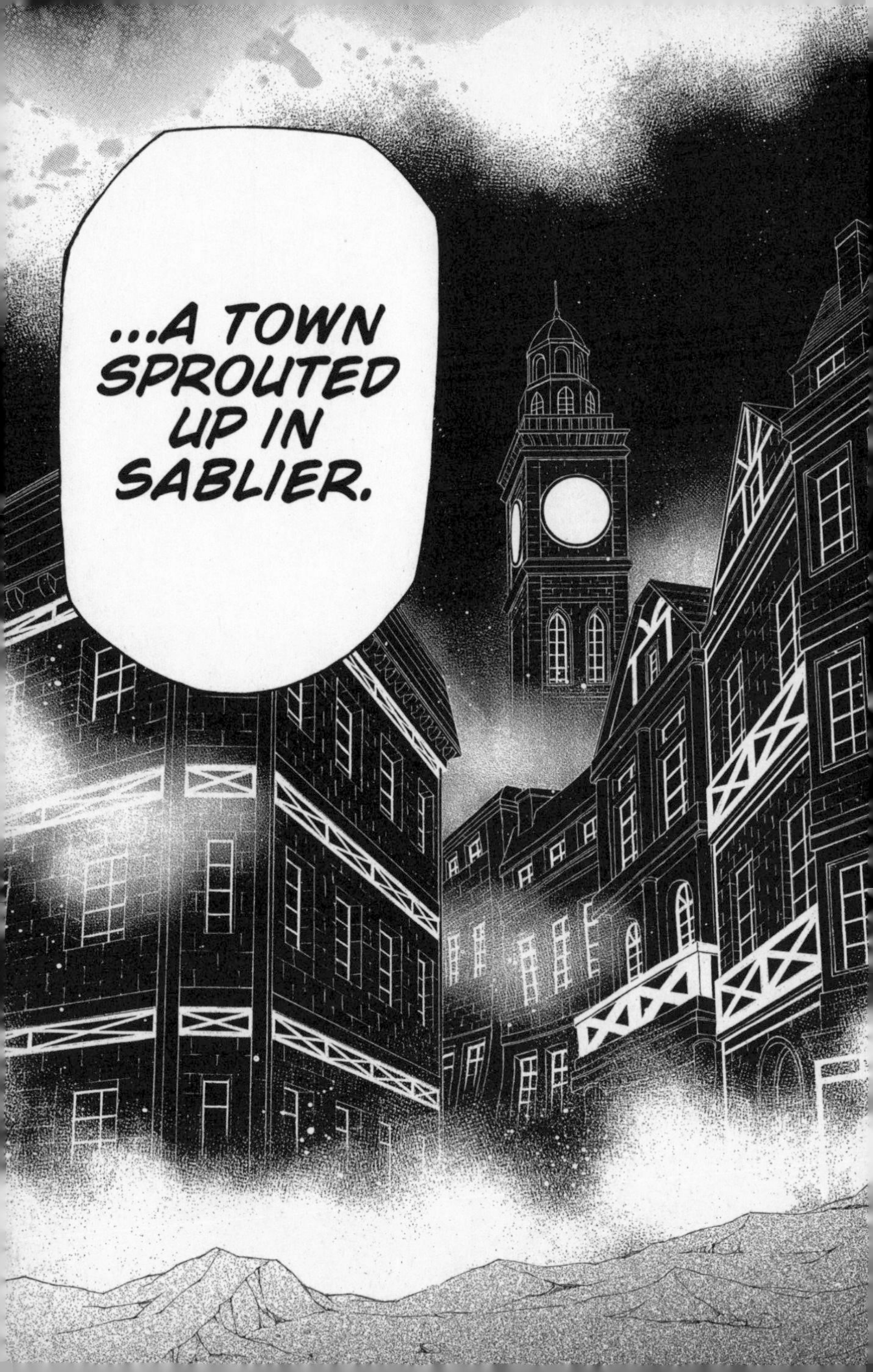
...A TOWN SPROUTED UP IN SABLIER.

Retrace : LXXXVII Starting point

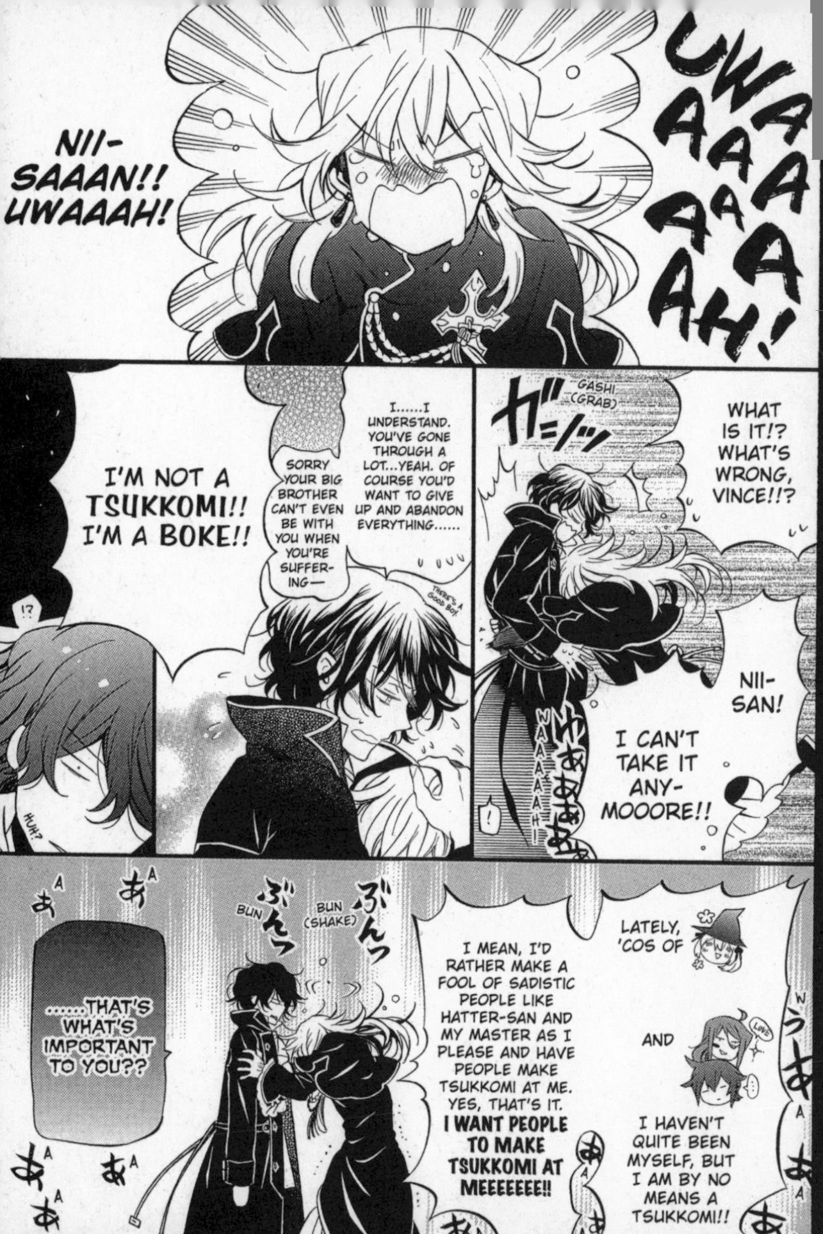

UWAAAAAAAAAH!
NII-SAAAN!! UWAAAH!
GASHI (GRAB)
WHAT IS IT!? WHAT'S WRONG, VINCE!!?
NII-SAN!
I CAN'T TAKE IT ANY-MOOORE!!
WAAAAAAAH!
I......I UNDERSTAND. YOU'VE GONE THROUGH A LOT...YEAH. OF COURSE YOU'D WANT TO GIVE UP AND ABANDON EVERYTHING......
SORRY YOUR BIG BROTHER CAN'T EVEN BE WITH YOU WHEN YOU'RE SUFFER-ING—
THERE'S A GOOD BOY.
I'M NOT A TSUKKOMI!! I'M A BOKE!!
!?
HUH?
LATELY, 'COS OF
AND
I HAVEN'T QUITE BEEN MYSELF, BUT I AM BY NO MEANS A TSUKKOMI!!
I MEAN, I'D RATHER MAKE A FOOL OF SADISTIC PEOPLE LIKE HATTER-SAN AND MY MASTER AS I PLEASE AND HAVE PEOPLE MAKE TSUKKOMI AT ME. YES, THAT'S IT. I WANT PEOPLE TO MAKE TSUKKOMI AT MEEEEEEE!!
BUN (SHAKE)
BUN
......THAT'S WHAT'S IMPORTANT TO YOU??

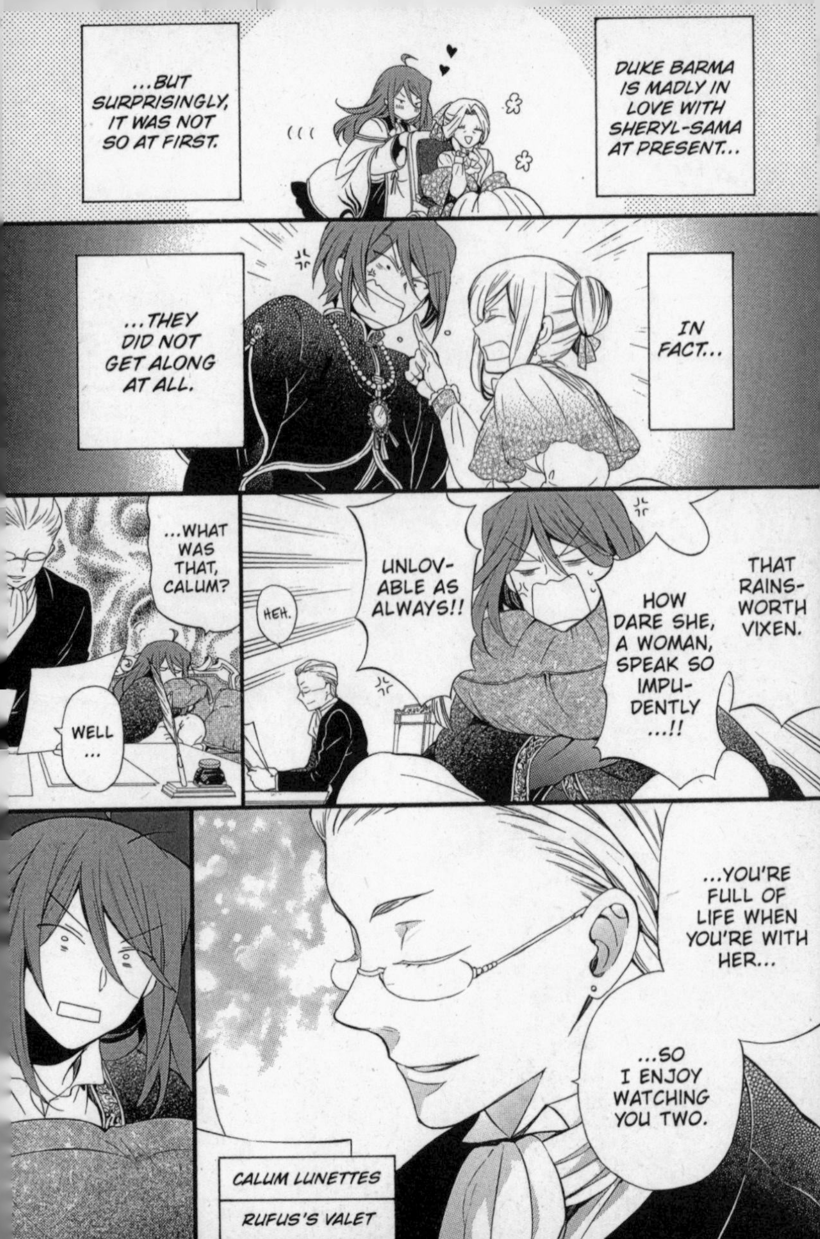
DUKE BARMA IS MADLY IN LOVE WITH SHERYL-SAMA AT PRESENT...
...BUT SURPRISINGLY, IT WAS NOT SO AT FIRST.
IN FACT...
...THEY DID NOT GET ALONG AT ALL.
THAT RAINSWORTH VIXEN.
HOW DARE SHE, A WOMAN, SPEAK SO IMPUDENTLY ...!!
UNLOVABLE AS ALWAYS!!
HEH.
...WHAT WAS THAT, CALUM?
WELL ...
...YOU'RE FULL OF LIFE WHEN YOU'RE WITH HER...
...SO I ENJOY WATCHING YOU TWO.
CALUM LUNETTES
RUFUS'S VALET

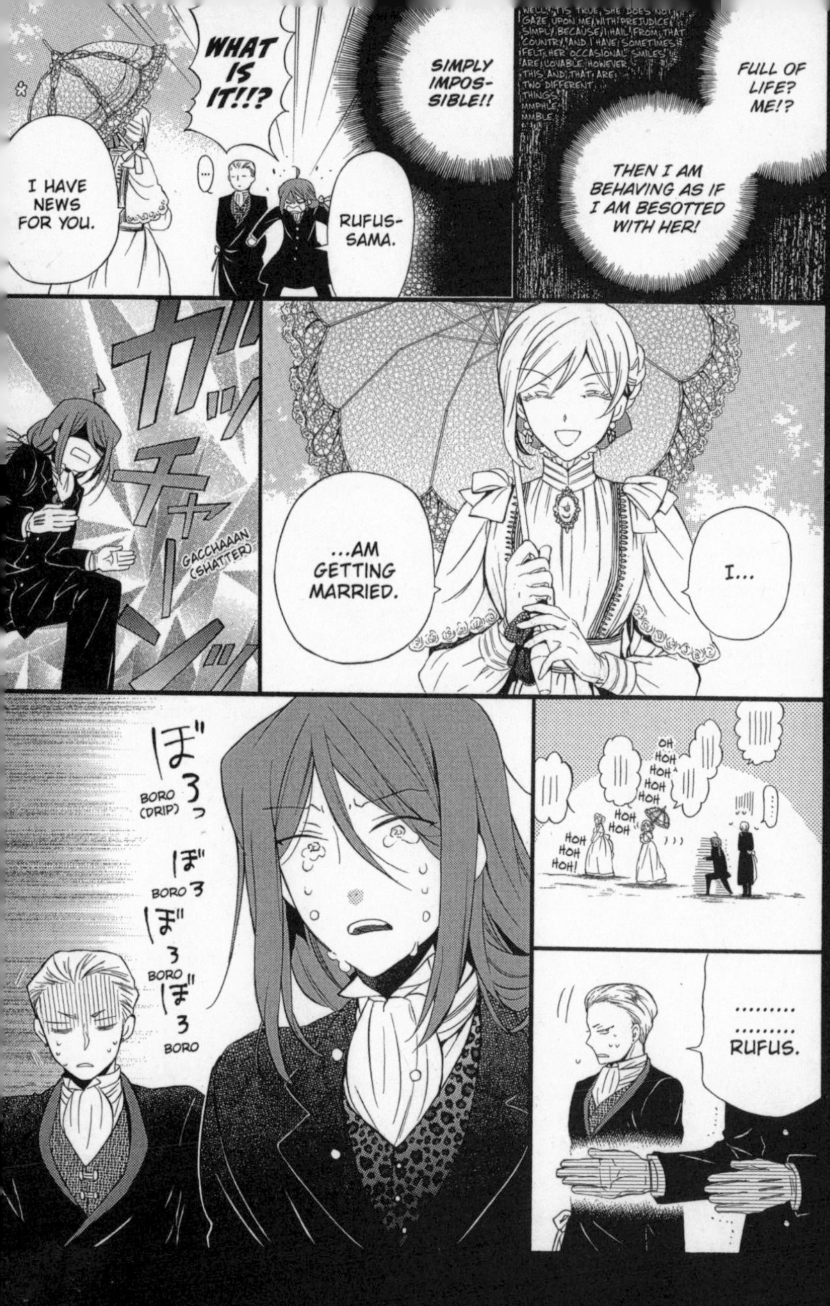
FULL OF LIFE? ME!?
WELL, 'TIS TRUE, SHE DOES NOT GAZE UPON ME WITH PREJUDICE SIMPLY BECAUSE I HAIL FROM THAT COUNTRY, AND I HAVE SOMETIMES FELT HER OCCASIONAL SMILES ARE LOVABLE. HOWEVER, THIS AND THAT ARE TWO DIFFERENT THINGS. MMPHLE, MMBLE.
THEN I AM BEHAVING AS IF I AM BESOTTED WITH HER!
SIMPLY IMPOSSIBLE!!
WHAT IS IT!!?
RUFUS-SAMA.
...
I HAVE NEWS FOR YOU.
I...
...AM GETTING MARRIED.
ガシャーン
GACCHAAAN (SHATTER)
!!!
OH HOH HOH HOH HOH
HOH HOH
HOH HOH HOH!
!!!
...
....
....
RUFUS.
ぼろっ
BORO (DRIP)
ぼろ
BORO
ぼろ
BORO
ぼろ
BORO

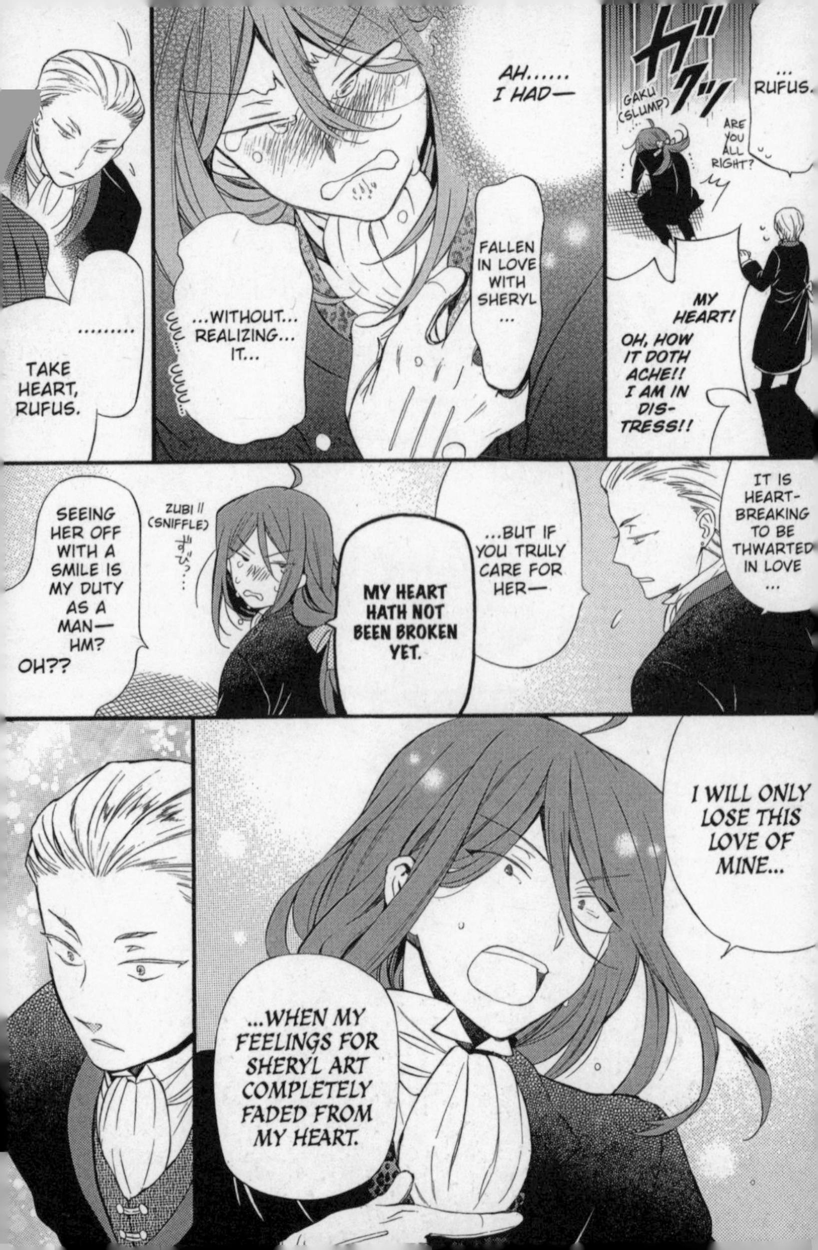
... RUFUS.
ARE YOU ALL RIGHT?
GAKU (SLUMP)
MY HEART! OH, HOW IT DOTH ACHE!! I AM IN DIS-TRESS!!
AH...... I HAD—
FALLEN IN LOVE WITH SHERYL ...
...WITHOUT... REALIZING... IT...
UUU... UUUU...
....
TAKE HEART, RUFUS.
IT IS HEART-BREAKING TO BE THWARTED IN LOVE ...
...BUT IF YOU TRULY CARE FOR HER—
MY HEART HATH NOT BEEN BROKEN YET.
ZUBI (SNIFFLE)
SEEING HER OFF WITH A SMILE IS MY DUTY AS A MAN—HM?
OH??
I WILL ONLY LOSE THIS LOVE OF MINE...
...WHEN MY FEELINGS FOR SHERYL ART COMPLETELY FADED FROM MY HEART.

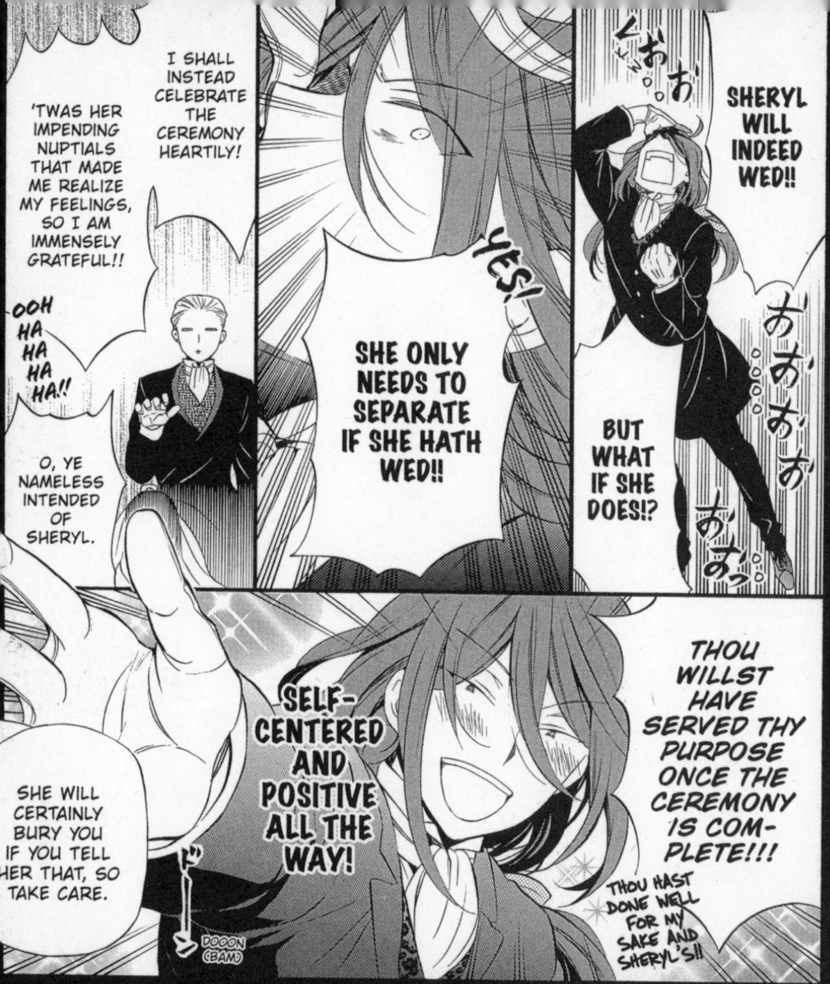
SHERYL WILL INDEED WED!!
BUT WHAT IF SHE DOES!?
YES!
SHE ONLY NEEDS TO SEPARATE IF SHE HATH WED!!
I SHALL INSTEAD CELEBRATE THE CEREMONY HEARTILY!
'TWAS HER IMPENDING NUPTIALS THAT MADE ME REALIZE MY FEELINGS, SO I AM IMMENSELY GRATEFUL!!
OOH HA HA HA HA!!
O, YE NAMELESS INTENDED OF SHERYL.
THOU WILLST HAVE SERVED THY PURPOSE ONCE THE CEREMONY IS COMPLETE!!!
THOU HAST DONE WELL FOR MY SAKE AND SHERYL'S!!
SELF-CENTERED AND POSITIVE ALL THE WAY!
DOOON (BAM)
SHE WILL CERTAINLY BURY YOU IF YOU TELL HER THAT, SO TAKE CARE.

Special Thanks!!

FUMITO YAMAZAKI
I WANT TO EAT GREEN CURRYYY!!!

SAEKO TAKIGAWA-SAN
WASN'T LIKE A CAT!!

KANATA MINAZUKI-SAN
YOU SHOULD JUST LIVE HERE.

YUKINO-SAN
I WANT TO MOVE PAST TAPPING YOUR KNEES FROM BEHIND AND FORCING YOU TO BEND THEM.

RYO-CHAN
…KKU IS WEARING A BEAR SUIT…!!?

MIZU KING-SAN
COMPLETELY DENIED SHUKU ASAOKA'S SOUVENIR (≡SMILE≡)

TADUU-SAN
YO, HEALTHY BODY!!! (I THOUGHT YOU'D RECEIVE THE MOST WARNINGS.)

YAJI
DO YOUR BEST IN THE CZECH REPUBLIC!!

SAYA AYAHAMA-SAN
YOU SHOULDN'T BE SHRINKING YET!!!

SHUKU ASAOKA-SENSEI
YOU'LL BE A PARAKEET IF YOU'RE EVER BORN AGAIN.

MIYUU-SAN
A REAL SAVIOR…!! MY MESSIAH!!!

MY FAMILY

MY EDITOR TAKEGASA-SAN
PLEASE SAY "HELLO" WHEN YOU ANSWER THE PHONE.

———— AND YOU!

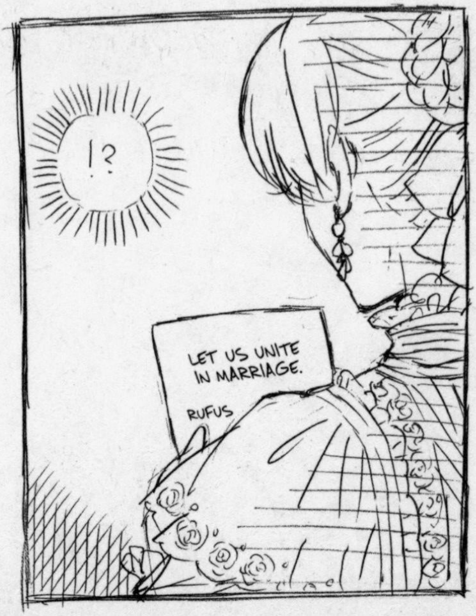
!?
LET US UNITE IN MARRIAGE.
RUFUS

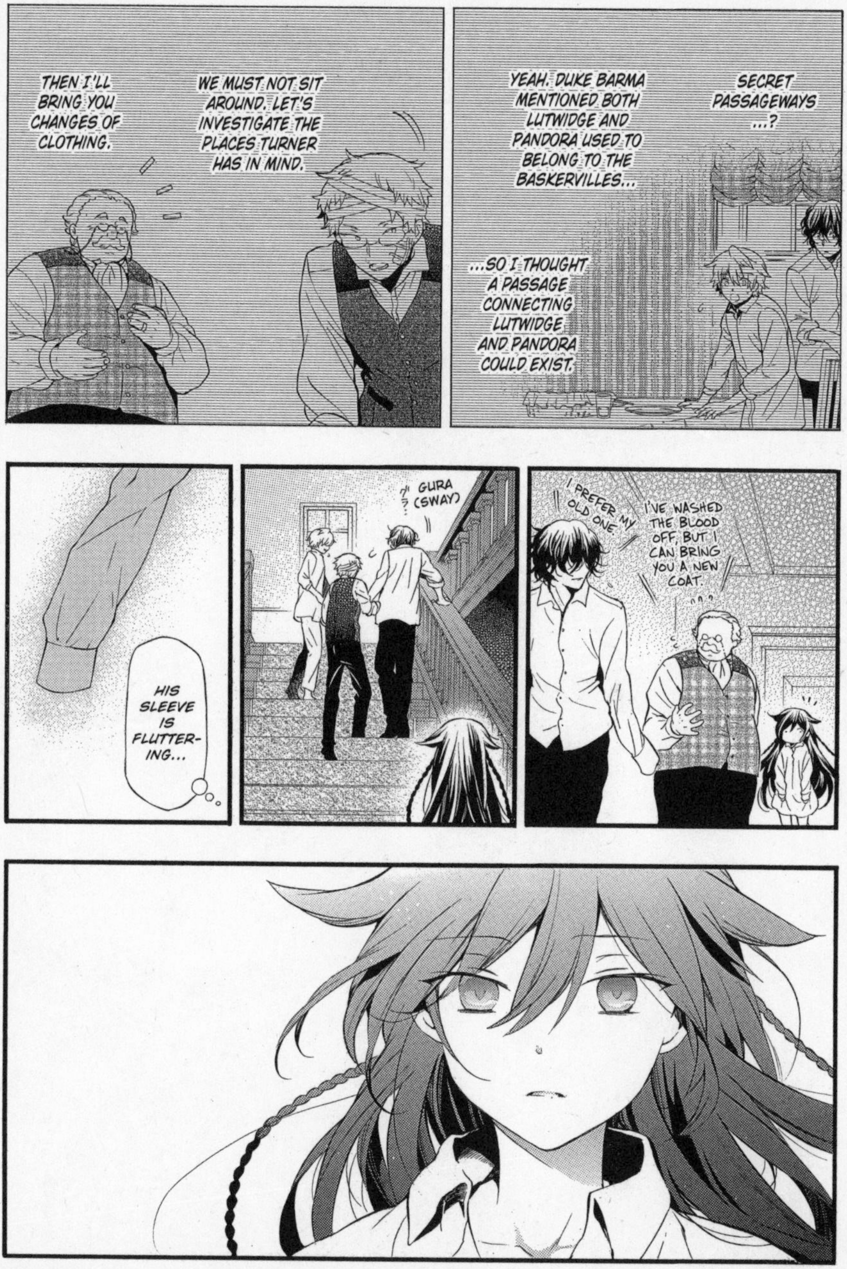
SECRET PASSAGEWAYS ...?
YEAH. DUKE BARMA MENTIONED BOTH LUTWIDGE AND PANDORA USED TO BELONG TO THE BASKERVILLES...
...SO I THOUGHT A PASSAGE CONNECTING LUTWIDGE AND PANDORA COULD EXIST.
WE MUST NOT SIT AROUND. LET'S INVESTIGATE THE PLACES TURNER HAS IN MIND.
THEN I'LL BRING YOU CHANGES OF CLOTHING.
I'VE WASHED THE BLOOD OFF, BUT I CAN BRING YOU A NEW COAT.
I PREFER MY OLD ONE.
GURA (SWAY)
HIS SLEEVE IS FLUTTERING...

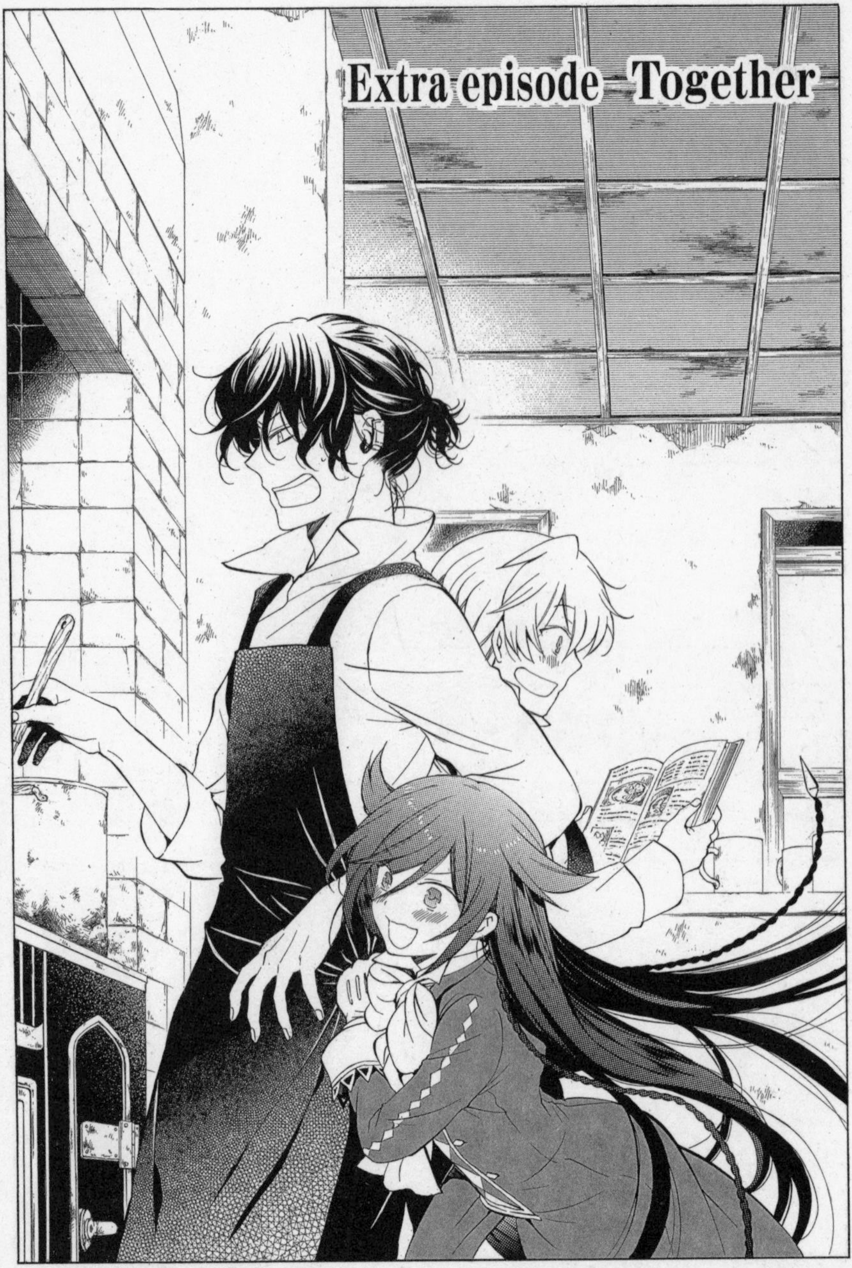
Extra episode Together

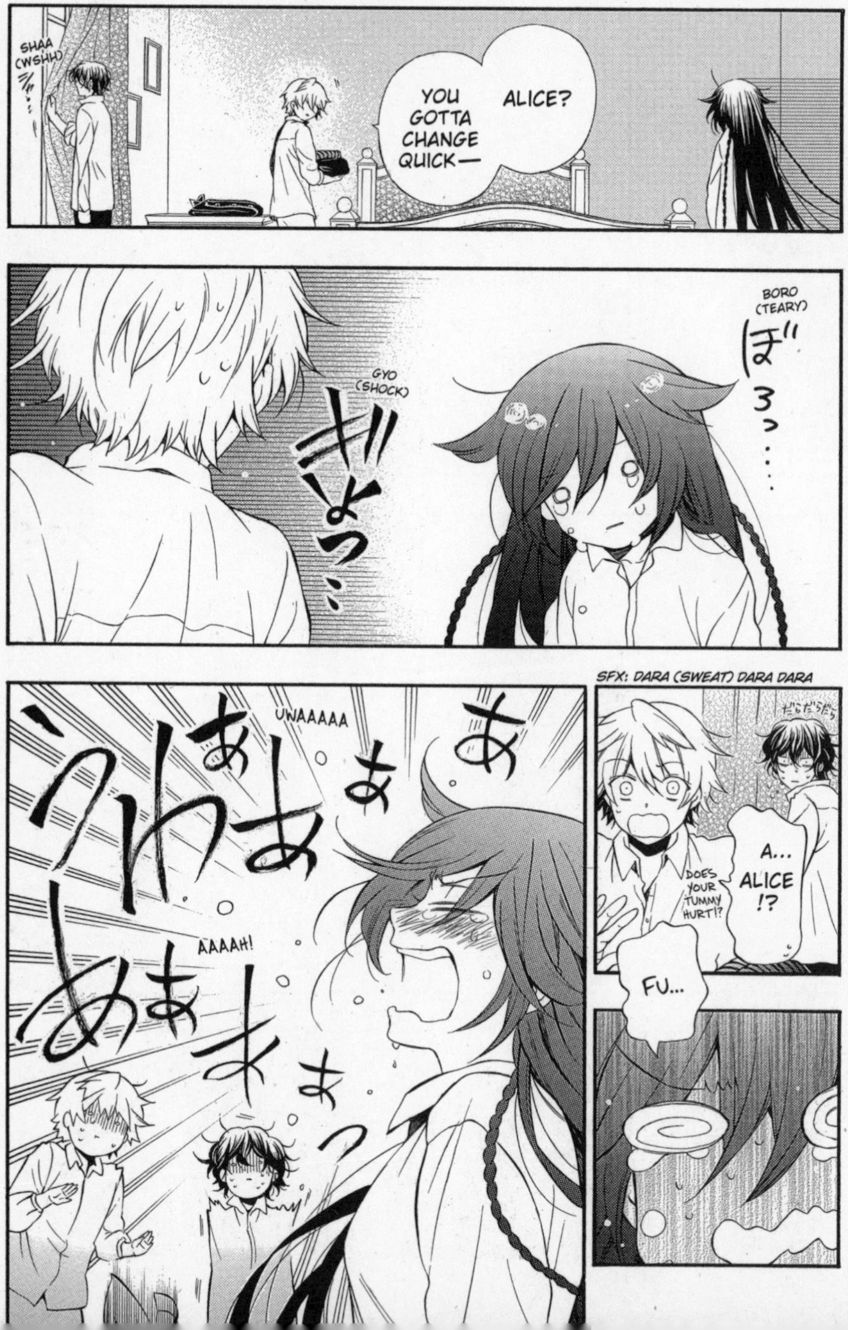
ALICE?
YOU GOTTA CHANGE QUICK—
SHAA (WSHH)
BORO (TEARY)
ぼろっ・・・
GYO (SHOCK)
ぎょっ
SFX: DARA (SWEAT) DARA DARA
だらだらだら
A... ALICE !?
DOES YOUR TUMMY HURT!?
FU...
UWAAAAA
AAAAH!

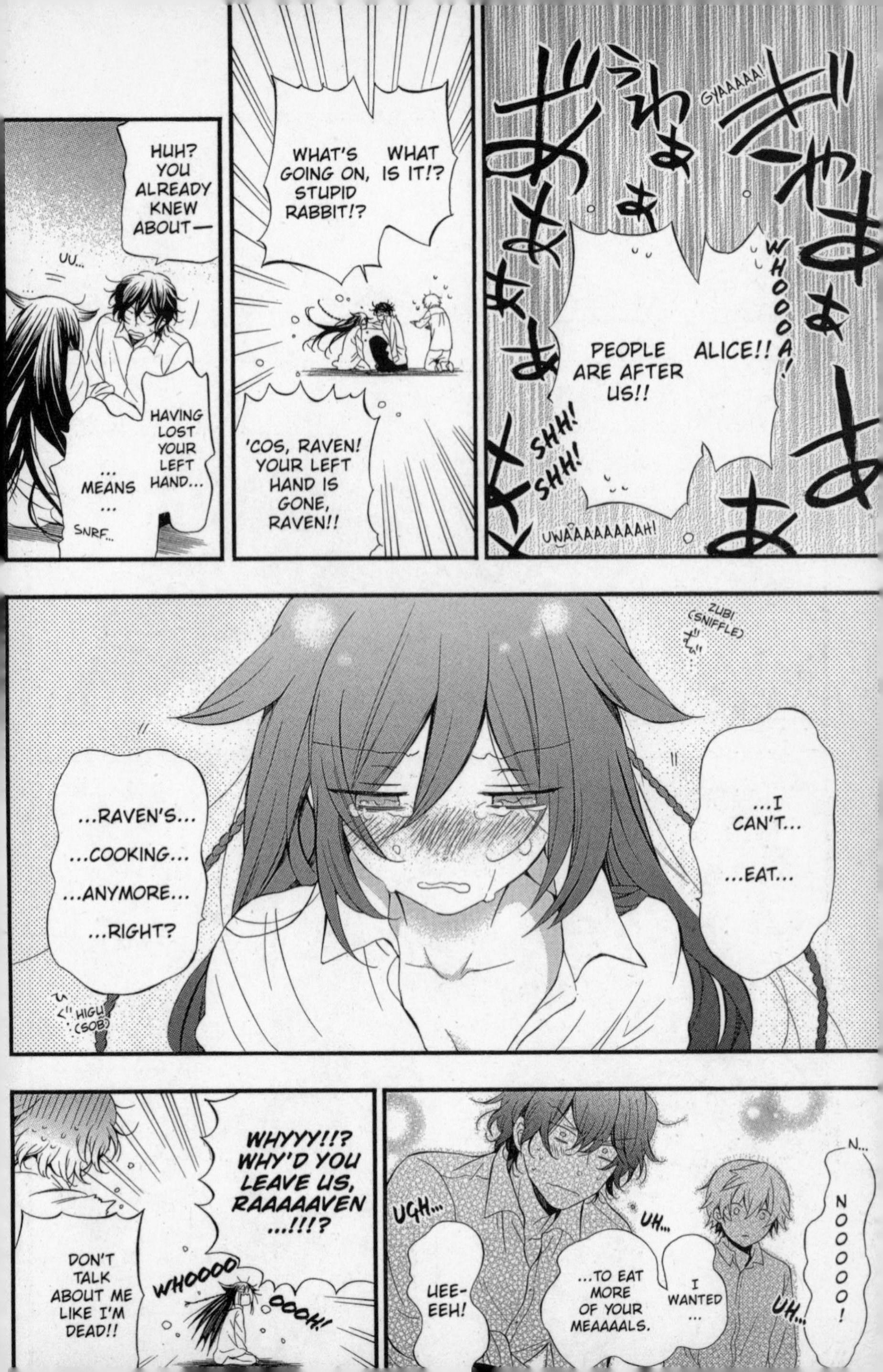
GYAAAAA!
WHOOOOA!
ALICE!! PEOPLE ARE AFTER US!!
SHH! SHH!
UWAAAAAAAAH!
WHAT IS IT!? WHAT'S GOING ON, STUPID RABBIT!?
'COS, RAVEN! YOUR LEFT HAND IS GONE, RAVEN!!
HUH? YOU ALREADY KNEW ABOUT—
UU...
HAVING LOST YOUR LEFT HAND...
...MEANS...
SNRF...
ZUBI (SNIFFLE)
...I CAN'T... ...EAT...
...RAVEN'S... ...COOKING... ...ANYMORE... ...RIGHT?
HIGU (SOB)
N... NOOOOOO!
UH...
I WANTED...
...TO EAT MORE OF YOUR MEAAAALS.
UH...
UEE-EEH!
UGH...
WHYYY!!? WHY'D YOU LEAVE US, RAAAAAVEN...!!!?
WHOOOO OOOH!
DON'T TALK ABOUT ME LIKE I'M DEAD!!

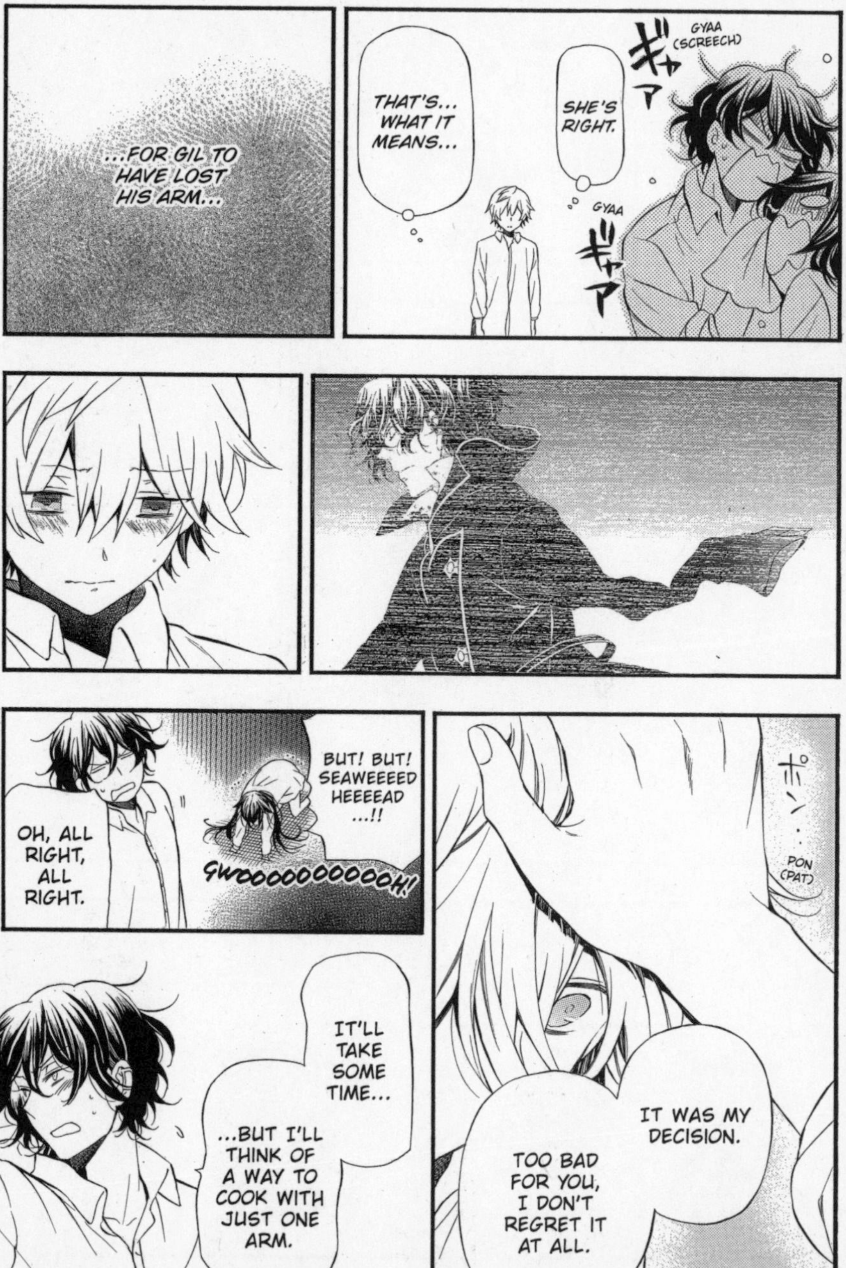
GYAA (SCREECH)
ギャア
SHE'S RIGHT.
GYAA
ギャア
THAT'S... WHAT IT MEANS...
...FOR GIL TO HAVE LOST HIS ARM...
ポン
PON (PAT)
IT WAS MY DECISION.
TOO BAD FOR YOU, I DON'T REGRET IT AT ALL.
BUT! BUT! SEAWEEEED HEEEEAD ...!!
GWOOOOOOOOOOOH!
OH, ALL RIGHT, ALL RIGHT.
IT'LL TAKE SOME TIME...
...BUT I'LL THINK OF A WAY TO COOK WITH JUST ONE ARM.

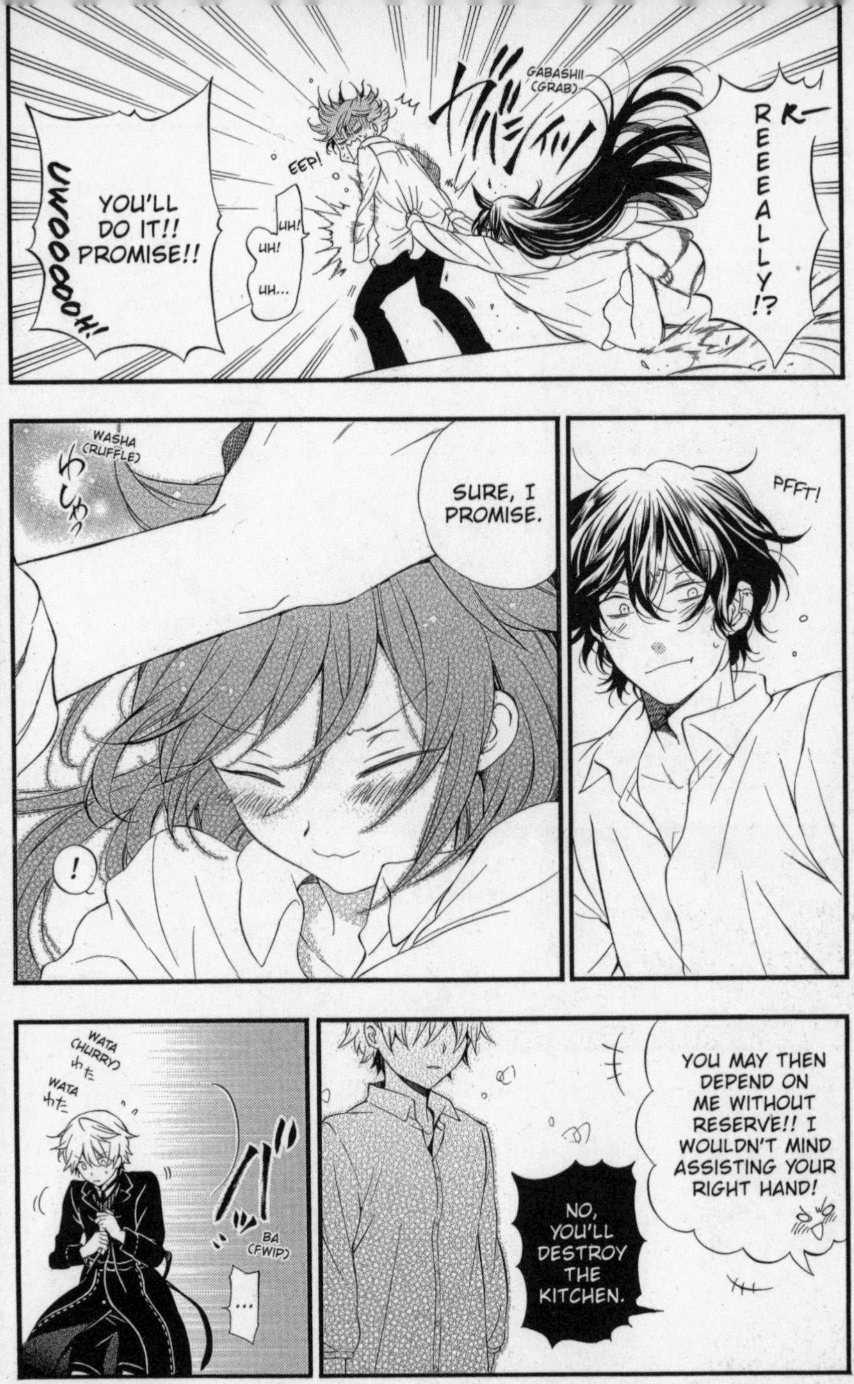
R— REEEALLY!?
GABASHII (GRAB)
EEP!
UH! UH! UH...
YOU'LL DO IT!! PROMISE!!
UWOOOOOOH!
PFFT!
SURE, I PROMISE.
WASHA (RUFFLE)
!
YOU MAY THEN DEPEND ON ME WITHOUT RESERVE!! I WOULDN'T MIND ASSISTING YOUR RIGHT HAND!
NO, YOU'LL DESTROY THE KITCHEN.
WATA (HURRY)
WATA
BA (FWIP)
...

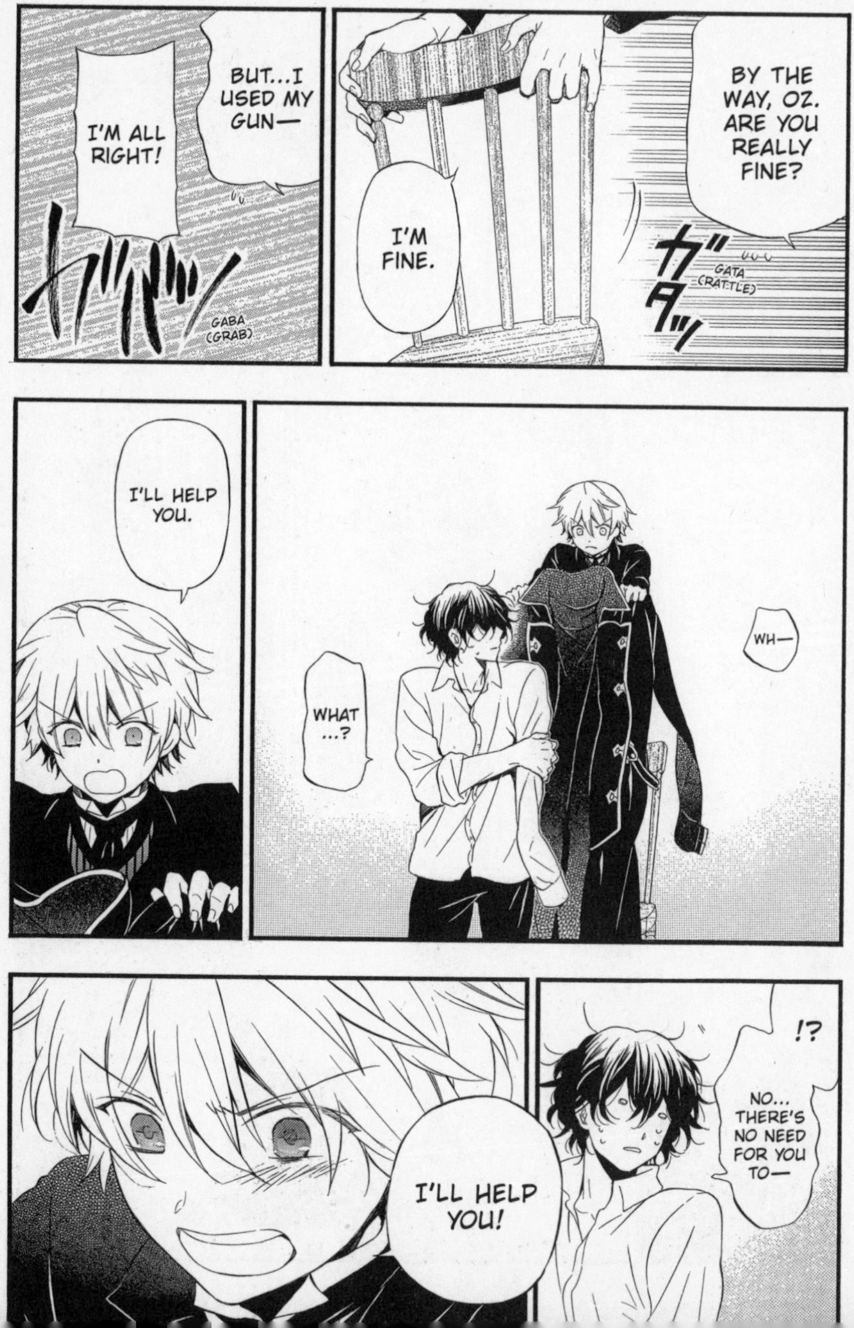
BY THE WAY, OZ. ARE YOU REALLY FINE?
GATA (RATTLE)
I'M FINE.
BUT...I USED MY GUN—
I'M ALL RIGHT!
GABA (GRAB)
WH—
WHAT ...?
I'LL HELP YOU.
!?
NO... THERE'S NO NEED FOR YOU TO—
I'LL HELP YOU!

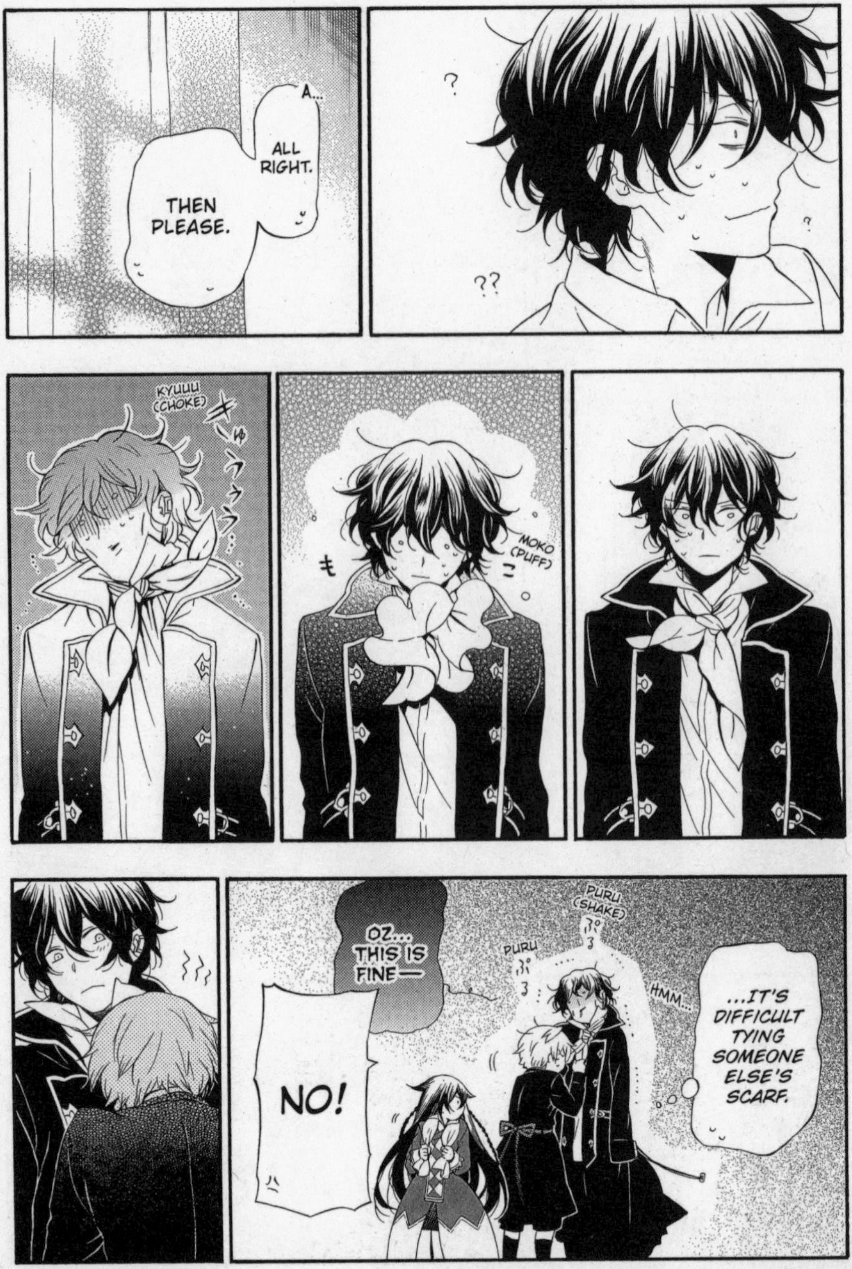
A...
ALL RIGHT.
THEN PLEASE.
MOKO (PUFF)
KYUUU (CHOKE)
...IT'S DIFFICULT TYING SOMEONE ELSE'S SCARF.
HMM...
PURU (SHAKE)
PURU
OZ... THIS IS FINE—
NO!

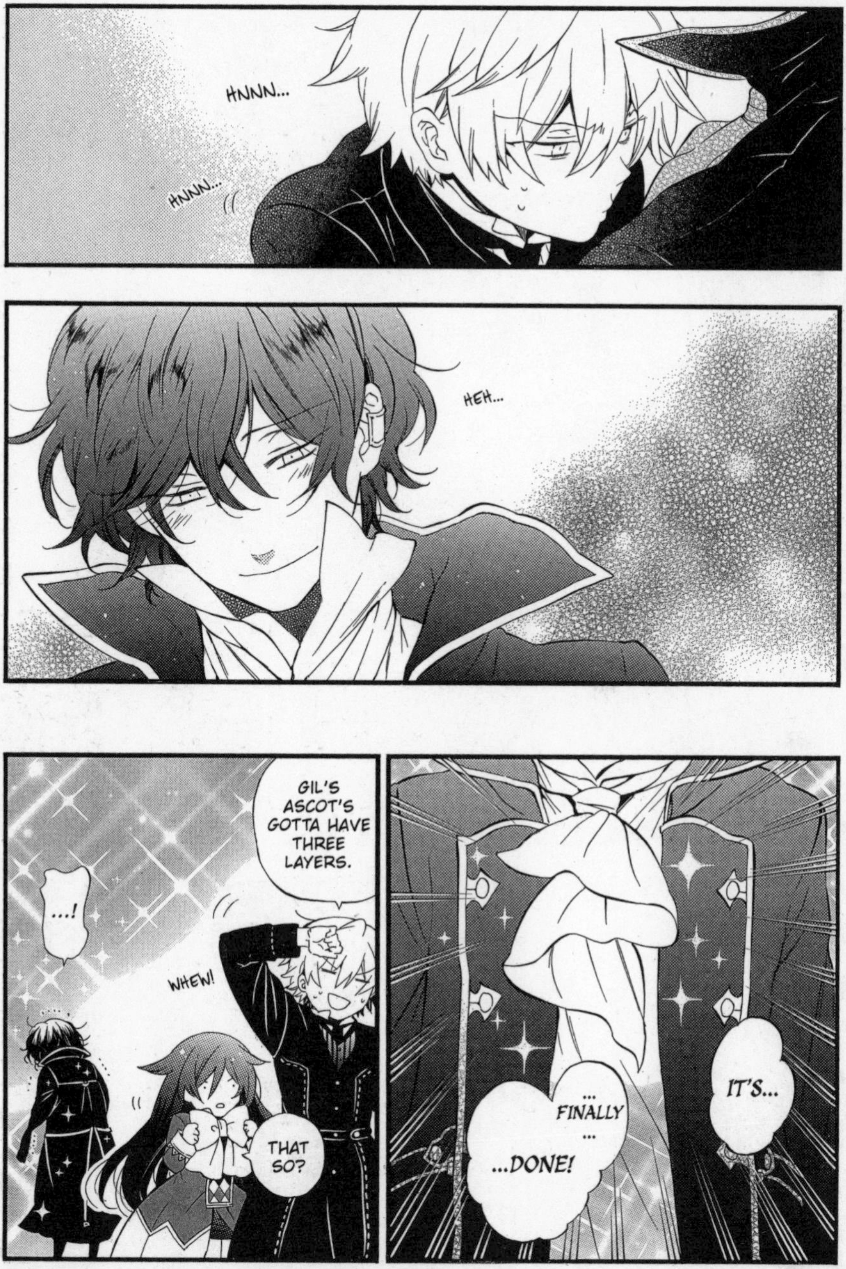
HNNN...
HNNN...
HEH...
IT'S...
...FINALLY...
...DONE!
GIL'S ASCOT'S GOTTA HAVE THREE LAYERS.
...!
WHEW!
THAT SO?

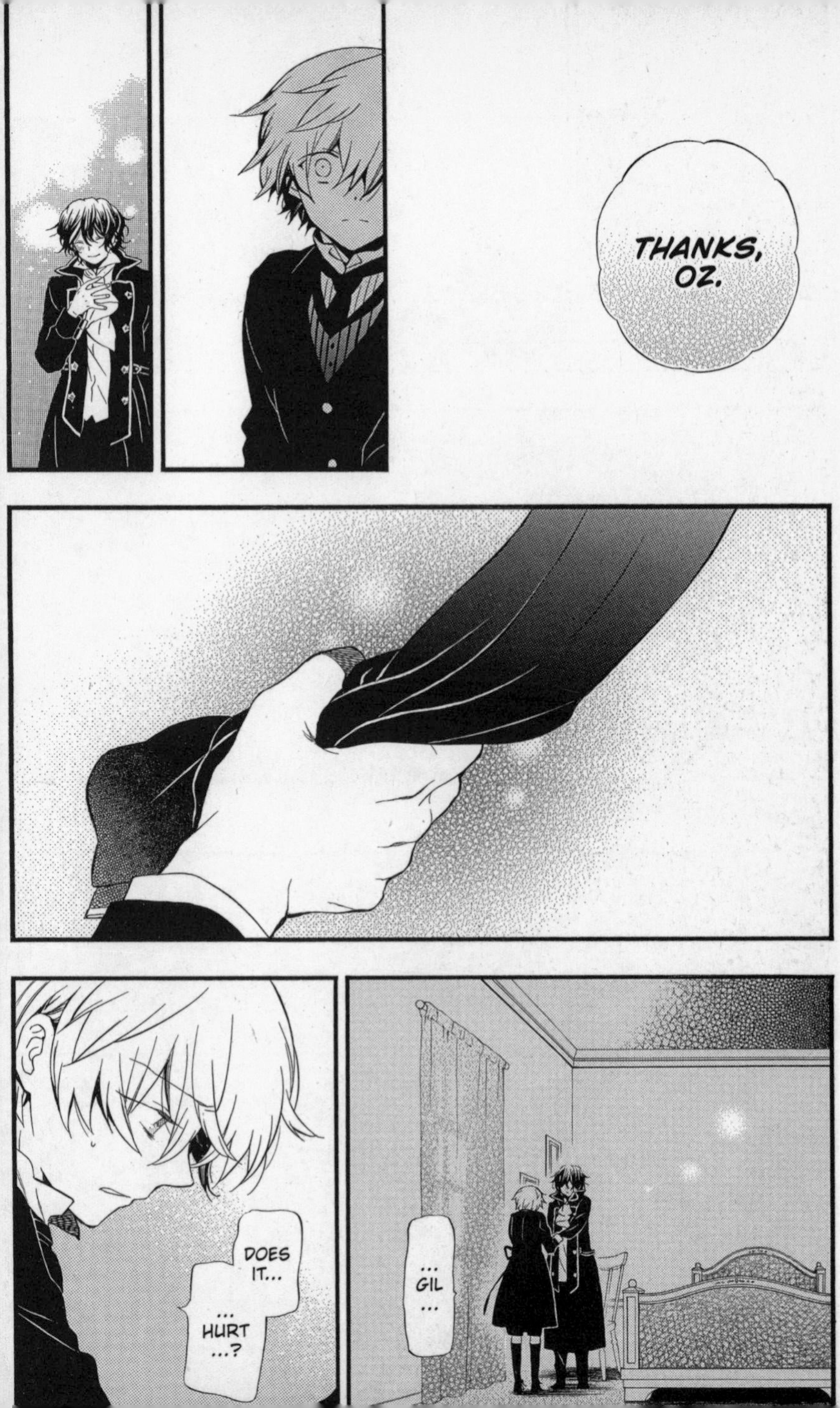
THANKS, OZ.
... GIL ...
DOES IT...
... HURT ...?

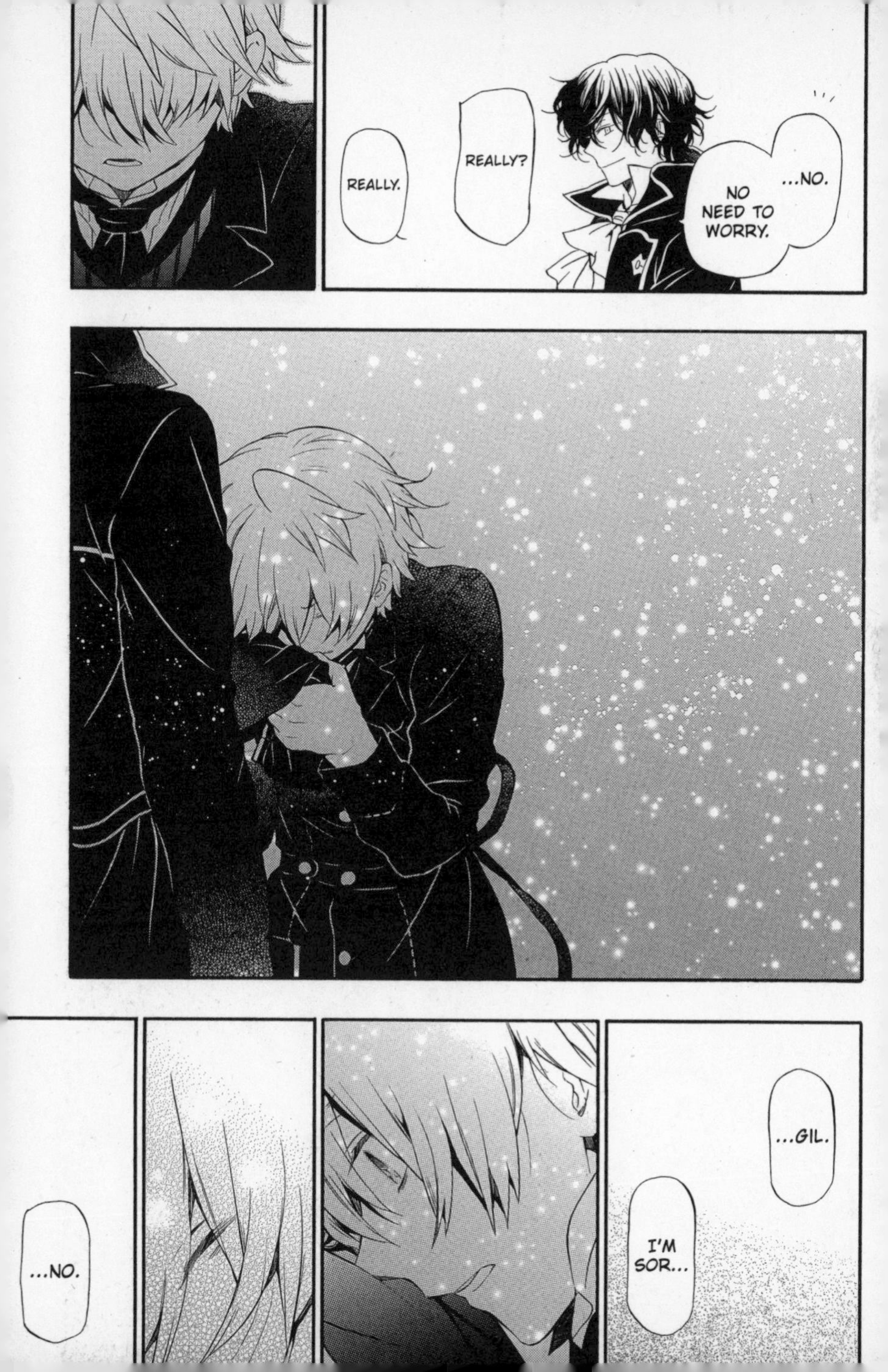
...NO.
NO NEED TO WORRY.
REALLY?
REALLY.
...GIL.
I'M SOR...
...NO.

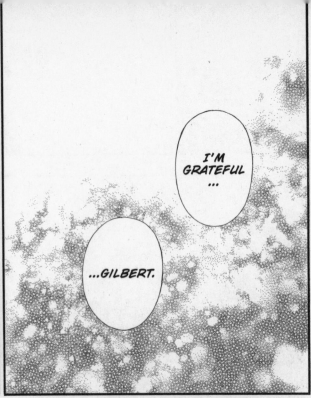

I'M GRATEFUL ...

...GILBERT.

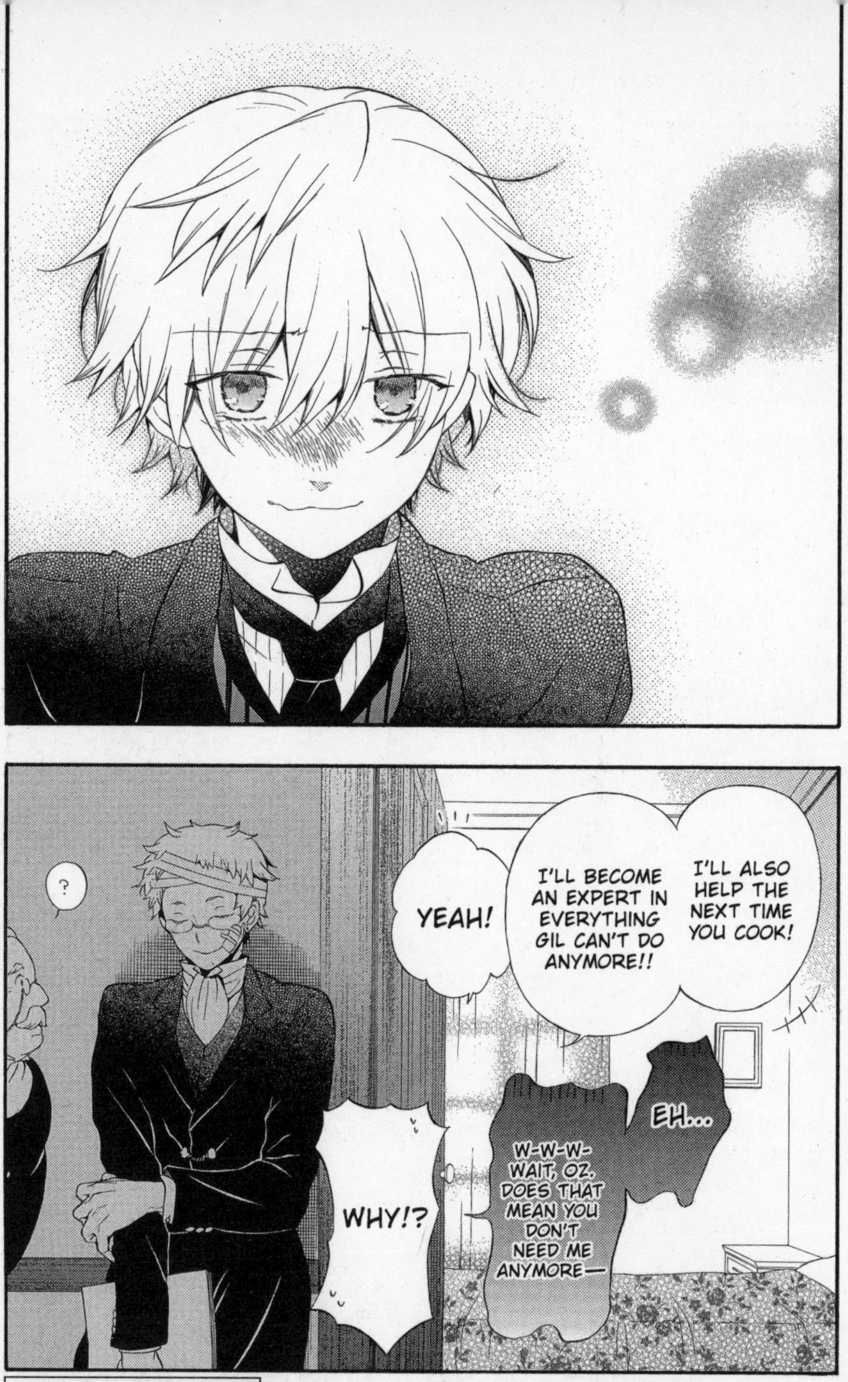
I'LL ALSO HELP THE NEXT TIME YOU COOK!
I'LL BECOME AN EXPERT IN EVERYTHING GIL CAN'T DO ANYMORE!!
YEAH!
EH...
W-W-W-WAIT, OZ. DOES THAT MEAN YOU DON'T NEED ME ANYMORE—
WHY!?
?

[Side Job] ① Hall staff ② Kitchen staff

①② Minimum 800¥/hr

[Hours] Work shifts between 7AM-1AM

[Responsibilities] ① General cafe duties such as working the counter and cash register. ② Cooking.

[Qualifications/Benefits] Experience not necessary. Senior high school students may apply. Commuting expenses provided. Uniforms provided. Midnight shift allowance. Meals provided. May arrange to be paid daily or weekly.

*You must wear your own black or brown leather shoes.

◆◆◆◆◆◆◆◆

Highly individual staff works at our old establishment which was founded a little over 100 years ago. We welcome people who want to discover their new selves! Tsukkomi are urgently wanted!

◆◆◆◆◆◆◆◆

HIDEAWAY CAFE **PANDORA CAFE**

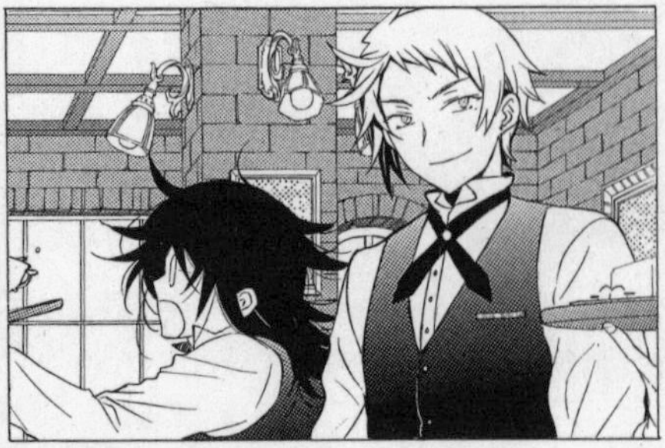

[Side job] Sales staff

Minimum 900¥/hr

[Hours] Work shifts between 11AM-7PM. Minimum 3 hours.
[Responsibilities] Product sales and customer service. Discussing the occult with the shop manager.
[Qualifications/Benefits] Intellectuals welcome. Commuting expenses provided. Costumes provided. Members of any religious denomination may apply. Invitations to Sabbaths sponsored by the shop manager.

MAGICAL ITEMS SHOP
MAGICAL GIRL CRAFT☆

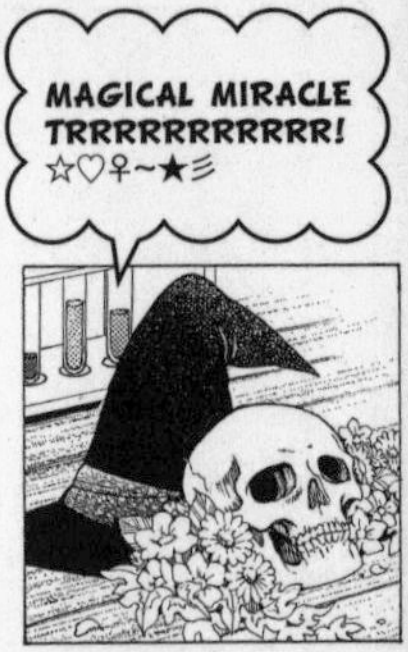
MAGICAL MIRACLE TRRRRRRRRRR! ☆♡♀~★彡

[Full-time] Office clerk

Minimum 500,000¥/month

[Hours] All day long.

[Responsibilities] Reim-san's assistant.

[Qualifications/Benefits] Commuting, meal expenses and other expenses provided in full. Pandora's uniforms provided.
- Must be at least 20 years old.
- Must be tough and have lots of energy.
- You'll be the next Reim Lunettes!

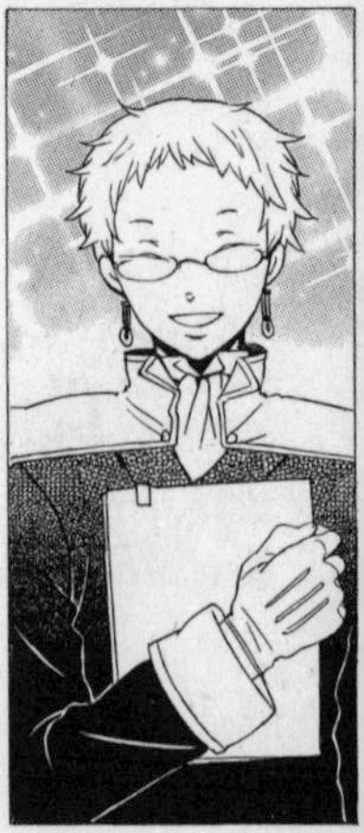
NOT TO WORRY. YOU CAN DO IT IF YOU RESIGN YOURSELF TO FATE!

Domestic Security Agency
PANDORA

[S/P/F] Production/Packing/Sales

① 900¥/hr ② 1000¥/hr ③ 200K¥/mo

[Hours]
① Work shifts between 8AM-8PM
② 8AM-8PM, 5-day work week
③ 6AM-10PM

[Responsibilities]
①② Production and sales of "Piyoko Master," our traditional and well-known sweets.
③ Developing new products. Sketching Master with artist Fang. Photo shoot events and stalking Master with Mama Lottie. Growing herbs with Dug-san. Walking the dogs with Lilly. Basking in the sun with Master.

[Benefits]
①② Commuting expenses provided. Uniforms provided. Meals provided. Pay raises available.
③ Company dormitory available at the Baskerville residence. All daily necessities provided. Annual company trip to the Abyss.

A STEP FROM SABLIER! TRANSPORTATION SERVICE BY JABBERWOCK AVAILABLE!

SINCERE CONFECTIONERY
Baskerville Family-San L.L.C.

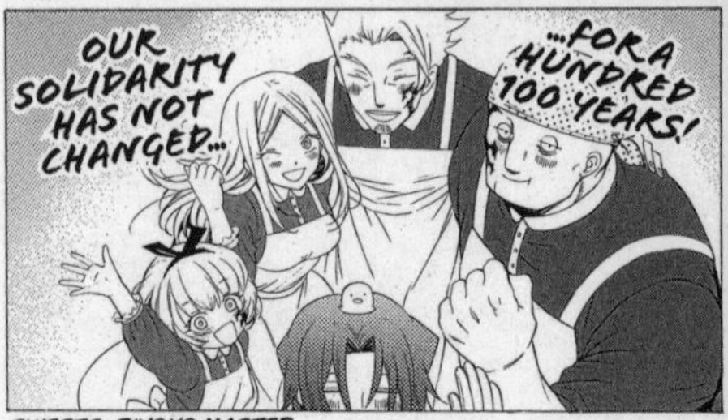
...FOR A HUNDRED 100 YEARS!
OUR SOLIDARITY HAS NOT CHANGED...

SWEETS: PIYOKO MASTER

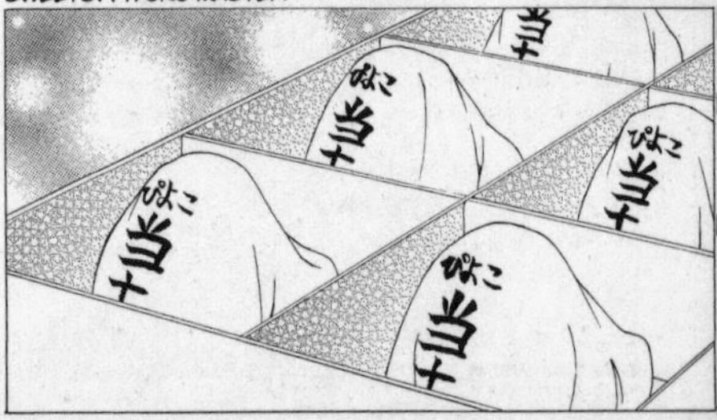

[Shift job] P.I. aide, Office clerk

Hourly wage negotiable

[Hours] Negotiable.

[Responsibilities] Negotiable.

[Benefits] Negotiable.

— A fun workplace where everyone's always smiling! —

Partner E: "I'm overwhelmed I can work with the great Break-sensei I respect! That alone makes me happy! I don't need any pay!"
The great sensei: "I prefer those who can make sweets."

BREAK PRIVATE EYE AGENCY

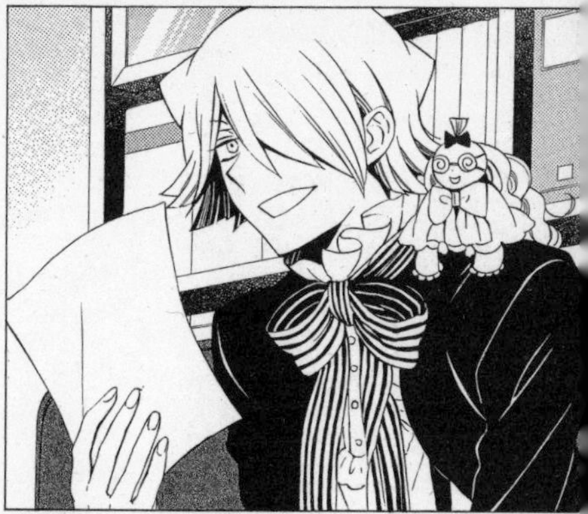

[Part-time] Childcare assistant

Minimum 1000¥/hr

[Hours] 7AM-4PM

[Responsibilities] Play well, study well, and sometimes scold the little pandas.

[Benefits] Commuting expenses provided. Aprons provided. Qualification allowance.

WHY DON'T YOU WATCH THE SMALL AND CUTE LITTLE PANDAS GROW UP WITH US? YOU'LL BE FINE EVEN IF YOU'RE NOT QUITE CONFIDENT! OUR KIND SENPAI WILL TEACH YOU FROM SQUARE ONE!

Social Welfare Corporation

Pandara Kindergarten

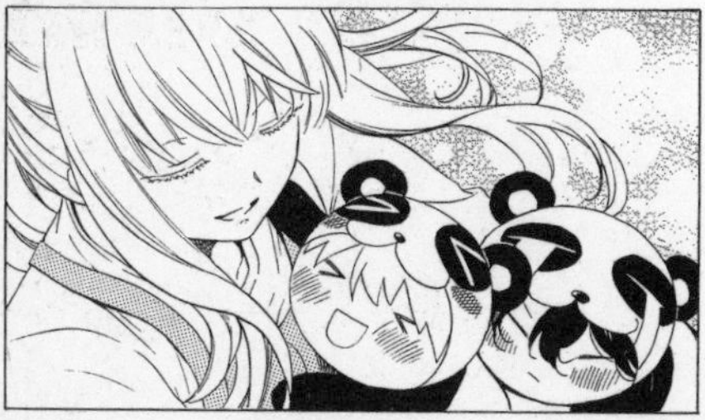

[Part-time] ① Hall staff ② Kitchen staff

①② Minimum 850¥/hr

☆OPENING STAFF WANTED!! LIVEN UP THE CAFE TOGETHER WITH YOUR COMRADES!! ☆★☆★

[Hours] 10AM-4PM, 4PM-9PM

★ Work in shifts
★ Can start from one day a week!!
★ We w-w-welcome beginners and permanent part-time jobbers!!
★ Four days of training provided.
★ Uniforms provided. Commuting expenses provided. Super-delicious meals provided ☆
★ Located in dreamy prime downtown of Reveil!!

Maidora Cafe

Reveil Flagship Branch

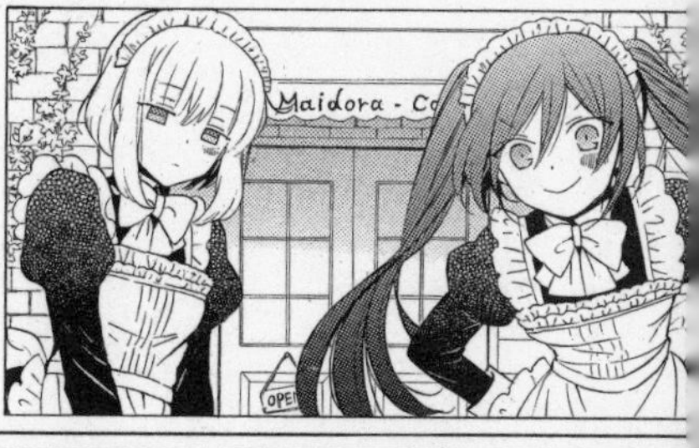

[Shift job] Academy cleaning staff

Minimum 730¥/hr

A rewarding job you can devote yourself to while peeping at the school lives of young and juicy boys and girls!

[Hours] 4AM-11PM
[Benefits] Madam Turner's breakfast. Use of student dining halls.

EDUCATION CORPORATION

LUTWIDGE SCHOOL

[Shift job] Operations assistant

Minimum 700¥/hr

[Hours] Work shifts between 11AM-2AM. Minimum 4 hours.
[Responsibilities] Accounting, answering phone calls, cleaning.
[Benefits] Commuting expenses provided (1500¥ max.)

We welcome kids who love music! You might be able to meet JUCKn!?

STUDIO

SABLIER

[Full-time] Items sales

Minimum 400,000¥/month

[Hours] 8AM-5PM
[Responsibilities] Selling Jack Vessalius-sama items on YuRaYuRa.com. Producing new Jack Vessalius-sama items.

By using every method available to pursue the faint remnants of Jack Vessalius-sama, our strong feelings will eventually go beyond the Abyss so we can use psychokinesis to uncover the private life of Jack Vessalius-sama that has been inscribed in the past.

ISLA YURA GROUP CO., LTD.

COMMON HONORIFICS

no honorific: Indicates familiarity or closeness; if used without permission or reason, addressing someone in this manner would constitute an insult.

-san: The Japanese equivalent of Mr./Mrs./Miss. If a situation calls for politeness, this is the fail-safe honorific.

-sama: Conveys great respect; may also indicate that the social status of the speaker is lower than that of the addressee.

-kun: Used most often when referring to boys (though it can be applied to girls as well), this indicates affection or familiarity. Occasionally used by older men among their peers, but it may also be used by anyone referring to a person of lower standing.

-chan: An affectionate honorific indicating familiarity used mostly in reference to girls; also used in reference to cute persons or animals of either gender.

PandoraHearts

I've begun taking English conversation lessons as a breather, as well as for future use. Someday, the me who has become perfectly fluent in English will be stylishly flying outside Japan here and there for my manga research. That's the me I'm dreaming of. All right, then let us begin by attending lessons every month. (I'm already somewhat defeated.)

MOCHIZUKI'S MUSINGS

VOLUME 21

PHEEW...

PandoraHearts

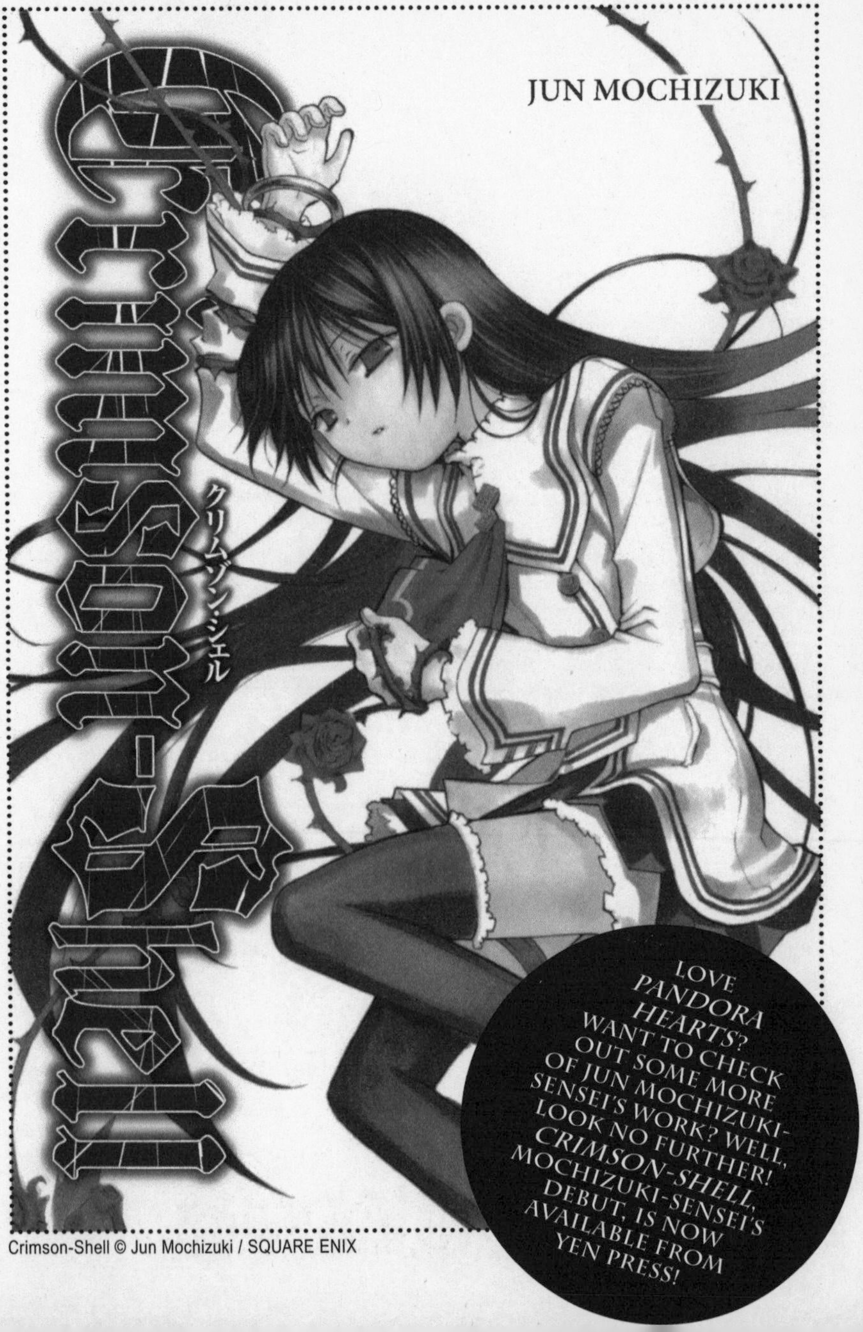
Crimson-Shell
クリムゾン・シェル
JUN MOCHIZUKI

LOVE *PANDORA HEARTS*? WANT TO CHECK OUT SOME MORE OF JUN MOCHIZUKI-SENSEI'S WORK? WELL, LOOK NO FURTHER! *CRIMSON-SHELL*, MOCHIZUKI-SENSEI'S DEBUT, IS NOW AVAILABLE FROM YEN PRESS!

PandoraHearts

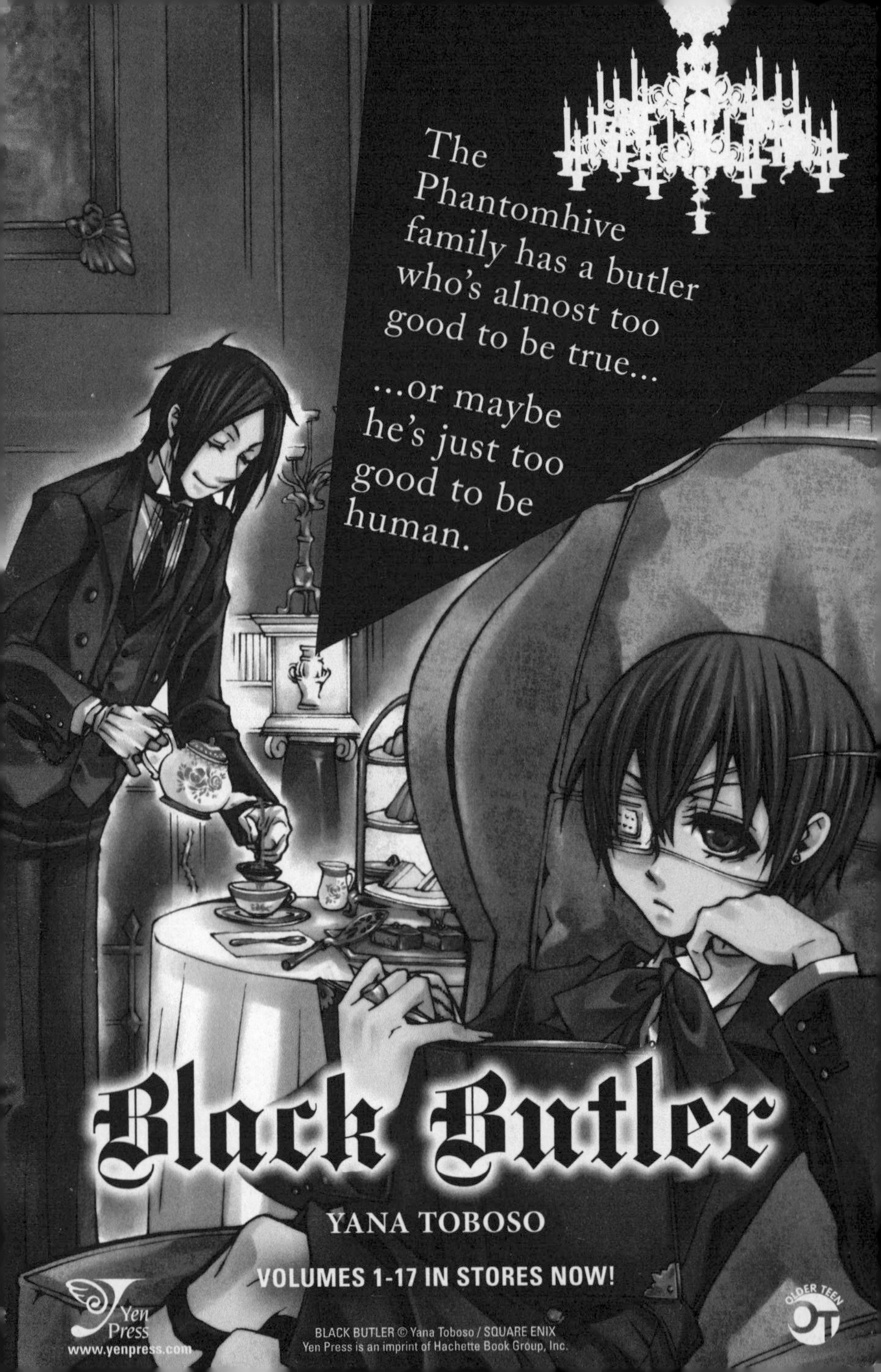
The Phantomhive family has a butler who's almost too good to be true...
...or maybe he's just too good to be human.
Black Butler
YANA TOBOSO
VOLUMES 1-17 IN STORES NOW!
Yen Press
www.yenpress.com
BLACK BUTLER © Yana Toboso / SQUARE ENIX
Yen Press is an imprint of Hachette Book Group, Inc.
OLDER TEEN
OT